Transnational Terrorism

Perspectives on Motives, Measures and Impacts

Transnational Terrorism

Perspectives on Motives, Measures and Impacts

Edited By

Chintamani Mahapatra

&

Amulya K. Tripathy

4831/24, Ansari Road, Darya Ganj,
New Delhi-110002
Tel : 23260807, 41563444
Fax : 011-41563334
E-mail: info@essessreference.com
url:http://www.essessreference.com

Reference Press
4831/24, Ansari Road,
Darya Ganj,
New Delhi-110 002.

Tel.: 23260807, 41563444
Fax: 41563334
E-mail: info@essessreference.com
www.essessreference.com

Rs.925/-

First Published - 2007

ISBN: 81-8405-036-4 (10 Digit)
978-81-8405-036-3 (13 Digit)

Published By Reference Press and printed at Salasar Imaging Systems

PRINTED IN INDIA

Contents

Dedicated to the memory of

Late Professor Emeritus M.S. Venkataramani

Doyen of American Studies in India

support to militancy in Kashmir. Indo-Pak relations also took a turn for the better, triggering off the peace process with the Indo-Pak Composite Dialogue in 2002. Amulya K Tripathy in third chapter has examined this aspect of the US war on terror in his contribution. He has traced the history of US policy towards Pakistan-sponsored terrorism in India and the gradual shift in US policy towards the same.

It is important to see how the US led war on terror has changed the contours of international politics. How has it affected US ties with other leading powers? How has it affected bilateral relations between countries involved directly or indirectly in the US-led war on terrorism? In the wake of the 9/11 incident, conflicting relations gave way to productive partnerships. Co-operation replaced competition in some instances, where mutual interest in the war on terror took precedence over clash of interest. Different cases of such changing relations have been dealt with in this book and the impact upon regional and global politics has been assessed. China which was viewed as a strategic competitor to the US emerged as a strong sympathizer of the American experience with terrorism. While US policy vacillated between containing and engaging the unbridled rise of China, the 9/11 attacks have removed such ambiguity in their bilateral relations. China, which is facing separatist movements in Xinjiang and Tibet, has extended its support to the US campaign against terrorism, thus avoiding unwarranted external criticism of its responses to these movements. One of the impacts of the post-9/11 era on US-China relations is reflected in the fact that major contentious issues between the two nations, such as human rights, humanitarian intervention and regional security have been put on the back burner. Both countries realize the importance of a co-operative bilateral relationship today, keeping in mind the huge economic and strategic considerations involved. Monika Chansoria in the fourth chapter of the book looks into the evolution of such a relationship between the two powers, the roadblocks they have crossed and attempts to chart out the future of Sino-US engagement. Pakistan, which has emerged as the frontline state on the US-led war on terror is also the most volatile region today. The interplay of various factors, internal as well as external, that have rendered Pakistan, a dangerous and a vulnerable state need to be critically assessed. Seema Sridhar in the fifth chapter scrutinizes the gradual course of Pakistan's complex and turbulent journey from being a harbinger of Islamic fundamentalism to the current situation of falling prey to its own policies.

US-Israel partnership against terrorism is perhaps the oldest of such partnerships in modern international history. This is a relationship which well predates 9/11 and in fact, it is this relationship which has spurred off vehement opposition to US policies in the Arab world. US cooperation with Israel has made the former a target of terrorist attacks from Islamic terrorist groups. It is pertinent to examine the nature of this relationship and how their respective vulnerabilities have drawn them closer in the fight against terrorism. In the sixth chapter, Ramesh Babu Kanneganti explores the nature, extent and scope of the US-Israeli co-operation in the fight against international terror. He has attempted to explain the intricate historical and political grounds on which this partnership is built.

The extension of the US led war on terror to Iraq has had tremendous impact on the international support for the war on terror. It has created stumbling blocks for the war in many ways. It is useful to understand how the intervention in Iraq has affected the nature of international terrorism. Iraq has become fertile ground for radical Islamist groups of different kinds. The post-regime change insurgency in Iraq needs to be placed in the context of the Shia-Sunni sectarian divide in the region. The sectarian uprising and prevailing confusion in Iraq has serious implication for terrorist networks in the Middle East, which needs to be taken into account in our attempt to understand the direction in which the international fight against terrorism is headed. Shelly Johny in the seventh chapter traces the development of these Sunni and Shia militant organisations and how they influence the Iraqi insurgency.

The quest of the developed world to have access to natural resources has led the major wars of the last century. Oil being the most sought after non-renewable natural resource, the attempt to ensure unhindered supply of oil from its sources has influenced the way nations behave in international politics. The US aspirations to have strategic hold over the oil rich Middle East, the reaction of the Islamist militant groups to US policy toward this region and the most recent US positions on violence and militancy in the region can be better explained in terms of the geo-strategic and economic importance of oil and its accessibility. It is perhaps one of the strong determinants of the continuing US-led war on terror and its extension to the Middle East after the bombing of Afghanistan. In the eighth chapter, Narottam Gaan looks into the geo-politics of fossil fuels and how the US finds itself in the imbroglio of terrorism and counter-terrorism.

The phenomenon of modern terrorism has come a long way. It has evolved from movements for self-determination, to social justice to anti-Americanism of this age. Saroj Kumar Rath in the ninth chapter traces the use of terror to different ends and lays down the characteristics that differentiate cases of post-9/11 terrorism from the incidents of pre-9/11 terrorism that had specific political ends, such as the Tamil Tigers in Sri Lanka and the Palestinian resistance against Israel. Motives for today's terrorism are varied. Terrorism today has access to weapons of mass destruction, chemical and biological weapons and high-tech equipment of communication. The ability to strikes at vulnerable targets, with precision and using modern technology for the same also characterizes today's terrorism.

Terrorism has become a concern for the United States after the September 11, 2001 attacks on the World Trade Centre towers and the Pentagon, the symbols of American economic and military might. The US became aware of the gravity of threat of terrorism only after 9/11 attacks. The terrorism that the US is fighting today needs to be placed in the context of the US foreign policy in the past decades, that has spurred off anti-Americanism, particularly in the Muslim world. It is important to look into the origins of Islamic terrorism leading to 9/11 terrorist attack and find out how far the United States global war on terror and its counter-terrorism policy has been effective in tackling terrorism. In the tenth chapter Ashok Sharma's chapter delves into the problems and drawbacks with the counter terror measures taken by the US. Off late the western world, particularly the United States and its European allies are making loud noises over the emerging terrorist threat to their respective interests. However, the Afro-Arab world for long has suffered a great deal due to a large number of terrorist activities. It is important that the world takes proper note of victims of terrorism in Asia and Africa and co-operates with these countries in combating terrorism. Jagdish Prasad Sharma takes a closer look at the issue of terrorism in the Afro-Asian world in Chapter 11.

What acts could be classified as terrorist acts? Are definitions absolute or are they perceptions, depending on who is defining? Sudhir Chandra Jena in chapter 12 brings out the different contours in defining terrorism and contradictions within the same. Various causes for this phenomenon are identified and analyzed. Terrorist acts, which were earlier sporadic in nature and limited to a few pockets of the world, have become frequent and all pervasive today. We need to look into the reasons for terrorism fast spreading to assume international character. Socio-economic deprivation, political instability, religious intolerance and fanaticism, ethnic strife and cultural alienation etc. make necessary condition for spread of terrorism. De-polarization of international politics in the post-Cold War era has to be examined to understand international terrorism. Is today's terrorism the result of weakening Third World voice against the supremacy of the developed West? According to this view, religious radicalism has emerged as a 'sole replacement' in the absence of a vocal Third World leadership against Western domination. It has become evident from the weakening of forums like the Non-Aligned Movement (NAM), in spite of their continuing relevance. In the thirteen chapter, Pradeep Harichandan delves into different points of view that attempt to explain the phenomenon of terrorism and attempts to analyze the impact of globalization on terrorism. It is also important to look into how the concept of national interest has been used by the US, consequentially leading to the spread of international terrorism.

Islamic radicalism and extremism as a violent, destructive, and murderous ideology has emerged as the new scourge of the free world. Apparently seeking to avenge centuries of humiliation of Muslims heaped by the imperialist West, this global movement has been using "Islam" for political benefit. It has put terror in the hearts of numerous men and women in various countries—regardless of what their governments may claim—and has created a widespread impression that the world is at war with Islam. "Islamic terrorism" is under the scanner of the Western media and there seems to be a search for explanations in the Holy Quran in support of terrorism. This, in turn, has forced Islamic scholars to make painstaking efforts to "prove" that Islam is actually a peaceful religion. Saumyajit Ray's article in the fourteenth chapter delves into the Scriptures—the Holy Quran—and the Islamic traditions (Hadith), and Muslim political history to understand the true nature of Islam in an attempt to unravel the links between Islamic faith and Muslim violence and find out the reason behind the success of Islamists in using their faith as a justification for their activities.

As the measures adopted by terrorists have changed drastically in the last decade, the threat of nuclear terrorism is increasingly becoming a reality. Since the US nuclear attacks on Hiroshima and Nagasaki during World War II, nuclear weapons have generated dread and awe in the minds of people and nations. Acquiring nuclear weapons brings prestige and power and enhances the status of a nuclear weapon power in the international community. It has changed the way nations perceive one another. Possession or lack of nuclear weapon capability determines a country's security and enlarges its bargaining tools in international diplomacy. Proliferation attempts have led to imposition of international economic sanctions, diplomatic quarantines and military interventions, wreaking massive humanitarian losses. It is not therefore unfathomable why terrorist groups would want to acquire such weapons and indulge in an ultimate demonstration of strength. However, this is not such a simple task, considering the stringent network of anti-proliferation mechanisms in place, which makes use of state of the art technology and intelligence. Implications of such an acquisition on the non-proliferation regime would be disastrous and have been pondered upon in this study. As the scale of this particular threat is unknown and is unprecedented, the dread of this possibility has surfaced. Sitakanta Mishra in the fifteenth chapter examines the different facets of nuclear terrorism, and feasibility of such a venture by terrorist organizations and answers the how, when and where questions.

Violence of extreme left outfits moves us to ask certain difficult questions related to the factors that have led to this form of terrorism and how the state has responded to this. Post-9/11, the question of terrorism, i.e. use of un-provoked violence against non-combatants, has assumed bigger significance. When all kinds of violence against the democratic-sovereign states are being categorized as 'terrorism' in the sixteenth chapter Arvind Kumar tries to look how India has tried to come to grips with it.

The different means used by terrorist groups have grown to include even the cyber space. Attacks against information, computer systems, computer programmes and data have been carried out by subversive groups or surreptitious agents, affecting the civilian population. Modern terrorism is techno-savvy and all possible means and methods have been explored by terrorist organizations, including the cyberspace. Cyber terrorism is extremely difficult to detect. It requires incredible amount of co-operation in intelligence sharing to prevent it and its overall consequences still remain unaccounted. This very complex phenomenon has been elucidated by Padmalaya Mahapatra in the seventeenth chapter of this book. The *modus operandi* of a cyber terrorist, its impact, detection and prevention mechanisms in place have been elaborated upon in the chapter.

Modern terrorism uses every avenue available for the attainment of its objectives and modern technology has offered them innumerable innovative ways of furthering their cause. Modern terrorism seems to flourish on publicity. They rely on the media to sensationalize their acts and draw wide attention to them. Media coverage of spectacular and gory attacks widens the scope of fear generated among the populace. In the eighteenth chapter Chitra Kanungo discusses how the media is used by terrorists to propagate their cause. She brings out the difficulty of the media in walking the tight rope and balancing its role by seeking to prevent terrorist groups from using it to fulfill their agenda and at the same time creating awareness by disseminating information at the fastest speed possible about terrorism among people.

Means employed by terrorists are as diverse as their

motives and objectives that they wish to attain. Violence has been perpetrated in many inventive ways sparing no channel available to do so. The perpetrator has effectively become the destroyer through the extreme process of self-annihilation, creating a new breed of terrorists called suicide bombers. Suicide terrorism has become an increasing phenomenon over the last two decades. Suicide attacks were witnessed in Lebanon, Kuwait and Sri Lanka in 1980's and spread to Israel, India, Panama, Algeria, Pakistan, Argentina, Croatia, Turkey, Tanzania, Kenya and many other countries in the 1990s. The multiplicity of these attacks strongly suggests that suicide bombings have become a preferred means to successfully infiltrate into the target population and cause enormous socio-political damage. It wreaks havoc in the minds of the people due to the magnitude of the injuries created and also about bomber's commitment to the cause if he or she is willing to resort to this extremity. Somehow, it seeks to justify their means and captures public attention towards their cause. Smitha in the nineteenth chapter draws attention to the Sri Lankan experience wherein the Tamil separatist group, the Liberation Tiger Tamil Elam (LTTE) has launched the maximum number of suicide attacks in the world within the country and its neighbourhood. The factors contributing to this phenomenon, its origins, the tactics employed and the governmental measures against it are furnished in this comprehensive study on terrorism.

The terrorist attack on the United States in September 2001 has exposed a new angle to the dynamics of modern terrorism. Nonetheless, no consensus yet exists among scholars, legal experts or political leaders on the exact meaning and definition of terrorism. While the international community has been critically sensitized on the catastrophic consequences of terrorist acts, the lack of unanimity in its definition poses a continuing challenge to the global community. Ashwini Kumar Tiwari in the final chapter of this volume discusses the conceptual dimension and definitional aspect of trans-national terrorism.

Tremendous amount of efforts went into compiling and editing this volume. It has been our endeavor not to edit the chapters in ways that would affect the message an author intended to convey in his or her own style and method. Our major effort has been geared to bring all these scholars together to present their respective views on a theme that is of continuing relevance to questions of peace and stability facing humankind. Significantly, scholars of diverse political convictions and theoretical orientations have contributed to this volume and have made it rich in content and substance. All credits for good work should go to individual authors. We are grateful to the members of our respective families for bearing with us even as we spent endless hours in reading, editing and arranging this volume. Meera and Nandini took good care of our children when we were busy with this work. Seema and Monika were of great help in the entire process of editing. Last but not the least, we are dedicating this volume to our late Professor Emeritus M.S. Venkataramani who was a major source of inspiration, support and intellectual guidance for decades.

Chintamani Mahapatra
Amulya K. Tripathy

List of Contributors

Chintamani Mahapatra
Associate Professor, Centre for Canadian,
US and Latin American Studies,
School of International Studies,
Jawaharlal Nehru University.

Christopher S Raj
Professor of American Studies at the Centre for Canadian,
US and Latin American Studies,
School of International Studies,
Jawaharlal Nehru University.

Amulya K. Tripathy
Senior Lecturer in Political Science,
D.A.V. College, Titlagarh,
Sambalpur University, Orissa.

Monika Chansoria
Research Associate at the Centre for Air Power Studies,
New Delhi.

Seema Sridhar
Senior Research Scholar at the School of
International Studies, JNU.

Ramesh Babu Kanneganti
Post-doctoral Visiting Fellow at Begin-Sadat
Centre for Strategic Studies, Bar-ilan University, Israel.

Shelly Johny
Research Associate at the Centre for Air Power Studies, New Delhi.

Narottam Gaan
Reader in Political Science, Badamba College, Utkal University, Cuttack.

Saroj Kumar Rath
Senior Research Scholar, School of International Studies, Jawaharlal Nehru University.

Ashok Sharma
Research Associate at the Centre for Air Power Studies, New Delhi.

Jagdish P Sharma
Head of the Department of Afro-Arab Studies, University of Delhi.

Sudhir Chandra Jena
Senior Lecturer in Political Science, MPC College, Baripada, Utkal University.

Pradeep Harichandan
Lecturer in Political Science, P.N. College Kurdha, Utkal University.

Saumyajit Ray
Lecturer at the Department of Journalism and Mass Communication, Kasturi Ram College of Higher Education, Guru Gobind Singh Indraprastha University, Delhi.

Sitakant Mishra
Research Associate, at the Centre for Air Power Studies, New Delhi.

Arvind Kumar
Senior Research Scholar, School of International Studies, JNU.

Padmalaya Mahapatra
Reader in Political Science,
Mizoram Central University.

Chitra Kanungo
Senior Lecturer in Political Science,
Emarti Devi Women's College,
Cuttack, Utkal University.

Smitha
Senior Research Scholar at the
South Asian Studies Division,
School of International Studies,
Jawaharlal Nehru University.

Ashwini K Tiwari
former Reader in B.J.B College,
Bhubaneswar, Utkal University.

1

India in the Midst of Terrorism

Chintamani Mahapatra

Is nuclear India safe in this era of growing threats posed by all kinds of terrorist groups? Is India's military machine sufficiently equipped to tackle the ever growing terrorist threats? India today is surrounded by countries afflicted with terrorism? Afghanistan, Pakistan, Nepal, Bangladesh and Sri Lanka—almost all of India's neighbours are facing this threat. Iraq and Indonesia in India's extended neighbourhood have also become the battleground of terrorism. So are Thailand and Indonesia.

India has also been waging a protracted war against terrorism within its own borders. No part of India appears to be safe, whether North, South, East or West. Perhaps no country in the world has lost more people in acts of terrorism than India since the end of the Cold War. As former American Ambassador to India Robert D Blackwill commented: "With respect to terrorism, India in the past 15years has lost more people to jihadi killers than any other nation in the world."[1] For a long time, India warned the international community of the rising threat of terrorism to regional security, even as it confronted with terrorism perpetrated by the ULFA in Assam, Khalistanis in the Punjab and a host of terrorist groups in Kashmir. With a timely awareness that terrorism is a transnational menace, India has long sought to sensitize the international community on the dangers of terrorism and at length spoke of cross-border terrorism in Kashmir, which could not be tackled without certain amount of international cooperation.

But India's views and appeals fell on deaf ears until the September 11, 2001 terrorist attacks on the United States. This incident exposed the vulnerability of a hyper power and the strength and resilience of terrorist outfits. When the Bush Administration commenced a global war against the perpetrators of the 9/11 attacks, numerous members of the international community came forward to assist the US in confronting this peril. But more than five years after that calamitous episode, the world appears to have become more insecure and unsafe than before.

The latest report on global terrorism released by the US Department of State has stated that terrorist acts in 2006 increased by 25 per cent from that of 2005. The locus of maximum terrorist acts has continued to be West Asia and South Asia. About 90 percent of all 290 high casualty attacks by the terrorist groups took place in this region.

It is note worthy that countries, which traditionally did not face this problem, have begun to do so. Pakistan, for instance, known for long as an incubator of terrorists, itself has become a victim of rising number of terrorist attacks in recent years, The North West Frontier Province of Pakistan, where Islamabad never exercised adequate control, is today under the command of terrorist organizations or their well-wishers. Terrorist activities have also expanded to other cities of Pakistan, such a Lahore and Karachi. Nepal, a peace loving Hindu Kingdom, recently fell victim to terrorist violence perpetrated by an ideological extremist organization, namely the Maoists. Certain parts of India too appear to be experiencing the widening grip of Naxalites—once again ideologically motivated militants.

Sri Lanka has been struggling with Tamil tigers, namely the LTTE, for decades without any real solution in sight. Isolation of the LTTE in the international community in the post-9/11 era failed to weaken this organization. LTTE, once known for its human bombs, has demonstrated its military muscle by launching air attacks on selected targets and launching naval attacks on the high seas. Recently the LTTE launched air attacks on selected targets, the most recent being oil storage tanks in Ceylon—the fuel depot of Ceylon Petroleum Storage Terminals Limited, a joint venture of the Indian Oil Corporation, the Government of Sri Lanka and the Ceylon Petroleum Corporation.

Bangladesh too has emerged as a battleground of terrorism. The Rapid Action Battalion of Bangladesh has been struggling to tame brutality and carnage carried out by the JMV or Jamaatul Mujahedin Bangladesh. Perpetual political instability in that country has presented the Bengali terrorist groups, including some terrorists from Northeastern India, to have a field day and a safe haven.

TERRORISM: NO LONGER DOMESTIC PHENOMENON

In this age of globalization, terrorist groups have world-wide network. The interface between drugs traders, criminal syndicates, small arms merchants and the terrorist organizations is facilitated by the information revolution and easier means of transport and communication across international borders. States have realized that terrorism is no longer a domestic phenomenon. They have cross-border as well as international connectedness. This makes it difficult for any single government to deal with such groups without international cooperation.

India has no doubt tried to engage the international community in its war against terrorism. India has counter-terrorism working groups with 16 countries, including the United States. It has also very actively engaged the European Union and the BIMSTEC countries in counter-terrorism measures. Yet the problem persists. Scholars have thrown much light on the causes of terrorism, law enforcement authorities have understood the modus operandi of terrorist organizations and governments have forged international cooperation, yet the menace is not under control and rather getting worse.

A casual reading of the annual reports of the Ministry of Home Affairs could create an impression that the situation is indeed improving in India and that the law enforcement agencies in India are doing pretty well. The 2006-07 annual report says: "The overall internal security and law and order situation in the country has remained largely under control during the year 2006-07. The level of violence in Jammu and Kashmir continues to show a declining trend. The overall security situation in the North Eastern States has shown signs of improvement with definite improvement in the situation in Manipur this year. Overall naxal violence in the affected States has been contained during the current year...."[2] However, a careful examination would reveal that the claimed decline in terrorist violence is actually marginal and does not indicate that we all can go to sleep peacefully. According to the report, "Terrorist-related incidents came down by 22%, killings of civilians by 21% and those of SFs by 33% during the year 2005 as compared to the year 2004. · During the year 2006, the number of incidents was lower by 16%, those of civilians killed by 30% and SFs killed by 20% over the corresponding period of the last year."[3] What do these figures suggest? The situation was relatively better than the previous year, but the terrorist danger by and large persisted. A couple of more terrorist incidents and the figures could show drastically different results. The report rightly brings out that: "A discernible change in violence profile after April, 2006 suggests a tactical shift against soft targets including minority communities, tourists and migrant labourers."[4] Indeed, to India's owes, its railways, shopping centres, temples, mosques, government buildings, legislatures, military barracks and several other places have come under the target of terrorist organizations. Which place in India is safe? Who is safe in India? India has lost two of its illustrious prime ministers in its struggle against terrorism!

SECURITY DILEMMA

India's security dilemma arises from its political geography partly, being in the centre of South Asia and sharing border with all South Asian countries. Anti-India terrorists seek safe havens and sanctuaries in neighbouring states and terrorist groups from other countries too have some illegal presence in India. The warning issued by a prominent national daily, The *Hindu*, is indeed timely. It says: "the time has come to remind the Congress-led government at the centre that foreign policy, even when it involves Sri Lanka, must be made in New Delhi—not in Chennai, and certainly not under the influence of pro-LTTE parties. It has become abundantly clear that the banned terrorist organization...has emerged as a security problem for India." India at one point of time militarily intervened in Sri Lanka at Colombo's invitation, but failed to tame the LTTE for a variety of reasons. Indian Prime Minister Rajiv Gandhi lost his life in a suicide attack by an LTTE activist. That South India cannot remain safe until terrorism ends in Sri Lanka is a foregone conclusion.

Bangladesh is partly responsible for instability and violence in India's Northeast. The ULFA terrorists have found a safe haven in that country and operate from the jungles of Bangladesh. So are several other terrorist organizations of the Northeast. But Bangladesh does not cooperate with India in counter-terrorism measures. Rather it rejects Indian claims that anti-Indian terrorist elements are making use of Bangladeshi territory as a sanctuary with the complicity of some Bangladeshi officials. More disturbing is increasing presence of other international Islamic extremist groups in Bangladesh. The radical Revival of Islamic Heritage Society based in Kuwait has a presence in Bangladesh. The Islami Bank in that country has close nexus with terrorist groups[5] . While Bangladesh has no problem in establishing close counter-terrorism cooperation with the US, it is not agreeable to forge similar ties with India.

Nepal was relatively a peaceful Himalayan Kingdom until

Maoist insurgency struck it in the recent past. India's help in containing Maoist violence in Nepal was certainly not adequate or praise worthy. The US actually made inroads into a security zone, which was the exclusive domain of India. Nepal has been slipping away from an area that India considered vital and the Chinese influence and the American presence have increased considerably in that country. India may have less to worry about American role in Nepal, but the fact remains that even Pakistan's dreaded ISI has expanded its presence in that country. Violence and instability in Nepal can easily spill over into India due to geographic and demographic factors. While the Maoists in Nepal have agreed on an interim arrangement of governance, the situation remains volatile. Political compromise to bring about democratic reforms in Nepal is indeed fragile.

However, India has more strategic vulnerability in its Northwest than any other part. Nepal, Bangladesh and Sri Lanka present enormous challenges in view of terrorism situation in their territories, but Pakistan remains central to India's core strategic concerns. Pakistan has been a sponsor of terrorism, incubator of terrorists and of late has become a victim of terrorist violence. Ten years of anti-Soviet insurgency in Afghanistan backed by the United States and executed through Pakistan's direct involvement in training and equipping the Afghan Mujaheedins was actually responsible for the outbreak of terrorism in Kashmir in 1989. Soon after Soviet troop withdrawal from Afghanistan, Pakistan promoted terrorism in Kashmir. Even after seventeen years Kashmir is not back to normal!

It is true that Pakistan failed in snatching away Kashmir by encouraging a low intensity conflict in Kashmir. But the bitter truth is India's opportunity cost of handling the law and order situation in that state. The 9/11 terrorist attacks on the US brought about a major transformation in US attitude towards terrorism in Kashmir. US pressure on President Pervez Musharraf was partly responsible for the current Indo-Pakistan peace process. But it appears that both India and the United States have rather put lots of eggs in Musharraf basket. The Bush administration did not allow Musharraf to go ahead with Pakistan's traditional policy of sponsoring terrorism in Kashmir. It was because tension along Indo-Pakistan border would obstruct Pakistani assistance to the US along Pakistan-Afghanistan border in dealing with the Al Qaeda and the Taliban rank and file. But the real danger would arise for India when Washington would begin to distance itself from the Musharraf regime.

GROWING CONCERNS OVER PAKISTAN

The Bush Administration went head over heels to praise President Musharraf for his cooperation in countering terrorism for years. But of late complications have developed. US Vice President earlier this year secretly stopped at Pakistan on his way to Afghanistan and conveyed to the Pakistani leadership that there was a growing concern in his country about Pakistan's inadequate support to the war against terrorism. A few weeks earlier US Defense Secretary Robert Gates visited Pakistan; held wide ranging discussions with the Pakistani President and voiced similar concerns.

As the winter was about to make way for spring to arrive, the American and other NATO forces grew restive, because of the intelligence reports as well as common sense calculations that the Taliban and other insurgent forces in Afghanistan would begin their Spring Offensive against the foreign occupying forces in their country. Five years after the remo val of the Taliban regime in Kabul, the US has found it difficult to bring peace to the strife torn Afghanistan. About fifty thousand NATO forces and several thousand American forces have not been able to eliminate the Taliban influence in Afghanistan. The land-locked country with pathetic socio-economic conditions is presenting a Himalayan hurdle for the best military forces in the world and becoming a quintessence of the limits of military power.

The Americans perhaps now realize it better as to how easy it was for them to "bleed the Soviets white" during the Soviet military intervention in that country during 1979-89. Several Afghan Mujaheedin groups were mobilized, trained, equipped and funded with the help of Pakistan's dreaded ISI to fight against the Soviet military. The American allies were fully with the US strategy against the Soviet intervention in that country. Even then, the Soviet Union could manage to hold ground for about ten years.

The contrast is crystal clear to day. There is a pro-American government in Kabul. The Afghan military has been raised, trained, equipped and supported by the US and the NATO forces. Pakistan this time is again with the US and battling against the Taliban forces. No major power is assisting the Afghan insurgents and the Taliban forces and yet five years have gone by without any sign of peace and stability in that country. However, as Pakistan came under renewed pressure, President Musharaff fought back; saying that his country had done the "maximum" and that other allies should step in and make "joint efforts" to guard the Pakistan-Afghanistan border. Interestingly, the West, which ignored, doubted or disbelieved India's consistent complaints against cross-border terrorism in Kashmir, has now been egging on Pakistan to stop movement of terrorist groups to Afghanistan from its border areas.

The US thus far has little option than to keep Pakistan on its side. Pakistan is a strategically located country, which is vital to US strategy against global terror. Soon after the US policy makers began to plan the response to 9/11 attack and the decision was taken to bomb Afghanistan, Secretary of State Collin Powell told President Bush that the US would not be able execute its plan "without Pakistan." But for Pakistan, the US war against terrorism would have been much more ineffective and the country's cooperation remains fundamental until that fight against terror comes to an end. The Bush administration for long viewed the Pakistani ruling regime, particularly General Musharraf as a trusted ally, a friend and an indispensable supporter of America's counter-terrorism strategy. But disappointment set in, as Musharraf began to distance himself from the US to some degrees perhaps to protect his skin. By blaming Washington for excessive pressure on him after 9/11, concluding agreements with the tribal leaders of Waziristan, believed to be supporters or sympathizers of the Taliban, inability to locate Osama bin Laden rumored to be in Pakistan and suspected ISI linkages with Taliban, Musharraf has raised many eyebrows in Washington's policy making circles. Questions are being raised in Washington about trustworthiness of General Musharraf.

One commentator has stated that Musharraf helps only to the extent it would ward off US pressures. Another commentator argues that evidence of nexus between the Pakistani intelligence and the militants is ample and that Pakistani army continues to rule the roost, while raising the bogey of threats from the militants. Moreover, Congressional leaders have begun to question the justification of massive US aid to Pakistan in the name of fighting militancy and terrorism. Lack of progress in the war against terror has led to linkages in a new bill, already passed by the House of Representative, between US aid and Musharraf's performance. The bill requires the US President to certify Pakistan's commitment to fight terror to enable that country to receive US assistance. Some Congressman question the rationale behind blind support to military dictatorship in Pakistan and question the Bush Administration's attempt to whitewash Musharraf's anti-democratic measures while simultaneously making statements after statements to promote democracy abroad. Pakistan's name hardly figures in the US agenda of promoting democracy.

The US Administration, however, is bound by its own compulsions. Pakistan is a country that can become an example of state failure, unless handled carefully. Its economy is in a dire state of affairs. Two-thirds of the Pakistani revenue is spent in paying interest to public debt and building the military every year. The country is largely agricultural and textiles account for 60% of that country's total exports. It is heavily dependent on external assistance and borrowing to sustain itself. The sectarian violence, rising incidence of terrorist bombings and a precarious governing system add to the country's long list of woes. But despite these difficulties, Pakistan's usefulness for fighting terror networks is still appreciated in the US. Pakistan is the hotbed of terrorist training camps and Pakistan-trained Islamic extremists can be found in the nook and corner of the globe. Unless the Pakistani government is co-opted in the war against extremism and terrorism, the task would remain unfulfilled. The dilemma for the Bush Administration is how to befriend Musharraf, while not generating anti-Americanism among the Pakistani people. The Pakistani opinion against the US policies is one of the worst in the world and massive amount of US assistance to that country has not won the hearts of people.

TALKING TO ENEMY

So long as Musharraf is with the US, the latter can have moderate influence on Pakistan to build peace with India and restrain anti-India terrorist activities from its soil. But should India rely too much on this aspect of counter-terrorism measures? How best to de-link Pakistan from anti-Indian terrorist organizations is a major challenge for India's counter-terrorism efforts. The urgency of India bilaterally dealing with Pakistan was more clearly demonstrated by the event better known as the 7/11 incident. On 11 July 2006, a series of seven bombs exploded in the Suburban Railway in Mumbai, India's finance capital, which killed 209 people and injured more than seven hundred. While the Indian police quickly saw the hands of Laskra-e-Tayyaba and Students Islamic Movement of India, it failed to book the perpetrators.

The findings of the 7/11 incident, among other things, should make us aware that in a rapidly changing world talking to the enemy needs to be designed as an important foreign policy and national security strategy of the country. The ISI's hand, according to the report of the investigation, was incontrovertible. This is the not the first time that Indian home ministry has discovered the invisible hand of the ISI in various terrorist activities around India. And it is not the first time that Pakistani Government has refuted the Indian charges. The world of western intelligence agencies and the intelligence community in India have long been conscious of the power and influence of ISI in Pakistani Governing Establishment and its role in fomenting trouble in India and Afghanistan. During the time of conflict and war, intelligence agencies generally assume greater power and influence even in democratic countries. At one time, the whole world, including sections of Americans, was concerned about the rising power and influence of the US Central Intelligence Agency. KGB was a powerful entity during the Soviet era with a gigantic international network. Israeli Mossad is considered a dreaded organization in the Middle East. But the ISI is unique in the sense that unlike in other countries, both democratic and communist, it has evolved into a government within a government in Pakistan. It has no democratic control because of weak political institutions, lack of democratic governance and lingering periods of military rule in that country. And, ironically, even the Pakistani Army seems to have had not much of a control over this agency.

Why did General Musharraf and his spoke-persons reject the findings of investigations citing ISI involvement in 7/11 incident in Mumbai so instantaneously? It was not because the Pakistani Government is sure of ISI's virtue, purity and innocence. It is partly because of the fear of isolating or antagonizing a powerful section of the Establishment and also because of ISI's functional role in Pakistani Government's strategic scheme against India in Kashmir and against the Karzai Government in Kabul. ISI, created in 1948 by a British Army Officer who happened to be the Deputy Chief of staff of the new Pakistani Army. Among other things, it was in charge of coordinating the intelligence functions of the three wings of the Pakistani military and its close links with the military goes back to its very inception. It was soon hijacked and used by General Ayub Khan, who came to power by staging the first military coup, to sustain the military regime by keeping a watchful eye on all opponents of the military. But it soon grew into a monstrous organization and its officers were not answerable to military or political leaders. According to its critics, it became a "state within a state." But the ISI always prospered under military rulers and grew in its power and influence within the country under General Yahya Khan's and General Zia-ul-Haq's military rule.

General Zia incidentally rose to the highest rank because of the support of the ISI Chief General Gulam Jilani Khan and he was instrumental in giving a free hand to the organization during his entire rule. He retained Gulam Jilani Khan as the ISI Chief even after his retirement. The Soviet invasion of Afghanistan and the decision of the US to turn Pakistan into a frontline state in waging a military struggle against the Soviet troops came as a golden opportunity for the ISI to expand its capabilities in covert and semi-military operations. As money and sophisticated weapons poured into Pakistan for training the anti-Soviet Afghan mujaheedins, the ISI had a field day. According to an estimate, the ISI "trained about 83,000 Afghan Mujahideen between 1983 to 1997 and dispatched them to Afghanistan." In the aftermath of the Soviet withdrawal from Afghanistan and the subsequent end of the Cold War with the disintegration of the Soviet Union, Pakistan made full use of the ISI to engineer the rise to power of the Taliban regime in Afghanistan. The US actually looked the other way when the Pakistani armed forces with the active participation of the ISI ensured the Taliban victory in the Afghan civil war. But like chicken coming home to roost, the Taliban regime was partly responsible for the 9/11 terrorist attacks on the United States.

As the US launched a global war against terrorism and once again converted Pakistan into a frontline state, the ISI appeared to be in for trouble. The ISI had hundreds of Taliban supports in its rank and file and Washington suspected if this organization would be of substantial and quality help in tracking down the al-Qaeda and Taliban members and sympathizers. Nonetheless, it was not practicable to isolate ISI, since it had good intelligence information on terrorist training camps, a large number of which were operating under its sponsorship or surveillance. It was clear that General Musharraf was not a willing and pleased partner of the US in the latter's war against the al-Qaeda and the Taliban. He was under pressure to follow Washington's instructions. What was known through American sources for years has been reconfirmed by Musharraf in his new and controversial book—*In the Line of Fire: A Memoir.* While Musharraf stood behind the Bush Administration and helped contrive the demise of the Taliban and received enormous kudos from American officials, top to bottom, the Taliban's resurgence is once again unfolding. Even the super terrorist, Osama bin Laden, appears to be healthy and hearty.

Washington was pleased when Musharraf replaced ISI head Lieutenant General Mahmood Ahmed Lieutenant General Ehsanul Haq weeks after the 9/11 incident and purged some of the Islamic fundamentalist elements from the important positions. But it was actually cosmetic. Now even American analysts are questioning the wisdom of investing so much on an individual—General Musharraf and do not believe that he is going to walk the extra mile in capturing Taliban leaders or eliminating Taliban as a force.

Before dubbing Taliban as a more dangerous threat than al-Qaeda in Europe, Musharraf had inked an agreement with the pro-Taliban tribal chiefs in the country's North Western Frontier Province. Unlike the Americans, Musharraf knows the Taliban and the ISI better. The clock has begun to tick against the Americans and Musharraf cannot afford to antagonize either the Taliban or their Godfather ISI.

What is the lesson for India? India had three options. First, it could wage a war against the perpetrators of 7/11. The geopolitical factors would not permit such an offensive. This option will be the hardest task and could offend the US as well, since Washington would not keep quiet over a potential Indo-Pakistan war amidst its own war against terror. Secondly, it could persuade General Musharraf to implement the newly agreed anti-terrorism mechanism and help capture and punish the culprit. But the end result was quite predictable. Musharraf would not be able to touch anti-India elements in the ISI without risking too much in politics and strategy. Thirdly, it could be realistic enough to hold dialogues with the ISI and aim at a new set of CBMs and mutual cooperation. But New Delhi did not do so. India actually should have woken up to the reality of the existence of a powerful pillar of Pakistan's ruling Establishment and open a dialogue with it for diplomatic solution of a quasi-military problem.

COUNTER-TERRORISM COOPERATION WITH THE US

While our peace process with Pakistan has not ensured any major improvement in terrorist threats, the emerging strategic partnership with the US has also not delivered much in this field. The debates on the nature, scope and consequences of the Indo-US nuclear deal has so dominated the agenda that cooperation over this crucial security issue of countering terrorism has remained overshadowed. India and the US established a forum to cooperate and coordinate efforts against terrorism in 2000, before the 9/11 terrorist attacks on the US. But when terrorism struck the US and India offered unconditional support, the Bush Administration chose to turn to Pakistan for help.

Islamabad promptly agreed to support Washington, soon after India extended its hand to the US, because Pakistan was afraid that it would otherwise become the target of Indo-US counter-terrorism offensive. By agreeing to support the US, the Musharraf regime protected Pakistan from possible US military action. Except token and cosmetic steps Pakistan did little concretely to stop cross-border terrorism against India. The US soon became more concerned about cross-border terrorism along Pakistan-Afghan border than along Indo-Pakistan border.

In May 2006, Assistant Secretary of State Richard Boucher had the following to say in his testimony before the House Subcommittee on Asia and the Pacific: "Both Pakistan and the U.S. understand that terrorism, in all its forms and manifestations, threatens us all. Following the September 11 attacks, the United States and Pakistan joined international efforts to fight the scourge of terrorism. We are grateful for Pakistan's strong and vital support in the war on terror. The sacrifices of Pakistan's troops in fighting extremists in the Federally Administered Tribal Areas are often underappreciated. We applaud those efforts and will continue to provide Pakistan with the support necessary to carry on the fight against terror."[6] In the same testimony, Boucher did not use the term counter-terrorism even once while speaking about India! He had nice things to say about Indian democracy, rising economic cooperation between the two countries and a lot more on the nuclear deal, but little on cooperation in the fight against terrorism.

Only a month earlier the so-called Indo-US Working Group on Counter-terrorism had met in Washington and the officials from India and the US had discussed wide ranging issues, including "bioterrorism, aviation security, advancements in biometrics, cyber-security and terrorism, WMD-terrorism, terrorist finance and money laundering and violent extremism." and agreed to "share information on a real time basis, respond to counterterrorism assistance requests expeditiously and collaborate to upgrade preparedness and capability to deal with acts of terrorism." Why did Boucher choose to ignore this issue?

It was because there was little concrete to report on this aspect of bilateral cooperation. For the United States, the war on terror launched in September/October 2001 is not yet over. The Bush Administration pledged then and has continued to do so to fight against terrorists of all kinds without any discrimination or prejudice. The 2006 *National Security Strategy Report* makes it clear that the US must stay on the offensive" and defeat the terrorists abroad so we do not need to face them here at home."[7]

Is India capable of such an offensive against the anti-India terrorist groups? In fact, India would receive no help from the US in tackling its terrorist threats, particularly those that are connected with Pakistan. The US response to such an Indian effort is predictable and will be along the similar line as was after the 13 December terrorist attack on the Indian Parliament. The Indo-US nuclear agreement, if implemented, is no doubt going to elevate the bilateral strategic partnership between the two countries. But lack of adequate cooperation in the field of tackling terrorism will turn Indo-US strategic partnership into almost a hollow one. The present and future threat that this nation is going to face is from terrorism. This is where India needs to seek cooperation from other countries, including the US. No macho show of domestic force can help us against terrorists. The US has realized it better. We need to do so.

The Bush administration claims now that "Al-Qaeda has lost its safe haven in Afghanistan. A multinational coalition joined by the Iraqis is aggressively prosecuting the war against the terrorists in Iraq. The al-Qaeda network has been significantly degraded. Most of those in the al-Qaeda network responsible for the September 11 attacks, including the plot's mastermind Khalid Shaykh Muhammad, have been captured or killed." The Indian Government, on the other hand, is waking up to the emerging reality that Al Qaeda is beginning to make in-roads into India. The reported Al Qaeda presence in Kashmir and the suspected Al Qaeda threat to blow up the Taj Mahal are but two significant examples. The content of Indo-US strategic partnership needs to be sufficiently expanded to include counter-terrorism cooperation. Like in the case of the nuclear deal, there will be concerns and apprehensions about US penetration of Indian security networks. But cooperation in this vital area is essential and sufficient cerebral activities can go into safeguarding India's national security secrets, even while cooperating with the important countries.

The Congressional Research Service brought out a report in February 2007 that has a long list of accomplishment in signing agreements and holding meetings. It says: "In November 2001, President Bush and then-Indian Prime Minister Vajpayee agreed that 'terrorism threaten not only the security of the United States and India, but also our efforts to build freedom, democracy and international security and stability around the world'. In 2002, India and the United States launched the Indo-US Cyber Security Forum to safeguard critical infrastructure from cyber attack. The June 2005 "New Framework for the U.S.-India Defense Relationship" lists 'defeating terrorism and violent religious exremism' as one of four key shared security interests, and it calls for a bolstering of mutual defense capabilities required for such a goal. An April 2006 session of the U.S. India Joint Working Group on Counterterrorism... ended with a statement of determination...to further advance bilateral cooperation...on such areas of common concern as bioterrorism, aviation security...."[8] But the actual cooperation in combating terrorism does not appear to be substantial. As has been mentioned earlier, the complex Pakistan factor will keep creating obstacles on the way of Indo-US relations. But that is not all. India will not be able to have all comprehensive world-wide cooperation with the US on counter-terrorism, because the US has a global approach and global threats, whereas India's concerns and interests are limited to the region. Secondly, the unilateral American approach to certain Islamic issues makes it almost impossible for India to join the US. The demographic profile of India with the second largest Muslim population in the world, India's economic interests in West Asia and geopolitical complexity of South Asia simply would not permit India and the US to come together on every aspect of this issue. The Indo-US counter terrorism cooperation should be robust, but should be confined to South Asia alone.[9]

CONCLUDING OBSERVATIONS:

While seeking international cooperation to combat terrorism is imperative, it is not sufficient. India needs to do a lot at home. In this regard, the observation made by the US State Department in its latest Country Report on Terrorism, 2006 is worth examining. It says: "India's counterterrorism efforts were hampered by its outdated and overburdened law enforcement and legal systems. The Indian court system was slow, laborious, and prone to corruption; terrorism trials can take years to complete. An independent Indian think tank determined that the thousands of civilians killed by terrorism in Jammu and Kashmir from 1988 to 2002 received justice in only 13 convictions through December 2002; most of the convictions were for illegal border crossing or possession of weapons or explosives. Many of India's local police forces were poorly staffed, trained, and equipped to combat terrorism effectively."[10]

As India marches ahead in the 21st century and increasingly plays a global role, the main threat to the country would come from within. India's emergence as an economic power house, its engagement of major powers of the world in matters of politics, economics and security and its intention to elevate India's profile in the international community could get punctured, unless the issue of current terrorism and potential ones is appropriately dealt with. The diversity of India and a transparent democratic structure make India proud but at the same time make it quite vulnerable to inter nal political and societal violence. The most disturbing phenomenon of the 21st century is the rising abilities of individuals and groups to cause violence. It poses one of the most formidable challenges to the concept of state sovereignty. The forces of globalization, open borders and technological innovation coupled with the physical empowerment of individuals and groups make democracies more and more vulnerable to terrorist attacks. The allocation of resources among people based on caste, religion, ethnicity, language and region to the satisfaction of diverse groups of people is not simple and painless in a democracy.

Can Indian democracy successfully do so? India is not equipped with the industrial bounties of the advanced industrial societies. India does not possess a totalitarian governing structure like that of the People's Republic of China. India is in the list of top fifteen industrial nations of the world. It is a potential permanent member of the UN Security Council and a prospective new member along with China of an extended G-8. It is now regarded as an IT superpower and an economic power house. But the other side of life in India is truly frightening. More than eighty percent of Indians live in less than two dollars a day. The conditions of the large number of Indian farmers are precarious. Majority of Indians do not benefit from the bounties of liberalization and rewards of globalization. India is thus full of potential terrorists. Disgruntled groups of individuals can come together on the grounds of caste, religion, region or other factors and resort to terrorist methods.

Last but not the least, the US war against global terrorism has reached the crossroads. The resurgence of the Taliban in Afghanistan, an apparent American war fatigue in Iraq, rising terrorist violence and political uncertainties in Pakistan, and unresolved strife in the Middle East and elsewhere are ominous signs of an uncertain future. What happens if the US withdraws its forces from Iraq? What will be in store for regional countries, if NATO decides to wind up its operations from Afghanistan? What will be the impact of Iran's emergence as a nuclear weapon power on the moral of Islamic radicals? Closer to home, what will be repercussions of a post-Musharraf political dispensation

on Kashmir and Indo-Pakistan peace process? Difficult days are ahead. Perspective planning is essential.

REFERENCES

1. "The Indian Imperative: A Conversation with Robert D Blackwill," *National Interest*, Summer 2005, p.12.
2. Government of India, Ministry of Home Affairs, Department of International Security, States, Home, Jammu and Kashmir Affairs and Border Management, *Annual Report, 2006-07*, p.7.
3. Ibid.
4. Ibid.
5. US Department of State, *Country Report on Terrorism*, 2006.
6. "The United States and South Asia; An Expanding Agenda," Statement of Richard Boucher, Assistant Secretary of State for South and Central Asian Affairs, before the Subcommittee on Asia and the Pacific of the House International Relations committee, 17 may 2006.
7. *The National Security Strategy of the United States of America*, 2006, issued by the White House, Washington, D.C.
8. "Indo-US Relations", *CRS Report for Congress*, Order Code RL33529, 13 February 2007.
9. For details see Chintamani Mahapatra, "The Muslim Factor in Indo-US Relations," *Indian Foreign Affairs Journal*, vol.1, no.4, October-December 2006.
10. US Department of State, *Country Report on Terrorism*, 2006.

2

US War on Terrorism: Intervention in Afghanistan and Iraq

Christopher S. Raj

On September 11, 2001, nineteen Saudi-born Islamic hijackers with box cutters and eluding security stunned the world, more particularly America when they with remarkable synchronism and accuracy, flew three fully fuelled jumbo aircrafts as human-guided missiles into designated and highly symbolic targets in New York and Washington. The fourth aircraft, which crashed in a Pennsylvania field, was believed to have been headed for the White House or the Capitol. In its emotional impact, September 11, may have been the most horrifying single day event in American history as Americans watched on television, in real time, the twin towers of the New York World Trade Centre and sections of Pentagon burn and collapse and more than 3000 of their fellow citizen die.[1] The day after September 11, General Richard Myers was asked at the Congressional hearings why the mightiest military in history had failed to protect the heart of American power from a band of men brandishing "box cutters". In those early shocked hours, the incoming Chairman of the Joint Chiefs of Staff had no ready reply but the unvarnished truth "we're pretty good if the threat is coming from the outside," Myers said. "We're not so good if it's coming in from the inside."[2]

PROCLAMATION OF NEW GLOBAL THREAT

President George W. Bush experienced 9/11 horrors as directly and as emotionally as any American. From the American President, Americans expected a convincing response. President Bush declared: "Make no mistake, the United States will hunt down and punish those responsible for these cowardly acts."[3] Bush and his foreign policy advisers suddenly faced an irreconcilable enemy and "new threat" to respond. During cold war years America had identified "Communism" as global threat. However, since the collapse of the Soviet Union in 1991, America had been celebrating that it had won the cold war and that the great clash of ideologies had ended. Surprisingly the post-Cold War phase also suddenly ended as America proclaimed new global threat when President Bush in his address to the joint Session of Congress and American people and world on 20th September 2001 announced that "our war on terror begins with al-Qaeda, but it does not end there. It will not end until every terrorist group of global reach had been found, stopped and defeated."[4] He reiterated that "only way to defeat terrorism as a threat to our way of life is to stop it, eliminate it and destroy it where it grows." Thus, since September 11, America had gone abroad in search of new "monster" (a term coined by then US Secretary of State John Quincy Adams in 1821) to destroy abroad—terrorist with hostile ideology, global in scope with uncertain duration, ruthless in purpose and terrorist methods. Before 9/11 many American policy makers and practitioners tended to view terrorism as a nuisance, individual entities but not a network nor as a major challenge to what the United States did in the world or a pressing threat at home.[5] All this changed in a single day on September 11.

Terrorism, since 9/11 was no longer one among a number of assorted dangers to the United States but declared a fundamental threat to America as well as to the world. Bush declared: "Every nation, in every region, now has a decision to make. *Either you are with us, or you are with the terrorist.* From this day forward, any nation that continues to harbor or support terrorism will be regarded by the United States as a hostile regime." The President vowed that the United States would find the perpetrators of the crime and would bring "our enemies to justice, or bring justice to our enemies, justice will be done." Indeed, Bush affirmed that "This is not, however, just America's fight. And what is at stake is not just America's freedom. This is the world's fight. This is civilization's fight." Many analysts and scholars have described these statements constituting the "Bush doctrine." Michael Hirsch's influential article in the Foreign Affairs Journal observes: "The Bush doctrine has been used to justify and a new assertiveness abroad unprecedented since the early days of the Cold War—amounting nearly to the declaration of American hegemony—and it had redefined US relationship around the world."[6] Hirsch affirms that "under the hammer of the Bush Doctrine," Pakistan was forced to relinquish its long-time support of the Taliban and its tolerance of al-Qaeda; and Saudi Arabia had to reckon that 15 of its own disaffected citizen belonging to fundamentalist Wahabi brand of Islam were the terrorists who had carried the horrifying attack. The third significant observation of Hirsh had been that the Bush doctrine has also "helped to reinvigorate relations with major powers such as China, Russia and India," each of which face its own terrorist insurgency all of which "are now on friendlier terms with Washington than with each other." Fourthly, Hirsh notes that the President had used the Bush doctrine to isolate Iraq, Iran and North Korea as an "axis of evil"—even though almost no one else around the world view them quite that same way—to declare America's right to pre-emptive attack anywhere. Thus while Hirsch summed up that "unilateralism" in American foreign policy had dawned, Michael Mandelbaum declared that the United States was no longer a mere superpower but a "hyper power"; and "moved into a more imperial mode" notes Barry Buzan.[7] Joseph Nye while affirming that the "United States is the most powerful nation on earth..." observed that "like Rome, the US is not invincible. Rome did not succumb to the rise of another empire, but to the onslaught of waves of barbarians. Modern transnational terrorists are the new barbarians."[8] Richard N. Haass, then Director, Policy Planning Staff of the State Department pointed out "the attacks were a grim reminder of how the march of globalization has raised the stakes from transnational threats. The murderers used cell phones, email and the internet to communicate. They moved money via wire. And they turned civilian airlines into flying missiles.... Transnational threat can present a clear and present danger to our way of life."[9]

Mark Penn, a pollster, who carried out polls for former President Clinton, posed the question in a survey whether people considered government "more or less relevant to their life since September 11." Significant overwhelming majority, precisely 69% responded "more relevant." For the first time since the Cuban missile Crisis, Penn concluded "this is an experience that makes the people fundamentally more positive about their government and leadership." Mark Penn findings were also corroborated by the *Washington Post* and *ABC* polls. Its finding were revealing as the poll established that the confidence of the people on the Federal government had escalated to its highest since 1996.[10] Such highly charged and mobilized public opinion in favor of federal government facilitated the Bush Administration to proclaim "terrorism" as national security "threat" and formulated instruments of "war on terrorism".

The Bush Administration's shift from economic liberation of post-cold war years to national security paradigm in post-9/11 was shrewdly executed. With national security legitimating its unilateralist proclivities under the slogan of war against terrorism, a fervently neoconservative White House found terrorism and terrorists a new threat and build a world around it. Discounting deterrence and containment as ineffective in the world of amorphous and ill-defined terrorist networks, the Bush

Administration justifyingly upheld bolstering the state's coercive and police power at home and to remilitarize American policy abroad. Hence, national security paradigm rapidly passed through three variants focused successively on:

* *Prevention:* building up domestic counter-terrorism (homeland security Measures taken after September 11, 2001).
* *Retribution*: legitimizing diplomatically sanctioned military force & formation of "alliance of willing" (intervention to destroy the Taliban government in Afghanistan).
* *Pre-emption:* implementing the unilateralist Bush Doctrine (war to achieve Regime change in Iraq).[11]

THE DECISION: WAR ON TERRORISM AND AL-QAEDA

On 15 September 2001, President Bush summoned his top national-security advisers to Camp David to decide America's retaliation for the terrorist attacks on New York City and Washington.[12] The statutory national security advisers to President, who are members of the National Security Council, (an institution created in 1947 to counter the Communist and the Soviet threat) included Vice President Dick Cheney, Secretary of State General Colin Powell, Secretary Defense Donald Rumsfeld, Director of Central Intelligence Agency (CIA) George Tenet, National Security Adviser Condoleezza Rice, Chairman of the Joint Chiefs of Staff Richard Myers. According to Time magazine, "Cheney's...relations with Bush is so close and so big that he is fixed weight who pulls policy in his direction...." [13] As Secretary of Defense in Senior Bush Presidency Dick Cheney has been working on a radically new foreign policy doctrine for the post-Cold war world. In 1992 when Defense Planning Guidance was published, it was called "Dick Cheney's master work".[14] In formulating the document substantial assistance was provided by Paul Wolfowitz then

Under Secretary of Defense in the Senior Bush's Presidency. The document assumed that the most important of America's unique qualities was its military dominance. The Cheney document also introduced the idea that unilateral military action, the preemptive use of force and the maintenance of a US nuclear arsenal strong enough to deter the development of nuclear programme elsewhere were now appropriate U.S. policies. It called on the United States neither to cultivate its own garden nor to pursue a world mission through multilateral organization that would define and legitimize common goals. Instead, it demanded of America only that it be, remain and act as the world's sole superpower. It is noteworthy that since 1997 "core ideas" of the Defense Planning Guidance document had become part of the Project for a New American Century (PNAC) as founding members of this Project included Cheney, Rumsfeld, Wolfowitz, I. Lewis Libby and Elliot Abrams.[15] PNAC'S vision, as articulated by its founders, anti-apologetically favors a Pax Americana backed by superior military power and a will to confront—unilaterally, if necessary—any emerging or potential regional or global power before it can threaten Washington's interest or position.; mostly hostile towards the United Nations; absolutely convinced of the fundamental moral superiority and redemptive mission of the United States abroad. It is significant to observe that in January 2001, member of PNAC who are often referred to as neoconservatives and unilateralists have become the national security advisers of President Bush: Cheney as Vice-president, Rumsfeld as Secretary of Defense, Wolfowitz as Deputy Secretary of Defense, I. Lewis as Cheney's Chief of Staff, Elliot Abrams as member of National Security Council Staff. This neoconservative group of Washington insiders got support from outside the administration, from members of PNAC and neoconservative groups including such personalities as former UN Ambassador Jeanne Kirkpatrick, "End of History" guru Francis Fukuyama, former CIA chief James Woolsey, syndicated columnist Charles Krauthammer, and Weekly Standard editor, William Kristol, Richard Perle, acting in his quasi-governmental role as Chair of the Defense Policy Board. The neoconservatives while sharpening the doctrine of intervention, pre-emptive strikes and unilateralism also addressed through Wolfowitz the aspect of how to handle Iraq. As early as 1990 Wolfowitz had been suggesting a policy of pre-emptive strike against enemy states like Iraq which is trying to obtain Weapons of Mass Destruction (WMD).[16] Charles Krauthammer and William Kristol as "new imperialist" were disappointed of the ending of the Gulf war in 1991 without any actions inside Iraq.[17] In January 1998 in formal letter to President Clinton signed by right-wing policy group called Project for the New American Century, including Wolfowitz and Rumsfeld urged "to enunciate a new strategy that would secure the interest of the U.S. and our friends and allies around the world. That strategy should aim, above all, at the removal of Saddam Hussein's regime from power."[18] Yet after assuming his current post as Deputy Secretary of Defense in 2001, Wolfowitz initially downplayed the wisdom of committing U.S. forces to oust Saddam. Only after September 11, Wolfowitz appreciated the need and urgency to remove Saddam before he would slip WMD to terrorists.[19]

Moreover, it appears that by that time Wolfowitz had evolved his project of great ambition—that an American intervention will make of Iraq "the first Arab democracy".[20] It envisions a post-Saddam Hussein Iraq—secular, middle-class, urbanized, rich with oil—that will replace the autocracy of Saudi Arabia as the key American ally in the Persian Gulf, allowing the withdrawal of United States troops from the Kingdom. The presence of a victorious American Army in Iraq would then serve as a powerful boost to moderate elements in neighboring Iran, hastening that critical country's evolution away from the mullahs and toward a more moderate course. Such an evolution in Tehran would lead to withdrawal of Iranian support for

Hezbollah and other radical group thereby isolating Syria and reducing pressure on Israel. This undercutting of radicals on Israel's northern borders and within the West Bank and Gaza would spell the definitive end of Yasser Arafat and lead eventually to a favorable solution of the Arab-Israeli problem.

With neoconservatives having significant clout in the Bush Administration, the only moderate force among the national security advisers appears to be Secretary of State Colin Powell supported by Richard Armitage, Deputy Secretary of State and Richard N. Haass, Director, Policy Planning Staff of Department of State. Powell has long taken exception to the conservatives' muscular brand of unilateralism, arguing instead that the U.S. should act in concert with allies. Colin Powell is no liberal or dove. As James Mann, a Senior writer-in-residence at the Centre for Strategic and International Studies wrote in the Washington Post: "Powell has been, throughout his career, a proponent of a strong national defense, an extensive military presence overseas and, more generally, a unique American role in the world....US troops should be sent into conflict only when vital US interests are at stake, where there is strong public support, where the objectives are clearly defined and limited, and where overwhelming force is used to accomplish the objectives."[21] It may be observed that inside State Department while reasonably harmony existed among Powell, Armitage and Haass, there existed fifth columnist in John Bolton, Under Secretary of State for Arms Control and international Security.[22] Bolton was more in tune with Cheney, PNAC's vision and Pentagon hawks than with Powell's relatively moderate and demeanor. Besides John Bolton had the support of Deputy Assistant Secretary of State for Near East Affairs Elizabeth Cheney, the daughter of U.S. president Dick Cheney.

Available reports indicated that on 15 September 2001 President Bush summoned his top national security advisers (possibly the member of the National Security Council) to Camp David to plot America's retaliation for the terrorist attacks on

New York and Washington. It seems all the advisers including Secretary Powell favored the decision relating to war on terrorism.[23] Such decision was spontaneously forthcoming because of the fact that 19 terrorists committed on September 11 most shocking traumatic atrocities in New York and Washington, and that the US had found in past precedence of such terrorist attacks on Americans in 1998 and 2000 linked to Osama bin Laden and al-Qaeda. But the question and debate was where this war should be pursued. As the group began to hammer out a strategy for war against Taliban and hitting Osama bin Laden in Afghanistan, Paul Wolfowitz took a different track. An Afghan war in his view had the makings of a quagmire. The larger threat to American security was sitting not in a cave in Afghanistan but in a Baghdad bunker. And so just four days after September 11, Wolfowitz with the support of Rumsfeld and Cheney urged Bush to go war against Iraq. According to CBS News Report, Rumsfeld while favored war on Taliban and hitting Osama bin Laden, did not want to exclude war against Iraq too. Moreover, the Pentagon sought in spite of the State Department's opposition, widening the war on terrorism to Iraq, even if there was no firm evidence linking Saddam Hussein to the September 11 terrorist attacks. However, Wolfowitz presentation perhaps did not convince or persuade President Bush or all his national security advisers. According White House NSC counterterrorism official, Richard A. Clarke (till 2003) pointed out that President Bush was interested to know whether Saddam had any link in spite of the intelligence officials reiterating that al Qaeda was involved.[24] Then CIA Director George Tenet had been holding the view that "al Qaeda is at war with" the US.[25] Secretary Powell seems to have persuaded the President that a larger war involving other countries would only alienate the Islamic world more particularly American allies in the Middle East. Consequently, it seems Bush decided in favor of a "war on terror" focusing on al-Qaeda and Taliban leadership in Afghanistan. This decision he shared with the nation on 20 September 2001, when he addressed the Joint Session of Congress.

Before leaving the office President Clinton in his official meeting with President-elect George Bush emphasized terrorism to be major "new threat" facing America...[26] He also instructed his NSC Advisor Sandy Berger to raise it with his successor as NSC Advisor Condoleezza Rice. However, in January 2001, the Bush Administration, really thought Clinton's recommendation that eliminating al-Qaeda be one of their highest priorities, well, rather odd, like so many of the Clinton administration's action from their perspective.[27] Moreover, Bush's Secretary of the Treasury Paul O Neil recently revealed that Bush from the first National Security Council meeting was focused on Iraq and elimination of Saddam Hussein.[28] This objective continued until the shocking episode of 9/11. Unable to directly link Iraq with the 9/11 episode, together with overwhelming intelligence identifying of al-Qaeda with 9/11 horror, and the need to quickly and successfully retaliate for restoring American image, presumably made Bush to declare "war on terror" and focus on al-Qaeda in Afghanistan. In his address to the nation and Joint Session, President Bush said: "Americans are asking: who attacked our country? The evidence we have gathered all points to a collection of loosely affiliated terrorist organization known as al-Qaeda. They are the same murderers indicted for bombing American embassies in Tanzania and Kenya, responsible for bombing of the U.S.S. Cole. Al Qeada is to terror what the mafia is to crime....This group and its leader—a person named Osama bin Laden—are linked to many other organizations in different countries, including the Egyptian Islamic Jihad and the Islamic Movement of Uzbekistan." President Bush also noted that the Al Qaeda had linkages with terrorist organization in as many as sixty countries. Its finger prints were claimed presumably by the Bush and his national security advisers to be all over the September attack. Such observation by the policy-makers was result of their awareness of America's past links and fostering of Islamic militants.

THE QUESTION NOW ARISES WHO CREATED THE AL-QAEDA AND FOSTERED OSAMA BIN LADEN

A few days after the attack on the World Trade Center and the Pentagon, a top official of the George Bush Administration told closed door gathering, "our chickens have come home to roost." [29] The candid submission was more than attempt to deflect the blame from the present administration. It was a tacit acceptance of the long-term failure of American foreign policy which used the "Islamic card"[30] as antidotes to Communist ideology and anti-Soviet campaign in Afghanistan since 1979. Sleigh Harrison from the Woodrow Wilson International Centre for Scholars created quite a furor in March 2001 when he stated that the American Central Intelligence Agency (CIA) worked in tandem with Pakistan to create the Taliban. "The CIA made a historic mistake in encouraging Islamic groups from all over the world to come to Afghanistan. The US provided $ 3 billion for building up these Islamic groups and it accepted Pakistan's demand that they should decide how this money should be spent'. Harrison claimed to have warned the CIA authorities against creating a monster which at a later period might run wild. However, the CIA obsession with defeating the Soviets proved to be myopic. As a result, "some 35,000 Muslim radicals from 40 Islamic countries joined Afghanistan's fight between 1982 and 1992. Tens of thousands more came to study in Pakistani madarsas." Eventually, CIA's facilitator Pakistan's Inter-Service Intelligence (ISI) recruited more than 100,000 foreign Muslim radicals including young Saudi student Osama Bin Laden, who subsequently through his front organization Maktab al- Khidamar (MAK) operationalised holy war "Jihad" against the Soviets forces in Afghanistan which then served American interest.[31] American action soon witnessed the revisitation of the story of

Frankenstein's monster displaying in real life as America also permitted the fostering of Islamic militant facilities within the US. For instance, mosques in New York were allowed in order to help train recruits for the Russo-Afghan war since 1979. It was only a matter of time before these cells turned on the US.

After successfully pursing his holy war "jihad" against the Soviet forces which withdrew from Afghanistan in 1989, Osama's indoctrinated Arab and Afghan mujahideen along with Pakistanis facilitated to power Taliban regime at Kabul. The White House counter-terrorism official Richard Clarke, pointed out that following the Soviet withdrawal, America quickly pulled out and abandoned the country to its fate. He observed: "Some Afghan and some Arab fighters (led by Osama) pondered what you could do with money, Korans and few good weapons. You could overthrow an infidel government. More important, you could destroy a superpower."[32] Bin Laden's al Qaeda struck the first blow against the United States in 1993 when a time bomb placed in the basement of WTC exploded resulting in the death of a large number of people and injuries to even a much larger number. In August 1998, Bin Laden declared that "our fight is now against America. I regret having lived this long. I have nothing to lose" and again four months later, he proclaimed, "I am not afraid of death. Rather, martyrdom is my passion because martyrdom would lead to the birth of 1,000s of Osamas."[33] In 1998, the al Qaeda struck another major blow with powerful RDX explosive at the American Embassies in Dar-e-salaam in Tanzania and Nairobi in Kenya resulting in death of many Americans. Though American intelligence had been tracking Bin Laden since 1995, it was only after the bombing in 1998 that President Clinton authorized all out hunt.[34] On 20 August 1998, the Clinton Administration launched a cruise missile attack against his headquarters in Khost and a pharmaceutical factory in Sudan which it claimed was producing substance for manufacturing chemical weapons. Moreover, the US had information that a meeting of nearly

hundred terrorist was to take place in Khost in which Bin Laden was going to attend. Bin Laden reportedly narrowly escaped with alerting by Pakistani intelligence. Two years later in October 2000 in Yemen the USS Cole was again attacked by members of Al-Qaeda and many American naval personnel were killed. In all these three major terrorist al-Qaeda's attacks the American reaction had been considering them as a single act of terrorism and were satisfied by bringing the suspect, including Bin Laden to justice by persuading the Taliban to hand over . Indeed this was the perspective of the intelligence communities in Europe. The terrorist organization cells were viewed as individual entities and were watched but were not viewed as a network. It was only after September 11 that the investigations revealed the existence of a net work of al Qaeda in sixty countries including at least in six European countries. (Belgium, Britain, France, Germany, Italy and Spain).

Once the Bush Administration identified the perpetrators of the September 11th catastrophe to be the terrorists linked to Al Qaeda and Osama bin Laden, President Bush on 20 September in his address to Joint Session of Congress declared a "a war on terror," and demanded of the Taliban leadership in Afghanistan that it turn over all the leaders of al-Qaeda terrorist group based in that country, close every terrorist training camp there, hand over all terrorists to appropriated authorities, and give the United States full access to terrorist training camps. "These demands are not open to negotiations or discussion," the President said. Moreover, the President warned that "the Taliban must act and act immediately. They will hand over the terrorists, or they will share in their fate." President Bush also revealed the goal of the "War on Terror" when he said "Our war on terror begins with al-Qaida, but it does not end there. It will not end until every terrorist group of global reach has been found, stopped, and defeated."

A TWO FRONT WAR: DOMESTIC & AFGHANISTAN

The United States began the war against international terrorism on two fronts: at home and in Afghanistan. The immediate effect of the September attacks on the domestic front was that partisan differences disappeared. On 14 September, the US Congress promptly passed resolution authorizing the President to "use all necessary and appropriate force" against "nations, organizations, and individuals who are involved in acts of terrorism or harbored people who were involved." The Senate approved the resolution by a unanimous 98 to 0 vote but the House adopted it by 421 to 1 vote. The lone dissenting vote was cast by Congresswoman Ms. Barbara Lee (Dem.Cal.). Ms. Lee's contention was that military action would not prevent further acts of violence against the country and she stood by her conviction.[35] The tolerance of dissent had gone to such an extent in the post September 11 America that Ms Lee's office reported receiving death threat after the vote. Nancy Gibbs wrote in the Time: "when dissent is made to seem unpatriotic, a little silver of democracy is dying." There was a spurt in hate crime and Muslim and Sikh Americans were attacked. The Congress approved a $40 billion package by a 96 to 0 vote for helping the victims and hunting the perpetrators of the attacks. The public opinion was solidly behind the tough stand being taken by the President. His approval rating after the September attack climbed up to 90 percent, the highest in six decades according to the Gallup that had been conducting the opinion polls. The country not only approved the waging of the war against terrorism but eight out of ten Americans supported the use of ground force, even if there were casualties. The President declared national emergency.

In a speech President Bush underlined the new reality. He said, "We've entered into a new period in our history...and the lives are not going to be as normal as they were in the past." American people understand, he said, "that this is going to take a long period of time, and they are prepared for that."[36] In the

House of Representatives, Congressman Don Young (Rep. Alaska) introduced a bill which was passed that had three main features: it provided for the assumption of complete control of airport security and screening, expansion of Federal Air Marshal Plan, and securing of cockpits and other security measures abroad air planes.[37] On 26 October 2001, the President signed another bill that gave the law enforcement officials additional powers of arrest, wire tapping and seizure to control the terrorist activities.

By an executive order on 24 September 2001, President Bush froze the assets and transactions of 27 terrorist organizations. Included in the list was Harkat-ul-Mujahideen, a terrorist organization that had been very active in Jammu and Kashmir. This was called a "a major thrust in the war against terrorism." President Clinton had issued similar edict against Al Qaeda but it had not effect. Analysts were quick to point out that network of Bin Laden not only operated through formal banking channels but through non formal channels were unlikely to be affected.

Meanwhile, on 19 September 2001, the first draft of what would be called the USA-PATRIOT ACT (the acronym abbreviates "Uniting and Strengthening America by Providing Appropriate Tools Require to Intercept and Obstruct Terrorism) is introduced in the Congress. However, due to Congressional opposition of its broad powers, the act is revised and introduced on 2 October. The "anti-terrorism" USA-PATRIOT Act was again not well received by all. Senate Majority Leader and future anthrax target Tom Daschle (Dem.) said that he doubted the Senate would take up the bill in one week timetable the administration wanted. Attorney General Ashcroft accused the Senate Democrats of dragging their feet. On 4 October, the Senate Judiciary Committee Chairman and future anthrax target Patrick Leahy (Demo) accused the Bush Administration of reneging on an agreement on the anti-terrorist bill and warned that "lawmakers" were overlooking constitutional flaws in their rush to meet the Administration's timetable.[38] Finally the PATRIOT Act was signed into law by President Bush on 26 October. It was passed without any public debate. Even though it ultimately took six weeks to pass the law, there was no hearing or Congressional debate. Congressman Barney Frank (Dem.) stated: "This was the least democratic process for debating questions fundamental to democracy I have ever seen. A bill drafted by a handful of people in secret, subject to no Committee process comes before us immune from amendment." Only 66 Congressman, and one Senator, Russell Feingold (Dem.) voted against it. Few in Congress were able to read summaries, let alone the fine print of 342 pages, before voting on it. Feingold stated, "the new law goes into a lot of areas that have nothing to do with terrorism and have a lot to do with the government and the FBI having a wish list of things they want to do...." [39]

Some of the important provisions of the PATRIOT Act are: (1) Non-Citizens can be detained and deported if they provide "assistance" for lawful activities of any group the government chooses to call a terrorist organization. Under this provision the Secretary of State can designated any group that has ever engaged in violent activity as a terrorist organization. (2) The government is not required to provide detainees with counsel, nor is it required make any announcement or statement regarding the arrest; (3) Immigrants can be detained indefinitely, even if they are found to not have any link to terrorism. They can be detained indefinitely for immigration violations or if the attorney general decides their activities pose a danger to national security. They never need to be given a trial or even a hearing on their status; (4) Internet service providers can be ordered to reveal the web sites and e-mail addresses that a suspect has communicated to or visited. The FBI need only inform a judge that the information is relevant to an investigation; (5) It lays the foundation for a domestic intelligence-gathering system of unprecedented scale and technological prowess." It allows the government to access confidential credit report, school records, and other records, without consent or notification. All of this information can now be given to the CIA, in violation of the CIA's mandate prohibiting it from spying within the US; (6) Financial institutions are encouraged to disclose possible violations of law or "suspicious activities" by any client. The institution is prohibited from notifying the person involved that it made such a report. The "suspicious" is not defined, so it is up to the financial institutions to determine when to send such a report; (7) Federal agents can easily obtain warrants to review a library patron's reading and computer habits; and (7) The government can refuse to reveal how evidence is collected against a suspected terrorist defendant.[40]

A national debate on balancing the national security and civil liberties has been ensuing ever since the passing of the USA PATRIOT and Department of Homeland Security Acts.[41] The many challenges raised by the war on terror make the debate about it multifaceted and complex. This complexity itself is perhaps one reason a simple "liberty versus security" framework has gained at traction. Instead of grappling with the many difficult issues involved, each side simply focused itself with single criterion of concern. Advocates of security see in government policies under the said acts to be justifiable and admirable for the security of the nation. The civil libertarians see these policies to be long train of abuses. From the pubic outcry over the Bush administration's measures to combat terrorism, libertarians suppose that America is well on the way to becoming a police state. A full page newspaper advertisement by the American Civil Liberties Union (ACLU) for instance, informs us that the PATRIOT Act, the administration's major security initiative, goes "far beyond fighting terrorism" and has "allowed government agents to violate our civil liberties—tapping deep into private lives of innocent Americans." From the libertarian Left, Anthony Lewis in the New York Times Magazine has charged President Bush with undermining safeguards for the accused in a way that Lewis "did not believe was possible in" US, while from the Libertarian Right, William Safire has protested the administration's effort to realize the "super snoop's dream" of spying on all Americans. Moreover, according to Ibrahim Hooper, a spokesman for the Council for the Council on American-Islamic Relations, American Muslims have already lost many of their civil rights. "All Muslims are now suspects," Hooper has protested bitterly. He pointed out that the most salient outward sign of this had been ethnic profiling that occurs routinely in US, particularly at airports but elsewhere as well—a form of discrimination widely considered to be self-evident evil.[42]

Meanwhile, Four States (Hawaii, Alaska, Maine and Vermont) and 331 cities (including New York City, Los Angeles, Dallas, Chicago, Philadelphia, Pennsylvania and Cambridge) have passed resolution condemning the USA PATRIOT Act for attacking civil liberties.[43] Arcata, California, is the first city to pass an ordinance that bars city employees (including police and librarians) from assisting or cooperating with any federal investigations under the USA PATRIOT Act that would violate civil liberties. The Bill of Rights Defense Committee is helping coordinate local efforts to pass such anti PATRIOT Act resolutions. The present debate has identified the conflict in five main areas of controversy: due process issues, extraordinary detention, and the civil rights of non-citizens, government secrecy, and the treatment of terrorist captives outside the United States. The first and greatest source of concern among civil libertarians arises from the expansion of police powers that make it easier for government agencies to conduct surveillance, use wiretaps and searches, obtain access to personal records, and track and question designated groups. As a result, the current civil liberties debate is distinctive for its novel focus on issues related to due process.[44]

Expanded scope for surveillance is an especially important feature of the Act. It gives police agencies new authority to conduct expanded telephone and Internet surveillance and loosens 1070s restrictions on the ability of the CIA to engage in domestic surveillance. Under the New Department of Justice guidelines that employ broad definition of terrorism, the FBI could monitor religious and political groups without specific evidence of wrongdoing in the name of national security. Moreover, the power of the police to track, monitor, and question individuals has also increased. Plans to fingerprint and track electronically Arab and Muslim non-citizens have been announced by the Department of Justice. The police have also been authorized to question thousands of Arab and Muslim men, without "individualized suspicion" wrongdoing. Already the Human Rights Watch has revealed that some 1,200 non-citizens mostly Middle Eastern, South Asian and North Africans have been secretly arrested and incarcerated in connection with the September 11 investigation.[45] The Human Rights Watch have also pointed out that the US government has held some detainees for prolonged periods without charges; impeded their access to counsel; subjected them to coercive interrogations; and overridden judicial orders to release them on bond during immigration proceedings. Added to the identified expanded police powers some controversial measures to unify and coordinate the operations of various branches of the government. Most notably, the USA PATRIOT Act authorizes the FBI and CIA to cooperate and share information much more closely; bringing together the work of intelligence and law enforcement agencies that had been intentionally separated a generation ago in order to protect civil liberties. To integrate the domestic policing effort in the war on terror, the Department of Homeland Security has been providing local law enforcement with much more information gathered from national law enforcement agencies. Finally, the Department of Homeland Security is also assessing the extent to which military forces may be used to aid civilian law enforcement effort, in the face of the 1878 Posse Comitatus Act prohibiting domestic use of the military.[46]

Advocates of security have pointed that when dangers increase, liberties shrink. That has been history, especially in Wartime. "And today we face dangers without precedent: mass movement of militant Islamic terrorist who crave martyrdom, hide in shadow, are fanatically bent on slaughter as many of us possible...ultimately we can hold down our casualties only by finding and locking up (or killing) as many as possible of the hundreds or thousands of possible al-Qaida terrorist whose strategy is to infiltrate our society and avoid attention until they strike....The urgency of penetrating secret terrorist cells make it imperative for Congress-and-the nation—to undertake candid, searching, and systematic reassessment of the civil liberties rules that restrict the government's core investigative and detention powers."[47] The advocates of security observed that US policy makers long have wrestled with civil liberties questions in times of crisis and those seeking restraints on individual rights often have prevailed.[48] Repeatedly it is being debated that the unusual character of this war and unique task facing the government especially as the enemy is a terrorist organization operating in part on the American soil, the response would be unavoidably at least as much as matter for law enforcement as for the military. In the end the forcible warning had been that after September 11, it is impossible to deny that very real possibility that a terrorist could detonate a nuclear bomb in an American city. Under such circumstances, the security advocates claim that anything but the most vigorous security policy (foreign and domestic) would be inexcusable

US INTERVENTION IN AFGHANISTAN

Although the war on terrorism has greatly raised the profile of democracy as a policy matter it has hardly clarified the issue. The United States faced two contradictory imperatives: on the hand, the fight against al-Qaeda tempts Washington to put aside its democratic scruples and seek closer ties with autocracies throughout the Middle East and Asia. On the other hand, U.S. officials and policy experts have increasingly come to believe that it is precisely the lack of democracy in many of these countries that helps breed Islamic extremism. Resolving this tension had been not easy task. So far, Bush and his foreign policy team have shown an incipient, albeit unsurprising, case of split personality: "Bush the realist" actively cultivates warm relations with "friendly tyrants" in many parts of the world, while "Bush the neo-Reaganite" makes ringing calls for a vigorous new democracy campaign in the Middle East.[49] With such uncomfortable dualism Bush sought his allies especially Muslim states (mostly authoritarian) to join the US in the war on terrorism against Bin Laden's al-Qaeda in Afghanistan.

The prevalent anti-American feelings in the Muslim world were delaying the campaign against terrorism beginning in Afghanistan. In an al-Jazeera talk-show that aired 10 July 2001 (Before WTC/Pentagon attacks) Bin Laden was portrayed as an Arab hero who stood up to the West.[50] Misperception also abounded after 9/11when many in the Arab world did not believe bin-Laden was responsible for the attack. For example, a regional Arab Opinion poll concluded that 31 percent respondent blamed Israel for the attacks on the US while only 27 percent blamed Bin-Laden.[51] Palestinians were particularly opposed to intervention in Afghanistan. A Bir Zeit University poll found 76 percent opposed to joining the US-led coalition and an even greater number, 89 percent, believed the United States was not justified in attacking Afghanistan. Even American allies like Egypt initially sought America proof of al-Qaeda's involvement in the 9/11 episode and was reluctant to participate in the US-led campaign. Indeed, Arabs hate America primarily because of American role in the Arab-Israeli dispute. A 2001 poll of Saudi, Kuwaitis, Emirates, Egyptians and Lebanese Arab concluded that 60 percent of the Arab public in those states claimed the Palestinian conflict as the "single most important issue of personal concern and hate America.[52]

In the context of existing anti-American Arab world public opinion, Secretary of State Colin Powell recognized the need for persuading the President that a larger war needed support of the America's Islamic allies and other Muslim countries in the Middle East for the removal of the regime in Afghanistan. This was not an easy task. For decades the United States had been in confrontation with major Muslim countries like Iran, Iraq, Syria and Libya. A number of terrorist groups like Hamas, Hezbollah, and Islamic Jihad violently opposed the American policy of blind support for Israel against the Palestinians. They had their bases in these countries. The United States had declared them to be "rogue states." Even American allies, Saudi Arabia and Egypt, strongly resented America's support for Israel. The ruling elite in friendly Arab countries maintained amicable relations with the United States but the masses regarded the United States as their enemy. What was noted by every one was that out the of nineteen terrorist identified for the September attack by the American intelligence fifteen were Saudis. The result was that even Saudi Arabia and Egypt found it difficult to extend full support to the United States led war against another Muslim country.[53]

Of all the Muslim countries the United States needed the cooperation of Pakistan and Central Asian Republic Tajikstan and Uzbekistan bordering Afghanistan for most of its military campaign. The Taliban had risen from Pakistan's madarsas. They had been helped in every conceivable way by the ISI to fight its way to power in Afghanistan. The geopolitical position of Pakistan and its closeness to the ruling Taliban regime invited American attention more than any other Muslim state. Reports indicated that President Bush directly spoke to President Musharraf and asked him to choose between joining the war against international terrorism or be treated as an enemy, a country on par with Afghanistan. Pakistan's President made his choice to be with the America for his country's national interest. In a telecast he explained the rational of his decision to the nation and claimed that he took the decision only after wider consultation with leaders of all sections of society.

Pakistan leader had calculated his options very well. The refusal to cooperate with the United States could invite more stringent economic sanction driving Pakistan to bankruptcy. On the other hand if Pakistan decided in favor of joining the war against terrorism, it could hope to reverse its economic decline with the assistance of the West. Its international debt could be written off or at least rescheduled. No wonder the jihadi group that he patronized would turn against him, which he could have calculated then could be managed. In hindsight it is proving his capabilities and also his mercurial participation in sharing intelligence on al Qaeda has not annoyed the American support of Pakistan. In fact Pakistan President Musharraf has created a great stake for America in sustaining his regime.

With the help of Britain and its Prime Minister Tony Blair, the United States made most strenuous effort to enlist the cooperation of the Islamic world. Blair visited the Middle Eastern countries four times within a month and a half to seek their support. The British Foreign Secretary jack Straw visited Iran, the first such visit in more than two decades, to persuade to join the war against global terrorism. But despite the fact that there was no love lost between the Taliban and Iran and that the latter was openly supporting the Northern alliance, the Jack Straw's effort did not go far. Iran did not want to be seen in company of the United States fighting against another Muslim country. In October 2001, Prime Minister Blair visited Syria for the first time in thirty years to enlist its cooperation in gathering intelligence about Bin Laden and his organization. Here too the British Prime Minister drew a blank as the Syrian President Assad strongly criticized the military campaign in Afghanistan that began on 07 October. Besides Assad told Blair that the West should not call the Palestinian struggle for independence and establishment of sovereign state as terrorism. He also decried the tendency to project the West Asia as the breeding ground of terrorists. [54]

The United States has close relations with Saudi Arabia.

The latter had permitted the United States to station its troops and set up communication and command center in the country during the Gulf war. Yet deeply conscious of the widespread anger of the masses against the United States it too was unwilling to throw itself in the US led war against terrorism despite the fact that bin Laden threatened the very existence of the Saudi rulers. To demonstrate its distance from the US policy the Saudis made it clear that they would not support American strike against any Arab country on the ground that terrorist organizations were known to operate from there. Even the Prime Minister Blair's personal visit to Saudi Kingdom did not produce open support for the war on terrorism in Afghanistan. Moreover, in a public snub, Saudi Arabian rulers declined to see him because of prevailing strong anti-West sentiment. After his visit to the Middle East Tony Blair concluded that the West was not winning the propaganda war and the message that the West was not at war with Islam was not getting through.[55] In order to reduce possible damages and hardening of opposition to the war, Prime Minister Blair invited Yasser Arafat to London and at the joint press conference supported the idea of a Sovereign Palestinian state side by side with Israel in peace and harmony. President Bush too came up with the statement that a Palestinian state had been always on the horizon of American policy. Its boundary could be settled through negotiations. However, on 7 November 2001 both Bush and Blair in a joint Press conference declared that resolution of the Palestinian issue was not a condition for winning the war in Afghanistan.

The "Operation Enduring Freedom" that began in Afghanistan was short war with several phases. The first began on 07 October 2001 and a month; the second ran through November and saw the Taliban lose control of the country; the third was characterized by intensive bombing of suspected al Qaeda strongholds in the Tora Bora mountain and cave complex in December. In a relatively short period, the US-led military offensive destroyed 11 training camps and 39 command centre.

Enduring Freedom also unseated Afghanistan's de facto ruling Taliban government, which sponsored al-Qaeda's presence in the country, and on 5 December 2001, UN Security Council recognized interim government under Hamid Karzai. On 13 June 2002, Afghanistan's Loya Jirga, or grand tribal Council, elected Karzai as the interim President.

Later in October 2004 Afghanistan's first nation-wide presidential election was held. An estimated 8.2 million ballots were cost in the historic voting on 09 October 2004. UN-Afghan election commission declared Hamid Karzai as President as he had won 55.5 percent of votes (4.2 million) against the closest rival former Education Minister Yunus Qanooni.[56] Surprising even after four years in 2007, the US-backed government of President Hamid Karzai has little credibility within the country. Afghans routinely refer to him as "the mayor of Kabul," since his authority does not extend much beyond the capital city, or more derisively as the "assistant to the American Ambassador," given his lack of real authority relative to US occupation forces.

The "Operation Enduring Freedom" was led by the United States under a "coalition of the willing" that included not only its allies, but many other countries that shared its objectives. Indeed, 136 countries have offered the US-led war varying forms of military assistance, and some 20 nations have deployed a combined 16,000 troops for operations in Central front.[57] The sky above Afghanistan was patrolled by some 40 fighter aircraft from five countries, while the Arabian Gulf had some 80 ships from 15 countries. While any country that has offered support since September 11 to the global war on terrorism has been called an ally, only 23 countries are formally obligated by treaty to defend the United States from an armed attack. These treaty allies include Australia, Japan, the Republic of Korea, the Philippines, Thailand, and the 18 countries that belong to the North Atlantic Treaty Organization (NATO). Following the collapse of Taliban regime and success of the Operation Endurance Freedom, in December 2001, 18-nation

International Security Forces (ISAF) had been created by the UN Security Council to support essentially to assist the interim Karzi Afghan government. In August 2003 NATO took over the command and coordination of ISAF. This is first mission outside the Euro-Atlantic area in NATO's history. The role of ISAF is essentially stabilization and reconstruction of Afghanistan. By the end of 2006, ISAF had only 18,000 troops from 37 countries with NATO members providing the core of the forces.[58] US contribute very less to this NATO forces. By end of 2006 there were 23,000 US troops in Afghanistan under the "Operation Enduring Freedom" which would be reduced to around 19,000 by the end of 2007. US withdrawing its profile from Afghanistan has led the European allies "think that the United States is trying to dump the Afghanistan counter-terrorism mission on them," says Mike Williams of the Royal United Services Institute for Defense Studies in London.[59] Meanwhile, the NATO's, ISAF does not explicitly have counter-terror mission, especially fighting Taliban, al-Qaeda, and narcotic warlords. Nevertheless, they are target of Taliban and al-Qaeda insurgents. Recently in June 2007 reports indicated that the Taliban insurgency attacks and military operations have surged.[60]

Despite al-Qaeda's curshing defeat in Afghanistan, Bin Laden's last publicly known address to his fighters in December 2001 had been that United States is a "paper tiger" and that "America is in retreat by the Grace of God Almighty and economic attrition is continuing up to today. But it needs further blows. The young men need to seek out the nodes of the American economy and strike the enemy's nodes."[61] Besides during 2002, terrorist incidents linked to al-Qaeda occurred in places as diverse as Tunisia, Pakistan, Jordan, Indonesia, Kuwait, the Philippines, Yemen and Kenya. Meanwhile, since 2006 and June 2007 reports have indicated that Taliban and al-Qaeda terrorists have regained their hold in some part of southern Afghanistan.

What is revealing is that the way the al-Qaeda continuing its international terrorism campaign even after their destruction in Afghanistan could be because of the retaining of three capabilities that had been critical to the success of 9/11. A RAND study states that the First of the capability was the ability to identify key vulnerability or gap in the defenses of its principal enemy—America—that could be mercilessly exploited (e.g., the US commercial aviation security structure). Second, was the effective use of deception on board the four hijacked aircraft where the passengers and crew were deliberately lulled into believing that if they behaved and cooperated as they were told—the standard operating procedure for crew and passengers on hijacked aircraft that historically had enhanced chances of survival—they would not be harmed? Third, suicide attack was employed to ensure the attack's success. None of these essential qualities was dependent on al-Qaeda having a base on operation in Afghanistan—and thus could likely be replicated in some future plan that successfully.[62]

TOWARDS INVASION OF IRAQ

The United States has sought to remove Iraq's Saddam Hussein from power since the 1991 Gulf war, although achieving this goal was not declared policy until 1998. Iraq's obstruction of UN Weapons of Mass Destruction (WMD) led to growing Congressional call for overthrowing Saddam Hussein. In January 1998, an obscure, ominous- sounding right-wing policy group called Project for New American Century (PNAC), affiliated with Dick Cheney, Donald Rumsfeld, Paul Wolfowitz and George Bush brother Jeb Bush, urged President Clinton to invade Iraq. In addition to Clinton, the group lobbied GOP leaders in Congress to push for Saddam's removal. "We should establish and maintain a strong US military presence in the region, and be prepared to use that force to protect our vital interest in the Gulf—and if necessary, to help remove Saddam from power," the group wrote to Representative Newt Gingrich and Senator Trent Lott in May 1998. A formal Congressional push for a regime change policy began with FY supplemental appropriation (signed on 1 May 1998) that among other provisions, earmarked $5 million in Economic Support Funds (ESF) for the opposition and $5million for a Radio Free Iraq, under the direction of Radio Free Europe/Radio Liberty. Radio Service began broadcasting in October 1998, from Prague. A clear indication of Congressional support for a more active US overthrow effort was encapsulated in another bill introduced in 1998: the Iraq Liberation Act (ILA—Signed into law on 31 October 1998) The ILA gave the President authority to provide up to $97 million in defense articles to opposition organization to be designated by the Administration. The Act's passage was widely interpreted as an expression of Congressional support for the concept of promoting an insurgency by using US air power to expand opposition-controlled territory. Indeed, the Iraq Liberation Act made the previously unstated policy of promoting regime change in Iraq, an official declared policy. A provision of the ILA states that it should be the policy of the United States to "support efforts" to remove the regime headed by Saddam Hussein. In mid-November 1998, President Clinton publicly articulated that regime change was a component of US policy toward Iraq. Thus by November 1998, the *Clinton Administration clearly stated that the United States was pursuing a policy beyond containment to promoting a change of regime in Iraq.*[63]

Soon after the "Operation Enduring Freedom" Campaign in Afghanistan, especially from January 2002, President Bush turned American attention and resources away from Al Qaeda to lead a crusade against Iraq's Saddam Hussein. Reports indicated that Bush had ordered the CIA and his senior military commanders to draw up details plan for military operation that could begin within months.[64] To justify this policy shift, President Bush and his aides have argued that the campaign against Saddam is a natural continuation of the war against terrorism. In his January State of the Union address to the

Congress President singled out Iraq, North Korea and Iran for seeking weapons of mass destruction. "States like these and their terrorist allies, constitute an axis of evil, arming to threaten the peace of the world," he said, adding the civilized world must act because the "price of indifference would be catastrophic." .It was clear that the Pentagon and White House war lobby was at work on President. Vice-President Cheney along with Wolfowitz urged the President that war against Iraq was urgent. He persistently warned that Saddam was stocking up on chemical and biological weapons.[65]

It appears by August 2002 the President had approved the military intervention for removal Saddam Hussein. A series of leaks from senior military brass that have growing increasingly distrustful of the adventurism of their civilian bosses marked the preliminary skirmishes in the conflict.[66] The war of words burst into the open when the elder Bush's national security adviser Gen. Brent Scowcroft, issued a broad warning against the idea of going to war with Iraq in the editorial pages of the staunchly hawkish Wall Street Journal arguing that "war against Baghdad would likely to destroy international cooperation in the war against terrorism"., Scowcroft also warned that "war could well destabilize Arab regimes in the region."

Once the Bush Administration had decided launch military intervention in Iraq to remove Saddam Hussein, the Administration engaged in preparing the public and the world to justify its actions. On 15 September 2002, President Bush unveiled the new National Security Strategy of United States of America. It is something of hodgepodge, speaking about primacy and balance of power. It talks about organizing coalition but also about not hesitating to act alone in self-defense. The most important aspect of the strategy is the statement that codifies all the new aspect of exceptionalism: It adopts the doctrine of preemptive action—while warning others not to use preemption as a pretext for aggression—and, making no mention of the United Nations in this context, presumes that the United States is the sole judge of the legitimacy of its own or anyone else's preemptive strikes. The document emphasized the deadly threat posed by weapons of mass destruction—should they fall into the hands of rouge states that "reject basic human values and hate the US and everything for which it stands." It promises to maintain whatever military capability is needed to defeat any attempt by state to impose its will on the United States or its allies, and to dissuade potential adversaries for building up their own forces to equal or surpass American. Last but not least, it reaffirms the determination to protect US national from the International Criminal Court. In sum, the Bush doctrine proclaims the emancipation of a colossus from international constraints (including from the restraints that the United States itself enshrined in network of international and regional organizations after Second World War). In this context, it amount to a doctrine of global domination.[67]

Armed with doctrine of pre-emptive strike, claiming that the Security Council resolution 1441 gives the United States to take military action against Iraq, and Congress passing a resolution authorizing President Bush to use force on Iraq, the Bush Administration even manipulated the intelligence evidence that Iraq acquiring fissile material for a nuclear weapons.[68] This aspect found its place in President Bush's State of the Union address in January 2003. In July 2003, explaining the intelligence manipulation George Tenet, the Director of CIA testified before the Senate Intelligence Committee after the war in Iraq concluded and Saddam removed, said that adhoc committee called the Office of special Plans, set up by Deputy Secretary of Defense Paul Wolfowitz, Assistant Secretary of Defense for Policy Douglas Feith and other high-profile hawks rewrote the intelligence information on Iraq that the CIA gathered and gave it to White House to help Bush build a case for war. It is surprising that the Pentagon and White House officials were so determined to launch the military campaign on Iraq, especially to obtain *enlarge zone of Democracy* that they did not bother when the European allies refused to support the war on Iraq. Thus the doctrine of pre-emptive strike proclaimed by America in the case of war on Iraq was manifestation of global domination even at the cost of emancipation from international constraints and allies counsel against war.

Now that the invasion of Iraq is completed and Saddam Hussein captured and hanged, the occupation of Iraq with about 138,000 troops for the past 3 years is increasing proving a costly war. Already more than 3628 American soldiers have died, which will increase. Moreover, failure to locate the WMD, insurgency in Fallujah, Karbala and Najaf and the grisly killing of American civilian and disgraceful Abu Ghraib prison episode have discredited Bush purpose of invasion of Iraq . Indeed it became major issue in the Presidential election when the Democratic Challenger John Kerry declared that in the pursuit of the war in Iraq "the President misled, miscalculated and mismanaged"; and also criticized that the war was "wrong war at wrong place and wrong time". By October 2004 the American nation was strongly polarized and was divided. On 30 October Bin Laden released a video tape which broadcast on the Arabi-language al-Jazeera network. Bin Laden declared that "your security is not in the hands of Kerry or Bush or al Qaeda. Your security is in your hands."[69] This was Bin Laden, in his first videotaped address in three years. But it seems this videotape crucially among other reasons influenced the American electorate on the 2 November 2004 Presidential election. The American voters re-elected President Bush overwhelmingly and challenger Kerry lost. The victorious President Bush in the first press conference on 04 November said: "I have earned capital in the campaign, political capital, and now I intend to spent it." He declared that he intend to spent it "winning the war on terror."

However, the developments from 2005 to June 2007 do not indicate that Bush is winning a war in Iraq. The Iraqi election that was held under the supervision of the United States did not unify Iraq as a democratic nation but actually strengthened sectarian divisions. Moreover the violence in Iraq–particularly in Baghdad—overwhelmed the political gains the Iraqis had made. Al-Qaida terrorist and Sunni insurgents have destroyed the peace and order in Iraq essentially to weaken the American presence. They blewp one of the holiest shrine in Shia Islam—the Golden Mosque of Samara—in a calculated effort to provoke Iraq's Shia population to retaliate. Their strategy worked. Radical Shia elements some supported by Iran, formed death squads. And the result was a vicious cycle of a sectarian violence that continues today. Meanwhile, ever since the Democratic majority in American Congress since the November 2006 elections, the President Bush's approval rating for handling the war hovering around 30 per cent only. Suddenly, real opportunities for the Public and the Congress have accrued to bring an end to the senseless US militar y adventure in Iraq. From January to March 2007, 20 pieces of resolution have been introduced in the Congress relating to war in Iraq.[70] Yet the President and his administration are aiming to stay for much longer in Iraq by redefining "victory" in Iraq once again—this time as permanent occupier. Defense Secretary Robert Gates told reporters on 01 June 2007 that he favors mutual agreement with Iraq in which "some forces of Americans...is present for a protracted period of time." Lt Gen. Raymond Odierno, in charge of daily military operations in Iraq supported this idea; comparing American involvement in Iraq to US continued military presence in South Korea. This type of "victory" was not what American signed up for as Bush led the nation to war.[71]

WAR ON TERRORISM OR ISLAM/MUSLIM WORLD?

On 16 September 2001, President Bush in the context of reassuring shocked nation said "this is a new kind of evil....And the American people are beginning to understand. This crusade, this war on terrorism is going to take awhile."[72] President Bush's reference to a "crusade" against terrorism evoked strong reactions in Muslim world especially in Pakistan and Indonesia. "A lot of people think that America is out to get Islam anyway," said Joshua Salaam, Director of the Council on American-Islamic Relations, in Washington.[73] The use of the world "crusade" said Soheib Ben sheikh, Grand Mufti of the Mosque at Marseille, France, "was most unfortunate." "It recalled the barbarous and unjust military operations against the Muslim World by Christian knight, who launched repeated attempts to capture Jerusalem over the course of several hundred years but failed."[74] Additionally, Bush declaring war on terrorism was "war between good and evil," shocked Europeans. "If this war takes a form that affront moderate Arabs opinion, if it has the air of a clash of civilization, there is a strong risk that it will contribute to Osama bin Laden's goal: a conflict between the Arab-Muslim world and the West." warned the Paris daily Le Monde.[75]

President Bush sought to calm American Muslims' fear of a backlash against them by appearing at the Islamic Centre in Washington on 17th September. There he assured Americans that "the face of terror is not the true faith of Islam. That's not what Islam is all about." Subsequently on 20 September in a major speech to the Joint Session of Congress, President Bush explained that the terrorist who attacked "our country" were "loosely affiliated terrorist organizations known as al-Qaida.... Al-Qaida is to terror what the mafia is to crime." Bush pointed out that these terrorist practices a "fringe form of Islamic extremism that has been rejected by Muslim scholars and the vast majority of Muslim cleric—a fringe movement that perverts the peaceful teachings of Islam." Bush also revealed that this group has been led by Osama bin Laden having linkages with many other terrorist organizations in sixty countries, including the Egyptian Islamic Jihad and the Islamic Movement of Uzbekistan. Bush also disclosed that Al-Qaida had extensive training camps in Afghanistan and that its leadership had great influence in Afghanistan by supporting Taliban regime in controlling most of that country. Hence, as part of his declared "war on terrorism" Bush demanded that Taliban regime close immediately and permanently every terrorist training camp in Afghanistan and handover every terrorist including leaders of al-Qaida.

President Bush address to Congress and nations had specific appeal and clarifications for the Muslim communities. He said:

> I also want to speak tonight directly to Muslims throughout the world: We respect your faith. It is practiced freely by many millions of Americans, and by millions more in countries that America counts as friends. Its teaching is good and peaceful and those who commit evil in the name of Allah blaspheme the name of Allah. The terrorists are traitors to their own faith, trying, in effect, to hijack Islam itself. The enemy of American is not our many Muslim friends; it is not our many Arab friends. Our enemy is a radical network of terrorists, and every government that supports them. Our war on terror begins with al-qaida...The terrorist practice a fringe form of Islamic extremism...a fringe movement That perverts the peaceful teaching of Islam. The terrorists' directive command Commands them to kill Christians and Jews, to kill all Americans.[76]

It is significant to observe that Bush not only excluded using the word "crusade", he and his administration consciously avoided giving any impression about the war on terrorism to be a war on Muslim world. Yet the Muslim world perceived that the war on terrorism was target on Islamic organizations and states, especially Afghanistan and Iraq.

Meanwhile, since September 11, 2001, a series of editorials and provocative articles have appeared in leading newspapers, journals and other media legitimizing the "clash of civilizations" thesis.[77] A decade-old debate has been renewed about whether the current "war on terror" is an inevitable, civilizational conflict between the forces of "Islam and the West." Reference to the "Clash of Civilizations" thesis first appeared in Bernard Lewis' 1990 Atlantic Monthly article: "Roots of Muslim Rage." Lewis argued that the West and the "Islamic World" would be inevitably locked in a "clash of civilizations" between Christendom and Islam:

> It should by now be clear that we are facing a mood and a movement far Transcending the level of issues and policies and the governments that pursue them. This is no less than a clash of civilizations—the perhaps irrational but surely historic reaction of an ancient rival against our Judeo-Christian heritage, our secular present, and the worldwide expansion of both.[78]

However, the "clash of civilizations" thesis is most commonly identified with Samuel Huntington. Huntington popularized this argument in his oft-cited 1993 article in Foreign Affairs, and his book, *The Clash of Civilizations and the Remaking of World Order,* published in 1996. Huntington argues that in the post-Cold war era, states will no longer be the principle actors in international relations. Rather, conflict between "civilizations" will take on the most important role. Huntington defines civilization as a cultural entity:

> ...a civilization is thus the highest cultural grouping of people and the broadest level of cultural identity people have short of that which distinguishes humans from other species. It defined both by common objective elements, such as language, history, religion, customs, institutions, and by the objectives self identification of people. [79]

Huntington suggests that future conflicts would occur along the cultural fault lines of differing civilization namely Western, Confucian, Japanese, Islamic, Hindu, Slavic-Orthodox, Latin American, and possibly African civilization. Particular importance is given to the relationship between Islam and the West: "on both sides the interaction Between Islam and the West is seen as a clash of civilizations." [80]

Soon after Huntington's propounding of the "clash of civilization" thesis, it was criticized by many as a simplistic and incomplete model for understanding the divisions and sources of conflict in the world today. Therefore, it cannot be a descriptive, analytical, and prescriptive tool for policy makers.[81] First, the "clash of civilizations" model is flawed by design because the notion of civilization still remains an amorphous and differentiated concept. Huntington also implies the unified development of culture and religion at the expense of differences within groups. Recognizing these conceptual ambiguities, civilizations cannot be described as hermetic, impermeable entities. As well, it is impossible to define civilization due to the constant interaction between Culture and their evolution over time. Islam's diverse interpretations confirm that it cannot be seen as a unified "civilization entity."[82]

Additionally the critics also upheld that conflict is solely the product of civilization is also problematic. Nevertheless the critics realized that there existed particularly kind of conflict, which could be characterized as a clash between the West and Islam between the "extreme" elements of Western and Islamic identities. Moreover, the critics have also pointed out that West is neither a unified entity nor antithetical to Islam.[83] They observed that Islam's evolution over time and its ability to creatively meet challenges has also been neglected in Western public discourse. At the same time, Western culture has sometimes been portrayed in superficial terms in the news media of many Muslim states. Another aspect the critics affirm the "clash of civilization" has failed to recognize is the hybridity between and other civilizations. For instances, while some diaspora communities in Western Societies may incorporate outward symbols of Westernization, they may retain elements of "older" culture.[84]

Some critics presume that "clash of civilizations" has been given incorrect label for other forms of conflict. It is assumed that Huntington may have been referring to a clash of empires rather than "civilizations." Some critics recognize that the global system being basically conflict prone, they have tried to describe the Huntington perception of conflict as a "clash within civilizations," for which two explanations are plausible:

* the "clash within civilizations" is a conflict between different ideologies within Islam, or a "struggle for the soul of Islam."; and
* the "clash within civilization" is the manifestation of economic globalization and "national, sub national, religious and tribal, particularism." [85]

Although these criticisms of "clash of civilization" have been made in the pre and post September 11 episode, the realities cannot be denied that in the twenty-first century, especially post-September 11, religion has become a crucial force and against all expectation in many part of the world, as a powerful, even shaping force.[86] Religion's presence has been particularly evident in conflict zones throughout the world—in Bosnia, Kosovo, Chechnya, Kashmir, other part of India and Pakistan, North Ireland, the Middle East, Sub-Saharan Africa and part of Asia. Indeed religion is often at the heart of conflict. It has been said that the Catholic Croats, Orthodox Serbs, and Muslims in the Balkans speak the same language and share the same race; the only thing that divides them is religion. Religion is the fault-line along which the side is dividing. The reason is simple. Whereas, broadly speaking, the twentieth Century was dominated by the politics of ideology, the twenty-first century is and will be dominated by the politics of identity—by the questions "who am I?" and "why am I here?"[87] Since the seventeen century the Western modernity discourses of the three great institutions—science, economics and politics—had been more procedural than substantive. They answer the question of "What"? and "How". They do not answer the questions "who" and "why". Therefore, when politics turns from ideology to identity, people turn to religion for the answers. The search for identity inevitably divides between every "us" is defined in contradistinction to a "them". Whether between Catholics and Protestants in Northern Ireland, Jews and Muslims in the Middle East, or Muslims and Hindus in India, identity divides.[88]

On 7 October 2001, as President Bush declared war on terrorism by initiating the military campaign and identified the militant Islam as primary threat to America emanating from Asia, specially West Asia, Osama bin Laden broadcast his statement that Americans and the British "have divided the entire world into two regions—one of faith, where there is no hypocrisy, and another of infidelity, from which we hope God will protect us."[89] Bin Laden's primary goal was to polarizing the Islamic world between *umma* (universal Islamic community) and the regimes allied with the United States. He expected that this would further the cause of Islamic revolution within the Muslim world Itself, in the Arab land, especially and in Saudi Arabia above all. Thus in his "Declaration of War" bin Laden lists 10 to 12 world hot spots where Muslims have recently died and attributed all of these deaths to a conspiracy led by the United States. And thus in another document, "Jihad Against Jews and Crusaders," bin Laden describes US policies towards the Middle East as "a clear declaration of war on God, His Messenger, and Muslims." [90] The magnitude of the attacks on New York and Washington make it clear that al Qaeda does indeed believe itself to be fighting war to save the *umma* from Satan, represented by secular Western culture.[91] Extreme though they may be, these views extend far beyond al-Qaeda's immediate followers in Afghanistan. Even a quick glance at the Islamist press in Arabic demonstrates that many Muslims who do not belong to bin Laden's terrorist network consider the United States to be on a moral par with Genghis Kahn. Take for instance, Muhammad Abbas an Egyptian Islamist who wrote the following in the newspaper *al Shaab* on September 21:

> Look! There is the master of democracy whom they have so often sanctified but who causes criminal barbaric, bloody oppression that abandons the moral? standards

> of even the most savage empires in history. In my last column I listed for readers the five million killed...because of the crimes committed by this American civilization that America leads. These five million were killed in the last few decades alone.

Similar feelings led another Al Shaab columnist that day, Khalid al Sharif, to describe the shock and delight that he felt while watching the World Trade Centre crumbling:

> Look at that! America, master of the world, is crashing down. Look at that! the Satan who rules the world, east and west is burning. Look at that! The sponsor of terrorism is itself seared by its fire.[92]

Apart from placing the current conflict as between Islam and West, especially America, al-Qaeda led and the general Muslim have framed the conflict in political and socio-economic terms too. Political factors contributing to resentment and alienation include : the operception of the US as hegemon; the lack of resolution to the Isralei-Palestinian conflict; the presence of American troops in Saudi Arabia. In addition, the Muslims perceive that the West and specially America hold double standards in foreign policy by supporting authoritarian regimes and military regimes and military intervention without regard to absolute justice threatens to undermine the democratization of Muslim societies from within. [93] As result, these political causes have exacerbated feelings of disempowerment in Muslim communities: "Democracies often get very bad press in the Arab and wider Muslim World because Britain and America have often said, 'we believe in freedom and democracy but you've got to have the Shah of Iran as dictators over you.'"[94]

Hence, the perception that Western powers preach democracy while supporting corrupt, authoritarian regimes has left many Muslims with a feeling of desperation and anger organize their opposition in the name of Islam. Indeed Islamic religious and social institutions are the only available vehicles for mass political mobilization.[95]

The Muslim communities in the West Asian is highly disillusioned by the American collusion and promotion of Islamic parties during the cold war and strongly opposed to them in the post cold war or post 9/11. During the much of the cold war the biggest US fear in the Middle East was secular Arab nationalism which seemed defiant to the West and friendly toward the Soviet Union. Therefore, Islamic movements were promoted by America and even Israel support of rise of Islamic movement that were competing with the PLO, only discover later that these movements gave birth to the militant HAMA.[96]

Moreover, in combating and defeating the Soviet presence and supported regime in Afghanistan, the United States through CIA trained hostile Islamic Mujahiddin and al Qaeda.. Today these very Islamic militant guerrillas have become terrorist and threat to America.

The growth of Arab media also played prominent role in highlighting Muslim grievance against the US. The "information revolution" of globalization has resulted in a new generation of Muslims even more aware of perceived injustices. For instance, al-Jazeera Television providing the Arab perception of the Arab Israeli conflict has contributed greater gap between American and Arab perception of the conflict. Such exposure of the gaps increases the credibility of "clash of civilizations."[97]

CONCLUDING OBSERVATIONS

Just as the Cold War was both real and a façade behind which the US pursued its two century march to global empire, the "war on terrorism" is simultaneously real and the distraction being used to mobilize the US people and international community to impose the Bush Administration's "arrangement (for) the twenty-first Century" with the aim of ensuring that the "the United States will continue to be the domination political, economic and military power in the world." [98] The massive and discriminate September 11 Terrorist attacks on New York's World Trade Centre and Pentagon were despicable criminal attacks against innocent civilian. Nevertheless, the episode gave the American policy-makers to formulate for the early years of twenty-first Century America's national security threat to be "terrorism" and the "war on terrorism" has become so pervasive and strident that it appeared (Secretary of State Adam's warning from the 1820s notwithstanding) that the United States had now gone abroad in search of monster to destroy. Thus, in the post-9/11 world "terrorism" has replaced the "Communism" of the cold war years as America's national security threat. It is significant to note when President Truman (in his address to Joint Session of Congress in 1947) describing the "Communism ideology and Communist" threat had used words like, "terrorist, terror, oppression and armed minorities" as the operation tactics of the Communism to undermine the democratic institutions and capture state power. President in his address to the Joint Session of Congress in September 2001 had not revealed any ideological threat but "the terrorists" who "practice a fringe form of Islamic extremism" to be nation security threat to America. It is significant to note that for combating terrorism American strategy and tactics of "war on terrorism" appears almost similar to strategy of "containment" adopted to combat communism in cold war years. The "War on terrorism" is pursued by increasing in defense expenditure, military and economic assistance to pro-US Islamic states, talk of Marshall Plan similar assistance to Afghanistan, building of "coalition of willing" and circumventing United Nations—all these aspects seem to be revisitation of strategy and tactics of containment.

It is now common knowledge that, with the assistance of the Pakistani military and Pakistani and Saudi intelligence, the US created the Islamic Mujahedeen including Osama Bin Laden to help drive the Soviets from Afghanistan. But contradictions have a way of asserting themselves. Having defeated the Soviet "infidels," Osama Bin Laden and other Mujahadeen returned to their native countries to find their corrupt national leaders still subservient to the "Christian" infidels in Washington. Osama and his Islamicist political forces perceived being besieged and homeland defiled by the intimidating, destructive and abusive US military bases continuing in Saudi Arabia and other Islamic countries and also supporting. Building on the model of Hezbollah, which forced Israel's withdrawal from Southern Lebanon by repeated terrorist attacks, small minority turned to asymmetrical terrorist warfare against the Imperial colossus on September 11.[99]

It is entirely reasonable and legitimate for a state and nation to defend its people from terrorist and other attacks. Yet, the Bush Administration squandered the massive post-9/11 outpouring of sympathy and support of the international community. The French press is no longer carries headlines that "we are all Americans."[100] Indeed, what the Bush policy has done more to isolate the United States than to isolate the terrorist. Moreover, the terrorist attacks were used to mobilize US popular opinion, to manipulate the US Congress, and to create coalition of the coerced in support of the US campaign to impose the "arrangement for the twenty-first century" in which the United States will continue to be the dominant political, economic and military power in the world." With re-election President Bush and his claim that election has given him "political capital," he has declared that he would vigorously pursue the "war on terrorism". Thus Bush-Cheney-Rumsfeld-Wolfowitz cabal had attempting reconsolidate US dominance of the worlds essential oil supplies by continued occupation of Afghanistan and Iraq and strengthening the network of military bases across West and Central Asia. However, the reverses in Iraq weakened the Cabal with the exist of Rumsfeld and Wolfowitz.

War on terrorism gave a strategic advantage for the US as that facilitated American military presence in Central Asia, an objective US desired eluded them during the Cold war. Because of the challenge of terrorism, US' erstwhile adversaries Russia and Central Asian Republics had common cause to unite. In the aftermath of 11 September, Russia accepted the US military presence and use of air bases in Uzbekistan, Kyrgyzstan and Tajikistan. But opposition to Russian President Putin's pro-US course is strong. The top echelons of the Russian armed forces and security services are traditionally anti-American. Therefore, the initial enthusiasm in which Russia allowed the American bases in Central Asia is changing. The Central Asian Republican states too are cautious about American military presence as they expect America to accept their limited version of democracy. Currently, the US is faced with a situation of America embracing Central Asian regimes for the sake of war against terrorism and regional security and stability including support of authoritarian, even dictatorial regimes and suppression of radical Islam. Choosing the lesser of two evils—radical Islam and corrupt dictatorships—will mean support for the latter, just as the United States has done in Egypt and Saudi Arabia. This would mean sweeping under the Carpet the systemic causes of instability which will eventually resurface.

Increasingly the US "war on terror" is understood by the Muslim as Americans are waging a war on Islam. President Bush use of the word "crusade" to describe the war on terror had reiterated the Muslim perception. In spite of the effort of the Bush Administration to communicate to Muslim World that "war on terror" is not against Islam and Muslim, it had not succeed to erase that perception of Muslim. Besides the US support for Israelis over Palestinians, President Bush's declaration of war on Taliban and al-Qeada and invasion of Afghanistan and Iraq, and American troops in Saudi Arabia have not only contributed to rising anti American sentiment in Central and West Asia but a "distinct feeling of a Judeo-Christian conspiracy against Muslims".

President Bush and his supporters have insisting that Iraq is a model of "democracy" that other countries in the region should emulate. Just as the Soviet gave "socialism" a bad name through their intervention and occupation of Afghanistan, the US intervention and occupation of Iraq along with subsequent events that have, in the eyes of many Muslims worldwide, tarnished the reputation of democracy. Democracy, alas, has become synonymous with war, chaos, domination by a foreign power, and massive human suffering.

It is alarming that the Bush Administration claim that there is no alternative to US policing the world for the sake of homeland security, international peace and for the American standard of living. According to his doctrine, spelled out by the White House in its National Security Strategy, the United States must maintain global military dominance and right of pre-emptive military strike against any country it regards as a current or even a potential threat. Bush's party leaders, his father's national security team, several Secretaries of State—including his own, and top military planner all advocated alternative to invasion of Iraq. Yet Bush evoking the doctrine of pre-emptive strike invaded Iraq without the support of European and Middle East allies and without evidence of Iraq posed a threat to US or the region. It is alarming because the first-strike doctrine ignores international law, dismisses the precepts and procedures of collective security established by the UN Charter, and establishes the United States as an international vigilante—acting at once a cop, judge and executioners.[101] It is dangerous not only because it will rush the United States into unnecessary wars but also because it provides a precedent for extraterritorial operations by other nations and non-state actors. Moreover, by demanding the right to act unilaterally, by changing the target from the perpetrators of 9/11 to purported "axis of evil," by scorning both multilateral alliances and the UN system, and by refusing to comply with international law in its treatment of prisoners captured in Afghanistan and elsewhere, the Bush administration is undermining the very cause it claims to serve.

REFERENCES

1 Bob Graham (2004) *Intelligence Matters: The CIA, The FBI, Saudi Arabia and the Failure of America's War on Terror* (Random House, New York), pp.xi,97; *International Herald Tribune* (Bangkok), 12 October 2001.

2. Michael Hirsh, (2002) "Bush and the World," *Foreign Affairs*, Vol. 81, no.5, September-October, p.29.

3. *International Herald Tribune*, (2001) (Bangkok) 12 September.

4. "Bush Announces Start of War on Terror," Official Text, Public Affairs Office, US Embassy (New Delhi) 20 September 2001, pp.4, 5.

5. Richard N. Haass (2002): "Defining U.S. Foreign Policy in a Post-Post Cold War World," Remarks to New York Foreign Policy Association, 22 April 2002, Text.

6. Hirsh, n.2, p.29.

7. Michael Mandelbaum (2002): "Inadequacy of American Power," *Foreign Affairs*, vol.81, no.5, September-October, p.61; Barry Buzan (2004): *The United States and the Great Powers* (Malden, M. A, Polity Press), pp.9, 154.

8. Joseph S. Nye (2004): "Hard Power, Soft Power and 'The War on Terror," in David Held and Mathias Koenigh Archibugi (eds), *American power in the Twenty-First Century* (UK, Polity Press), p.114.

9. Richard N. Haass, (2002): "Defining U.S. Foreign Policy in a Post-Post-Cold War World," Remarks to New York Foreign Policy Association, 22 April, Text.

10. *The Washington Post* (2001): 13 October (Electronic version).

11. Stephen Clarkson and Maria Banda (2004): "Paradigm Shift or Paradigm Twist? The Impact of the Bush Doctrine on Canada," *Foreign Policy in Focus* (Washington, D.C.) 1 March, pp.1-2; *http://www.fpif.org/fpiftxt/77* (Accessed on 24 February 2006).

12. Ramesh Ratnesar, "Paul Wolfowitz: Bush's Brainiest Hawk," *Time*, Vol.161, no.3, 27 January 2003, p.36

13. "Partnership of the Year: GeorgeBush-Dick Cheney," *Time*, 30 December 2002—6 January 2003, p.46.

14. Stanley Hoffmann, "The High and the Mighty: Bush's National-Security Strateg y and the New American Hubris," The American Prospect, Vol.13, no.24, 13 January 2003, p.1.

15. Jim Lobe, "Hawks Take Aim at Iraq," *Foreign Policy in Focus* (Washington, D.C) 30 November 2001, p.3.

16. Ratnesar, n.19, p.37.

17. Hoffman, n.21, p.2.
18. "PNAC Letter to President Clinton," www.newamericancentury.org/clinton.htm
19. Ratnesar, n.19, p.37.
20. Mark Danner, "The Struggle of Democracy and Empire," *The New York Times,* 08 October 2002.
21. James Mann, "The Left and Rights have the Secretary All Wrong, " Washington Post, 1 September 2002
22. Jim Lobe, "A Hawk Nests in the State Department," Asia Times on Line, 8 August 2003.
23. Michael Howard, "What's in a Name? How to Fight Terrorism," Foreign Affairs, Vol.81, no.1, January-February 2002, p.8; Jim Lobe "Hawks Take Aim to Iraq," Foreign Policy Focus, 30 November 2001; Secretary of State Colin Powell, "Seizing the Moments," Department of State, November 2001.
24. Richard A. Clarke, Against All Enemies: Inside America's War On Terror,(Free Press, 2004), p.32.
25. Ibid., p.227.
26. Ibid., p.225.
27. Ibid., p.226
28. Secretary Paul O Niel Interview: CBS News 60 Minutes, 10 January 2004. Secretary O Niel statement is part of the book titled: "The Price of Loyalty" by Ron Suskind
29. B.K. Shrivastava, "War on Terrorism"(unpublished Manuscript—2002), pp.11,12.
30. "CIA Worked in Tandem with Pak to Create Taliban," Times of India, 7 March 2001; Barnet R.Ruben, "Afghanistan under Taliban," Current History (Phildephia), Vol.98, no.625, p.80.
31. Ahmed Rashid, "Taliban: Exporting Extremism," Foreign Affairs (New York), Vol.78, no.6, November-December 1999, p.31.
32. Clarke, n.31, pp.52, 53, 54.
33. Bruce Hoffman, Al Queda, Trends in Terrorism and Future Potentialities: A Assessment (RAND, Santa Monica, 2003), p.13.
34. Time. 08 October, 2001, p.26.
35. The New York Times, 19 September 2001 (Electronic Version).
36. "US to Tighten up Its Visa Policy, Bush Says," Official Text, 30 October 2001.
37. The Bill was passed by the Congress on 1 November 2001. The Washington Post, 2 November 2001.

38. Paul Thompson, "Erosion of Civil Liberties." *www.cooperativeresearch*.org/timeline, 9 December 2003, p.3

39. LosAngeles Times 30 October 2001; Chicago Tribune, 1 November 2001.

40. Thompson, n.45, p.3; San Francisco Chronicle, 12 November 2001, 8 August 2002; The Washington Post, 4 November 2001; Thomas F. Powers, "Can We Be Secure and Free?" Public Interest, 22 March 2003, p.23. www.lexis.com/research

41. On 20 September 2001 President Bush announced a new Cabinet-level Office of Homeland Security, located at the White House. Later on 25 November 2002 President signed legislation creating the Department of Homeland Security consolidating nearly 170,000 workers from 22 Agencies including Coast Guard, the Secret Service, the Federal Security Guards in airport and Customs. However, FBI and CIA most prominent anti-terrorism agencies, will not be part of the Department. For details see "Senate passes Homeland Security Bill," Washington Post, 20 November 2002; Richard A. Best Jr., Homeland Security: Intelligence Support (Congression Research Service Report) 6 August 2003..

42. Thomas F. Powers, "Can We be Secure and Free?" Public Interest (New York) 22 March 2003, p.5d; *www.lexis.com/research* (Reterieved on 29 August 2003); Robert H. Bork, "Civil Liberties After 9/11", Commentary, July-August 2003, Vo.116, no.1, p.29.

43. Bork, n.49, p.29; http://en.wikipedia.org/wiki/USA_PATRIOT _ACT (Retrieved on 10 October 2004).

44 Powers, n.49, p.32.

45. "United States: Abuses Plague September 11 Investigation: Cheks on Government Authority Should be Restored," Human Rights Watch Press Release (New York), 15 August 2002, p1.

46. Powers, n.49, pp.32-33.

47. Stuart Taylor, "Rights, Liberties and Security," The Brookings Review (Washington, D.C.) Vol.21, no.1, Winter 2003, p.1. (retrieved on 29 August 2003).

48. Adriel Bettelheim and Elizabeth A. Palmer, "Balancing Liberty and Security" Congressional Quarterly, Vol.59, no.36, 2003, pp.2210-2214.

49. Thomas Carothers, "Promoting Democracy and Fighting Terror," Foreign Affairs, January-February 2003, p.84.

50. Brent J. Talbot, "The Arab perception and Consensus Problem: Implications for US Policy in the Middle East," INSS Occasionsl paper 48, USAF Institute for National Security Studies (INSS), USAF, Academy, Colorado, February 2003, pp.5-6.

51. Ibid.
52. Ibid, p.3.
53. B.K.Shrivastava, "War on Terrorism" (Unpublished Manuscript—2002), pp.11,12.
54. The Hindu, 01 November 2001.
55. Ibid., 13 October 2001.
56. Detroit Free Press, 27 October 2004 (Electronic Version).
57. Paolo Pasicolan and Balbina Y. Hwang, The Vital Role of Alliance in the Global War on Terrorism," The Heritage Foundation Backgrounder, No.1607 (Washington D.C) 24 October 2002, p.l.
58. Paul Gallis (2006): NATO in Afghanistan: A Test of the Transatlantic Alliance (CRS Report to US Congress, Washington D.C.), pp.1-3.
59. Christian Science Monitor, 31 January 2007.
60. Baltimore Sun 24 June 2007.
61. Bruce Hoffmen, Al Qaedaa, Trends in Terrorism and Future Potentialities: An Assessment (RAND, Santa Monica, 2003), p.11.
62. Ibid., p.12.
63. "Iraq: US Regime Efforts and Post-War Governance," Congressional Research Service Report 2003, pp.2,10,11 and 13.
64. "Secret US Plan for Iraq War," Guardian 2 December 2001.
65. "Cheney's Long Path to War," News Week 21 November 2003.
66. Jim Lobe, "Washington Goes to War," Foreign Policy in Focus, 20 August 2002, p.1.
67. Stanley Hoffman, "The High and the Mighty," The American Prospect, Vol.13, issue 24, 13 January 2003, p.4.
68. Jim Lobe, "Pentagon Office Base for Neoconservative Network Manipulating Iraq Intelligence," Foreign Policy in Focus, 15 September 2003, pp.1-2.5
69. Washington Post, 31 october 2004.
70. Travis Sharp (2007) "Moving the Chains: Congress and the War in Iraq," Foreign Policy in Focus, 12 March, pp.3-5.
71. Adil E. Shamoo and Bonnie Bricker (2007) "Victory in Iraq?" Foreign Policy in Focus, 21 June, p.1.
72. Le Monde (Paris) 17 September 2001.
73. Washington Post, 18 September 2001.
74. Le Monde 17 September 2001.
75. Ibid.

76. Bush Announces start of a "war on Terror" 20 September 2001, Public Affairs Office, US Embassy, New Delhi.,21 September 2001.
77. Canadian Department of Foreign Affairs and International Trade (DFAIT) &Canadian Centre for Foreign Policy Development, Canada and the Muslim World: Summary Report From Expert Meeting (Ottawa, 22002), p. 3.
78. Bernard Lewis, "Roots of Muslim Rage," The Atlantic Monthly, September 1990, on line:www.theatlantic.com/issues/90sept/rage.htm.
79. Samuel P. Huntington, "Clash of Civilization," Foreign Affairs, Summer 1993, p.24.
80. Ibid., pp.25,26.
81. DFAIT, n.120, p.4.
82. Ibid., p.5.
83. Mushirul Hasan, "Discussion Paper for Thinkers Treat: Clash of Civilization?: September 9-11 and Its Aftermath," on line: www.ccommons.net/ccipd-thinkers2002/main.phtml
84. DFAIT, n.120, p.5.
85. Benjamin Barber,"Can Democracy Survive the War Against Terrorism?" on line: www.cfp-pec.gc.ca
86. Jonathan Sacks, "The Dignity of Difference: How to Avoid the Clash of Civilization," Orbis, Vol.46, no.4, 2002, p.601.
87. Ibid., p.602.
88. Ibid.
89. Michael Scott Doran, "Somebody Else's Civil War," Foreign Affairs, January/February 2002, p.23.
90. Ibid., p.29
91. Ibid., p.28.
92. Ibid.
93. DFAIT, kn.120, p.6.
94. Karen Armstrong, "Can Democracy and Open Societies Overcome the Cause of Conflict in Divided World," on line: www.cfp-pec.gc.ca
95. Shelby Tehami, "American Foreign Policy Toward the Muslim World," SAIS Review, Vol.221, no.2, Summer-Fall 2001, p.3.
96. Ibid., p.2.
97. Paul Lalor, "Lessons from Israel and Palestine," on line: www.cfp-pec.gc.ca.
98. The Quotation is from Vice President Richard Cheney, Nicholas

Lemann, "The Quiet Man," the New Yorker, 2 May 2001.

99. Joseph Gerson, "The War on Terrorism Washington's Imperial Agenda in Asia." Online: *www.afsc.org/newsengland/pesp/korea.htm* (retrieved on 27 November 2003).

100. Ibid., p.3.

101. Foreign Policy in Focus "on Fateful Choice: Global Leader or Global Cop." On line: www. Socialcritic.org/terror.hlm (Retrieved on 07 November 2004).

3

American Response to Pakistan's Cross-border Terrorism

Amulya K Tripathy

Terrorism has been an age old phenomenon, which has acquired a distinct dimension with the advancement in mass media, communication, technology and other forces of globalization. Terrorism directly affects the foreign policy of a country. Before terrorist attacks on the World Trade Centre and the Pentagon in the United States, India had been facing the problem of terrorism since its independence. Terrorism has been the design of Pakistan's consistent anti-India strategy, beginning with its refusal to accept the constitutionally validated and democratically endorsed accession of Jammu & Kashmir to India.

For a long time Pakistan relied on military confrontation as exemplified by the high and low level wars waged in 1948, 1965, 1971[1] & 1999 to settle the Kashmir issue in its favour. After failing abjectly in this endeavour, the anti-India forces in Pakistan decided to foment terrorism and religious extremism as the principal means to instigate separatism in Kashmir. India has long accused Pakistan of funding, training and arming Muslim militants in Kashmir, a charge persistently denied by Pakistan. Moreover, Pakistan was also supporting the Khalistan movement in the 1980s to destabilize the Punjab. No actions were taken by the US and other powers against Pakistan.

Pakistan began to distinctly sponsor cross-border terrorism in the 1980's[2]. It first began in the Punjab. Though Islamabad could not succeed here, it acquired experience to perfect its techniques in the promotion of terrorism or low intensity conflict (LIC) in Jammu & Kashmir where there were greater possibilities of its success.

After the 9/11 attack in the US, the issue of cross border terrorism assumed an important dimension in Indo-U.S. relations. Before that the US was fully supporting Pakistan, though Pakistan was directly /indirectly supporting terrorist activites in India. Apart from that, Islamabad's support to the Taliban in Afghanistan was not a secret. Afghanistan under a friendly Taliban government provided Pakistan with strategic depth in the evetuality of a war with India and also provided Pakistan with easy access to the Central Asian Republics[3]. The US air attacks on Afghanistan which led to massive Afghan and Pakistan casualties confirmed Pakistan's involvement in the Taliban project. The Jehadi groups in Pakistan are the most aggressive among a growing array of activists and organizations challenging the crumbling state institutions. The Jihadis have played a major role in transforming South Asia into world's most volatile region and Pakistan into one of the world's most explosive country. The impoverished South Asian nation is home to at least 128 camps for militants dedicated to retrieving Kashmir and widening the size of the Islamic world[4]. But according to Indian estimates there are at least 150 terrorist training camps in Pakistan, Afghanistan and Pakistan Occupied Kashmir. They all receive extensive patronage from the Pakistan state apparatus in terms of logistics, arms and ammunitions and monetary help. So Pakistan's involvement in terrorist activities has been very clear from the beginning. But due to the shadow of the cold war, no proper pressure was applied upon Pakistan by the US to stop helping the terrorists. This was again proven in Pakistan's cross-border incursions into Kargil, along with Pakistani attempts to take the vital territory by force[5]. Above all, the Chief objective of Pakistan has been to create a Muslim-majority state in South Asia by annexing Kashmir. Little attention appears to have been paid to how this state would look like or exactly how "Islamic" it would be. Pakistan still debates vigorously on how fully their state should reflect Islamic law or the Koran[6]. But it is an evident fact in India that Muslims are enjoying more rights and liberties. Not only that, they are more free and comfortable than Muslims in Pakistan. In spite of that, Pakistan has been supporting Harkat-ul-Mujahideen, Jaise-e-Muhammad, Laskar-e-Jhangvi Pakistan, Sipah-e-Shahaba Pakistan and notorious Lashkar-e- Tiaba(LeT) who are very active terrorist groups operating in Kashmir and different parts of India.

However, all this changed for India and the rest of the world on September 11, 2001 when terrorists attacked the symbols of power and prosperity of the only super power. By declaring a war on international terrorism, US President Gorge W Bush built an international coalition of willing parties to fight this war. The Afghanistan campaign began on the night of October 7, 2001, with a programme of air strikes aimed initially at destroying the Taliban's limited air defences and communications infrastructure[7]. In this war, many Taliban and Al Qaeda defenders were killed and some including Mullah Muhammad Omar and other senior leadership left the city and went into hiding, ending the Taliban rule in Afghanistan. Many Al-Qaeda defenders escaped death or capture and fled across the border into Pakistan[8].

If September 11 shattered 'American smugness over the invulnerability of its homeland and changed the world,' the December 13 attack on the Indian Parliament, the heart of Indian democracy shook the confidence of India. But the result was quite different. The international community, particularly the US, did not make much noise against the attackers on the

Indian Parliament, who were supported by Pakistan. Ironically, the US President George W Bush later, while lending powerful verbal support to India's right to defend itself from terrorist attacks, made the shocking statements that Lashkar-e-Toiba (LeT) was 'Kashmir- Based' and 'Stateless'. However he added that Lashkar had 'targeted' both India and Pakistan and indeed 'undermined' the Pakistani President General Parvez Musharraf , and therefore India, Pakistan and the US should take it on jointly. It clearly showed American softness towards Pakistan. But immediately after the 9/11 attacks, India had offered support and help to the US. Of course, Pakistan followed India's example under pressure. Fortunately, the US had to shift its stance soon enough and acknowledge that the LeT operated from bases in Pakistan and asked General Musharraf to 'crack down' on Lashkar, Jaish-e-Mohammad(JeM) and other terrorist outfits in Pakistan.[9] But little was done by Musharraf, to demonstrate to the US that he was indeed taking corrective action. He warned the Jaish's supreme, Maulan Azhar , after keeping him under house arrest for precisely two days, and then allowed the LeT to shift its office from Lahore to Pakistan occupied Kashmir.

South Asia has been one of the worst affected regions by terrorism, which could not be taken into consideration by the UN or the Western Countries. The reason could have been the continuing shadow of the Cold War. During the Cold War period, Pakistan was a close ally of the US and India was more inclined towards the USSR. After the collapse of the USSR, India improved ties with the USA. But the 9/11 incident changed the situation for the better in US-India relations.

Earlier, terrorism landed from across the borders mercilessly, took thousands of innocent lives in India. But the international community led by the US and other Western countries had double standards in shedding their tears over the loss of life and remained mute. When innocents were killed, concerns were expressed, but when some terrorists were killed in counter- insurgency measures, there was a hue and cry. The accusation of violation of human rights, which the US was hammering on India, was thus highly discriminatory in nature. The attitude of the US and its Western allies has been however changing towards India after 9/11 attacks.

The September 11 terrorist attack was an event of international significance for several reasons. First, those who were killed – nearly 3000 belonged to over 60 countries. Second, terrorist groups had developed an international networking, where money came from different sources, and so did weapons.

PAKISTAN'S ROLE IN KASHMIR

Kashmir is one of the important factors of India – Pakistan tension, which led to three wars over the last six decades after both countries got independence in 1947. The background of the merger of Jammu and Kashmir with India is widely known to everybody. Since then, Pakistan has been trying to capture it through war or with other means. During the Cold War the US was openly supporting Pakistan on the Kashmir issue.

Both the United States and Pakistan are guilty of having contributed to the creation of Islamic Fundamentalism and Terrorism in Afghanistan. The Soviet occupation of Afghanistan in December 1979 provided the US with a good opportunity to take revenge against the Soviet Union for its humiliation in Vietnam. The *Mujahideen* and mercenaries from several Muslim countries were given military training in Pakistan by the ISI and arms supplied by the US.,[11] which Pakistan successfully used against India in terrorist activities in Kashmir and other parts. Though terrorism in India, sponsored by Pakistan has been in existence since the 1980's, post –9/11 witnessed more than four major terrorist attacks. The military Government of General Pervez Musharraf doubtlessly confronts severe obstacles in any effort to root out Islamic extremism on its own soil. Islamists carry weight in the country and are said to be beyond Government control. In addition, the army feels an irresistible temptation to use terrorists in its campaign against India, especially in the state of Jammu and Kashmir. As a result, Pakistan has sought to let, what India calls, cross- border terrorism in Kashmir continue.

Either with Islamabad's connivance or tacit approval, or despite its genuine willingness to stop them, groups directly linked with Pakistan and Pakistan based extremists have perpetrated ever more intolerable attacks against India. On October 1 , 2001, Lashkar-e-Toiba and Jaise–Mohammad (which were soon designated as terrorist organizations by the US) trained and financed by Pakistan, organised a brazen assault on the Jammu – Kashmir Legislative Assembly. On December 13, the attempted terrorist attack on the Indian Parliament triggered the deployment of Indian forces to the Indo-Pak border. The third was the attack on the American Centre in Calcutta on January, 22, 2002 and the fourth was the attack on an Army Camp at Kalu Chak on May 14, 2002.[12] Despite Pakistan's assurances of a crack down , terrorist violence continues, including the massacre of 24 Kashmiri Hindus, later followed by several attacks on the military personnel. The recent bomb blast in a local train of Mumbai in July 2006 proved that the terrorist activities sponsored by the Pakistan based organizations, have shown no signs of ending. When the WTC and Pentagon were attacked, immediate action was taken by the United Nations and the US. Terrorism is terrorism, whether it strikes New York or Jammu. To please President Bush, Musharraf ensured speedy trial and conviction of Ahmad Omar Saeed Sheikh, charged of kidnapping and killing US Journalist Daniel Pearl. In this terror – ridden setting, what is regrettable is the Pakistani President's indifference to Indian pleas. Terrorist activities in Kashmir and different parts of India have increased in the Post September 11 era rather than decline.

The attack on Jammu & Kashmir Assembly which resulted in loss of 29 lives provoked Farooq Abdullah, the then

Chief Minister of J&K, to demand action against the culprits, even at the risk of a nuclear war with Pakistan.[13] Immediately the then Prime Minister Vajpayee told the US Government that India's patience was wearing out. Though the Bush Administration condemned the attack on J&K Assembly as a 'terrible terrorist attack', it did not show much interest in punishing the culprits. Further, Pakistani involvement was also found in the attack on the Indian Parliament and at other places in the country. The international coalition took no proper action was taken against Pakistan. Rather the Bush administration tried to delink the attack on the American Centre, Calcutta in January 2002 from Indo-Pak Conflict and argued that it was not a terrorist attack However, it was later confirmed from the interrogation of Aftab Ansari that ISI and some Pakistan based terrorist groups were involved in the attack.

The question is for whose interest action would be taken to put an end to the terrorist activities in India. Both countries should realize some basic facts. Firstly, Pakistan should realize that it cannot snatch Kashmir from India by force. Also, India should realise that PoK cannot be brought back. Secondly, both countries need to divert their attention to other common interests, such the basic needs of people and address economic and social issues. After the sanctions imposed by the US, the Indian economy could persist unaffected. But Pakistan faced very tough problems on the economic front. This indicated the vulnerability of Pakistan. The confidence building measures and cooperative efforts to solve their basic problems would serve the interests of both India and Pakistan.

It is true that no Pakistani Government, either democratically elected or military, can stay in power without the raising the Kashmir factor. This domestic compulsion has been there since independence. Islamabad wrongly believed that the US will always back them on the Kashmir issue. As the international situation changes, US policies also change. On the other hand, India is beset with a contradiction in Kashmir.

It claims that Kashmir is a bilateral issue and that no third party has any role there. But India has consistently been complaining that the US does not do enough to stop Pak-sponsored terrorism in Jammu & Kashmir. Pakistan strongly pleads for US mediation in Kashmir, which is unacceptable to India. In the changed circumstance of post-9/11 era, the Kashmir problem needs to be resolved by both countries, through negotiations and workable compromise.

BANGLADESH NEW BASES OF ISI SPONSORED TERRORISM

After expulsion of the Al-Qaeda and Taliban in Afghanistan and lack of official support for Al-Qaeda in Pakistan, these groups had to find new areas of operation. Due to increased pressure from the US after September 11, flow of funds to terrorist groups has slowed significantly. This factor forced Al-Qaeda and its allied organizations to find new bases and sources of finance in remote areas where US intervention is not easy or likely. Many African countries, Bangladesh, Nepal and some South American countries are the favored destinations. In South Asia, Bangladesh and Nepal became the centre of terrorist activities by Al-Qaeda, Lashker-e-Toiba and Jaish-e—Mohhmad, with the direct support of the ISI. Bangladesh Muslims are generally followers of moderate Islamic norms and the fundamentalist trends noticeable lately are not a part of natural process, but a deliberate attempt by the Al-Qaeda led Islamic *Jihadi* groups to change cultural values. The rise of Jamaat-e-Islamic had affected a significant segment of the population and given rise to sectarian and religious violence. Anti-India voices in Bangladesh and a large number of anti-Indian armed separatist groups maintaining safe havens in Bangladesh is a worry-some development for India. The government of Bangladesh remained mute spectators to the operations of United Liberation Front of Asom(ULFA) and National Democratic Front of Bodoland (NDFB) from its soil.

There are many cases which show the involvement of Pakistan sponsored terrorism in Bangladesh and Nepal, which are operating against Indian interests. It indicates the double standards of Pakistan in dealing with terrorism. Though the US has been provided with evidence of Pakistan's involvement in terrorism in this region, no concrete action has been taken by Washington against it thus far. The infiltrators from Bangladesh entering India, who are residing in Muslim dominated places in Maharastra and elsewhere in India, coupled with illegal migration into India have been persisting unchecked for decades, thanks to those Indian politicians who considered these foreigners not as a potential terrorist threat to the country, but as valuable minority votes to win the elections.

It is evident that both countries have lack of confidence in each other while addressing the issue. Both should break the chicken-and-egg cycle that prevents even a starting point for discussions. Pakistan says, 'settle Kashmir and normal co-operative relations will follow'. India responds, 'start normalising relations, and options regarding Kashmir unthinkable today can become feasible'. The Kashmir problem should not be allowed anymore to check positive movement in other bilateral relations.

US ROLE

American policy in South Asia has been gradually changing in the Post Cold War era, more drastically after the terrorist attacks of 9/11. The US today has befriended both India and Pakistan to combat terrorism in the region. Without checking cross- border terrorism along the Indo-Pak border and Pakistan sponsored terrorism from the bases of other countries like Nepal and Bangladesh, it would be impossible for the US to root out terrorism in South Asia.

No doubt, the US took the help of Pakistan as a front runner state to fight Al Qaeda terror in Afghanistan since September 2001. The Indian fight against cross-border terrorism should however not be avoided and undermined. Throughout the Cold War period, US involvement with Pakistan had always come at the cost of improved relations with India. For the first time, despite its heavy reliance on Pakistan the Bush administration has managed to avoid its rift with India, which seems dexterous in the Bush administration's South Asia policy.[14]

Indo-US relationship which was often contentious and sometimes turbulent throughout the years of the Cold War, now appears more balanced. The policy makers of both countries have moved to a number of bilateral and global issues during the last couple of years like military to military contacts, lifting of sanctions and other issues. Moreover, both the US and India have engaged in a civilian nuclear energy co-operation agreement and India has been recognized as a responsible nuclear power. A robust Indo-Pak relationship could help promote stability in South Asia and remove its troubled environs. Both Washington and New Delhi have common interests in combating terrorism, avoiding war between India and Pakistan, and resolving the festering Kashmir dispute all of which are inextricably linked-and to future strategic co-operation against a potentially revivalist China.[15]

The 585 page National Commission on Terrorist Attacks upon the United States Report that investigated the plot, design and circumstances leading to the 9/11 attacks on the US has also highlighted the involvement of Pakistan with the Al-Qaeda: 'Pakistan did not break with the Taliban until after 9/11, although it was harbouring Bin Laden'.[16] It also asserts that Pakistan benefited from the Taliban-Al-Qaeda relationship as Osama Bin Laden's camps trained fighters for Pakistan's ongoing struggle with India over Kashmir[17].

Even after being aware of relevant facts, US policy in South Asia and particularly over India's concerns over cross-border terrorism remained unchanged. American involvement in the region is there for its own interest. The US has always tried to dissuade both countries (India and Pakistan) from fighting wars. Foreign policy is not based on emotional factors, but is based on the interest of a country, which the US follows. So long as the US is in the forefront of the war against terrorism, India ought to follow the strategy of using all diplomatic levers to achieve the goal of eradicating terrorism without fighting a war with Pakistan. At the same time, India has to retain the option of use of coercive power in case the US fails to end the scourge of terrorism in South Asia. India has suffered at the hands of Pakistan sponsored terrorists for such a long time-over two decades –and has been accustomed to the US role of double standards. Yet the US-led war against global terrorism has its greater impact than Indian war against terrorism in the last two decades. Though President Bush does not miss a single opportunity to praise Musharraf's contribution to the war against terrorism, he also tries to recognize that cross-border terrorism against India launched by Pakistan must be controlled and ended. Lastly, it is also a fact that, American policy towards India has been improving in the post September 11 era and there is hope for greater success in dealing with terrorism.

NOTES AND REFERENCES

1. A.B.Vajpayee, "We shall Triumph Over Terrorism", *World Focus,* Vol.23,No.9, Sept.2002.
2. P.M. Kamath, "India's War Against International Terrorism in the Twenty First Century: Issues , Challenges and Evolving A Strategy", *India Quarterly,* Vol.LVIII No.2 April-June , 2002.
3. Kalim Bahadur, "Is Pakistan A Terrorist State?", *World Focus,* Vol.23,No.1,January 2002.
4. Ibid P.P.7
5. AshleyJ.Jellis,C Christine Fair, and Jamison Jo Medby, "Limited Conflicts under the Nuclear Umbrella: Indian and Pakistani Lessons from the Kargil Crisis (Santa Monica, Calif: RAND, 2001)
6. Stephen P. Cohen, "The Jihadist Threat to Pakistan" , *The Washington Quarterly,* Vol.26 , No.3 Summer, 2003.
7. Stephen Biddle, "Afghanistan and the Future of Warfare", *Foreign Affairs,* Vol.82No.2, March/April 2003.

8. Ibid P.P.34
9. J.K.Baral, J.N.Mohanty, "The U.S. War Against Terrorism: Implications for South Asia", *Strategic Analysis*, Vol.26 , No.4 October-December 2002.
10. K.Shanker Vajpayee, "Untangling India and Pakistan", *Foreign Affairs*, Vol.82 No.3 May/June 2003.
11. *The Hindustan Times*, November 5, 2001.
12. Sumit Ganguly, "India and Pakistan in the Shadow of Afghanistan", *Current History*, April, 2002.
13. Josy Joseph, "India, U.S. to discuss China Formally for First Time", *India Abroad*, October 11, 2002.
14. The 9/11 Commission Report. Final Report of the National Commission on Terrorist Attacks Upon the United States, Executive Summary, P.7
15. Ibid.

4

Changing Contours of US-China Relations in the Aftermath of 9/11

Monika Chansoria

BACKGROUND

Sino-American relations in the period prior to September 11, 2001, could best be described as being one where the differences between the People's Republic of China (PRC) and the United States (US) were prevalent, though there still was reason to be positive since the two nations were reaping the benefits of the economic convergence of interests of the 90s. But at the same time, the two countries found themselves in sustained conflict with one another owing to numerous issues of strategic divergences such as the US missile defence plan in Asia, the perennial issue of Taiwan coupled with Chinese human rights violations especially after the Tiananmen Square incident.

Subsequently, during the 2000 US Presidential election campaign, Republican candidate, George W. Bush vehemently denounced Clinton's 'engagement policy' vis-à-vis China. He argued that, given China's ideological preferences and ill-conceived ambitions, it was inappropriate for the US to regard it as a strategic partner. Rather, he viewed China as a strategic competitor and lashed out at the Clinton administration for allegedly putting more emphasis on relations with China than with Japan, the most important ally of Washington in Asia, claiming that this compromised American security interests in Asia. He also announced that the policy of strategic ambiguity with regard to Taiwan was outdated. If elected president, Bush vowed to clarify the policy so that the US could more effectively help Taiwan defend itself.[1] Upon entering the White House, President Bush honored his campaign promises by assuming a tougher position on China than that of his predecessor.

After assuming office, the Bush White House brought into office a wide-ranging critique of the outgoing (Clinton) Administration's Asian policies. President Bush appeared to be pursuing what was termed as 'ABC' (anything but Clinton) set of policies.[2] It focused towards a swing from cultivating engagement with China to highlighting the centrality of America's alliance with Japan. Bush Administration felt that its predecessor had in fact been too solicitous of China's sensibilities and too naïve about the potential threat that China might pose both to Taiwan and the future US role in the region.

Bilateral relations between Washington and Beijing were marked by worsening pungency during this period when the first major foreign policy challenge for George W. Bush's Administration came on April 1, 2001 during which an EP-3 US Navy reconnaissance aircraft, on a mission to collect signals intelligence collided in mid-air with a Chinese F-8 fighter over the South China Sea, off the coast of Hainan Island. The Chinese aircraft broke up and crashed into the sea and its pilot was lost. Consequently, the Chinese authorities detained the American crew and US-China relations were plunged into turmoil yet again.

Beijing demanded an apology that was initially not agreed to by the Bush administration. Although, later Secretary of State Colin Powell wrote a letter to Chinese Vice-Premier Qian Qichen early on April 5 that included a statement of regret regarding the apparent loss of the Chinese pilot as well as the

US aircraft entering Chinese air-space. It hoped for the release of the crew as well as returning the aircraft.[3] The crew was finally released on April 12, 2001. Barring anything else, the EP-3 plane incident did manage to depict that Chinese pragmatism indeed had prevailed. On the American side this experience showed that astute-diplomacy could resolve knotty issues, but the incident, seemed to have confirmed the hard-liners' view of China as a dangerous and confrontational adversary.[4] It was occurrences such as the one mentioned above, due to which the bilateral relationship was largely out of balance prior to 9/11. Moreover, Washington was busy drafting the new *Quadrennial Defense Review Report*, which treated China as a potential threat and outlined measures that the US should adopt in order to cope with it.[5]

It was against this background that 9/11 occurred. The horrors of the terrorist attack on the US redefined history forever since the magnitude of the September 11, 2001 attacks on the World Trade Centre and the Pentagon were unprecedented in the history of global terrorism. Boeing aircrafts, hijacked almost simultaneously from airports on the American East Coast, were crashed into the symbols of American establishment and enterprise—the 110-storey twin towers of the World Trade Centre in New York and the Pentagon, outside Washington D.C. Another Boeing 747 crashed about 130 kms from Pittsburgh, Pennsylvania sending shock waves around the globe.

SINO-AMERICAN RELATIONS SINCE 9/11

The September 11 terrorist attacks raised the prospects for a fresh start to Sino-US ties. It was hoped that increased cooperation in the area of counter terrorism could help rebuild a stable bilateral relationship despite the major differences between the two nations over human rights and humanitarian intervention coupled with regional security issues. In sync with this anticipation, the Chinese reaction to the 9/11 incident came in the form of Chinese President Jiang Zemin conveying a message to his US counterpart expressing sympathy to the American government and the people for the attacks against the US and took a strong position in support of the US efforts to combat international terrorism. Furthermore, the Chinese Foreign Ministry spokesman Zhu Bang Zao stated, "The Chinese government has always denounced and opposed all terrorist acts of violence."[6] Moreover, at the United Nations (UN), China voiced its concerns over terrorism with Chinese permanent representative Wang Yingfan stressing in the Security Council, "International terrorism causes tremendous losses of life and property of innocent civilians and seriously endangers human society and political and economic order of countries, thus constituting a serious potential danger against international peace and security." He further went on to add, "China supports the UN in strengthening its work in preventing and fighting terrorism and favors continued strengthening of cooperation among member states."[7]

Following the coordinated terrorist incidents of September 11, the ensuing death and destruction and the declaration by President Bush announcing the launching of a global war on terrorism, China offered cooperation in this worldwide counter-terrorism struggle. On September 12, China voted in favour of United Nations Security Council Resolution 1368 condemning the terrorist threat. Its vote for Resolution 1368 was particularly momentous in that it was the first time China voted in favor of authorizing use of international force. Thus the bilateral ties between Washington and Beijing experienced some improvement, something that was difficult to envisage prior 9/11.

Clearly, in the wake of the September 11, 2001 terrorist attacks, the PRC and US foreign policy calculations appeared to be changing. This apparent shift was deftly displayed during the ninth Asia-Pacific Economic Cooperation (APEC) meet held at Shanghai in October 2001, where a joint statement was issued to counter terrorism. The statement affirmed, "Leaders consider the murderous deeds as well as other terrorist acts in all forms and manifestations... as a profound threat to peace...........and a direct challenge to APEC's vision of a free world."[8] Moreover, Chinese President Jiang Zemin said, "Terrorism should be cracked down upon, whenever and wherever it occurs, whoever organizes it, whoever is targeted and whatever forms it takes."[9]

Later in a meeting with President Jiang Zemin in Shanghai, President Bush thanked China for its speedy reaction to express its clear and firm support for the US and for its efforts to cooperate in this regard. President Bush stressed that his Administration attached high importance to US-China relations and that China was by no means an enemy of the US, noticeably displaying a marked departure from the earlier rhetoric.

On the contrary, he viewed China as a friend, and his Administration was committed to developing cooperative relations with China.[10] President Bush reiterated at the APEC Summit that there were differences between the two countries; however, his Administration was going to deal with these differences on the basis of mutual respect and candor. This yet again marked a lucid swing of stance from the earlier position that Bush had with regards to China. "The Chinese share our resolve to shut down the global terror network linked to Osama bin Laden... We are pleased with the cooperation we have received from China since September 11," said Frank Taylor, the State Department's Ambassador at large for counter-terrorism.[11]

While China's support for increased international cooperation in combating terrorism was clear, its attitude toward the use of force in response to 9/11 remained ambivalent. Reacting to the air strikes launched by US and Britain against Al-Qaeda hideouts Afghanistan, China stressed that attacks against terrorism should be aimed at specific targets to avoid injuring innocent people. It gave an impression that China was attempting to play a balancing act. Although, China appeared wary about US' war on terrorism, and said that US President George W. Bush's comments in his State of the Union address, on January 29, 2002 in which, he clubbed North Korea, Iran and Iraq as an 'axis of evil' suggested the US was preparing the ground for widening its war on terrorism. China refuted this statement by saying that no such 'axis' existed between the three Asian nations.[12]

Though, American and Chinese perspectives on the threats and challenges emanating from failing states have been converging, especially post-9/11, the Chinese regime has been rather cautious in extending its political support to the Bush Administration's war on Afghanistan and China has in fact bolstered its military forces along the border with Afghanistan. Moreover, Beijing has been anxious about the direct intervention of the US into the strategic and resource-rich Central Asian region.

Besides, the meet of the Association of South – East Asian Nations (ASEAN) in July 2002, left China bothered with regards to a prospective counter–terrorism pact between the US and the ASEAN, in turn giving Washington additional clout in Southeast Asia, where Beijing has been extensively cultivating ties to assert its regional position. According to Zhu Feng of Beijing University, in case fighting terrorism led to a stepping up of military exchanges between the US and Southeast Asian countries, then China would be worried as it would not want to see the US using its war against terrorism to set up military bases in Southeast Asia and have troops stationed there. As a matter of fact, such action would be interpreted by Beijing as a threat partly targeted at China, which in the past has used its military prowess to try to intimidate Taiwan.

According to few security analysts, "...it appears that China's support of the war against terrorism does not and will not fundamentally alter the Sino-US relationship."[13] There are others who question the sustainability of Sino-US cooperation [in the anti-terror struggle].[14] However, the 9/11 attacks made

Beijing more aware of potential direct threats to its security. Bordered by a number of states that have provided safe haven to terrorists, including Afghanistan, Pakistan, and some Central Asian states, China also began to recognize the urgency of responding to the dangers and challenges emanating from weak and failing states, including emerging or worsening transnational, nontraditional threats.[15]

Despite the sharing of numerous common interests on the issue of tackling international terrorism, Sino-US cooperation to respond to terrorism faced certain limits. A key US concern was the Chinese initiative to equate separatist movements with terrorism, regardless of whether separatist groups used political means or terrorist attacks. Washington, in all probability is unlikely to endorse Chinese efforts to define the ongoing separatist movements in Xinjiang and Tibet as acts of terror. Over all, it can be implied that China has cautiously adopted a supportive stance. China obviously will not be keen to see US military forces entrenched for long near its Central Asian borders which could be attributed to the fact that China faces an ongoing separatist insurgency among the ethnic Uighur minority—a Turkic-speaking, predominantly Muslim community—in the sensitive and remote northwestern Chinese province of Xinjiang, abutting the Central Asian republics.

Significantly, during the 2001 APEC Summit, official Chinese media reported that during their meeting on the fringes of the APEC summit, President Jiang Zemin and Russian President Vladimir Putin agreed, "Chechnya and East Turkistan terrorist activities are part of international terrorism." However, on the other hand, President Bush reiterated the US position without specifically referring to Uighur terrorism and said, "The war on terrorism must never be an excuse to persecute minorities... Ethnic minorities must know that their rights will be safeguarded—that their churches, temples and mosques belong to them."[16] This statement was widely viewed as a caution to China that the issue of terrorism should not be mingled with the contentious issues of human rights violations, ethnic cleansing and suppressing the ongoing separatist movement in Xinjiang.

CRISIS IN THE XINJIANG PROVINCE

Beijing has long claimed to be confronting "religious extremist forces" and "violent terrorism" in the Xinjiang Province. Xinjiang is critical to the economic ambitions of the PRC. Significantly, the province makes up more than one-sixth of China's landmass, but more importantly has rich, untapped deposits of oil, natural gas and minerals. China is currently trying to attract investment for a massive natural gas pipeline project, costing more than a whopping $US14 billion, being built from the province to Shanghai. In addition, China also perceives Xinjiang as its gateway to the huge oil and gas reserves of Central Asia with Chinese companies already seeking foreign partners to construct pipelines from fields in Kazakhstan and Russia.

Much like Tibetans, the Uighurs in Xinjiang, have struggled for cultural survival in the face of a government-supported influx by Chinese migrants, as well as harsh repression of political dissent and any expression, however lawful or peaceful, of their distinct identity. Some have also resorted to violence in a struggle for independence.[17] However, Chinese authorities have not discriminated between peaceful and violent dissent and their fight against "separatism" and "religious extremism" has been used to justify widespread and systematic human rights violations against Uighurs, including many involved in non-violent political, religious, and cultural activities.

According to the *Amnesty International Report,* repression had broadened and intensified following a national conference in Beijing, which identified "ethnic separatist forces, religious extremist forces and violent terrorist forces... as the main priorities in 'political and legal work' for the year 2002."

Crucially, Xinjiang remains the only province in China where execution of political prisoners is common. According to the *Amnesty International Report*, over 200 people were executed between 1997 and 1999.[18] It is Chinese activities such as these that are likely to erode the goodwill produced by cooperation in the war against terrorism.

PRC's remote northwestern Xinjiang province has a long historical association with China. The region was dominated by rival warlords along with being occupied by other forces for much of the first half of the 20th century. The Kuomintang did not establish its control of the region after the 1911 nationalist revolution and the local Turkic elites declared an independent Eastern Turkistan Islamic Republic twice during the interwar period. The Uighurs, who look and sound more like Turks than Han (ethnic) Chinese, enjoyed a brief period of independence in the 1940s, declaring themselves as the Republic of East Turkistan. On the last occasion in 1944, Stalin backed the "independent" republic as a buffer state and provided limited aid. However, the Communists re-established control soon after coming to power when the peasant armies of Mao Zedong seized power in 1949 and Xinjiang soon after was occupied and proclaimed a "national autonomous" region. But as in Tibet, the Stalinist regime in Beijing failed to overcome the region's economic and cultural backwardness and sought to exploit the region's resources with scant regard for local sensibilities.[19]

In fact, most of China's nuclear tests were carried out in this province. The exploitation of mineral resources and the opening up of the region for cotton production brought an influx of ethnic Chinese which dramatically altered the province's ethnic balance and reduced the Uighurs to second-class citizens. In 1949, Xinjiang had 3.2 million Uighurs a compared to a paltry 140,000 Chinese. Today, Xinjiang has a population of 18 million and is home to numerous Turkic-speaking Muslim ethnic groups, of which the Uighurs, numbering eight million, is the largest followed by the second largest group of Kazakhs numbering at 1.2 million. The percentage of Han Chinese population has grown from 6 percent in 1949 to 40 percent at present with a staggering 7.5 million people.

Through the 1990s, Beijing was apprehensive with regards to the emergence of unrest and terrorism in its largely Uighur Muslim-inhabited region of Xinjiang, since the Uighurs share more cultural affinity with central Asia than with rest of China. In Xinjiang there is widespread economic and cultural resentment of the Han Chinese resulting in Uighur militancy aided by pan-Islamic elements—possibly the Taliban-Al Qaeda combine-and several terrorist acts.[20] China continuously has stepped up efforts to convince the outside world that there is a direct link between the US-led war on terror and its own fight against Muslim separatists. But many remain unconvinced by Beijing's latest claims against those accused of carrying out a series of bombings and assassinations in its biggest and most politically restive region. In the past, China revealed as little as possible about the sensitive issue of separatist violence in Xinjiang. Nevertheless, China seems to be coming out of the closet as far as Xinjiang and terrorism are concerned.

China has identified four groups that reportedly are threatening China's security. They include the Eastern Turkistan Islamic Movement (ETIM), which the US and the UN agreed to ban in 2002. In addition, China's first ever "terrorist" list included the Eastern Turkistan Liberation Organization (ETLO), the World Uighur Youth Congress (WUYC) and the East Turkistan Information Centre (ETIC). Both WUYC and ETIC support the creation of an independent state for Xinjiang's Muslims. There are grounds for believing that Washington and Beijing have tangible evidence linking ETIM to the Taliban in neighbouring Afghanistan and Osama bin Laden's Al-Qaeda network. In recent years a large number of Uighurs have crossed the border from Xinjiang into Pakistan, Afghanistan and Central Asia and have come into contact with Al-Qaeda and other groups.[21]

The September 11 attacks on America and the subsequent US invasion of Afghanistan simply compounded the tensions in Xinjiang as it did throughout the region. Beijing no doubt was pleased that the US military destroyed the bases of operations for at least some of the armed Uighur groups active in Xinjiang, though simultaneously, China was concerned about the consequences of a string of US military bases on its doorstep and the potential for Washington to manipulate Uighur separatism into a pretext for a more direct intervention in Xinjiang.

After September 11, 2001, the Chinese government charged that Uighur groups had links with the Taliban in Afghanistan and claimed that they were receiving support from numerous radical Islamist organizations. On October 10, 2001, for instance, Chinese Foreign Ministry spokesman Sun Yuxi's declaration, "China hopes that efforts to fight against East Turkistan terrorist forces should become a part of the international efforts and should also win support and understanding" must be seen in this light.[22]

Beijing expected the international community to accept its post-9/11 crackdown in Xinjiang as part of the global war on terrorism. The Chinese State Council in January 2002 issued a *Report* titled *East Turkistan Terrorist Forces Cannot Get Away with Impunity* that detailed the extent of terrorist activities since 1990. The report listed more than 200 incidents that resulted in 162 deaths and 440 injuries, and included bombings, assassinations, armed assaults on government organizations, poison and arson, establishing training bases, and plotting riots such as the Yining incident in February 1997.[23] However, on August 26, 2002, while visiting Beijing, US Deputy Secretary of State Richard Armitage stated that Washington recognized one Uighur organization, the East Turkistan Islamic Movement, as a terrorist organization and had placed it on the list of terrorist organizations because it had committed acts of violence against unarmed civilians. The group was not placed on the top priority list of terrorist organizations but rather on the broader list of groups subject to financial sanctions. Nonetheless, Armitage's discussions with Chinese leaders included the need for Beijing to respect the rights of Uighurs.

Many of the human rights advocates have in fact stressed that since September 11, the Chinese government has expanded its suppressive policy toward the Uighurs under a more acceptable pretext i.e. suppressing terrorism. China claimed that the Uighur activists were inspired, encouraged and supplied by terrorist organizations, particularly by al-Qaeda and the Taliban stationed in neighboring Afghanistan.[24] In yet another instance, China exploited the US "war on terrorism" to step up its crackdown when on November 14, 2001, Chinese vice-premier Qian Qichen told the UN Commission for Human Rights—which had complained in the past about alleged human rights abuses in Xinjiang—that over 1,000 Islamic extremists from the province had received terrorist training in Afghani camps operated by Osama bin Laden's Al Qaeda network.[25]

For more than a decade, Xinjiang has been rocked by demonstrations, bombings, and political assassinations. According to a recent government report, Uighur separatists were responsible for 200 attacks between 1990 and 2001, causing 162 deaths and injuring more than 440 people. In the largest single incident, in 1997, as many as 100 people may have been killed during a pro-independence uprising in the town of Ili, with the government and the separatists blaming each other for the fatalities. These incidents have occurred despite the best efforts of the Chinese authorities to suppress them. As part of their continuing 'strike hard' campaign against crime, for example, Chinese police reported the arrest of 166 separatist "terrorists" and other "major criminals" in a series of raids carried out in Urumqi, Xinjiang's capital.[26]

Notably, since September 11, tens of thousands of extra Chinese troops were moved into Xinjiang, both to bolster border posts and to enforce martial law conditions. According to a

November 19, 2001 article by the official *Xinhua News Agency*, a campaign against "major threats to social security" was ordered in September. The most prominent threats were listed as "infiltration and sabotage by hostile overseas forces...disturbance by nationalist splittism forces and religious extremists and terrorists".[27] After October 7, 2001, the Chinese Government, which previously had been playing down the frequent incidents of violence in the Xinjiang-Uighur Autonomous Region (XUAR) did a round about and instead started playing them up. They attributed it to the East Turkistan terrorists who formed part of the international terrorism network and hence were projected as a legitimate target of the international coalition.[28]

However, the United States had warned Chinese officials that the anti-terror campaign should not be used to suppress legitimate political dissent among China's Muslim populations. In a visit to Beijing in December 2001, for instance, the State Department's counter-terrorism expert, Francis X. Taylor, said that Washington did not believe Muslim separatists in China who supported an independent East Turkistan were part of the global anti-terror network. But on August 26, 2002, US Deputy Secretary of State Richard Armitage announced that Washington had added the ETIM to its list of terrorist groups thereby raising questions behind the motivations of the unexpected US move.

Besides, *The Washington Post* quoted one unnamed diplomat as suspicious that the move appeared to be a trade-off for PRC support in the UN Security Council for the US campaign against Iraq.[29] On August 28, 2002, officials at the US Embassy in Beijing further announced they had evidence that the ETIM was plotting a terrorist bombing of the US Embassy in Bishkek, Kyrgyzstan. Furthermore, on September 11, 2002, the United Nations announced that, at the request of both the United States and China, it was placing the ETIM on a UN list of terrorist organizations, requiring that all UN members freeze the group's financial assets and ban its members from entry.[30] This flow of events aptly demonstrated that both Washington and Beijing were in fact playing a well-orchestrated bargain game plan and trying to extract as much concessions from each other as they possibly could.

THE ROAD AHEAD

China appears to be facing a serious dilemma in crafting its response to the US war on terrorism. On the one hand, it wants to be spotted as resolute and unfailing in its political support for action against terrorism while on the other, it does not want to be closely associated with the US military actions [such as the US involvement in Iraq] that violate state sovereignty and invite retaliation. This could well be cited as a prime reason to explain Beijing's ties to nations such as Iran that are driven by a host of geo-strategic, commercial and foreign policy considerations.[31] One motive for Chinese efforts to develop diplomatic and economic relations with Iran could well be to prevent it from supporting separatist groups in Xinjiang.

With the passage of time since 9/11 it did increasingly become understandable that in the context of the international war on terror, Beijing has had to make some difficult choices. Nevertheless, the period following the twin tower attacks, witnessed the launch of an effective consultation mechanism on anti-terrorism. Numerous rounds of anti-terrorist consultative meetings have been held between Washington and Beijing covering domestic, regional and international anti-terrorist expertise since. There are notable indications of the growing security and law enforcement links between China and the United States. Moreover, the two nations signed an agreement to open a Federal Bureau of Investigation (FBI) liaison office in Beijing during Attorney General John Ashcroft's 3-day visit to China in October 2002.[32]

Further, in July 2003, Chinese customs officials and US signed an agreement in Beijing to cooperate in the Container

Security Initiative. Under the agreement, US officials would be stationed at ports in the cities of Shanghai and Shenzhen. The task of the personnel would be to certify that containers bound for US destinations were free of weapons or dangerous materials, which could be used by terrorists.[33] Furthermore, fund flows of suspected international terrorist organizations were blocked effectively. In fact, Sino-US Anti-terrorist Financial Working Group conducted a large number of consultations after the September 11 terrorist attacks. Financial authorities of China's mainland and Hong Kong cooperated closely and successfully froze funds of suspected terrorist organizations.

By all means it does appear understandable that since September 11, 2001, Beijing and Washington have expanded their cooperation, deepened consensus and made some achievements in the fight against international terrorism. The two countries have made an effort to cement the base for further cooperation. However, the two countries have rather diverging views on anti-terrorism regarding the definition and roots of international terrorism. Although China supports the US-led anti-terrorist campaign, but at the same time it emphasizes that military means should not violate state sovereignty and international laws. It deems that, without hard proof of a threat, preemptive military actions are not only dangerous, but will also have future repercussions. Above all else, military actions against terrorism should take into account the protection of civilians.[34] Probably sensing this existent thin line between friction and cooperation, Aaron Friedberg opined that the two countries never actually resolved any long-standing disputes while agreeing to cooperate on terror; it was merely a partnership of convenience.[35]

Indeed, the cooperation on terrorism did not entirely mean that the US diminished its pressure on China pertaining to issues such as human rights violations or political reform. The terrorism that most directly continues to threaten Beijing occurs within the context of ethnic separatist activity among non-Han minorities in the PRC, particularly the Muslim Uighurs in the Xinjiang Province. Statements by Chinese officials about terrorism also commonly emphasize the need to combat not only the "symptoms" but also the "root causes" of terror by working toward alleviating poverty and promoting prosperity in developing countries. This sentiment is consistent with China's long-standing effort to style itself as a "principled" country that promotes just treatment of the Third World.[36] It is reflective of the Chinese perspective according to which, the Bush Administration has often relied too heavily on military approaches to fight terrorism.

There has been growing sentiment that the US is waging a war against Islam. More significantly, Samuel P. Huntington, to a large extent had forecast the cultural and religious context in which a 9/11-type incident could well emerge. In the immediate aftermath of 9/11, he wrote that the attack was indeed an attempt by Osama bin Laden to draw the US and the West into a full-fledged clash of civilizations with Islam. While Huntington advocates tolerance and mutual understanding, he sees the West increasingly in conflict with Islam. In broader perspective, the events of September 11 and their aftermath abruptly brought down the curtain on the post-Cold War US foreign policy that was dominated for almost an entire decade by the themes of non-proliferation, globalization and humanitarian intervention.

Apparently, the Chinese government became more assertive in its approach including accepting rationales for international military intervention in some cases (such as in Afghanistan), thus coming more into alignment with US perspectives on these issues. This shift in the Chinese perspective on terrorism reflected, more generally, a significant change in Chinese strategic thinking and foreign policy. While still insisting on the primacy of the UN, the Chinese government, under the new leadership of President Hu Jintao and Premier Wen Jiabao, downplayed its prior insistence on "noninterference" and adopted a more flexible, open, and proactive foreign policy, signaling that even though the substance of Sino-US relations had not altered considerable since September 11, 2001, the atmospherics most certainly had.

Rising from the ashes of September 11, America was ushered through a 'gate of fire' into a new realism about the world according to former UN Secretary General Kofi Annan. Accordingly, any future American foreign policy orientation might consider refashioning its key relationships with the war on terrorism becoming the fulcrum. The changing connotations of its association with China aptly substantiate this reality. At the beginning of the new century, the development of a constructive and cooperative relationship between China and the United States appeared critical to the interests of the two countries and the world. However, the context of 9/11 did indeed accelerate the process in that united by the common cause of anti-terrorism, increased stakes in bilateral cooperation and greater responsibilities in world affairs, the two countries might just be compelled to find more productive ways to deal with the perils of global terrorism.

REFERENCES

1. For more details on Bush's Presidential Campaign see, *The New York Times*, p. A10, February 26, 2000.
2. For more details see, Kenneth Leiberthal, "The United States and Asia in 2001: Changing Agendas," *Asian Survey*, vol. 42, no. 1, January–February 2002, pp. 1-2.
3. As cited in, John Keefe and Susan V. Lawrence, "A Tale of 'Two Very Sorries' Redux: US–China Relations," *Far Eastern Economic Review*, March 21, 2002, pp. 31-32.
4. Lieberthal, n. 2, p. 6.
5. A sanitized version of the report was however released after September 11, 2001. The report clearly showed as to how the Pentagon was thinking about China prior to the 9/11 attacks, for instance in a passage the report suggests, "Although the United States will not face a peer competition in the near future, the potential exists for regional powers to develop sufficient capabilities to threaten stability in regions critical

to US interests." For more on the Report see, *Quadrennial Defense Review Report,* Department of Defense, September 30, 2001.

6. Cited in *Xinhua News Agency* Press Release, September 11, 2001.
7. *Xinhua News Agency,* September 13, 2001.
8. "APEC issues joint statement", Text published in the *The Asian Age,* October 22, 2001.
9. Ibid.
10. "President Jiang Zemin and President Bush Hold Talks", available at *http://www.peopledaily.com.cn* October 19, 2001.
11. Erik Eckholm, "Official Praises China for Its Cooperation in Rooting Out bin Laden Terror Network", *The New York Times,* December 7, 2001.
12. As cited in *China Daily,* February 1, 2002.
13. Denny Roy, "China and the War on Terrorism", *Orbis,* vol. 46, no. 3, Summer 2002, p. 518.
14. Thomas J. Christensen, "China," in Richard J. Ellings and Aaron L. Friedberg, eds., *Strategic Asia 2002-03: Asian Aftershocks,* (Seattle, WA: National Bureau of Asian Research, 2002), p. 81.
15. Banning Garrett and Jonathan Adams, *US-China Cooperation on the Problem of Failing States and Transnational Threats,* Special Report, no. 126, September 2004, United States Institute of Peace.
16. Cited in B. Raman, *US and Terrorism in Xinjiang,* Paper no. 499, South Asia Analysis Group, July 2002.
17. "China: Human Rights Concerns in Xinjiang", *Human Rights Watch Backgrounder,* October 2001.
18. *Amnesty International Report* 2003 available at *http://web.amnesty.org/web/web.nsf/report2003/chn-summary-eng/$FILE/china.pdf*
19. For more details see, John Chan, "*China's 'War on Terrorism'—Brutal Repression of Ethnic Unrest in Xinjiang*", available at *http://www.wsws.org/articles/2002/aug2002/chin-a08.shtml,* August 8, 2002.
20. *The Asian Age,* September 16, 2001.
21. Tim Luard, "*China's Changing Views of Terrorism*", at *http://news.bbc.co.uk/2/hi/asia-pacific/3320347.stm,* December 15, 2003.
22. Chinese Foreign Ministry Statement, quoted in *China Daily,* October 11, 2001.
23. On February 5, 1997, dozens of people were killed and seriously injured when the Chinese security forces reportedly opened fire on ethnic Uighur demonstrators and brutally broke up a peaceful demonstration

in the city of Gulja (Yining) in the Xinjiang Uighur A utonomous Region of China. Large number of people were arrested during the demonstrations, many detainees were tortured, thereby causing a great deal of unrest the following day. In addition, also see, Gaye Christoffersen, "Constituting the Uyghur in US-China Relations: Geopolitics of Identity Formation in the War on Terrorism", *Strategic Insights,* vol. 1, no. 7, September 2002.

24. Hooman Peimani, "Beijing's harsher Uighur Policy: A Shot in Two Feet", at *http://www.atimes.com/china/DD24Ad01.html,* April 24, 2002.

25. James Conachy, "China's Stake in the US War on Terrorism", at *http://www.wsws.org/articles/2001/nov2001/chin-n26.shtml,* November 26, 2001.

26. For more details see, Chien-peng Chung, "China's 'War on Terror': September 11 and Uighur Separatism", *Foreign Affairs,* July/August 2002.

27. *Xinhua News Agency*, Press Release, November 19, 2001.

28. Chung, n. 26.

29. *The Washington Post*, August 27, 2002.

30. China-US Relations, *Congressional Research Service Issue Brief for Congress,* IB98018, March 14, 2002, [Updated].

31. Jing-dong Yuan, "The War on Terrorism: China's Opportunities and Dilemmas", at *http://cns.miis.edu/research/wtc01/china.htm,* September 25, 2001.

32. Statement issued by the *US Department of State*, Office of the Spokesman, October 2002.

33. Andrew Scobell, "Chinese Foreign Policy and the War on Terror", *Terrorism Monitor,* vol. 2, no. 2, January 30, 2004.

34. Wang Baofu, " Feeling Secure: China and the United States Cooperating in Anti-terrorism", *Beijing Review available* at *http://www.bjreview.cn/EN/200437/World-200437(B).htm*

35. Aaron Friedberg quoted in Natalia Rigol, "A Game of Giants: The Future of Sino-US Relations", *Harvard International Review,* vol. 27, no. 1, Spring 2005.

36. Denny Roy, "Lukewarm Partner: Chinese Support for US Counter-Terrorism in Southeast Asia", at *http://www.apcss.org/Publications/APCSS/pdf,* March 2006.

5

Terrorism and Pakistan: Tracing the Course from Harbinger to Victim

Seema Sridhar[1]

"He that killeth with the sword must be killed with the sword"
— *The Bible [Rev 13:10]*

The terrorist attacks of 9/11 that caused devastation in the United States and the rest of the world. Its reverberations were felt across continents, upon the political and strategic dynamics of several regions. It was one such reverberation that Pakistan, which was one of the only three countries to recognize the Taliban regime in Afghanistan, emerged as the frontline state on the US led war on terror. The preponderance of Pakistan in the US war on terror has been consistently underscored by unfolding events in terrorism, wherein Pakistan has completed the cycle providing safe sanctuary for terrorism to becoming a victim of its own policies in fostering terrorist groups. The country's significance in this regard has been aptly brought out by Nicholas Burns, the US State Department's Under Secretary for Political Affairs in his November 2006 statement "It is in South Asia where our future success in the struggle against global terrorism will likely be decided — in Afghanistan and Pakistan."[2] All the ingredients of a natural ally have been bestowed upon Pakistan. Its strategic positioning in South Asia, bordering on Afghanistan, Iran and Central Asia, particularly the al-Qaeda operating in the region, a history of teaming up with the US to fight the Soviets in Afghanistan by training the *mujahdeen* and the consequent knowledge and intelligence about the major terrorist networks in the region, contributed to Pakistan being the 'chosen one' to ally with the US on the war on terror. This paper seeks to analyze the trajectory of Pakistan's war on terror and delve into the manifold factors that are intertwined with the broad issue of terrorism in Pakistan. The study, based on empirical analysis traces the passage of the Islamic state form being a sanctuary for religious fundamentalism to the current state of affairs where it is bearing the brunt of its own policies of fostering the double-edge sword of Islamic extremism.

ROOTS OF TERRORISM IN PAKISTAN: A BACKGROUNDER

> "....The majority of religious scholars are very enlightened people, but the extremists who are carrying out these protests think they are the sole custodians of Islam. They looked at the Taliban as if they were the renaissance of Islam and at those who were against the Taliban as if they were, God forbid, not Muslims. But these people have no respect for human rights... and the Pakistani people were let down by these so-called religious scholars." — *Pervez Musharraf*[6]

Pakistan has been a haven for Islamic fundamentalist groups and terrorist groups since its inception. According to the Council on Foreign Relations Report of December 2005, Pakistan's military and Inter-services Intelligence (ISI) both include personnel who sympathize with—or even assist—Islamist militants. ISI has provided covert but well-documented support to terrorist groups active in Kashmir, including the al-Qaeda affiliate Jaish-e-Mohammed, which investigators linked to the December 2001 attack on the Indian parliament and the

February 2002 murder of Wall Street Journal reporter Daniel Pearl[4]. President Pervez Musharraf made promises to stop Kashmiri militants from crossing into the Indian-held sector of Kashmir, but India insists Musharraf has yet to stop the terrorists' movements[5].

The root of Pakistan's nationhood is derived from Deobandi[6], a type of Islamic fundamentalism. This movement, which began as a reformist movement in India against British oppression, gradually evolved into the idea of the formation of a Muslim state. Islamic fundamentalism in Pakistan found a fertile breeding ground in the large network of *madrassas,* which were part of the Deobandi movement in Pakistan. The inception of the Taliban movement has been traced to the Deobandi *madrassas* in Pakistan.

Islamic orthodoxy in Pakistan gained firm hold in Pakistan when the process of Islamisation of the State began by Zia-ul Huq[7]. In his quest for legitimizing his regime, he turned to the support of right wing Islamist groups, bringing in a more stringent Wahabi Islam from Saudi Arabia. The Soviet intervention in Afghanistan in 1979 facilitated Gen Zia's Islamist goals eventually being combined with the US directed objective of forging ties with the Afghan *mujahideen.* An intricate interwoven network emerged between the Afghan *mujahideen,* domestic religious groups in Pakistan, and the Pakistani State, all supplied with arms and financed by the US Extremist violence spread swiftly from Afghanistan to Pakistan owing to the unbridled availability of arms combined with an expanding fanatic cadre.

Pakistan's acceptance of and support for hard-line Islamists within the country and beyond its borders finds its origins the in ethnic Pashtun ties that cross the Afghani-Pakistani border. After the Soviet withdrawal, the struggle among rival extremist groups started to deepen, while competing for power and influence intensified. Pakistan began to officially support specific hard-line Islamist groups after the Soviet withdrawal, to assist them in establishing and maintaining their control over Afghanistan. The infrastructure of *madrassas* and training centres began to train students in Islamic ideology, train militants for waging jihad against neighbouring India, to incite separatist violence in Punjab and later Kashmir. Pakistan's military and Inter Services Intelligence (ISI) both include personnel who sympathize with—or even assist—Islamist militants. ISI has provided covert but well-documented support to terrorist groups active in Kashmir, including the al- affiliate Jaish-e-Mohammed, which was linked to the December 2001 attack on the Indian Parliament[8].

The end of the Afghan war brought about transformation not only in Pakistan's external policy towards its neighbours, but also within its domestic realm. Large numbers of Afghan refugees migrated to major urban centres in Pakistan, particularly Karachi, increasing the ethnic strife in the multi-ethnic commercial hub which had a huge population of *Muhajirs*[9]. It led to large settlements of refugee camps in the North Western Frontier Province, which became a recruitment camp for Islamist militant organizations, trained by the *madrassas* in combat operations, as they adopted a violent interpretation of Islam. It was also in the interest of the State to keep these organizations active, to be used surreptitiously for creating mayhem in neighbouring countries and also to support the ruling elite whenever a crisis for legitimacy arises, which incidentally has been quite regular in the history Pakistani politics. It was in this backdrop that the 9/11 triggered off an about turn in the State policies, and Musharaff's famous U-turn on terrorism only brought to the fore, that the policy of fostering extremist outfits, was indeed a double-edged weapon. What followed was a crisis of stability within Pakistan, somewhat held together by the firm American support to the military rule of General Pervez Musharraf.

PAKISTAN, THE FRONTLINE STATE

> "....Pakistan rejects terrorism in all its forms and manifestations. Pakistan will not allow its territory to be used for any terrorist activity anywhere in the world. We have been taking measures against terrorism from the beginning, not because of any outside pressure. Even television shops in India were crowded with viewers. We were already carrying out these measures when a terrorist attack was carried out in America on 11 September. After 11 September we joined the international coalition against terrorism and I am delighted that the majority of Pakistani people supported this decision. I however regret that some religious extremist groups resented this decision. I further regret that this opposition was not based on religious principles, but based on personal interests and party interests...."
>
> — *Pervez Musharraf*[10]

Musharraf became the most bankable bet for the US in its Afghan mission. The 9/11 Commission identified President Musharraf's military regime as the best hope for stability in Pakistan and Afghanistan[11]. It has recommended that the United States make a long-term commitment for continuation of the wide-ranging support for Islamabad, which it is already receiving, so long as Pakistan shows its commitment in fighting extremism and adheres to the policy of "enlightened moderation." A strong military controller who was also arm twisted into compliance with the US *diktat* into the US led joining the international coalition against terrorism suited American interests well. Democracy was yet again compromised for expediency in US foreign policy and the military leader was given full support to take all possible measures to ensure that American objectives in the region could be pursued unhindered. A free reign in terms of amendments of the Pakistani Constitution was taken up by Musharraf to give him extra-ordinary powers to implement certain policies, which would have otherwise been greeted by staunch opposition to the extent of threatening his own position. Pakistan was declared a major non-NATO ally of the US and was given huge benefits, monetary and military. This move of course came with a huge price, that of antagonizing the groups that Pakistan had hitherto nurtured and the 'betrayal' was not taken lightly by the groups that Pakistan clamped down on. Post 9/11 alliance with the US marked the unleashing of the wrath of terrorism on Pakistan.

Pakistan became the staging area for the war in Afghanistan. President Musharraf's sweeping policy shift away from Islamic extremism began with the severing of all official ties to the Taliban in September 2001 and culminated in a landmark January 2002 speech[12] in which he vowed to end Pakistan's use as a base for terrorism of any kind, criticized religious extremism and intolerance in the country, and banned numerous militant groups, including Lashkar-e- Taiba and Jaish-e-Muhammad which have been responsible for numerous terrorist attacks in Kashmir and other parts of India[13] . Sweeping police reforms were instituted, immigration control system was upgraded, new anti-terrorist finance laws were brought about by Islamabad. About 3,300 extremists were arrested in the immediate aftermath of 9/11 and detained, though at least one-third of these have since been released, including the founders of both Lashkar-e-Taiba and Jaish-e-Muhammad.[14]

Over flight rights to coalition aircraft, let US forces use two Pakistani airfields, and intelligence was shared about suspected terrorists. Pakistan worked with the Federal Bureau of Investigation (FBI) to capture suspected al- and Taliban fugitives who fled into northern Pakistan—including al-operations chief Abu Zubaydah and the alleged September 11 mastermind Khalid Shaikh Muhammad—and in some cases committed its troops to hunt down al- holdouts. The massive It is widely believed that Pakistan has been allowing the United States to conduct low-level military or military support operations in Pakistan's western border regions since April

2002[15], following the massive US bombardment of Afghanistan's Tora Bora region in late-2001[16] and Operation Anaconda in Afghanistan's eastern Shah-i-Kot mountains in March 2002 prompting two waves of up to 5,000 al-Qaeda fighters fleeing into Pakistan.[17] Subsequent reports claimed that most of these al-Qaeda fighters were evacuated from the area by Pakistani military aircraft and in the company of "dozens of senior Pakistani military, including two generals"[18]

The US provides Pakistan huge amounts of aid every year since 9/11, in International Narcotics and Law Enforcement (INCLE) Emergency Response Funds that continue to be used for border security and related law enforcement efforts.[19] Apart from supplying numerous instruments to bolster Pakistani security forces, including used transport helicopters, short- and long-range radios, and vehicles (trucks, tractors, SUVs, and motorcycles) to increase mobility, it has also made available to Pakistan, sophisticated communication and surveillance equipment. The equipment is to be used in efforts to track down suspected terrorists and those involved in drug trafficking. Also, the United States is undertaking to train Pakistani police investigators and is helping to establish a national fingerprint database modeled on that of the FBI. Funding for the Criminal Information Database and for road-building projects in the Federally Administered Tribal Areas has been lavished upon the US strategic ally. The United States also supplied to Pakistan the Personnel Identification Secure Comparison Evaluation System (PISCES), for installing a national personal identification system, which could make real-time comparisons of photographs and other personal details with the FBI database in order to track the movements of Islamist militants. Pakistani customs and finance officials are trained by US as part of the effort to track foreign flow of money into charitable and religious institutions.[20] It has been roped into US non-proliferation efforts by being made to implement regulations for a new export control law, including adoption of enforcement regulations and establishment of a new export licensing body.[21]

In return for its cooperation, Pakistan receives immense financial aid from the United States. It is one of the largest recipients of U.S. security assistance, poised to receive $1.5 billion of Foreign Military Financing from the US from 2005 to 2009[22] . It is the process of receiving F-16 aircraft from the US, after lengthy negotiations[23] . In June 2004, President Bush designated Pakistan as a Major Non-NATO Ally, making Pakistan one of a select group of nations outside of NATO that have the benefit of a variety of military and financial advantages conferred by the United States[24] . To prove its allegiance to the US initiatives against terrorism, it has joined the Container Security Initiative thereby, agreeing to pre-screen all maritime cargo destined for the United States through the port of Qasim, for smuggling of terrorist weapons[25] .

The London bombings of July 2005 brought to the fore to its Western allies, the insufficiency of Pakistani efforts at tackling terrorism. After the London bombings, in which the bombers were of Pakistani decent—and at least one of the suspects visited a Pakistani *madrassa*—a new approach was outlined for cracking down on extremism[26] . Several new stringent steps were announced which were supposed to curb this menace substantively by Musharraf, who was weighing under immense pressure from the US. Over 200 suspected Islamist militants were detained. Hate sermons from mosques began to be monitored; all *madrassas* were required to be registered and foreign students were to be expelled; inflammatory material were clamped down upon; and militant groups were prohibited from collecting funds. However tangible difference in outcome was not to be seen and burden of showing results has been consistently piling up on Musharraf's shoulders. He is placed in a precarious position of limited control over these outfits which threaten not only his own position, but also his life.

Pakistan has taken action against several outfits identified by the US and its initiatives include detaining operatives and designating active groups suspected of financing terrorist activities. Yet Pakistan's political, military regulatory structures and efforts fall short of American expectations and of course remain insufficient for a fully effective anti-terrorism policy. There still lacks any efficient mechanism of monitoring the activities and movements of foreigners in NWFP and means to keep an account of foreign charities.

US MILITARY PURSUIT IN THE 'LAND OF THE PURE'

The extension of US military operations into Pakistan's territories has been a matter of grave provocation for the extremists. A series of intermittent attacks on the Federally Administered Tribal Areas (FATA) of Pakistan has created a furor among the media, the human rights organizations and the general public. The strikes on select targets believed to be key al-Qaeda operatives, is a natural extension of the American hunt for the al-Qaeda in Afghanistan. A large number of operatives on the American most wanted list are suspected to have taken refuge in the vast tribal lands of Pakistan. The tribal areas are ruled by the special Frontier Crimes Regulation Act (FCRA), implemented by their respective political agents, representatives from the federal government. These hinterlands, bordering on Afghanistan have not been conquered by any army, even that of Pakistan.

Military operations, if any, in the area are carried out with close cooperation with the local tribal lords. The consent for such cooperation needs to be given by the local *Jirga*, or council. The rules, procedures and codes of conduct applicable to the rest of Pakistan are not applicable here and the local tribal chieftains have their own autonomy and their loyalty is won by the political agents by paying them huge amounts of money. Pakistan's far-flung tribal areas have been a training ground for insurgents and a focal point for concerns over terrorism, particularly since the 9/11 attacks. President

Musharraf has found himself trapped between constant US demands to clamp down on militants in the tribal lands and antagonism from his own army against fighting the tribesmen. The region's predominant ethnic Pashtuns have strongly resisted Pakistani rule just as they fought British control during colonial times. The region has proved to be a safe haven for the Afghan and Pakistan Taliban, al-, Chechens, and the Islamic Movement of Uzbekistan among others.

The Taliban has grown to assume leadership roles in certain parts of the tribal lands, particularly the agencies of North and South Waziristan and Bajaur. The Pakistani government seems to be vain attempts at balancing US concerns by hardening its standpoint on al- on one hand and adapting a conciliatory posture with the Taliban, which works with other extremist groups in a complex interdependent network.

President Musharraf, buckling under severe US pressure, initiated counterterrorism operations by deploying 80,000 Pakistani troops for the operation, aimed mainly in the agencies of North and South Waziristan. The operation was unsuccessful and became very unpopular with the Pakistani armed forces, comprising of Pashtuns as the second largest ethnic group. Since 2004 the Pakistani troops remain stuck in the quagmire of turning against their own establishment's creation or showing results to the Americans and thus have not achieved anything concrete, whereas the conflict has accentuated in the course of the years.

The presence of US military surveillance equipment over Pakistani territory has long been speculated upon, but denied by both the Pakistan government and the US State Department. The attack on Bajaur agency of the Federally Administered Tribal Areas in Pakistan in January 2006 confirmed US military activities in the region though it was officially denied then. CIA drones targeted an area where Ayaman-al Zawahiri, al-Qaeda's number two was believed to have been present.[27] The strikes reportedly killed three foreign militants and triggered off strong opposition in the volatile tribal areas. The State's response was taciturn, leaving the tribes feeling betrayed and angry. An enraged mob of five thousand protestors had to be dispersed with tear gas and gun fire and the reporters of the incident were arrested by the political administration in Bajaur. The operations in the tribal agencies only compounded the problem of terrorism by brewing vengeance among the extremists and the tribesmen under their influence. The conflict aggravated placing Musharraf in an uncomfortable situation, warranting a compromise with the tribesmen, a step that was seen as counter-productive by the US as it enabled the Taliban to remain.

Thus came into being the Miramshah Agreement with North Waziristan tribal leaders and members of the Taliban, in September 2006. The provisions of the agreement included troop withdrawal by Islamabad, release of 165 militants, economic compensation for losses and right to the tribesmen to carry small weapons. An end to infiltration of militants from across the Afghan border and prevention of attacks on the military were promised in return. However, the Pakistani government has little means to ensure compliance and its means for enforcement are limited, given the threat of aggravating the extremists. The agreement is seen as a compromise and as playing into the hands of militants. The Taliban continues to regroup and reinforce itself and incursions into Afghanistan are on the rise. This continues be a menace to Musharraf and to the state of security within Pakistan.

In another such covert military operation in October 30, 2006, the Zia-ul-Uloom *madrassa* in Chinagai, a border village in the Bajaur agency of FATA was attacked by two missile strikes bringing to a grinding halt a similar peace agreement that was being worked out with the tribesmen[28]. The attack, supposedly targeted against the al-Qaeda and pro-Taliban elements, killed 82 people and resulted in a vehement public outcry, ignited by the media and non-governmental organizations about human rights violations and the banning of the entry of journalists into the region. Though Pakistani government claimed responsibility for the attack, it was widely speculated that it was a joint operation of the US and NATO forces[29] .

The Pakistani forces may not have the required technical expertise of the US, but they could provide crucial intelligence on the ground scenario. Better cooperation would foster better results, but it is the American distrust of the Pakistani willingness to act decisively upon the al-Qaeda which seems to have forced such strikes. Pakistan has little choice but to cover up the US exercises as its own to prevent the backlash from several domestic quarters. In this backdrop, misgivings about US incursions into the tribal areas are looked upon as betrayal by the State inviting the fury of the extremists who are already irked by military operations in the tribal areas and the Pakistani support to the US in its war on terror.

THE REPRISAL

> *"…. Violence and terrorism have been going on for years and we are weary and sick of this Kalashnikov culture... The day of reckoning has come. Pakistan has become a soft state where law means little, if anything."* — *Pervez Musharraf*[30]

Terrorist strikes on Western targets in Pakistan became pronounced after 9/11. A series of attacks on Churches, Christian missionary schools, hospitals and charities began with the first post-9/11 attack on Westerners in a Catholic Church bombing in Bahawalpur, which claimed the lives of 17 Christians, including five children in October 2001[31] . The United States Consulate in Karachi was attacked repeatedly, in June 2002[32] and again in February 2003 by unidentified gunmen, injuring many and killing two policemen[33] . The February 2002 kidnapping and subsequent murder of Wall Street Journal reporter Daniel Pearl is believed to have spurred an intensified US focus on law enforcement in Pakistan and efforts to assist local security forces in tracking and capturing Islamist militants in that country's urban centers. The attacks on American establishments such as Pakistan-American Cultural Centre and the residence of the US Consul General in Karachi in May 2004 with two successive car explosions, killing two persons and wounding thirty three persons[34] only proved the extremists' persistence in violent expression of anti-Americanism. Western business enterprises such as Kentucky Fried Chicken (KFC), gas stations owned by Royal Dutch and Shell Group and Caltex were attacked, with serial bomb blasts at twenty-one gas stations in May 2003[35], injuring many showed the loathing for anything western- its people, religion or business concerns. In yet another attack by the al-Qaeda on the US Consulate in Karachi in March 2006[36], a US diplomat was killed and several wounded. The Islamists were driving a point across loud and clear- the Americans were not welcome and would be driven out at any cost. Al-Qaeda links are suspected in numerous other violent anti-Western and anti-Christian attacks in Pakistan, wherein they have been actively involved or have aided and abetted Pakistani militant outfits in carrying on the attacks.[37]

The attacks are no longer limited to western targets. The terror trial has been unleashed upon fellow Muslims of Pakistan, as a violent expression of defiance against Islamabad's diktats. Soon after Pakistan pledged its support to the US, the Interior Minister Moinuddin Haider's brother was killed in a suspected terrorist attack in Karachi. A bomb blast at a residential area in Orangi Town, Karachi, leaving nineteen persons injured. Attacks on *madrasssas* in tribal areas also provoked the wrath of religious parties such as the Muttahida Qaumi Movement (MQM) and Muttahida Rabita Committee which accused the government of selling out to the US. Since civilian casualties were involved, the Pakistani Government's muteness was interpreted as total apathy for its citizens and the fundamentalist forces took advantage of the public outcry. Such incidents only strengthened anti-American feelings and gave credibility to the extremists in demonizing the State.

Attacks have been most pervasive in the NWFP, the tribal

agencies and in Karachi, which has also been the victim of Shia-Sunni sectarian violence in Pakistan. To name a few instances-In Feb 2004, a suicide bomber is killed and four worshippers sustain injuries in an attack on a mosque in the Satellite Town area of Rawalpindi. It is in the post-9/11 scenario that suicide bombers emerged in Pakistan. In June 2004 a group of seven to eight unidentified terrorists ambush the convoy of Corps Commander, Karachi, Lt. Gen. Ahsan Saleem Hyat, near the Clifton Bridge in Karachi, killing at least 11 persons, including seven Army personnel and three police personnel, and injured 12 others. In March 2006, a suicide bomb attack at Nishtar Park in Karachi killed at least 57 people, including prominent Islamist clerics, and injured more than 200 people[38] . This was a day before the scheduled visit of American President George W Bush to Pakistan. In what is believed to be the biggest terrorist attack since Pakistan's support to the US war on terror, a suicide bomber blew himself up at an army-training centre at Dargai in the NWFP, killing 42 and injuring 39 recruits of the Punjab Regiment Centre (PRC) and their instructor in November 2006. Several such attacks have taken place in the NWFP and FATA with ruthless regularity, since the deployment of troops to the border region. Army personnel, vehicles, garrisons, government officials have invariably been the targets. The attacks are only going to intensify in numbers and magnitude, if dramatic measures are not taken to address the menace. The overwhelming feeling in the American strategic circles off late is that Pakistan is not doing enough.

The Taliban is on a gradual but meticulous expansion and consolidation drive in the FATA and NWFP. After completely taking control of the tribal areas, particularly north and South Waziristan and Bajaur, facilitated by the peace agreements with the government, it is now looking towards settled districts of the NWFP[39] . The rampant violence in Bannu, Tank and DI Khan districts, involving forcible recruitment of school students into their cadres for the Taliban's Spring

Offensive in Afghanistan in March this year would indicate the same. The imposition of strict Islamic codes and attacks on music shops, barber saloons, kidnapping of businessmen and NGO workers for ransom demands points to the growing lawlessness in these districts, and the Taliban just waiting to sweep into the space of the unofficial law enforcers there.

However, the complexity of the problem of Pakistan's saga with terrorism leaves no easy options. President Musharaff's support to the war against terror has proved to be perilous not only to his position, but also to his life. President Musharraf himself has escaped two assassination attempts- the first on 14 December 2003 when an explosive device went off at the Chaklala Bridge near Jhanda Chichi in Rawalpindi approximately two minutes after the departure of his convoy; the second, less than two weeks later, on 25 December 2003 when at least 18 persons were killed and forty others are injured in Rawalpindi[40]. There were conjectures about the real hold that the military ruler has over his army, after the abortive attacks on him, as the army has far reaches into the terrorist network and in turn would be able to use those connections to threaten him, as military coups have been almost a norm in Pakistan. But he has proved all speculations to be wrong by managing to stay in power and biding to American expectations, while keeping the army in tow. President Musharaff faces the tough task of balancing the tight rope as he has to take decisive action against the militant outfits in the FATA and NWFP, who have the support of the Pashtuns.

SECTARIAN CLASHES- ADDING TO WOES

Pakistan has been historically plagued by one of the worst sectarian conflicts, and the State is responsible for its unfolding in the region in many ways. The people of Pakistan are paying the price for it, in terms of unbridled sectarian violence over the years. The divide between political, social, religious and terrorist violence is very murky in Pakistan. They are formed based on either ethnicity or sectarianism and have tremendous influence over the political setting in Pakistan. Not only are violent outbursts between organizations of different sects common, but also between organizations of the same sect, for pre-eminence over the other. A sort of "gang war" between different schools has been going on in Pakistan and terror attacks in public places, killing innocents have been an unfortunate, loathsome show of power for these outfits.

The earliest among such sectarian outfits, yielding political clout and resorting to violence in Pakistan, has been the Muttahida Quomi Movement (MQM), a progression of the *Muhajir* Quomi Movement. An offshoot of this called the Haquiqi Mohajir Quomi Movement (HMQM), owing to differences among the factions emerged strong in the early nineties, only to get entangled in a violent war to establish supremacy over the urban territory if Sindh, where the largest concentration of the *Muhajir* community was found. After a tough stance taken by the State against these outfits in the late nineties, when the MQM lost most of its cadres and ammunition, the violence subsided.

Sectarian violence has its roots in a Shia-Sunni conflict for political assertion within Pakistan in the seventies, when Islam became a tool for political legitimacy and power, during General Zia's Islamisation drive. Shia and Sunni elements, which had earlier made a united effort to get the Constitution, amended so as to recognize Ahmediyas[41] as non-Muslims, engaged in a violent struggle for suzerainty. The prime motive was to get sole recognition for their sect through the Constitution. Several organizations from both sects, such as Tehrik-e-Jafria Pakistan[42] and Sunni outfits as the Sipah-e-Sahaba Pakistan[43] came into existence to fight one another. Lashkar-e-Jhangvi (LeJ), an offshoot of the SSP is a terrorist outfit, and several other Sunni organizations came into existence indulging in sectarian violence, though not classified as terrorist organizations. They have targeted places of worship, socio-religious outfits, sectarian leaders, workers and people of the rival sect. With Sunnis comprising the majority in Pakistan and most extremist outfits rendering support to the Taliban, the Sunni dominance has been obvious and their attempts to impose their codes has been raucous.

Some of the more recent incidents of sectarian violence instigating large scale clashes include the assassination of Maulana Azam Tariq, leader of the outlawed Sunni group Sipah-e-Sahaba Pakistan (SSP) and Member of National Assembly, is assassinated along with four others in Islamabad in October 2003[44]. In one of the large scale attacks in 2004, a procession of Shias was attacked by Sunni extremists in March in Quetta, Baluchistan killing at least 47 persons and leaving more than 150 wounded. Following this, in May the same year, the pro-Taliban Sunni cleric and chief of Binoria mosque in Karachi, Mufti Nizamuddin Shamzai, was killed and his son, nephew and driver are wounded, when armed men ambushed their vehicle in front of the mosque[45]. What followed in October 2004 was yet another attack on a gathering of Sunnis, assembled to mark the first anniversary of the killing of Sunni leader and SSP chief Maulana Azim Tariq by twin explosions, killing forty people and wounding hundred[46]. More recently, April 2005 witnessed large scale violent clashes between the two rival sects in Kurram agency in FATA, where armed groups of rival combatants attacked each other's villages with heavy weapons. The clashes lasted for several days, over a week and they take a toll on the already burdened army, fighting the foreigners in the tribal areas. The attacks were long drawn and intense to the extent of one town, Lower Kurram, being reportedly being fired by around 2000 missiles, bringing down over 250 houses[47].

Rampant sectarian clashes in 2007 in the FATA have added fuel to the fire of the ongoing fight on terrorism. A region, strewn with complex power relationships, torn by violence, plunged into questions of shifting loyalties, where being beheaded is the price to be paid for any inkling of disloyalty,

the sectarian violence has added to the woes of Pakistan, leaving the region extremely vulnerable.

BALOCHISTAN INSURGENCY- BREWING TO THE BRIM

Separatism and secessionism have been the anathema for post-colonial nation-states, whose national identities were politically constructed in order to resist colonialism. Many identities that have been deemed to be lost over the course of time or have been silenced at the point of a gun are bound to resurface. The right catalyst ignites the surge of a lost nationality to be regained at any cost. After nearly three decades of the nationalist voices being stifled by Pakistani military repression in Balochistan in a long drawn confrontation between 1973-77, the catalyst came in the form of large scale developmental projects, planned by the federal government in the province.

Fredrick Grare identifies three reasons for the Baluch crisis- expropriation, marginalization and dispossession.[48] The most sparsely populated province of Pakistan is endowed with vast natural resources that have thus far not been made available to the local populace to benefit from. Sui gas, which was supplied to Punjab almost two decades before Quetta, the provincial capital had to get gas supply because a military garrison was stationed there. The town of Dera Bugti is still the only one to receive gas supply owing to the military presence there. The Baluch have a very small role to play in the construction of the Gwadar port as it is a project of the federal government. The coming of outsiders to work on these projects alters the ethnic composition while depriving them of employment opportunities. Hence developmental activities are seen as schemes to benefit only the military. The killings of Chinese engineers working on the Gwadar plant have brought to international attention, the ongoing insurgency in Balochistan. The violence took a definitive turn when a lady doctor, Shazia Khalid working in Sui was raped by an army Captain, later exonerated by the military establishment in 2005[49]. The tribes who wanted to draw attention to the case fired eight rockets that that crashed into a Frontier Constabulary camp near Kohlu while Musharraf was addressing a rally in the area, in December 2005. An aggravated Musharraf ordered a crackdown on Nawab Akbar Bugti, one of the most influential *Sardars* or chieftains, leader of the dominant Bugti tribe and the lynchpin of the Baloch nationalist movement. Since then, the army operations intensified and the 80 year-old Bugti, a former Chief Minister of Balochistan, had been orchestrating the armed insurgency, from the underground. The killing of Bugti, along with 38 insurgents, under suspicious circumstances, in an encounter in the Chalgri area of Bhamboor Hills in Dera Bugti District on August 26, 2006 has set the terror trial ablaze in all twenty two districts of the province. The conflict in the province is further exacerbated by inter-tribal rivalry such as those between the Marris and Mengals, as well as intra-tribal feuds, such as those hampering the naming of a successor to Bugti within the Bugti tribe itself. The tribal *jirga* organized soon after Bugti's death agreed to abolish the *Sardari* system and accepted Islamabad's writ in the province. Thus, dissent and factionalism mar the evolution of a consolidated movement, but the violence continues unabated and the supply of arms through drugs money persists. Now, the Baloch cause has found a martyr, whose death could unify the factions and avenge the military onslaught on their territory which translates into a complete dismissal of their grievances[50].

In 2005, according to official data, there were 187 bomb blasts, 275 rocket attacks, 8 attacks on gas pipelines, 36 attacks on electricity-transmission lines and 19 explosions on railway lines[51]. The attacks have been carried out with the intention of upsetting communication links of the province with the rest of Pakistan and to break the infrastructure. Commercial enterprises involving harnessing of natural resources within the province have been particularly targeted. The Baloch Liberation Army

(BLA), a militant organization responsible for several attacks lacks the wherewithal to launch an all out war against the Pakistani Army. However, the violent attacks perpetrated are bringing to a grinding halt, the economic activities of the province and are denying the rest of Pakistan from utilizing their resources.

The Pakistani establishment has been trying to sell the ambush in Balochistan to the public as a move to 'emancipate' the Baluch people from the tyrannical rule of the *Sardars,* who have always been at conflict with one another[52]. However they have been united in their stand against Islamabad's writ of repression and exploitation of their homeland. The Baluch, who have traditionally been opposed to the *mullahs,* are also enraged at Islamabad's conscious policy of establishing thousands of *maddrassas* in the province preaching fundamentalism. And in a move to sabotage a nationalist movement, the Baluch uprising has been equated with Islamist extremism, which the rebels find detrimental to their secular cause.

The situation in Balochistan has far reaching consequences for the US war on terrorism as two bases Pasni and Dalbandin in the territory are being used for operations against the al-Qaeda. The Taliban are also operating out of Balochistan. Besides, the obvious economic cost which Pakistan has to bear due to the conflict in Balochistan, the strategic implications of this are very significant. Continuing violence against the Pakistani military hampers the hunt for the al- Qaeda in the territory. On the other hand, Islamic fundamentalism is being fostered by the establishment in order to destabilize the Baluch insurgency, and therefore is counter-productive for the military's task of fighting terrorism. The blot on the sincerity of Pakistan's willingness and ability to tackle fundamentalist forces has been so transparent in its handling of the Balochistan case. Fredrick Grare's report also contends that the US might want to use the Baluch nationalists against the *mullahs* if the situation calls for such an alliance[53]. The manifold implications of the crisis in Balochistan includes, a ludicrous complication of the war on terrorism due to Islamabad's policies there reeking of double standards as well as an undue disruption of developmental activities on which the strategic interests of both Pakistan and China lie, such as the Gwadar Port, Sui and other projects. The Gwadar port which is crucial to Pakistan for an access of its hinterlands to the Arabian Sea and beyond as the Karachi port is susceptible to blockade by the Indian Navy in the event of an Indo-Pak stand-off. The Gwadar, would connect Afghanistan and Central Asia to the Arabian Sea, making Pakistan an indispensable strategic point of contact. Besides, the Baluch insurgency threatens the stability of Pakistan, which is already pulled in several directions, with violence spreading to all of its provinces, as has been delved upon in the above sections.

CAN THE GORDIAN KNOT BE UNTIED?

> "....First we have to rid ourselves of hatred, of religious intolerance. We have to rebuild and realise that a mind cannot be opened by oppression... You cannot change hearts and minds through force..." —*Pervez Musharraf*[54]

Pakistan seems to have completed the full cycle in evolving from a perpetrator to a victim of its rulers sanction to violence and terrorism. The larger issue of the border dispute between Pakistan and Afghanistan hangs like a noose above his head, before taking any drastic measures. The danger of Pashtun mobilization across the Durrand Line[55] and the traditional demand for autonomy could resurface if the people are pushed over the brink by the Pakistani Army. Since the Pashtuns are an ethnic minority in Pakistan, the threat of secessionism is to Pakistan and not to Afghanistan, where they comprise the majority. How Musharraf handles the Pak-Afghan border issue would be a key determinant in the future of the pursuit of al-. This is again shaped by several internal and external factors.

India's close linkages with the current Karzai government on Afghanistan are an irritant to Pakistan's relations with the latter, and the fear that antagonizing the Karzai government would only push him closer to India drives the policy of molly coddling Afghanistan. However, domestic compulsions in Pakistan, keeping in mind the powerful *mullahs* and Islamic fundamentalist forces, who have been asserting their brute power, giving away wanted militants to the Karzai regime is not practicable for the former. President Karzai's repeated allegation that Pakistan is not doing enough and violence is increasing in Afghanistan due to crossing over of the al-Qaeda operatives from the Pakistani side of the porous border has heightened the tensions between the two neighbours. Pakistan resents loosing the leverage that it had with Afghanistan through the Taliban. The inaction on the part of Pakistan over the list of the wanted al-Qaeda terrorists to Pakistan by calling it outdated and irrelevant has once again exposed the unwillingness of the Pakistani establishment to act decisively on this aspect[56].

There has been a resurgence of the Taliban after a respite of about two years. There is every reason for the US and Afghanistan to be deeply concerned, that the gains made in Afghanistan immediately after OEF (Operation Enduring Freedom) might be dissipated, according to Ashley Tellis, a prominent expert on South Asian Affairs[57]. However, what needs to be borne in mind is that the gains in Afghanistan were only illusory as they did not eradicate the networks of the Taliban, but merely shifted them to the neighbouring Pakistan, where they found safe haven to regroup, and avenge their Afghan setback against the state that nurtured them and then turned their back on them, owing to the expediency of real *politick*-Pakistan.

The insurgency in Balochistan and sectarian strife throughout the country are adding fuel to the fire, in a melting pot, that the state of Pakistan has become. These issues have become intricately inter-woven with Islamic terrorism in Pakistan. What needs to be seen is how adept would Musharraf be at disentangling them, if at all he does want to. The US war on terror seems to be dependent on a one-man show-Musharraf's promises and his continuance in power. With Islamic fundamentalist parties asserting themselves and coming to power in rigged elections in the provinces, is a deterring the US from insisting in democratic reforms in the state. While trying to brand the insurgent Baluchi movement as 'terrorism' Pakistan's stand on the issue of Kashmir stands terribly diluted, highlighting its double standards, in refusing to acknowledge the violence in Kashmir as terrorism. Pakistan's condemnation of the military presence in Kashmir calling it the 'occupying army' now lacks any weight, with the presence of 123,000 troops in Balochistan, supported by helicopter gun-ships, artillery and the Air Force, to combat the insurgency. Around 80,000 troops are stationed in the FATA to pursue the al-Qaeda and the difference in number of troops deployed is indicative of which conflict Pakistan holds more urgent to tackle at the moment-dismembering the Taliban networks in FATA or ruthlessly silencing the uprising in Balochistan by placing it under the umbrella of 'terrorism'. The deliberate propagation of *madrassas* in the province to *Islamize* the tribes there depicts that it is in the interest of the Pakistani establishment to harbour the Taliban network in Balochistan to counter suspected Iranian influence. Pakistan's ISI also suspects Indian involvement in the province and this is another driving force for Pakistan to concentrate its resources there, to trounce any foul play by Iran or India. The bitter lesson of the secession of Bangladesh in 1971 has made Islamabad to be brutally repressive of any groups challenging the writ of the State. Islamabad is facing aggressive confrontation in Balochistan, FATA, NWFP and the Northern Areas, which could threaten the very idea of a Pakistani State, whose identity was imposed in 1947 over provinces which were intrinsically diverse in language, ethnicity and culture.

Preserving the idea of Pakistan becomes the first and foremost consideration for Islamabad. If fostering fundamentalist elements is going to help them do so as it has done in the past, the policy will be pursued with hardnosed meticulousness, whether the Americans like it or not. Thus the war on Islamic extremism takes a beating yet again. Since Pakistan's strategic interests are surmount and not fastening the noose too tight on the Taliban is part of these interests. Unfortunately, Pakistan's unavoidable alliance with the US would continue to make victims of the Pakistani people, of terror attacks, until clear dramatic decisive action is taken against the terror network.

Musharraf's growing unpopularity after the controversial extra-constitutional sacking of the Chief Justice, Iftikhar Choudury, and the building public opinion against him do not auger well for his position[58]. If Musharraf looses his stronghold, it is not known whether a successor regime would be able to deal with the situation any differently. He is stuck in a catch-22 situation where doing more on the terror front does not suit the establishment's interest, while maintaining pro-US status-quo only invites retaliation from the fanatics. This compounded with the multifarious odds stacked up against him in terms of the Baluch uprising, and growing sectarian violence, Pakistan is headed towards disastrous instability. If the logic of cause and effect is applied to the case of Pakistan's rendezvous with terrorism, it simply follows that its policies have eventually paid off by backfiring on the state. The vicious cycle cannot be broken as the key to avert further terrorist attacks on it citizens seems to lie in continued support to these outfits; the harder the crackdown, the more vociferous the backlash.

REFERENCES

1. Seema Sridhar is Senior Research Scholar at the School of International Studies, Jawaharlal Nehru University.
2. "U.S. Policy in South Asia," November 27, 2006. See, http://www.state.gov/p/us/rm/2006/76984.htm
3. "Musharraf speech highlights", BBC News, South Asia, January 12,

2002. See, http://news.bbc.co.uk/1/hi/world/south_asia/1757251.stm.

4. "U.S. journalist Daniel Pearl is dead, officials confirm", www.cnn.com See, http://archives.cnn.com/2002/WORLD/asiapcf/south/02/21/missing.reporter/index.html.

5. 'Terrorism Havens: Pakistan', *Council on Foreign Relations Report,* December 2005.

6. Deoband is a town a hundred miles north of Delhi where a madrassa, Dar-Ul-Ulum was established there in 1867. The Deoband School has sought to purify Islam through literal and austere interpretations of the Koran and oppose western influences as amoral. It inspired the Taliban movement. See, www.globalsecurity.org

7. General Zia-ul-Haq, who was appointed Chief of Army Staff in 1976 came to power after he overthrew ruling Prime Minister Zulfikar Ali Bhutto, in a bloodless military coup d'état on July 5, and imposed martial law in Pakistan. He was the head of state of the Islamic Republic of Pakistan from July 1977 to August 1988.

8. Statement made by Home Minister, L. K Advani on the terrorist attack on Parliament House on December 13, 2001. See, http://www.indianembassy.org/new/parliament_dec_13_01.htm

9. *Muhajirs* are the Urdu speaking Muslims refugees from India who settled in Pakistan after independence in 1947. The term finds its origin in the Arabic word, *Muhajirum,* meaning refugee or emigrant. *Muhajirum* was coined for the people who left Mecca for Medina along with Prophet Muhammad.

10. Musharraf's televised address to the nation on 12 January, 2002. See, http://news.bbc.co.uk/1/hi/world/south_asia/1757251.stm.

11. The National Commission on Terrorist Attacks upon the United States (also known as the 9-11 Commission) was an independent, bipartisan commission created by congressional legislation and the signature of President George W. Bush in late 2002. On July 22, 2004, the ten member Commission, headed by Thomas H.Kean released its public report. It was closed on 21 August 2004 after releasing two staff monographs on the same day. See, http://www.9-11commission.gov/ http://www.9-11commission.gov/report/911Report.pdf

12. "Musharraf speech highlights", BBC News, South Asia, January 12, 2002 See, http://news.bbc.co.uk/1/hi/world/south_asia/1757251.stm.

13. ("Designation of Foreign Terrorist Organizations," US Department of State Press Release, December 26, 2001). In January 2003, the United States added to the FTO list the Pakistan-based Lashkar-i-

Jhangvi – a group held responsible for "numerous deadly attacks in Pakistan," including the January 2002 kidnapping and murder of Wall Street Journal reporter Daniel Pearl.

14. "Musharraf Says Heads of Two Extremist Groups Did Nothing Illegal," *Agence France-Presse,* March 2, 2003.

15. Dexter Filkins, "F.B.I. and military unite in Pakistan to hunt al-Qaeda," *New York Times,* July 14, 2002.

16. Philip Smucker, "Villages pay price as US bombs go awry", *The Telegraph,* December 4, 2001. See, http://www.telegraph.co.uk/news/main.jhtml?xml=/news/2001/12/04/war04.xml

17. At least one subsequent report claimed that most or all of these Al fighters were evacuated from the area by Pakistani military aircraft and in the company of "dozens of senior Pakistani military, including two generals"

18. Seymour Hersh, "Transcript: Jane Wallace Talks With Seymour Hersh," Now With Bill Moyers, Public Broadcasting Service, February 21, 2003. See, http://www.pbs.org/now/transcript/transcript_hersh.html.

19. US Department of State Report for FY 2002 See, http://www.state.gov/documents/organization/17782.pdf

20. K Alan Kronstadt, "US-Pakistan Relations", Issue Brief for Congress, IB 94041, *Congressional Research Service,* 24 September 2002.

21. Fact Sheet: United States and Pakistan: Long-Term Strategic Partners, Office of the Press Secretary, March 4, 2006.

22. K. Alan Kronstadt, "Pakistan and Terrorism: A Summary", *Congressional Research Service Report for Congress,* Order Code RS22632, March 27, 2007.

23. Peter Baker, "Bush: U.S. to Sell F-16s to Pakistan", *Washington Post,* March 26, 2005 See, http://www.washingtonpost.com/wp-dyn/articles/A800-2005Mar25.html

24. Qudssia Akhlaque, "US pledges long-term strategic partnership: Pakistan designated major non-NATO ally", *Dawn,* 19 March 2004. http://www.dawn.com/2004/03/19/top3.htm

25. "Proliferation Security Initiative (PSI): Combating Illicit WMD Trafficking", British American Security Information Council. See, http://www.basicint.org/nuclear/counterproliferation/psi.htm

26. Luke Harding and Rosie Cowan "Pakistan militants linked to London attacks", *The Guardian,* July 19, 2005. See, http://www.guardian.co.uk/attackonlondon/story/0,,1531453,00.html

27. Jason Burke and Imtiaz Gul "The drone, the CIA and a botched

attempt to kill bin Laden's deputy", *The Observer*, 15 January 2005. See, http://observer.guardian.co.uk/world/story/0,16937,1686918,00.html

28. Anwarullah Khan, "82 die as missiles rain on Bajaur", *Dawn*, October 31, 2006.
29. "US military intelligence used in Bajaur raid", *Dawn*, October 31, 2006.
30. Musharraf's Speech Highlights, BBC World, January 12, 2002. See, http://news.bbc.co.uk/1/hi/world/south_asia/1757251.stm.
31. "Trained terrorists behind Pakistan church slayings", CNN World, October 28, 2001. http://archives.cnn.com/2001/WORLD/asiapcf/south/10/28/pak.christian.shooting/index.html
32. "11 killed in a car bomb attack near US consulate in Karachi", *The Hindu*, July 15, 2002.
33. "3 die in attack on US Consulate in Pak", *The Tribune*, February 28, 2003.
34. "Police suspect terror group linked to Karachi car blasts", *Daily Times*, May 28, 2004
35. "Karachi under heightened security", *Daily Times*, May 20, 2003.
36. "Qaeda claims US consulate blast in Karachi", *Daily Times*, May 1, 2006.
37. "Militants' Lair Raided, 12 Arrested in Pakistan," *Chicago Tribune*, August 29, 2002.
38. Arman Sabir and S. Raza Hassan, "Karachi hit by terror attack, four killed: US diplomat among dead, 54 injured", *Dawn*, March 3, 2006.
39. D Suba Chandran, "Violence in Tank, NWFP - Taliban's Look East Policy", *Peace and Conflict*, Vol. 10, No. 4, April 2007.
40. "Significant Terrorist Incidents, 1961-2003: A Brief Chronology", Office of the Historian, Bureau of Public Affairs, US Department of State, March 2004. See, http://www.state.gov/r/pa/ho/pubs/fs/5902.htm
41. The Ahmadiyas are an Islamic sect who follow the teachings Mirza Ghulam Ahmad Qadiani (1835- 1908), the holy man of Punjab who founded the Ahmadiyya Muslim Jamaat in 1889.
42. This was originally named Tehrik Nifaz-i-Fiqah-i-Jafria, which means Movement for the Implementation of Fiqah-i-Jafria, a school of Islamic jurisprudence professed by the Shias,
43. This was originally called Anjuman Sipah-i-Sahaba Pakistan and was founded by Maulana Haq Nawaz Jhangvi, in Jhang district of Punjab.
44. Mohammed Asghar and Baqir Sajjad Syed, "Azam Tariq gunned down

in Islamabad", *Dawn,* October 6, 2003.

45. "Musharraf, Jamali appeal for calm", *Dawn,* May 31, 2004
46. "Editorial: Carnage in Multan", *Dawn,* October 8, 2004.
47. "Pakistan Timeline", South Asia Terrorism Portal See, http://www.satp.org/
48. Fredrick Grare, "Pakistan: The Resurgence of Baluch Nationalism", *Carnegie Papers,* South Asia Project, No. 65, January 2006.
49. "Pakistan: Fear for Safety: Dr Shazia Khalid (f), medical doctor", *Amnesty International Library,* UA 35/05, PUBLIC AI Index: ASA 33/002/2005, February 15, 2005. See, http://web.amnesty.org/library/Index/ENGASA330022005?open&of=ENG-PAK
50. Nirupama Subramanian, "Balochistan blaze", *Frontline,* Volume 23, Issue 18, September 22, 2006
51. Alok Bansal, "Balochistan Liberation Army: Playing to its Strength", *Peace and Conflict,* Vol. 9, No.9, September 2006.
52. "Editorial: Development and political expression in Balochistan", *Daily Times,* February 5, 2006. See, http://www.dailytimes.com.pk/default.asp?page=2006%5C02%5C05%5Cstory_5-2-2006_pg3_1
53. Fredric Grare, "Pakistan: The Resurgence of Baluch Nationalism", *Carnegie Papers,* South Asia Project, No 65, January 2006, p.4.
54. "Musharraf speech highlights", BBC News, South Asia, January 12, 2002. See, http://news.bbc.co.uk/1/hi/world/south_asia/1757251.stm.
55. The Durand Line is the poorly marked 2,640 kilometer border between Afghanistan and Pakistan, named after the then Foreign Secretary of British India. The line, which is unclear in sections of the FATA, intended to divide the Pashtuns, marking the territories of Afghanistan and British India. However, since Indian independence and the creation of Pakistan in 1947, the legitimacy of the continuation of the Durrand line has been repeatedly questioned by the Afghans, who do not recognize it as their border.
56. "Editorial: General Musharraf's salvo on Afghanistan", *Daily Times,* March 7, 2006.
57. "Bush's 'Mediation' of Karzai, Musharraf Dispute Highlights Seriousness of Problem", Interview of Ashley J Tellis, Senior Associate, Carnegie Endowment for International Peace, by Bernard Gwertzman, Consulting Editor, Council of Foreign Relations, 28 September, 2006. See, http://www.cfr.org/bios/3348/bernard_gwertzman.html?page=5
58. "Pakistan muffles media as supporters hail judge", *Indian Express,* June 2, 2006.

6

US-Israel Cooperation against West Asian Terrorism

Ramesh Babu Kanneganti

Both the United States and Israel have been facing terrorism for decades. Modern terrorism actually has roots in the Middle East; and Israel and the US have been targets of terrorist attacks at least since 1970's. While the US faces terrorism of various kinds, Middle Eastern political violence and terrorist activities have a direct correlation to the US policy towards the Palestinian issues, US strategic cooperation with Israel and with the very existence of the state of Israel.

MIDDLE EASTERN TERRORIST GROUPS: ORIGINS AND NATURE

Middle Eastern Terrorist groups and their state sponsors have been the focus of US counter-terrorism policies for several decades. Since the 1970's, Middle Eastern groups or states have conducted several major acts of terrorism against US targets. The US is convinced that terrorism is used as an instrument by several states to achieve certain international objectives. Out of seven states, which appeared in the US State Department's list of state sponsors of terrorism, five happen to be from the Middle Eastern region. They are Iran, Iraq, Libya, Syria and Sudan.

Middle Eastern terrorist groups as well as their state sponsors differ in their goals, objectives, and ideologies. For example, some radical Islamic groups aim at derailing the Arab-Israeli peace process, while others state their main objective as the overthrow of secular governments in their countries of origin. The five Middle Eastern states in the terrorism list, like the groups they reportedly sponsor, differ in their objectives and in their degree of involvement in terrorism. The State Department's annual report on terrorism has labelled Iran as the most dangerous state sponsor of terrorism. In contrast, the report characterizes Sudan as primarily a harbor of terrorist groups and training camps rather than an active perpetrator of terrorism. Iran and Sudan use paramilitary and terrorist groups to promote radical Islamic ideology. Syria, on the other hand, is led by an authoritarian nationalist and secular government that appears to support terrorist groups as levers in its negotiations toward a peaceful settlement with Israel and other regional issues. Iraq uses terrorism to strike at people or institutions, such as international relief workers, that symbolize international sanctions imposed on Iraq for the invasion of Kuwait.[1]

STRUCTURE, ACTIONS AND METHODS

Terrorist groups in the Middle East have diverse origins, ideologies, and organizational structures. But they can be roughly categorized into traditional and new- generation groups. Traditional groups date back to the late 1960's and early 1970's and the majority of these were formally or informally linked to the PLO. Typically, they are also relatively bureaucratic in nature and maintain a nationalistic or Marxist agenda. In contrast most new generation groups arose in 1980's and 1990's. These have fluid organizational forms, and most of them rely on Islam as a basis for their radical ideology.

The traditional, bureaucratic groups have survived to this date, partly through support from states such as Syria, Libya and Iran. The groups retain an ability to train and prepare for terrorist missions; however, their involvement in actual operations has been limited in recent years partly because of successful counter terrorism by Israeli and western agencies. In contrast, the newer and less hierarchical groups, such as Hamas, the Palestinian Islamic Jihad (PAJ), Hizbullah, Algeria's Armed Islamic group (GIA), the Egyptian Islamic group (IG), and Osama Bin Laden's Arab Afghans, have become the most active organizations in and around the Middle East.

TRADITIONAL GROUPS

Traditional terrorist/extremist groups in Middle East include the Abu Nidal Organization (ANO), the Popular Front for the Liberation of Palestine (PFLP), and three PFLP related splinters- the PFLP- General Command (PFLP-GC), the Palestine Liberation front (PLF), and the Democratic Front for the Liberation of Palestine(DFLP).

The ANO was an integral part of the PLO until it became independent in 1974. It has a bureaucratic structure composed of various functional committees.[2] The activism it displayed in 1970's and 1980's has lessened considerably. Owing to a lessening of support from state sponsors and to effective counter terrorist campaigns by Israeli and Western intelligence services,[3] the very existence of these organizations has recently been put to question.[4]

George Abbas founded the PFLP in 1967 as Palestine Liberation affiliated organization. It has traditionally embraced Marxist ideology and remains an important PLO faction. However, in recent years it has suffered considerable losses from Israeli counter terrorist strikes.[5] The PFLP General Command split from the PFLP in 1968, an intern-experienced schism in the mid-1970. This splinter group, which calls itself PLF is composed of three sub-groups and has not been involved in high profile acts since the 1985 hijacking of Italian cruise ship Achill Lauro.[6] The PLFP was subjected to another in 1969, which resulted for the Democratic Front for the Liberation of Palestine. The DFLP resembles a small army more than a terrorist group-it's operatives are organized in battalions, backed by intelligence and Special Forces.[7] DFLP strikes have become less frequent since the 1970's, and since late 1980's it has limited its attacks to Israeli targets near borders.[8]

What seems evident here is that old generation of traditional, hierarchical, bureaucratic groups are on the wane. The reasons are varied, but the point remains the way that the old way of waging terrorism is being superseded by a new way that is more attuned to organizational, doctrinal and, technological needs of the information age.

NEW GENERATION GROUPS

The new generation of Middle Eastern groups has been active both in and outside the region in recent years. In Israel and the occupied territories, Hamas and to a lesser extent the Palestinian Islamic Jihad have considerable strength. These groups have been conducting suicide bombings killing hundreds of people and injuring several more.[9] Exploiting a strong presence in Lebanon the Shiite Hizbullah organization also stages a number of attacks against Israeli defense forces troops and Israeli citizens in Galilee.[10]

Recently, the loosely organized group of Arab Afghans-radical Islamic fighters from several North African and Middle Eastern countries, which forged cooperation during the Afghanistan crisis of 1980s,[11] has come to the fore as an active terrorist outfit. One of the leaders and founders of the Arab Afghan movement, Osama bin Laden, a Saudi entrepreneur who bases his activities in Afghanistan[12] is suspected to have sent operatives to Yemen to bomb a hotel used by US soldiers on their way to Somalia in 1992, of plotting to assassinate the President of Philippines in 1994 and Egyptian President Hosni Mubarak in 1995, and of having a role in the Riyadh and Khobar blast in Saudi Arabia killing 24 Americans in 1995 and 1996.[13] US officials have pointed to Bin Laden as the mastermind behind the US Embassy bombings in Kenya and Tanzania, which claimed the lives of more than 260 people, including 12 Americans.[14]

In varying degrees, these groups share the principles of network organizations-relatively flat hierarchies, decentralization and delegation of decision making authority, and lose lateral ties among dispersed groups and individuals.[15] For instance, Hamas is loosely structured, with some elements working openly through mosque and social service institutions to recruit members, raise funds, organize activities, and distribute propaganda. Palestinian security sources indicate that there are ten or more Hamas splinter groups and factions with no centralized operational leadership.[16] The Palestine Islamic Jihad is a series of loosely affiliated factions, rather than a cohesive group.[17] The pro-Iranian Hizbullah, acts as an umbrella organization of radical Shiite groups, and in many respects is a hybrid of hierarchical and network arrangements. Although the structure is highly bureaucratic, interaction among members are volatile and do not follow a rigid line of control.[18] According to the US Department of State, Egypt's Islamic Group is a decentralized organization that operates without a single operational leader,[19] while the GIA is notorious for the lack of centralized authority.[20]

Unlike traditional terrorist organizations, Arab Afghans are part of a complex network of relatively autonomous groups that are financed from private sources forming a kind of international terrorist internet.[21] The most notorious of their leaders is Osama Bin Laden, who uses his wealth and organizational skills to support and direct a multinational alliance of Islamic extremists. At the heart of this alliance is his own inner core group, known as Al-Qaeda (THE BASE), which sometimes conduct mission on its own more often in cooperation with other groups and elements in the alliance. The goal of the alliance is opposition on a global scale to perceived threats to Islam, as indicated by Bin Laden's 1996 declaration of a holy war against the United States and the West. In the document, Bin Laden specifies that irregulars-light highly mobile forces using guerrilla tactics, will fight such a holy war,.[22]

Even though Bin Laden finances Arab Afghan activities and directs some operations, he apparently does not play a direct command and control role over all operatives rather, he is a key figure in the co-ordination and support of several dispersed activities.[23] For instance, Bin Laden founded the 'World Islamic Front' for jihad against Jews Crusaders".[24] And yet most of the groups that participate in this front (including Egypt's Islamic Group) remain independent, although the organizational barriers between them are fluid.[25]

From a net war perspective, an interesting feature of Bin Laden's Arab Afghan movement is its ability to relocate operations swiftly from one geographic area to another, in response to changing circumstances and needs. Arab Afghans have participated in operations conducted by Algeria's GIA and Egypt's IG. Reports in 1997 also indicated that Arab Afghans transferred training operations to Somalia, where they joined the Islamic Liberation Party (ILP).[26] The same reports suggest that Arab Afghan movement has considered sending fighters to Xinxiang Uighur Province in Western China, to wage a holy war against the Chinese regime.[27] This groups' ability to move and act quickly (and, to some extent, to swarm) once opportunities emerge, hampers counter terrorist efforts to predict its actions and monitor its activities. The fact that Arab Afghan operatives were able to strike the US embassies in Kenya and Tanzania substantiates the claim that members of this network have the mobility and speed to operate over considerable distances. Although the organizational arrangements in these groups do not match all the basic features of the network ideal, they stand in contrast to traditional groups. Another feature that distinguishes the newer generations of terrorist groups is their adaption to information technology.[28]

Middle Eastern Foreign Terrorist Organizations (FTO's) Designations

Group	*Description*	*Activity Level*
Hizballah(party of God)	Lebanon, Shiite Islamist	Active
Hamas	Palestinian Islamist	Active
Palestinian Islamic Jihad	Palestinian Islamist	Active
Popular front for the liberation Of Palestine (PFLP-GC)	Nationalist Palestinian	Moderately Active
Democratic Front for the Liberation of Palestine	Marxist Palestinian	Sporadically Active
Palestine liberation front (PLF)	Nationalist Palestinian	Generally Inactive
Abu Nidal Organization (ANO)	Nationalist Palestinian	Generally Inactive
Kach	Jewish Extremist	Sporadically active
Kahane Chai	Jewish Extremist	Sporadically active
Islamic Group	Egyptian Islamic opposition	Active
Al-Jihad(Islamic Holy War)	Egyptian Islamic opposition	Active
Armed Islamic Group	Egyptian Islamic opposition	Active
People's Mojahedin Organization of Iran	Leftwing Iranian opposition	Active
Kurdistan Worker's Party	Kurdish, anti turkey	Active
Al-Qaida (Bin Laden Organization)	Multinational. Afghanistan-Based Islamist	Highly Active

Source: Kenneth Katzman: " *Terrorism: Middle Eastern Groups and State Sponsors, 1999", August* 9, 1999, CRS Report for Congress, (The Library of Congress, Washington DC, 1999), p.3.

TERRORISM AND INFORMATION REVOLUTION

Terrorism seems to be evolving in the direction of a violent netwar. Islamic fundamentalist organizations like Hamas and the Bin Laden network consists of groups organized in loosely interconnected, semi- independent cells that have no single commanding hierarchy.[29] Hamas exemplifies the shift away from a hierarchically oriented movement base to "great leader" (like the PLO and Yasser Arafat).[30]

The internet concept is consistent with patterns and trends in the Middle East, where the newer and more active terrorist groups appear to be adopting decentralized, flexible network structures. The rise of networked arrangements in terrorist organizations is part of a wider move away from formally organized, state sponsored groups that may have strategic guidance but enjoy tactical independence. Related to these shifts is the fact that terrorist groups are taking advantage of information technology to coordinate the activities of dispersed members. Terrorists not only wage information warfare, but also support their own-networked organizations.[31]

While a comprehensive empirical analysis of the relationship between a) the structure of terrorist organizations and b) group activity or strength is beyond the scope of this paper,[32] a cursory examination of such relationship among Middle Eastern Groups offers some evidence to support the claim that terrorists have been preparing to wage netwar. The Middle East was selected for analysis mainly because terrorist groups based here been active in targeting US government facilities and interests, and these were involved in the bombings of Khobar Towers, and the American embassies in Kenya and Tanzania.

Information Technology (IT) is an enabling factor for networked groups. Terrorists use internet, not only as a weapon, but also to coordinate and support their activities. Middle Eastern terrorist groups provide examples of information technology being used for a wide variety of purposes, multi-organizational networks and as a tool for both coordination and disruption. Terrorists in the Middle East have been increasingly using satellite communications, e-mail and world wide web.[33]

Arab Afghans in particular, appear to have made use of latest adopted information technology. According to reporters, who visited Bin Laden's headquarters in a remote mountainous area of Afghanistan, they found these computers, communications equipment, and a large number of disks for data storage.[34] Egyptian Afghan computer experts are believed to have helped devise a communication network that relies on the world wide web, e-mail, and electronic bulletin boards so that the extremists could exchange information without running a major risk of being intercepted by counter terrorism officials.[35]

Hamas is another major group that uses the Internet to share operational information. Hamas activists in the US for instance, use chat rooms to plan operations and activities.[36] Operatives use e-mail to coordinate activities across Gaza, the West Bank, and Lebanon. Hamas has realized that information can be passed securely over the internet because it is next to impossible for counter terrorism intelligence officers or operatives to monitor accurately the flow and content of internet traffic. Israeli security officials, otherwise so talented, also find difficulties in tracing Hamas messages and decoding their content.[37]

In 1990s, counter terrorist operations have led to discovery of several terrorist organizations, such as the Armed Islamic Group (GIA) using computers and diskettes with instructions for the constructions of bombs.[38] According to reports, the GIA uses floppy disks and computers to store and process instructions and other information for its members, who are dispersed in Algeria and Europe.[39] Furthermore, the internet is used as a propaganda tool by Hizbullah, which manages three world wide web site-one for the central press office at www.hizbollah.org, another to describe its attacks on Israeli targets at www.moqawama.org and the last for the news and information at www.almanar.com.ib.[40] British Islamic activists having linkages with Middle Eastern groups also use the world wide web to broadcast their news and attract funding; and make use of the internet as an organizational and communication tool.[41]

The review of patterns and trends in the Middle East substantiates the worries and concerns that the "new terrorism" is evolving in the direction of net war, along the following lines.[42]

* An increasing number of terrorist groups are adopting networked forms of organization and relying on informational technology to support such structures.
* Newer groups (those established in the 1980's and 1990's) are more networked than traditional groups.
* A positive correlation is emerging between the degrees of activity of a group to which it adopts a networked structure.
* Information technology is as likely to be used for organizational support as for offensive warfare.
* The likelihood that young recruits will be familiar with information technology implies that terrorist groups will be increasingly networked and more computer-friendly in future than they are today.

9/11 AND AFTERMATH

While terrorism and terrorist attacks against US targets are not new, the attacks on the World Trade Centre in New York and the Pentagon in Washington on September 11, 2001, changed the US views on terrorism and the world. On September 11, 2001, in an apparently well- financed/ coordinated attack, hijackers rammed jetliners into each of the New York based World Trade Center's Twin Towers and ultimately collapsed them. A third hijacker airliner ploughed into the Pentagon and a fourth hijacked airliner crashed near Pittsburgh, raising speculation that a related mission- aimed at the Capitol or White House- had failed. In the absence of a final death toll from New York city, the US State Department's Patterns of Global Terrorism 2001, (revised February 2002) calculates the direct and indirect economic costs of the destruction of the World Trade Center at $ 83 billion in 2001 dollars.

The Administration's response to the September 11 events was swift, wide ranging and decisive. Administration officials attributed responsibility for the attack to Osama Bin Laden and the Al-Qaida organization. A full-scale campaign was launched, using all elements of national and international power, to go after Al-Qaida and its affiliates and support structures. The campaign involved rallying the international community, especially law enforcements and intelligence components to shut down. Al-Qaida cells and financial networks. A US military measure, Operation Enduring Freedom, was launched in early October 2001 against the Taliban regime-, which had harbored Al-Qaida since 1996, and against Al Qaida strongholds in Afghanistan. A total of 136 countries offered a range of military assistance to the US, including over-flight and landing rights and accommodation for US Forces. As a result of Operation Enduring Freedom, the Taliban was removed from power, all known Al-Qaida training sites were destroyed, and a number of Taliban and al-Queda leaders were killed or detained. In March 2002, ground troops from the US and five nations commenced Operation Anaconda, designed to raid remote Al_Qaida hiding places and to crush the Qaida leadership. Yet, top Al- Qaida leaders Osama Bin Laden and Ayman al Zawahari as well as the Taliban's Mullah remnants of the organization. US military and intelligence forces in Afghanistan and elsewhere reportedly have killed or captured more one-third of Al- Qaida, but Muhammad Omar apparently remains at large.

In addition to the 7,000 US troops deployed in Afghanistan, US forces were dispatched to Yemen, the Philippines and the former Soviet Republic of Georgia to train local militaries to fight terrorist. The Administration sought congressional approval to use of US military aid to Colombia to support the Colombian Government's "Unified Campaign Against narcotics trafficking and terrorist activities and other threats to its national security". Until then such assistance was restricted to supporting counter drug operations in Colombia.

In the context of this campaign, the United States stepped up intelligence sharing and law enforcement cooperation with other governments to root out terrorist cells, which were operating in several places, including in Western Europe and the US Much terrorist fundraising and banking also occurred in Western Countries. By early December 2002, an aggressive international law enforcement effort resulted in detention of 3,000 terrorists and their supporters in more than 100 countries and in freezing of $21 million in terrorists' assets in some 600 bank accounts around the world, including $36 million in terrorists' assets in some 600 bank around the world, including $36 million in terrorist assets in some 600 bank accounts around the world, $36 million in the United States alone.

The massive US war against terror networks generated an encouraging sign, which was evident in willingness of certain state sponsors of terrorism to distance themselves from extremists groups that they had supported in the past. For Example, Libya began to "sending signals that it wanted to get out of terrorism business" and it offered to compensate the families of the victims of the bombings of Pan-Qaeda training camps on its territory. Both Libya and Sudan also offered to share intelligence information on Al Qaida's activities with US authorities. Interestingly, exactly two months after the September 11 attack, even North Korea signed international conventions against terrorism, albeit with reservations: the 1999 International Convention against the Taking of Hostages.

Until recently, terrorism was primarily viewed by the US as an international and foreign policy issue. In 2001, approximately 63% of all terrorist acts worldwide were carried out against US citizens or property compared to 23% in 1995, according to the US Department of State; and the vast majority of these acts took place on foreign soil. State Department data indicate that between 1991-2001; 100 American nationals were killed in terrorist attacks outside US territory. However US governmental perception of terrorism, as primarily an overseas issue, dramatically changed after 9/11

On May 21, 2002, the State Department released its annual report on trends in international terrorism, Patterns of Global Terrorism 2001. According to the report, a total of 3,547 people were killed in international terrorist incidents in 2001, the highest death toll from terrorism ever recorded. Most of the deaths were associated with the September 11 attacks. In terms of the number of attacks by region, Latin America ranked first, as in previous years; Asia ranked second; Africa third; and the Middle East fourth. Almost 90% (191) of the 219 attacks US Citizens or interests occurred in Latin America, and most of these (178) were bombings of a multinational oil pipeline by leftist guerrillas in Colombia.

2001 still listed seven state sponsors of terrorism: Cuba, Iran, Iraq, Libya, North Korea Sudan and Libya. The Report pointed out that, of the seven Libya and Sudan were closest to being taken off the terrorism list and also noted that Iran, North Korea, and Syria made "limited moves" to cooperate with the international community's campaign against terrorism". However, both Iran and Syria continued to support groups such as HAMAS and Hizballah that vehemently oppose the Middle East peace process.

The State Departments terrorism reports provide comprehensive information on global terrorist activities. As has been mentioned earlier, the number of terrorist activities against the US is more in its own hemisphere than in the Middle East. But this does not nullify the significance of the threat. Terrorist activities that threaten peace, prosperity and stability of Israel and create turbulence in the oil-rich region of the world cause additional concern because of their implications for US domestic politics and international economic stability.

SOUL SEARCHING

While enormous amount of research and studies have been undertaken on various aspects of terrorism, 9/11 sparked a new awareness in the US of the need for in-depth soul searching. Why is the US so hated in the Muslim World? What factors produce terrorists in the Middle East? The answer to some of these questions was partly given by Osama bin Laden, the mastermind of 9/11 incidents.

"THE SWORD FELL"

Releasing a videotape statement less than a month after 9/11 and around the time the US would begin bombing of Afghanistan, Osama bin Laden provided some clues about the motivation behind his terrorist attacks. His said on 7 October 2001:

Here is America struck by God Almighty in one of its vital organs, so that its greatest buildings are destroyed. Grace and gratitude to God. America has been filled with horror from north to south and east and west, and thanks be to God. What America is tasting now is only a copy of what we have tasted.

Our Islamic Nation has been tasting the same for more 80 years, of humiliation and disgrace, its sons killed and their blood spilled, its sanctities desecrated.

God has blessed a group of vanguard Muslims, the forefront of Islam, to destroy America. May God bless them and allot them a supreme place in heaven, for he is the only one capable and entitled to do so. When those have stood in defense of their weak children, their brothers and sisters in Palestine and other Muslim nations, the whole world went into uproar, the infidels followed by the hypocrites.

A million innocent children are dying at this time as we speak, killed in Iraq without any guilt. We hear no denunciation, we hear no addict from the hereditary rulers. In these days, Israel tanks rampage across Palestine, in Ramallah, Rafah and

Beit Jala and many other parts of the land of Islam, and we do not hear anyone raising his voice or reacting. But when the sword fell upon America after 80 years hypocrisy raised it head up high bemoaning those killers who toyed with the blood, owner and sanctities of Muslims.

The least that can be said about those hypocrites that they are apostates who followed the wrong path. They backed the butcher against the victims, the oppressor against the innocent child. I seek refuse in God against them and ask him to let us see them in what they deserve.

I say that the matter is very clear. Every Muslim, after this event, after the senior officials in United States of America starting with the head of International infidels, Bush and his staff who went on a display of vanity with their men and horses, those who turned even the countries that believe in Islam against us- the group that resorted to God, the Almighty, the group that refuses to be subdued in its religion.

They have been telling the world falsehoods that they are fighting terrorism. In a nation at the far end of the world, Japan, hundreds and thousands young and old, were killed and this is not a world crime. To them it is not clear issue. A million children in Iraq, to them this is not a clear issue.

But when a few more than ten were killed in Nairobi and Dar es Salam (Capitals of Kenya and Tanzania, were the American embassies were bombed in 1998), Afghanistan and Iraq were bombed and hypocrisy stood behind the head of international infidels: The modern world symbol of paganism, America and its allies.

I tell them that these events have divided the world into two camps the camp of faithful and the camp of infidels. May God shield you and us from them?

Every Muslim must rise to defend his religion. The wind of faith is glowing and the wind of change is blowing to remove evil from the peninsula of Muhammad, peace be upon him. As to America, I say to it and its people and few words: I swear to God that America will not live in peace before reigns in Palestine, and before all the army of infidels depart the land of Muhammad peace be upon him. God is the greatest and glory be to Islam.[43]

Several American analysts have tried to debate and discuss the factors responsible for anti-American terrorism in the Middle East. Two scholars are worth quoting here. Steven Simon and Daniel Benjamin have also thrown some light on this crucial question: According to them,

The United States is resented for its cultural hegemony, global political influence, and overwhelming conventional military power. Its cultural reach threatens traditional values, including the organization of societies that privilege males and religious authority. It offers temptation blurs social, ethical and behavioural boundaries, and presages moral disorder. America's political weight is seen as the hidden key to the durability of repressive regimes that fail to deliver prosperity while crushing dissent. Its support is cited to explain the power of Israel to oppress Muslims and degrade Islam. American military prow ness is used to kill Muslims, as in Iraq, or is withheld to facilitate their extermination, as in Bosnia.

The American cultural challenge to Islamic societies stands for a broader Western commitment to secularization, the relegation of religion to the private sphere, and a focus on the here and now instead of on either a hereafter for individuals, or a messianic era in which the righteous as a collective will partake.

It is not so much the fact of this frontal assault on traditional values as its success in luring Muslims from the true path that angers the jihadists. Led astray by the West, Muslims forsake the beliefs and practices that once won for them world hegemony and would do so again if believers resisted the temptation of secularism and moral relativism and returned to their roots.

The socioeconomic decline of much of the Arab and larger Muslim world plays an indirect role in generating the new terrorism. It contributes to the disparity in power, influence, and prosperity that fuels resentment. But for the most part, the participants in the jihad against the United States have not been poor. This is true of al-Qaeda operatives and, as we have seen it was true of takfiri renegades in Egypt as well. Some may be the victims of frustrated expectations. Having anticipated an financially secure middle-class lifestyle, they find they cannot attain it in a region that has failed to mesh gears with other globalising economies. This is economic misery of a sort, but not the relentless, grinding poverty afflicting half the region's population. The link between socioeconomic trauma and terrorism lies in how the imagery of poverty fuels the anger of middle-class terrorists. Revolutionaries from the mid-nineteenth century through the end of the twentieth were similarly motivated.

Daniel Benjamin and Steven Simon, *The Age of Sacred Terrorism*, (Random House Inc.: New York, 2002), pp. 407-408.

Kurt Campbell and Michele A. Flournoy arguments are equally significant. The authors have pointed out:

There are some 21 to 23 countries in the Middle East, depending upon how states wish to align themselves at any given time. They sweep across North Africa, from Morocco to Egypt, cover the Levant, and then cover the Arabian peninsula and the northern Gulf, ending in Iran. All of the Middle Eastern states do have much in common. All but one-Israel- are principally Islamic. All but two-Israel and Iran- are primarily Arab. ...Most Middle Eastern states also have very young populations. Roughly four out of ten Middle Easterners are 14 years old or younger. The result is a flood of young men and women entering the labour market, most with limited educational preparation for competing in a modern economy and who are pouring into labour markets that are already saturated owing to a lack of broad economic development. In many countries, formal and disguised unemployment for young men between 18 and 25 equals or surpasses 30 per cent. ...This failure to develop, as well as active structural social turmoil, are compounded by the failure of secular ideologies to offer either economic or political success. Pan-Arabism, socialism, communism, secular nationalism, and capitalism have all failed in most of the Middle East. There has been no successor to Nasser in the Arab world, and no leader to compensate for defeat in the Arab-Israeli conflict, failed national economies, and a steady loss of status. US The Iranian revolution became a symbol of conflict between the regions people and the US-backed oppressive leaders but has ended in a popular backlash, symbolized by the election of President Khatami and paralyzed by power struggles between the Khatami and hard-line factions.

Other wars and civil conflicts have compounded the problem. The Arab-Israeli wars still go on in the form of second Intifada, and the images of Israeli tanks attacking Palestinian youths and of Arab funerals have come to be seen as symbols of US support for an oppressive Israel. The Iran-Iraq conflict and the Gulf war have left a lasting legacy: first, the large-scale use of weapons of mass destruction, and, second, policies that many Arabs see as a US-led impoverishment of the Iraqi people.

However, there are some critics who blame the past US policies for the current anti-US terrorism and point out that several of the US administrations themselves had cultivated some Islamic extremist organizations. And today, the talk seems to have turned against the US The following clearly speaks louder on this line of analysis.

TWIN OCCUPATIONS

Iraq has had an interesting connection to Middle Eastern terrorism and Islamic extremism. Iraq's victory in Iraq-Iran war had allowed Saddam to claim leadership of the Arab world, especially of the downtrodden while Saddam Hussein's misadventure into Kuwait made him extremely unpopular among the Arab masses. It was short lived. The crushing defeat of the Republican guard, unprecedented sometimes imposed on the Iraqi people, violation of Iraqi sovereignty by the Western power by establishing southern and northern no-fly-zones: and more significantly, the eventual suffering of the Iraqi people erased the memory of Kuwaiti crisis and generated sympathy for the Iraqi people among the masses as well as the terrorist organizations.

The earlier hope that the road to winning Jerusalem would be through Baghdad, meaning the expected Iraqi role in the process, was dashed to the ground when the US opened the second front in its war against terror by militarily intervening in Iraq and removing Saddam Hussein from power. However, the tall claim of the US that its forces aimed at liberating the Iraqi people sounded hollow when it appeared that the US forces were slowly turning into an occupation army. All these measures, completely sidelining the United Nations and further alienating the Iraqi people added fuel to the terrorist organizations to justify anti-Americanism and violence.

The road to Jerusalem and Middle East peace was supposed to lead through Baghdad but now Arabs see two occupations- one Israeli, one American. For the Arab World, the twin scenarios of occupying armies wreaking havoc on their people were a painful indication of American foreign policy in disarray. "Every day we see these terrible parallels- American tanks facing Iraqis, Israeli tanks facing Palestinians", says Jihad Al Khazen, a columnist and the former editor and chief of al Hayat, the Arabic language daily in London. "For peace, for the future of the region, there is a sense among Arabs that everything has been brought to a dead end".[44]

"The Road to Jerusalem", the mantra went, led through Baghdad. Neo Conservatives and other hawks within the Bush administration expected that the United States would win support in the Arab World through a massive show of force, and that Israel would be more comfortable making peace with the Palestinians once Saddam was removed. Instead, the region now seems to be growing more violent and America's image in the Arab world had been further tarnished." Not only have we validated and emboldened our enemies, but we have also shamed our friends", said an embittered US State Department official." Arab moderates who trusted our ideals feel betrayed and abandoned".[45]

As the White House began to tweak its Iraq policy- and took less strayed view of the situation there- demands grew for reconsiderations of the Arab- Israel conflict as well. Many American diplomats, particularly Arabists have long been frustrated over the US Middle East policy, worried that it had been hijacked by ideologues. Some began to speak up. In 2001 April, 53 former US officials accused the White House of sacrificing Americasn credibility in the Arab World and endangering its diplomats and troops because of the Bush administration's unstinting support for Sharon." By closing the door to negotiations with Palestinians and the possibility of Palestinian State, you have proved that the US is not an even-handed peace partner," The letter said: "A return to time honored American tradition of fairness will turn the present tide of ill will in Europe and the Middle East- even Iraq".[46]

The administration countered that it had just been trying to shake up the ever- sputtering peace process, and remained committed to Palestinian state. But few in the region found that argument persuasive. Israel's bloody incursion into Gaza and the White House's indifference to it angered critics, including some within the US Government. Even as Israeli tanks and troops were storming into Rafah, Bush told the American Israel Public Affairs Committee (AIPAC), the main pro- Israel lobby Group, that "Israel is a democracy and a friend and has every right to defend itself from terror".

How did the Bush administration- that came to office with reputation as a group of 'Arab friendly oil guys'- come to take this tack? A good part of Bush's stance is shaped by conviction, and personal history. Bush has long been an admirer of Sharon-at least since the Israelis took the then Texas governor on a helicopter tour over the West Bank in 1998. At their first meeting in the Oval House in early 2001, Bush recalled that helicopter trip." He's got marvelous sense of history", Bush told reporters." Our nation will not try to force peace. We will work with those responsible for peace".[47] Within three months, the White House National Security team included Elliot Abrams, a neo conservative who had promoted the idea of strengthening ties between American Jews and conservative Christians. Abrams first joined the National Security Council as senior director for democracy and human rights, but took over the Middle East portfolio in December 2002.

By the time of Abraham's ascent, the September 11 terrorist attacks in the US had drowned Bush into a closer embrace with Sharon. Bush saw stark parallels between Palestinian suicide bombings and Qaeda terror and adopted Sharon's position that there could be no serious negotiations and no Palestinian state without new Palestinian leadership. Sharon's expansion of settlements and his rejection of Palestinian demands for available state became secondary concerns.

A State Department official took a hard line position and insisted there could be no peace process until Palestinians proved their bonafide in fighting terrorists.[48] That insistence helped seal the fate of Mahmoud Abbas, the Palestinian prime minister who quit in September 2003 in frustration at the lack of progress along the roadmap to a Palestinian State. By refusing to press Sharon to declare a settlement freeze and remove illegal outposts, critics said, the white house fatally weakened Abbas and doomed the peace plan to failure.

TERRORIST VIOLENCE VERSUS PEACE PROCESS

From all points of analysis on Middle Eastern terrorism, Israel happens to be the common factor. While no major war has taken place between Arabs and Israelis since 1973, low-level violence against Israeli lives and property has never ceased. Several Arab states have not gone beyond "lip service" to the Palestinian cause, but non-governmental support to the anti-Israeli terrorist organizations has increased over the years. The resentment against the US blind support to Israel in the United Nations, on ground and in the form of huge international assistance is endemic in the Arab world. Together with this, the cable television and internet have brought Israeli military actions against the Palestinians to Arab drawing rooms and have generated anti-US sentiments and fueled terrorist activities.

Successive US administrations tried to remain an active partner in the Arab-Israeli peace process to make existence of Israel acceptable to Arab governments. But of late, peace process has been used as a method to dissuade anti-US terrorism.

In this context, the Israel- Palestine peace process and the rise of terrorist activities has always been interrelated. One may notice that whenever the failure of peace process was evident, the terrorist activities have also risen quickly. The failure of Bush administration in successfully resolving the Israel Palestine conflict through its peace plans has led to more violence in the Middle East Osama Bin Laden's statement immediately after September11 attacks on Al-Jazeera TV, substantiates this linkage. It is quite evident that Bin Laden represented the peole who had deep-seated grievances against the way the US has been handling the Israel-Palestine peace process. Laden argued that Israel was an extension of US imperialism in the Middle East.

COMBATING TERRORISM

Whatever may be the root causes of terrorism in the Middle East, the US has been following a determined policy to deal with Islamic extremism and anti-US terrorism around the world, especially since 9/11. More specifically in the Middle East, a commission was set up quickly to understand this problem and to recommend appropriate measures.

The 9/11 commission recommendations have been divided into two basic parts: what to do, and how to do it.

What to do?

According to 9/11 commission report:

* Attack terrorist and their organization
* Prevent the continued growth of Islamic Terrorism.
* Protect against and prepare for terrorist attacks.
* Make homeland security funding contingent.

How to do it? A Different way of Organizing Government

* Unity of effort: A National Counter Terrorism Center.
* Unity of effort: A National Intelligence Director.
* Unity of effort: Sharing information
* Unity of effort: Congress

Unity of effort: Organizing Americas Defense in the United States.[49]

As of today, the broad US policies in combating terrorism are the following:

* The US Government is opposed to domestic and international terrorism and is prepared to act in concert with other nations or unilaterally when necessary to prevent or respond to terrorist acts.
* The US Government considers the practice of terrorism by any person or groups a threat to its national security and will resist the use of terrorism by all legal means available.
* States that practices terrorism or actively support it will not do so without consequence. If there is evidence that a state is mounting or intends to conduct an act of terrorism against the country, The United States will take measures to protect its citizens, property, and interests.

* The United States will make no concessions to terrorists. It will not pay ransoms, release prisoners, change its policies, or agree to other acts that might encourage additional terrorism. At the same time, the United States will use every available resource to gain the safe return of American citizens who are held hostages by terrorists.

The United States will act in a strong manner against terrorists without surrendering basic freedoms or endangering democratic principles, and encourages other governments to take the same stands.[50]

Indeed, cooperation with Israel appears to be an indispensable part of US strategy to deal with terrorist activities in the Middle East. While Israel has often complicated the US desire to improve relations with friendly Arab regimes Israel is a real partner in the concrete battle against various kinds of terrorist outfits.

Israel has both the resources and the expertise to deal with terrorism since it has been facing this menace since its inception as a state in 1948. For the US, facing terrorism at home is a new phenomenon. Never before, in America's history, has it faced terrorist attacks on its homeland, even though US overseas bases and embassies were attacked. Had it not been for the 9/11 attacks the US would never have realized the gravity of the menace of terrorism. One of the most significant contributions Israel has made to US security has been shared intelligence. The truth is the US has little alternative, but to depend on Israel for much of its Middle Eastern human intelligence because the CIA's capability has diminished. In post revolutionary Iran, the CIA no longer had a presence and CIA's Lebanon station was virtually wiped out in the 1983 after the bombing of the US embassy in Beirut. The US relies on the Mossad and either Israeli intelligence agencies for information about terrorism, radical Islamic movements, proliferation and other Middle East related events.

For many years, Israel played a key role in assisting US intelligence through the capture and transfer of Soviet Weapons systems. For instance, Israel supplied the US valuable intelligence on Soviet fighters and their avionics. This occurred as recently as 1989 after the Syrian pilot defected in an advanced model of 1 MIG-23 and American officials were allowed to examine the plane.

Today, these strategic ties are stronger than ever. To cite a few examples:

* In Early 1997, Israel linked up to the US missile warning satellite system, which will provide Israel with real-time warning if a missile is launched against it.
* Joint military exercises are regularly held. In November 1996, US Marines held Training exercises in the Negev.
* A joint Anti- Terrorism Working Group was created.
* A hotline was established between the Pentagon and the Israeli Defense Ministry.
* The United States continues to fund research and development of Israeli weapons systems and military equipment, including the Arrow missile, the Nautilus Tactical High Energy Laser, the Barak ship self defense missile system, Bradley Reactive Armor Titles, Crash – Attenuating Seats, the have – Nap missile and Unmanned Aerial Vehicles.[51]

The success of CIA's use of Armed RQ-IA predator unmanned Aerial vehicles (UAV), made my General Atomics, to track and kill fleeing Al Qaeda operatives in Afghanistan has brought much attention to the fairly new piece of military technology and has led Pentagon officials to reassess the role of the unmanned aerial vehicle in future of defense strategy. The role of the UAV on the Urban Battlefield has become increasingly important, especially with its capability to identify likely locations for snipers. This capability of precision aerial reconnaissance of the UAV is the best way to identify these prime locations as well as to aid in the creation of maps of streetscapes with topographical features, all real ground commanders in real time. According to an Israeli officer, using UAV is a necessary step before troops are inserted into a city. Additionally, UAVs play a critical role in finding elusive mobile targets such as missile launchers.[52]

Seminars and meeting between health professionals on handling Biological and chemical weapons crisis as well collaborative efforts with law enforcement of both countries set a new standard of cooperation in 2002. In the wake of September 11, 2001, the New York Police Department (NYPD) chose to take approach to the threat of terrorism. At the end of May 2002, the NYPD investigators underwent training in Israel to detect and find out bombers. This was the first time, a US Police Department has been trained by military experts, who have had the unfortunate experience of handling suicide terrorism in the past. In the post-9/11 world, parades, sporting events, and other events that cause traffic jams are now seriously viewed as potential targets for terrorist attacks. The NYPD has sought to become as knowledgeable as possible on strategies and means of prevention of future attacks.[53]

As part of this counter terrorism programme a team of 10 high ranking law enforcement officers from several major US Cities toured Israel to have a dialogue and exchange practical knowledge and expertise in deterring terrorism. New security developments led Israel to buy US manufactured mobile devices that contain X- ray units and instrumens that sniff out explosives specifically involved in blasts on schools and public transportation.[54]

While security concerns grew significantly over the last couple of years, so to did teams of doctors and nurses, adequately qualified and prepared to respond to the effects of a massive attack such as 9/11. A new delegation of medical professionals toured the emergency facility and Israel's Soroca Medical Center on August 15, 2002. The Pentagon announced collaboration with Israeli units in research and development. Information receiced by the Israeli police helped the NYPD counter-terrorism bureau to send out warning to all city precincts.[55]

The US Strategy, as laid out by President Bush has three main factors: first, to disrupt terrorist activities in order to prevent attacks; second, to deny sanctuary to terrorist groups; and number threethird, to bolster US capabilities for combating terrorism. The war on terrorism was recognized as one across multiple fronts. In addition to the military front,there are critical activities underway on the diplomatic, intelligence, humanitarian, economic, law enforcements fronts.[56]

According to the 9/11 Commission report, Final Report of the National Commission on Terrorist Attacks upon the United States, more than 2600 hundred people died at the World Trade Center, 125 died at the Pentagon, 256 died on the foreplanes. The death toll surpassed that at Pearl Harbor in December 1941.[57] Four years after 9/11 the debate continues about how to protect America in this new era.

Both the US and Israel have come together to fight terrorism since 9/11. Both the countries have recognized the need to counter terrorist activities with full force. Their strategies may vary under different circumstances, although their final goal is to create a terror free world order.

REFERENCES

1. James P. Wooten, "Terrorism: IS Policy Options", Washington D.C.: library of Congress, CRS Report, 1995, P. 7.
2. Office of the Coordinator for Counter Terrorism, Patterns of Global Terrorism, 1996, US Department of State, Publication 10433, April 1997.
3. John Murray and Richard H. Ward (eds), *Extremist Groups,* Office of International Criminal Justice, (Chicago: University of Illinois, 1996), p. 34.
4. Youssef M. Ibrahim," Egyptians Hold Terrorist Chief, official asserts", *New York Times,* August 26, 1998.

5. Murray and Ward, *Extremist Groups*, p. 42.
6. *Patterns of Global Terrorism*, 1996, and Murray and Ward, *Extremist Groups*, Ibid.
7. Murray and Ward, *Extremist Groups*, p. 49.
8. *Patterns of Global Terrorism*, 1995, 1996, 1997.
9. For Instance, in 1997 Hamas operatives set off three suicide bombs in crowded public places in Tel Aviv and Jerusalem. On March 21, a Hamas satchel bomb exploded at a Tel Aviv café, killing three persons and injuring 48.
10. See "Hizbullah," Israeli Foreign Ministry, April 11, 1996. Available on the internet at http://www.isreal-mfa.gov.il.
11. Arab Afghans Said to Launch Worldwide Terrorist War", Paris al-Watan al-Arabi, FBIS-TOT-96-010-L, December1, 1995, pp.22-24.
12. William Gertz, "Saudi Financier Tied to attacks", *Washington Times*, October23, 1996.
13. Tim Weiner, "US Sees Bin Laden as Ringleader of Terrorist Network", *New York Times*, August21, 1998; M. J. Zuckerman, "Bin Laden Indicted for Bid to Kill Clinton", *USA Today*, August21, 1998.
14. Pamela Constable, "Bin Laden Is Our Guest, So We Must Protect Him", *Washington Post*, August21, 1998.
15. There is a difference between deliberate and factional decentralization. Factional decentralization-prevalent in older groups-occurs when subgroups separate themselves from the central leadership because of differences in tactics or approach. Deliberate or operational decentralization is what distinguishes network agents from others, since delegation of authority in this case occurs because of the distinct advantages this organizational arrangement brings, and not because of lack of consensUS
16. "Gaza strip, West bank: Dahlan on Relations with Israel, Terrorism", Tel Aviv Yedi'ot Aharonot, FBIS-TOT-97-022-L, February 28, 1997, p.18.
17. The Leader of the PIJ's most powerful faction Shaqaqi, was assassinated in October 1995 in Malta, allegedly by the Israeli Mosad. Shaqaqi's killing followed the assassination of Hani Abed, another PIJ leader killed in 1994 in Gaza. Reports that the group has been considerably weakened as a result of Israeli counter leadership operations are balanced by the strength demonstrated by the PIJ in its recent terrorist activity. See "Islamic Group Vows Revenge for Slaying of its Leader", *New York Times*, October 30, p.9.
18. Magnus Ranstorp, "Hizbullah Command leadership: its Structure,

Decision making and relationship with Iranian Clergy and Institutions", Terrorism and Political Violence, Vol.6, No.3, Autumn 1994, p.304.

19. Patterns of Global Terrorism, 1996.
20. "Algeria : Infighting Among Proliferating Wings of Armed Groups", London al-Sharaq al- Aswat, FBIS-TOT-97-021-L, February 24,1997, p.4.
21. David B. Ottaway," US considers Slugging it out with International Terrorism", *Washington Post*, October17, 1996, p.25.
22. Saudi Arabia: Bin Laden Calls for' Guerrilla Warfare" Against US Forces", Beirut Al- Diyar, FBIS- nES-96-180, September 12, 1996.
23. It is Important to Avoid equating the Laden network solely with Bin Laden. He represents key node in the Arab Afghan terror Network, but there should be no illusions about the likely effect on the network of actions taken to neutralize him. The network conducts many operations without his involvement, leadership, or financial- and will continue to be able to do so should be killed or captured.
24. "Militants Say There will Be More Attacks against US," European Stars and Stripes, August 20, 1998.
25. For Instance, there have been reports of a recent inflow of Arab Afghans into Egypt's Islamic Group to reinforce the latter's operations. See Murray and Ward, 1996, and "The CIA on Bin Laden", Foreign Report, No.2510, August27, 1998, pp.2-3.
26. This move was also influenced by the Taliban's decision to curb Arab Afghan activities in the territory under its control as a result of US Pressure. See "Arab Afghans Reportedly Transfer operations to Somalia", Cairo al- Arabi, FBIS-TOT-97-073, March 10, 1997, p.1.
27. Afghanistan, China: Report on Bin – Laden Possibly Moving to china", Paris al- Watan al- Arabi, FBIS-NES- 97-102, May 23, 1997, pp.19-20.
28. While it is possible to discern a general trend toward an organizational structure that displays several features of a network, and to observe substantial differences (and many hierarchy/ networks hybrids) in how organizations make their specific design choices. Different designs depend on contingent factors, such as personalities, organizational history, operational requirements, and other influences such as state sponsorship and ideology.
29. Analogously, right- wing militias and extremist groups in the United States also rely on a doctrine of "Leaderless resistance" propounded by Aryan nationalist Louis Beam. See Beam, 1992; and Kenneth Stern,

A Force Upon the Plain: The American Militia Movement and the Politics of Hate, Simon and Schuster, New York, 1996. Meanwhile they have been shifting away from centralized "dons" to more networked structures. See Phil Williams, "Transnational Criminal Organizations and International Security: Drug- Trafficking Networks", *Current History*, April 1998, pp.154-159. As noted earlier social activist movements long ago began to evolve 'segmented polycephalous' other peaceful activist groups supported an insurgent group in Mexico, see David Ronfeltd and Armando Martinez, "A Comment on the Zapatista Netwar", in John Arquilla and David Ronfeldt, 1997, pp.369-391.

30. It is important to differentiate notions of information age networking from earlier ideas about terror as consisting of a network in which all nodes revolved around a Soviet core (Claire Sterling, The Terror Network, Holt, Rinehart& Winston, New York, 1981). This view has generally been regarded as unsupported by available evidence (see Cindy C. Combs, Terrorism in the twenty-First Century, Prentice-Hall, credit to the possibility of the rise of terror networks that were bound more by loose ties to general strategic to the possibility of the rise of terror networks that were bound more by loose ties to general Strategic goals than by Soviet control (see especially Thomas L. Friedman, "Loose- Linked Network of Terror: Separate Acts, Ideological bonds, Terrorism, Vol.8, no.1, Winter 1985, pp.36-49).

31. Michael Whine, "Islamist Organisations on the Internet", Draft circulated on the Internet, April 1998 (www.ict.org.il/articles).

32. Group activity is a proxy for group strength, and is expected to be significantly correlated with strength. The relationship may not be perfect, but it is deemed to sufficiently strong for the purpose.

33. "Saudi Arabia: French Analysis of Islamic Threat", Paris al- Watan al' Arabi, FBIS- NES-97-082, April 11, 1997, pp.4-8.

34. Afghanistan, Saudi Arabia: Editor's Journey to meet Bin Laden Described", London al-quds al'- Arabi, FBIS-TOT-97-003-L, November 27, 1996, p.4.

35. Arab Afghans Said to launch Worldwide Terrorist war", 1995.

36. "Israel: US Hamas Activists Use Internet to Send Attack Threats", Tel Aviv IDF Radio, FBIS-TOT-97-001-L, 0500GMT October 13, 1996.

37. Israel: Hamas Using Internet to Rely Operational Messages", Tel Aviv Ha'aretz, FBIS-TOT-98-034, February 3, 1998, p.1.

38. "Italy: Security Alerts Following Algerian Extremists' Arrests", Milan II Giornale, FBIS-TOT-97-002-L, November 12, 1996, p.10.

39. "Italy: Vatican City: Daily Claims GIA ' Strategist' Based in Milan", Milan Corriere delta Sera, FBIS-TOT-97-004-L, December 5,1996, p.6.
40. "Hizbullah TV Summary 18 February 1998," Al-Manar Telivision World wide Webcast, FBIS- NES-98-050, February 19, 1998. Also see" Developments in Mideast Media: January- May 1998," Foreign Broadcast Information Service (FBIS), May 11, 1998.
41. "Hizbullah TV Summary 18 February 1998," Al-Manar Telivision World wide Webcast, FBIS- NES-98-050, February 19, 1998. Also see" Developments in Mideast Media: January- May 1998," Foreign Broadcast Information Service (FBIS), May 11, 1998.
42. "Islamists on Internet", FBIS Foreign Media Note-065EP96, September 9, 1996. Similar propositions may apply to varieties of netwar other than the new terrorism.
43. John Prados, *America Confronts Terrorism: Understanding The Danger and How To Think About It*(Chicago Ivan R. Dee, Publisher, 2002) p.5.
44. *Newsweek*, May 31 2004, p.22.
45. *Newsweek*, May 31 2004, p.24.
46. Ibid.
47. *Newsweek*, May 31 2004, p.22.
48. *Newsweek*, May 31 2004, p.24.
49. Ibid.
50. *Public Report of the Vice President's Task Force on Combating Terrorism*, February 1986, p.7.
51. http://www.us-israel.org/jsource/US-Israel/special.html. 27/10/02.
52. *Washington Post*, 9/23/02.
53. *The New York Daily News*, 19th October 2002.
54. *The Jerusalem Post*, 30 May, 2002.
55. www.jinsa.org
56. US Ambassador to Israeli Daniel C. Kurtzer, "The American Campaign Against Terrorism: Global & Regional Implications" Tel Aviv University, November 4, 2001. http://www.usembassy-isreal.org.il/publish/mission/amb/110401.html.
57. www.state.gov

7
Sunni-Shia Militant Movements in Iraq

Shelly Johny

INTRODUCTION

It has often been said that the September 11 terrorist attacks in the United States heralded a new age, where there is an increased likelihood of large scale terrorist attacks. According to the United States, this dramatic event has necessitated a response in the form of the 'war on terror'. But it is necessary to ask, if September 11 was such an unexpected and dramatic event which changed the world or if it is the culmination of a process that had been going on since the 1990's. The 1990's witnessed a drastic rise in the number of terrorist attacks by Sunni militant groups in West Asia and other parts of the world. These include the insurgencies waged by radical Sunni militant groups against the governments in Egypt and Algeria, attacks against US troops in Saudi Arabia and the bombings of US embassies in East Africa in 1998. Regarding the World Trade Centre in New York, the followers of the blind Egyptian cleric, Sheikh Omar Abdul Rahman, had made a failed attempt to destroy the building in 1993. In the light of the last incident, it can be said that the attempts by Sunni militants to destroy the World Trade Centre, the symbol of US economic strength, had begun in the 1990's itself. The September 11 attacks should be seen as the grand finale of a process of radical Islamist activism that has been going on since the 1990's.

The terrorist attacks of 2001 and the US 'war on terror' have a 'cause' and 'effect' relationship. In the same way, the 2001 attacks were not properly understood by placing it in the context of the previous decade, the consequences of the 'war on terror', which will have its impact on the coming decades, is likely to be misunderstood. One of the reasons for the invasion of Iraq by United States was the presumed link between the regime of Saddam Hussein and Al Qaeda. Therefore, it can be said that the invasion of Iraq was a part of the 'war on terror'. More than three years after the invasion, it would be worthwhile to have a look at how the invasion has affected the nature of trans-national terrorism in today's world. By now, it is well known that Iraq has become a magnate for radical Islamist groups of various shades. This does not mean that the insurgency in Iraq is one that is led by foreign nationals. On the other hand, there is enough evidence to prove that majority of the insurgents in Iraq are indigenous Iraqis who were formerly members of the Iraqi armed forces under the Baathist government. Many of them were former Special Republican Guards and still retain the weapons that they had when Saddam's government fell.[2] The purpose of this article is not to know about the exact nature of the insurgency in Iraq. But it is to understand how Sunni and Shia militant organisations developed in the context of the Afghan War and the Iranian Revolution and what impact the Iraqi insurgency is having on the radical Islamist network in West Asia today.

THE RADICAL SUNNI GROUPS AND THE AFGHAN WAR

The American invasion of Iraq has created the conditions for Sunni militant groups like the Al Qaeda to go into Iraq and use the situation there to recruit new militants. As mentioned earlier, the majority of the insurgents fighting in Iraq are indigenous Iraqis. These insurgents are fighting the occupation because of a number of reasons, the most important of which is the fear among Iraqi Sunnis of the loss of political influence in a new system of governance dominated by Shias and Kurds.[3] But at the same time, the occupation of Iraq has provided foreign militants the opportunity to directly fight American troops, which is an appealing prospect to radical Sunnis all over the world. This option was not available to militant groups before 2003. Earlier, organisations like the Al Qaeda had to conduct bombing campaigns against US interests like military bases and embassies in Saudi Arabia and East Africa. But now, with US forces spread out over a larger area in Iraq, militant organisations can fight a protracted guerrilla war against their enemy and keep improving their tactics. In order to understand the implications of the insurgency in Iraq on radical Islamist groups it is important to know how this phenomenon developed as a result of the Afghan War of the 1980's.

Before the Soviet invasion of Afghanistan, fundamentalist Islamist movements had already developed in countries like Egypt and Pakistan. The Muslim Brotherhood of Egypt and the Jamaat-i-Islami of Pakistan were the most important organisations during this period. But these organisations mostly worked within their specific environments and there was very less co-operation between them. But an important development was the formulation of a more radical Islamist activism by certain sections of the Muslim Brotherhood led by Sayyid Qutb. He advocated war against rulers who did not adhere to their concept of an Islamic state. It was such in a situation that the Soviet Union invaded Afghanistan at the end of 1979. Even before the invasion, neighbouring Pakistan under Zia-ul-Haq had already begun a process of Islamicisation. The invasion gave Zia the opportunity to call for a grand Islamic alliance against the Soviets. The nature of international politics during that time also created an environment suitable for the creation of such an opposition movement.[4] The Cold War rivalry between the United States and the Soviet Union was going on at that point of time. The United States believed that the Afghan crisis was an apt situation to support a guerrilla war against the USSR and weaken that country.[5]

Volunteers from all over the Islamic world heeded Zia's call for a holy war against the Soviets and they arrived in Pakistan in order to prepare themselves to fight in Afghanistan. The effort was funded by Saudi Arabia while the US provided the weapons and training.[6] Pakistan was used as a base by various Islamist organisations along with the support of the Pakistani army and the ISI. Thousands of Afghan refugees who had fled from their country because of the invasion were mobilised for the effort. They were provided charitable and educational services by Islamist organisations in therefugee camps.[7] This effort for a Jihad against the Soviets also influenced the fortunes of Islamist fundamentalist organisations. When Zia-ul-Haq came to power in 1977, his government had begun to promote organisations like the Jamaat-i-Islami as a part of its wider agenda of adopting an Islamic identity.[8] In the aftermath of the Soviet invasion of Afghanistan, the process gained greater speed and prominence. Along with the Jamaat, the government also supported organisations like the Jamiat-ul-Ulema-i-Islami and Markaz-ud-Dawaa-wal-Irshad. These organisations began to play a more influential role in Pakistani politics.[9]

After a prolonged guerrilla war that lasted almost a decade, the Soviets withdrew from Afghanistan in 1989. What was the impact of the Afghan War on the Sunni Islamist network? When the drive for mobilisation for the war was going on in Pakistan, thousands of Muslim volunteers came from places as far away as Algeria and the Philippines. Even during the Crusades that were fought from the eleventh century to the thirteenth, such a gathering of Muslims from all over the Islamic world was not possible because of limitations in travel and communication. Though the Muslims ultimately won the Crusades, it did not end the rivalries between ethnic groups like the Arabs and Turks. By the time of the Afghan War, the various Muslim territories had gone through a traumatic period of colonisation and domination by various European colonial powers. The need for Muslim solidarity and brotherhood had increased among Muslims all over the world. The various Islamist organisations from Pakistan and abroad tried to create this solidarity among the Afghans and foreign volunteers from different parts of the world. In spite of the efforts of the fundamentalist organisations, the situation at the ground level was different. The Arab fighters who came to be called as the local Afghans viewed 'Afghan-Arabs' with distaste and suspicion. The Arabs also had sense of superiority while interacting with the locals. But the Islamist organisations managed to create a level of co-operation between the two sides. Moreover, the Arab fighters from prosperous Gulf countries brought in much needed funds to the war-zone. The activities of the Islamist organisations also helped in the spread of radical Islamist ideology among Afghans who believed in a moderate form of Islam.

In the same way as the government of Pakistan, the Saudi Kingdom had also introduced a programme of giving more importance to Islamic principles during the 1980's. This was a response to the capture of the Grand Mosque at Mecca by a group of Muslim fundamentalists in 1979. The grievances of the rebels included the perceived decline of Islamic values among the Saudi royal family and the threat to Islamic values because of the rapid pace of modernisation in Saudi society due to the oil wealth. After the incident, the Saudi government introduced measures to give more importance to Islamic values in the education system and give more powers to the religious clergy. This process resulted in increasing the influence of religion among the Saudi youth during the 1980's. Adhering to Islamic principles began to be seen as highly necessary in Saudi society. Jihad is an important concept in Islamic thought. The two kinds of jihad are the internal jihad and external jihad.

Internal jihad refers to the spiritual cleansing of oneself whereas external jihad means fighting an authority that oppresses Muslims. The Soviet Union, which invaded Afghanistan, was seen as an atheist entity, which was oppressing fellow Muslims in Afghanistan. Religious Saudi youth saw this as an opportunity to fulfill a religious duty by fighting a holy war in Afghanistan. It was precisely because of this reason that many of the foreign volunteers who fought in the Afghan war came from rapidly Islamicising countries like Saudi Arabia and Pakistan.

As the foreign fighters interacted with each other they realised that they all faced the same problems back in their home countries. Most of them had repressive governments ruling back home. The foreigners felt the need for better co-ordination among the Islamist organisations of the various Muslim countries. This feeling gave birth to a new Pan-Islamist movement that later developed into the Al Qaeda. This is why Al Qaeda managed to attract recruits from other radical militant groups like the Egyptian Al Jihad and various Pakistani outfits. The various Islamist fundamentalist organisations developed their own militias, a process which had a profound impact on conflicts which were fought in Muslim countries during the 1990's. The Jamaat-i-Islami developed links with the Hezb-i-Islami in Afghanistan which is led by Gulbuddin Hekmatyar. In Kashmir the Jamaat supported the Hizbul Mujahideen. The militant wing of the Jamiat-ul-Ulema-i-Islami is the Harkat-ul-Mujahideen. A faction of the Harkat-ul-Mujahideen, led by Maulana Masood Azhar later on split off to form the Jaish-e-Muhammad. The Markaz-ud-Dawa-wal-Irshad's militant wing is the Lashkar-i-Tayabba.[10] The parent organisations provided educational and charitable facilities and thereby recruited people for their militant wings.

By fighting in the Afghan war, the various Sunni militant groups gained valuable military experience. They learnt how to use firearms, make bombs and use sophisticated communication technologies.[11] They also got access to sophisticated and powerful weapons. The Americans provided them with anti-aircraft Stinger missiles and the CIA trained them in their use. Soviet weapons also fell into the hands of the militant groups after a successful mission. In this manner they managed to get weapons from both the superpowers. These weapons would help them to fight in conflicts during the 1990's. The Afghan war was a conflict where the Islamist militants realised the necessity of advanced technology to fight a more powerful enemy. They learnt to reconcile the use of modern technology with an ideology that espoused recreating the Caliphate that existed more than one thousand and three hundred years ago. The Sunni militant groups managed to develop strong links with the Pakistani army and the ISI who provided them with aid in the future to continue their holy war not just in Afghanistan but also in neighbouring areas like Kashmir and Central Asia. During the Afghan War, the Soviet Red Army was the largest army in the world. The withdrawal of the Soviets convinced the Sunni Islamist groups that they could defeat a superior enemy using tactics similar to the one that they had used during the war.

THE POST-AFGHAN WAR PERIOD

The period following the Afghan War saw the collapse of the Soviet Union and the end of the Cold War that had lasted for almost fourty five years. It created an entirely new situation in international politics. The collapse of the Soviet Union saw the formation of new Muslim majority states. These included the five Central Asian republics and countries like Azerbaijan and Georgia. The citizens of these new states were coming to terms with a political system that discouraged the practice of religion and had lasted for more than seven decades. They were in the process of re-discovering their identities which included Islam. The Islamist organisations saw this as an apt opportunity to spread their ideology in these new states. Beyond the region, the former communist controlled Yugoslavia split into new countries. Identities based on ethnicity and religion, which was submerged in a socialist environment, began to emerge in a powerful manner. It resulted in a civil war between the various ethnic communities which included the Bosnian Muslims. Radical Islamist militants began to enter into that region and propagate their views.

The radical Islamists who had fought in the Afghan War went back to their countries and began to organize themselves in order to wage opposition activities against their governments.[12] In the Philippines they joined either the Moro Islamic Salvation Front or the Abu Sayyaf group which had split off from the former. In Indonesia the Islamists joined the Jemaah Islamiyya. An election in Algeria in which the Islamists won the majority was cancelled by the Algerian government which was controlled by the military. Islamist organisations like the Islamic Salvation Front and the Armed Islamic Group launched war against the government. The civil war was extremely violent and nearly resulted in a complete breakdown of the country.[13] Islamist organisations in Egypt like the Al Jihad and the Al-Gamaa al-Islamiyya launched a campaign of assassinations and bombings against the Egyptian government. The conflicts in Algeria and Egypt lasted for almost the whole of the 1990's. An Islamist fundamentalist government came to power in Sudan in 1989. Islamist Palestinian opposition movements like Hamas and Palestinian Islamic Jihad began to gain more influence during this period.

In the wider Islamic world there was an increase in the activities of the radical Islamist organizations. A separatist movement had emerged in the Indian state of Jammu and Kashmir. Though the movement was launched by nationalist elements, they later on came to be taken over by Islamist groups. Along with Kashmiri Islamist organisations, the different militias of Pakistani fundamentalist organisations began to be active in that state during the 1990's.[14] In Afghanistan the Taliban, which was an Islamist fundamentalist movement began to capture vast swathes of territory from Mujahideen organisations which had fought during the Afghan War. The Taliban had been trained and funded by the Pakistani ISI.[15] They had received support from Saudi Arabia as well.[16] They followed a puritanical form of Islam derived from the teachings of Muhammad Abd al-Wahhab, an eighteenth century religious reformer who was active in what is now Saudi Arabia. Wahhab's teachings were also the official faith of the Kingdom of Saudi Arabia. By the end of the 1990's, the Taliban controlled almost the whole of Afghanistan including the capital Kabul. The various Islamist movements in Central Asia also began to organise opposition movements against their respective governments. They in turn received support from the Taliban. With such huge support, radical Islamist groups began to be active as far away as in Chechnya and Dagestan in southern Russia.

Terrorist attacks against US targets were also increasing during this period. These include the various attacks against US troops in Saudi Arabia. But the most important development with regard to the radical Islamist movement was the emergence of the Al Qaeda. The organisation is led by Osama Bin Laden who was a Saudi and his deputy was an Egyptian called Ayman al Zawahiri. Both of them had fought in the Afghan War of the 1980's. Bin Laden announced the formation of an umbrella movement called the 'International Islamic Front for Jihad against Jews and Crusaders' shortly before the bombings of the US embassies in East Africa in 1998.[17] Later on, Al Qaeda claimed responsibility for the attacks. In many ways Al Qaeda was different from the other radical Islamist organisations which were active in their respective countries. It had a particular agenda for the whole Islamic world and not just for one country. That agenda was the establishment of an Islamic Caliphate. Bin Laden saw the stationing of American troops on Saudi soil as a sacrilege to the Islamic faith as the two holiest places of Islam, Mecca and Medina were in Saudi Arabia. This was the reason why he began to oppose the Saudi government.[18] After he was expelled from Saudi Arabia he went over to Sudan. But he was finally given refuge by the Taliban government in Afghanistan.[19]

In Afghanistan, the Al Qaeda, under the protection of the Taliban, organised training camps for Islamist militants from all over the Islamic world. The training camps were spread out in the territories of both Pakistan and Afghanistan. These camps created a pool of radical Islamist fighters who could be sent to any conflict that involved Muslims be it in Kashmir or Bosnia. The Al Qaeda's world view made it to act in a different way from the other Islamist organisations. As it identified the United States as the arch enemy of the Muslims it conducted attacks against US targets anywhere in the world. The Al Qaeda conducted attacks against the US Navy in Yemen and Al Qaeda fighters began to fight Saudi security forces. It also made attempts to attack US interests in Pakistan. The most spectacular operation of the Al Qaeda was the September 11 attacks. It won the widespread support of the public in Muslim countries when its camps were targeted by the US as a response to the attacks against the American embassies in East Africa. Al Qaeda was seen as the only organisation capable of taking on the might of the United States. Al Qaeda was also different from the other Sunni radical movements in its use of the media and other facilities like the internet in its war against the US.

By the second half of the 1990's, the various radical Islamist organisations began to be collectively called the Islamist International similar to the Communist International or the Comintern of the Cold War. With a heightened pace of activity among the various radical Sunni organisations during the 1990's it was believed that the first decade of the twenty first century would be an era in which their power and influence would grow further. But this was not to be. The military campaign launched by the Islamists in Algeria and Egypt was brutally crushed by their respective governments. The Sudanese regime was beset with internal divisions. As the Islamist opposition movements in Central Asia winded down, the situation in Kashmir settled into one of protracted warfare with fewer and fewer gains for the radical Islamists. As a response to the September 11 attacks, the US invaded Afghanistan and toppled the Taliban regime. This event led to the fleeing of remnant Taliban and Al Qaeda members to the border region between Pakistan and Afghanistan. With their camps out of action, the Al Qaeda could not train any more new recruits. The only exception during this period was the situation in Saudi Arabia. But since the last two years there have been lesser shooting clashes between Saudi security forces and Al Qaeda fighters in that country.

This does not mean that Islamist organisations have completely disappeared from the scene. Islamist parties like the Muslim Brotherhood and the Hamas won elections in Egypt and the Palestinian territories respectively. On the radical Islamist scene, there were terrorist attacks in Britain and Spain. But on the whole, the beginning of the twenty first century saw a lesser pace of activity among radical Islamists than the 1990's. The biggest failure of the Islamists was the inability to establish an Islamic Republic anywhere in the Islamic world especially in West Asia. In the background of the September 11 attacks it is easy to be mislead into a feeling that radical Sunni organisations have become all powerful and pervasive. The success of these organisations must be judged in the light of what has happened to the causes that were taken up by them during the 1990's. As mentioned earlier, the various struggles launched by the Islamists have been crushed by the authorities. This means that September 11 took place at a time when the radical Islamist movements were going through a declining phase. The invasion of Afghanistan unraveled all the efforts of these movements from the 1990's onwards. This is why 2003 can be seen as the end of a phase in the history of militant Sunni movements. But considering the opportunities that these same movements have received in Iraq since the invasion, 2003 can be seen as the beginning of a new phase for the radical Islamists.

RADICAL SHIA MILITANT MOVEMENTS AND THE IRANIAN REVOLUTION

In the same way as the Sunnis, a radical Islamist movement developed among the Shias as well. But before going into details about nature of Shia militancy it is necessary to understand the reasons for the split that occurred between the Sunnis and the Shias. The schism between the Sunnis and the Shia happened after the death of Prophet Muhammad over the question of his succession. While the Sunnis believed that only elders of Prophet Muhammad's tribe should be his successors, the Shia claimed that only the direct descendents of the Prophet had the right to succeed him. As the prophet had no sons, the Shia wanted the Prophet's cousin and son-in-law, Ali to be the Caliph. Ali finally became the fourth Caliph. After his assassination, the Caliphate passed on to the hands of Muawiya, a cousin of Uthman, the third Caliph and after that to Muawiya's son Yazid. When Ali's second son, Hussein and his followers tried to take the Caliphate from Yazid's hands, they were defeated and killed near Karbala in Iraq in 680.[20] Since that time, the Sunnis and the Shias have remained separate sects and great rivals. Shias form almost hundred percentage of the population in Iran while they constitute around sixty percentage of the Iraqi population. They are also a majority in Bahrain and form a significant minority in Lebanon. In the rest of the Islamic world they are a minority with little political influence.

Traditionally, the Shia clergy has not played a very significant role in politics in spite of their activities in Iran during the early part of the twentieth century and their involvement in the anti-British revolt in Iraq during the 1920's. This changed with the anti-Shah movement in Iran during the 1960's and the 1970's. The Shia clergy led mass demonstrations against the Shah and Ayatollah Khomeini began issuing political statements favouring an Islamic political system. In 1979 the Shah was toppled and an Islamic Republic was established in Iran. Ayatollah Khomeini became the Supreme Leader of Iran. One of the main objectives of the revolutionary Iranian government was the export of its revolution beyond its borders. The Islamic Revolutionary Guards Corps (IRGC), an armed force separate from the Regular Armed Forces, was created and entrusted with the duty of spreading the revolution to other parts of the Islamic world. The biggest success for Iran in this effort was in Lebanon where there was a considerable Shia population. A process of the radicalisation of the Lebanese Shia had already begun there under Ayatollah Musa al-Sadr from the end of the 1950's. Ayatollah Sadr's activities were mainly charitable and educational in nature. It later on blossomed into a movement with an armed militia known as the Amal.[21]

With the arrival of 1,500 Iran's revolutionary guards in Lebanon in the early 1980's, the politicisation of the Lebanese Shia was taken up on an entirely different scale. The IRGC united the various Shia factions and created a new and powerful movement in its place which later came to be called Hezbollah or the "Army of God". Iran's efforts to spread the concept of *Vilayat-e-Faqih* or the rule of the Islamic jurisprudent in Lebanon were clear from the outset itself. The IRGC tried to recreate the Iranian social conditions in Lebanese towns in the Bekaa Valley where they had influence. Such places were filled with visible signs of Iranian influence like Persian hoardings and women clad in the *hijab*.[22] Because of Iran's good relations with the Syrian regime, the training and arming of Hezbollah cadre by Iran was a major success. Syrian airspace was used by Iran to airlift arms to the Hezbollah. Iran armed Hezbollah with Tube-Launched Optically-Tracked Wire Guided Missiles (TOWs) and other deadly weapons which it had received from America via Israel for the release of American embassy hostages in Tehran in the infamous Iran-Contra affair.[23] Hezbollah became a powerful guerrilla movement during the Lebanese civil war and put up the toughest resistance to Israeli forces which had invaded Lebanon.

Shia militants, inspired by Iran, were responsible for

deadly suicide bomb attacks against American and French forces which had come for peacekeeping efforts in Lebanon.[24] This led to the withdrawal of American and French forces from Lebanon. They also kidnapped Western citizens and kept them as hostages. The most active phase of Shia militancy was the 1980's. By the time of the early 1990's, it became obvious that Iran's attempt to spread the revolution was not a success. There were a few bomb blasts in the Gulf countries that were linked to Iran's intelligence agencies. A Shia rebellion in north-east Saudi Arabia was put down by the government. In spite of Iran's partial success in Lebanon, its efforts could not succeed in Iraq where Shias formed the majority. It was expected during the Iran-Iraq war that the Iraqi Shia would join the side of Iran. But such hopes did not materialise Moreover, Saddam Hussein's huge security network was a big hindrance to Iran's effort's to spread the revolution in Iraq. Any attempt by the Iraqi Shia clergy to organise opposition activities was brutally crushed by the Baathist government. Iraqi Shia political organisations like the Daawa Party were persecuted by the Baathists and they were forced to flee to Iran.[25] An attempt by the Iraqi Shia to revolt after the Kuwait crisis was brutally crushed by the Iraqi armed forces while the victorious American led coalition stood by and watched.

But this did not mean that Iran's attempts to support Islamist opposition activities ended during the 1990's. Iran's support extended to the Palestinian Islamic Jihad and Hamas. Iran built up relations with the Islamist fundamentalist regime of Sudan. Hezbollah's resistance which lasted for the whole of the 1990's finally led to the withdrawal of Israeli forces in 2002. At the same time, Iran's hopes of establishing an Islamic Republic in Lebanon could not be fulfilled. As Lebanon was a multi-cultural and multi-religious society, Hezbollah realised that it was impractical to showcase itself merely as a Shia militant movement. It adopted a more pragmatic policy and began to showcase itself as a party that could meet the nationalist aspirations of Lebanese from different backgrounds.[26] With regard to Iran's efforts in Iraq, Iran's success in establishing its influence among the Iraqi Shia would have been an important milestone in its efforts to establish its hegemony in the Islamic world. Changes in Iranian politics also prompted successive Iranian governments to lessen its hard line stance on regional and international issues. It can be said that the early 1990's saw a decline in Shia militant activism in West Asia. But just as in the case of Sunni militant organisations like Al Qaeda, the invasion and occupation of Iraq created new opportunities for the Islamic Republic of Iran.

IMPLICATIONS OF THE IRAQI INSURGENCY ON SUNNI AND SHIA MILITANT MOVEMENTS

The benefits for Sunni militant organisations from the Iraqi insurgency have been already mentioned earlier. Even though most of the insurgents are local Iraqis, there are an increasing number of foreigners coming to fight in Iraq. Among the foreigners, majority of them are Saudis.[27] This could be because of the geographical proximity of Saudi Arabia to Iraq and the inability of security forces to monitor such a huge border that can be easily crossed. Even before the arrival of the foreigners, local Sunni radical groups like Ansar al-Islam were already active. Sunni clerics in pre-dominantly Sunni cities like Falluja and Ramadi had already begun preaching during Friday sermons on the need to resist the occupation.[28] One of the main Sunni militant movements fighting in Iraq is the Al Qaeda in Iraq, which had been led by Abu Musaab al-Zarqawi who was killed in a US air strike. Most of these Sunni militant groups favour bringing about a civil war in Iraq by attacking Shia targets. They believe that an Iraq beset by chaos and destruction would result in a withdrawal of US troops from the country. The Sunni militant groups have been conducting their campaign in accordance with this belief.

In the initial period, the targets of these militant

organisations included US troops and the assets of the United Nations. Al Qaeda in Iraq also bombed the embassies of any country that either send troops to Iraq or developed relations with the interim Iraqi administration. Later on, the targets of the Sunni militant groups included Shias, government officials and foreigners visiting Iraq. These groups also bombed Shia holy shrines during religious gatherings which resulted in a huge number of casualties. One such attack killed Ayatollah Muhammad Baqr al-Hakim, who was the leader of the Supreme Council for Islamic Revolution in Iraq (SCIRI). SCIRI is a Shia political organisation. But what was interesting was the spreading impact of the Iraqi insurgency on the neighbouring regions. Iraqi insurgents from Al Qaeda in Iraq were responsible for bomb blasts conducted in the Jordanian capital of Amman. These were visible signs that the influence of Sunni militant groups were spreading as a result of the Iraqi insurgency. As mentioned earlier, Saudi security forces have managed to reduce the number of Al Qaeda members in Iraq in recent times. But Sunni militants are gaining more experience and adopting newer tactics while fighting American troops in Iraq. As majority of the foreign fighters are from Saudi Arabia, the risk of battle-hardened Sunni militants coming back and conducting even more deadly attacks in Saudi Arabia and other neighbouring Muslim countries is very huge. This could spell a strengthening of Sunni militant movements in the West Asian region.

The invasion of Iraq has also strengthened Shia militant movements in that country. The American occupation has given various pro-Iranian Shia political organisations the opportunity to come to Iraq and actively involve in Iraqi politics which wouldn't have been possible during the rule of Saddam. Most of these Shia organisations have their own militias. The militia of the Supreme Council for Islamic Revolution in Iraq (SCIRI) is the Badr Corps which was trained by the Islamic Revolutionary Guards Corps (IRGC), an Iranian paramilitary force. Likewise, some of the Shia clerics like Ayatollah Muqtada al-Sadr have their militias which are more indigenous in nature with little or no Iranian support. Al-Sadr's militia is the Mahdi Army. As the US allowed most of the pro-Iranian political organisations like the SCIRI and the Dawaa Party to take part in Iraqi politics, none of these movements are active in the guerrilla war against America. This is not the case with the Mahdi Army which sees the Americans as occupiers and has fought pitched battles with US troops and Iraqi government soldiers. There are reports of co-operation between the Sunni militants and Al-Sadr's Mahdi Army.[29]

The fact that organisations like the SCIRI and Dawaa Party are not involved in the guerrilla insurgency does not mean that the radicalisation and militarisation of the Iraqi Shia is not taking place. There are growing instances of Shia militias like the Badr Corps, who are a part of the Iraqi Interior Ministry, rounding up Iraqi Sunnis, torturing and executing them and finally dumping the bodies. The power and influence of Shia militias are only bound to grow in the future because of the Shia networks which were created after the Iranian revolution of 1979. As both the Badr Corps of the SCIRI in Iraq and the Hezbollah of Lebanon were trained by the Islamic Revolutionary Guards, these two movements are likely to build relations with each other. Such an alliance could also include Sadr's Mahdi Army and the Dawaa Party. The possibility of such an event is very high as the Islamic Republic of Iran has always viewed and continues to view Israel as an arch rival. One of the Iranian slogans during the Iran-Iraq war was that the way to Al Quds (Jerusalem) was through Iraq. As the Syrian regime has been a long time ally of the Islamic Republic, the Shia militant movements will have little hindrance in building networks and increasing their influence across the region.

DRAWING A PARALLEL

One particular year can be considered as very crucial to the history of Sunni and Shia militant movements. The beginning of 1979 saw the Iranian Revolution and the establishment of an Islamic Republic in Iran. This event marked the origin of Shia militant movements in West Asia. The invasion of Afghanistan by the Soviet Union took place at the end of the very same year. The invasion galvanised support for a Holy War against the Soviet Union and helped in the linking up of various Sunni militant groups from different parts of the Islamic world. The militant phase of the Shia in West Asia ended by early 1990's. One of the main reasons for this was the inability of the Islamic Republic to win over the Iraqi Shia to accepting their concept of a theocratic government. As mentioned earlier, the Sunni militant movements had become severely weakened by the time of the September 11 attacks because of the brutal crackdown by governments in various Muslim countries. The Iraqi insurgency has given both Sunnis and Shia the opportunity to revive their respective militant movements. Irrespective of the presence of US troops in Iraq, the Islamic Republic has got an occasion to spread its ideology beyond its western borders. Likewise, Sunni militant movements have once again gained avenues to link with each other to fight a holy war in a major West Asian country – Iraq.

Owing to varied historical experiences of Sunnis and the Shia, the religious or theocratic structures of the two sects developed in a way that is very different from each other. The Shia developed an elaborate hierarchical clergy system whereas it was just the opposite in the case of the Sunni. The Sunni clergy did not have as much importance in the religious and cultural unlike their Shia counterparts. This variation also reflected on the way the militant movements of the two developed. As the development of Shia militant movement began with the ascendancy of the Shia clergy to state power in Iran, the fortunes of the movement were tied to the varying influence of the Iranian state. The huge network of Sunni militant movements was initially created with the help of states like Pakistan and Saudi Arabia. But during the course of the war the network itself adopted a non-state character. This meant that the patron states had little control over this phenomenon once it was created irrespective of the attempts made by state agencies like the Pakistani ISI to control it. Also, as a result of the lack of an organised structure among the Sunni clergy, the Sunni militant movements like the Al Qaeda could have an international impact by decentralising and organising itself into small cells.

There is a feeling that the Iraqi insurgency is not bound to have much impact on Sunni Islamist militancy in the wider region as majority of the insurgents are Iraqis. But it must be remembered that the foreign fighters in Afghanistan also numbered much lesser than the local Afghans. But what must be understood is the impact that the Afghan War had on the growth of Sunni militant movements in the wider Islamic world. In the decade that followed the war, countries like Algeria and Egypt were hit by a wave of radical Islamist militancy. After the end of the war in Afghanistan, Sunni militant groups could find a safe haven and organise military training camps in that country as long as it was in civil unrest or ruled by an Islamist fundamentalist regime. Considering the fact that radical Islamist movements had to shift base from Afghanistan as a result of the American invasion, it will be in their interests that Iraq remains unstable. In the present situation in Iraq, it is very difficult for them to create a Sunni Islamist theocracy in that country. This must be one of the reasons why they want to create a civil war like situation in Iraq. Only in such a situation can Sunni militant groups remain active in the country.

CONCLUSION

What are the likely implications of the increasing influence of Sunni and Shia militant movements due to the insurgency in Iraq? We are already witnessing the signs of what is likely to come in the future. As both sects go through a phase of radicalisation and militarisation, a civil war in Iraq between the two sides is highly likely. There are daily reports of dead bodies being found from Iraqi cities as a result of abductions and executions conducted by militant groups. Most of them bear visible signs of torture. We have examples of what has happened to societies in other Muslim countries which have gone through the same process. Religious sectarian groups in Pakistan have wrecked havoc on each other. In the long run, Shia political organisations might have success in bringing about a system of governance in Iraq that is influenced to a certain extend by an Islam from a Shia theocratic perspective. But even this is not going to be easy considering the multi-ethnic and multi-religious nature of Iraqi society. The leverage of Iran is bound to increase in the West Asian region and it can have more say in matters pertaining to Lebanon and Palestine. The status quo in Lebanon is not likely to change much in the near future though with Iraq opening up to Shia political activism, Hezbollah might have a larger theatre to operate.

Regarding the Sunni militant groups, their increasing influence is likely to affect a political setup that has existed since the time nation states were created in that region. The two kinds of political systems that have existed in most of the nations in the region, besides the notable example of Iran, are monarchies and military dictatorships. Though these systems have faced strong criticism for their style of functioning it has to be accepted that they have provided some kind of stability in the region. The Baathist government of Iraq was one of the most stable one in West Asia. By invading and toppling that regime, America has created space for non-state actors like the radical Sunni Islamist movements. Unlike the case of the Shia militant movements, the Sunni militants are likely to have lesser success in establishing a theocracy in any of these countries. But if the insurgency leads to an American withdrawal from Iraq, the appeal of the Sunni militants, who formed the core of the resistance to the occupation, is likely to increase among the Arab public creating new challenges for the governments in the region.

REFERENCES

1. The author is a Research Associate, Center for Air Power Studies (CAPS), New Delhi. He is also a Doctoral Candidate in West Asian Studies Division, School of International Studies, Jawaharlal Nehru University, New Delhi.
2. Ahmed S. Hashim, *Insurgency and Counter-Insurgency in Iraq*(London, Hurst and Company, 2006), p.170.
3. Ibid, pp. 60-65.
4. Rizwan Hussain, *Pakistan and the Emergence of Islamic Militancy in Afghanistan* (Hampshire, England, Ashgate Publishing Ltd., 2005), p. 107.
5. John K. Cooley, *Unholy Wars: Afghanistan, America and International Terrorism* (New Delhi, Penguin Books India Ltd., 2001), p. 19.
6. n. 3, p. 117.
7. Ibid, p. 119.
8. Ibid, p. 96.
9. Ibid, p. 117.
10. K. Santhanam and et al, *Jihadis in Jammu and Kashmir*(New Delhi, Sage Publications, 2003), pp. 94-224.
11. n. 3, p. 122.
12. n. 4, p. 57.
13. Ibid, p. 6.
14. Ibid, p. 225.
15. Ahmed Rashid, *Taliban: The Story of the Afghan Warlords*(London, Pan Macmillan Ltd., 2001), p. 184.
16. Ibid, p. 201.
17. n. 4, p. 229.
18. Ibid, p. 228.
19. Ibid, p. 7.
20. n. 1, p. 233-234.
21. Augustus Richard Norton, "Aspects of Terrorism in Lebanon: The Case of the Shia", *New Outlook*, Vol. 27, No. 1 (1984), p. 20.
22. Shimon Shapira "The Origins of Hizballah", *The Jerusalem Quarterly*, (1988), p. 125.
23. John Bulloch and Harvey Morris, *The Gulf War: Its Origins, History and Consequences*(London: Metheun London Ltd., 1989), p. 222.
24. Ibid, p. 93.

25. n. 1, p. 247.
26. A. Nizar Hamzeh, "Lebanon's Hizbullah: From Islamic Revolution to Parliamentary Accomadation", *Third World Quarterly*, Vol. 14, o. 2 (1993), pp. 323-324.
27. Jonathan Stevenson, "Demilitarising the 'War on Terror', *Survival*, Vol. 48, No. 2 (2006), pp. 37-54.
28. n.1, p.113.
29. n.1, p.262.

8

Geo-politics of Fossil Fuels and Terrorism

Narottam Gaan

The role of oil as a factor in strategic policy and action of the United States harks back to the day the US started embarking on massive industrialization based on fossil fuel technology. What dared president George Bush to mount an attack on Iraq is not even the remotest crying wolf for democracy, world peace, and security to which Iraq's alleged possession of weapons of mass destruction is purported to be a threat. In a world where many nations, including the US, are in possession of lethal weapons of mass destruction, pilloring Iraq for the pur pose stands paradoxical and reveals America's double standard. Behind the shenanigans of Americas' sabre rattling with Security Council resolving in its support was heard the loud concern of the United States for the treasure chest of Iraq's oil on which Saddam Husain sat. The other permanent members of Security Council to have a stake in Iraq's oil.

The implicit understanding found in the whole hearted support of the countries of the UN to Washington- anti Saddam drive or lack of adequate opposition to it is the American assurance that the countries standing in American good stead in stripping Iraq of Saddam Hussain and replacing it with American favoured Iraq National Congress (INC) would get a fair share in the post-Hussain Iraq's oil Caucasus. While giving countenance to this American stance the leader of INC, Ahmed Chalab is reported to have said that he favoured the creation of a US led consortium to develop Iraqi oil fields. This means the American companies will have a big shot at Iraqi oil [1]. The earlier agreements with Iraq reached by many countries like India, Italy, Vietnam, and Algeria to extract oil are already in the back burner due to the UN sanctions.

OIL AS A FACTOR IN STRATEGIC POLICY AND ACTION

The US, which had dominated the oil industry prior to World War II accounting for 60 percent of global production in 1938, ceased to be self-sufficient after 1945[2]. Its interest in Middle East oil increased accordingly. By 1954, the US had acquired a 40 percent share of Iranian oil, which was earlier controlled entirely by the United Kingdom, and soon afterwards a 100 percent share of Saudi Arabian oil. In addition, development rights to Kuwaiti oil. Kuwait had known reserves second only to Saudi Arabia were then shared equally but the US and the UK. The oil deposits of Saudi Arabia, discovered by the US companies before World War II comprised one fourth of the then global reserves, putting the US ahead of any other nation in terms of Middle Eastern oil concessions. In the post-world war II industrialized economies had heavy dependence on intensive use of fossil fuels, for effective functions of energy, transportation, chemical industries and maintenance of military establishment.

The US moves in 1958 to protect its domestic oil industry by imposing import restrictions did stimulate domestic production until about 1970[3]. However, the main exporter nations responded to this denial of free access to their largest market, and to the concomitant decline in the value of their oil, by creating in 1960 the Organization of Petroleum Exporting Countries (OPEC). A combination of collective strength of the OPEC, and growing demand for oil in western countries and

Japan were among the factors that spiralled oil prices after 1970, but the key reason was the rapid increase in demand for oil imports by the US after 1970. Before the fourth Arab-Israeli war of 1973, the delivered price of crude oil in the US and other countries more than doubled in one year. Subsequent imposition of an oil embargo by the OPEC against countries, considered by the organization to be sympathetic towards Israel, plus a major increase in the price of Iranian oil resulted in a fourfold increase in the price of oil during 1973. The cost of a barrel of crude oil rose from US $3 in 1972 to US $12 by 1974[4].

GEOPOLITICAL SIGNIFICANCE OF THE GULF

This oil shock galvanized the US and the West to formulate an aggressive plan to free themselves of the clutches of OPEC. Securing supplies of oil from diverse sources other than the Middle East, increasing domestic production and importing from varied sources, were the essential elements of this strategy. Finding alternative sources of energy gained currency to ensure energy security. About 30 years down the line, the industrialized countries are yet to cut the gordian knot of OPEC- their economies have kept growing on the strength of imported oil. When the US began trying to diversify its oil sourcing and increase domestic production in 1973, it imported about 35 percent of the petroleum it consumed. At present, it imports more than 50 percent. As energy demand soared by 17 percent during the 1990s, domestic oil production went up 2 percent only. And oil accounts for 40 percent of the total energy use in the US today [5]. Though Canada, Mexico and Venezuela each supply the US oil, Saudi Arabia remains its biggest supplier of crude oil. In 1977, OPEC accounted for one third of the total US oil consumption. In the mid- 1980s the figure fell to below 13 percent. And then it started climbing again. At present, OPEC accounts for half of the US oil imports- roughly one fourth of total consumption – and about half of that comes from the Persian Gulf. Middle East accounts for 67% of total oil depots in the world. There is not yet any evidence of the US breaking loose of its heavy dependence on oil imports from the Middle East. On the contrary, the percentage of US oil imports from the Persian Gulf and OPEC cartel is going to increase. Why is this so ?

RESPONSE TO EXTERNAL UPHEAVAL, NOT INTERNAL CHANGES:

By the persistence of focus on unhindered access to external resources in terms of geopolitics, the United States always concentrates its attention on external matters, rather than internal changes as a response to changing international circumstances[6]. Constructing the Gulf solely in terms of arena of geopolitical importance because of its supplies of petroleum ignores the demand side of the energy situation. As Among Hunter Lovins have pointed out repeatedly, the easiest option for US foreign policy in the Gulf is energy efficient automobiles and roof insulation in North American buildings[7]. The United States and Western countries including Japan will continue to remain vulnerable to political developments in the Gulf, if they do not take serious measures to reduce oil consumptions. If the United states wants to be serious about reducing the degree of its political vulnerability to domestic and international upheaval in the Middle East, then it must take appropriate measures to reduce its oil consumptions and rethink its pattern of development and life style[8]. This means rethinking the focus on a pattern of development based on fossil fuels, as the main thrust of its foreign policy. Since this kind of new thinking is not in sight at present in the United States, the dependence of US on oil imports from the Middle East is likely to increase. This is seen in the very deposition of Spencer Abraham, the US Energy Secretary, before a committee of the House of Representatives on March 6, 2002 : " over the last 12 months we have seen energy supply shortages ; natural gas and gasoline price spikes in the Midwest and California ; and terrorist attacks within our borders ... the budget request of $21.9 billion addresses the new security challenges we face after the events of September 11, as well as increased concern regarding our dependence on foreign oil, and the security of our critical energy infrastructure [9].

REJECTION OF KYOTO PROTOCOL: CAVING IN TO FOSSIL FUEL BASED INDUSTRIES

President Bush rejected the Kyoto protocol on the plea that it would hamper its economy. This shows America is not really committed to reduction of emission of co_2 to the atmosphere as agreed to at Kyoto. He was alleged to have acted under the pressure of his close link with big oil, automobile and energy companies in the US. The US based global climate Coalition founded in 1989 with American Petroleum Institute, Shell oil, Exxon, General Motors and more than 40 other corporations as members is the biggest think tank putting pressure on government [10]. About 80 percent of the oil and gas industry's political contributions in the US was to the present ruling party i.e. the Republican Party. To reduce co_2 emissions means rolling up fossil fuel based industries and technologies. Since these oil and gas executives and industries have taken over the reigns of the government today, no evidence of their being wound up is in the offing. Therefore, the US dependence on fossil fuels will continue to increase.

Newsweek stated in its 14 May 2001 issue: "Not since the rise of railroads more than a century ago, has a single industry (energy) placed so many foot soldiers at the top of a new administration"[11].

The National Resource Defense Council, a public interest group in the US said that, the Bush – Cheney energy plan was the culmination of a process that hinged on cosy business connections, secret deals and industry campaign contributions. At best, the energy industry has undue influence on major governmental decisions that will continue to affect all Americans[12].

FISHING IN TROUBLED WATERS OF THE MIDDLE EAST

Thus, the US and Western countries dependent on oil from Middle East have a stake in this region. Whenever a crisis or conflict has arisen in this region, the US has made its presence felt in this region, to prevent it from culminating into a situation that would disrupt oil supplies, impell Arab countries to put oil embargo or raise price of the oil. The 1967 oil embargo by the oil producing countries and 1973-74 oil crisis further reinforced American presence in this region. Its goal has been to protect the US and Western interests. The situation in the Middle East is grave and complex. The conflict between Arab countries plus Palestine and Israel show no signs of ending. There are also the difficult relations between a number of the Arab countries themselves: between Egypt and Libya; between Syria and Iraq ; between Yemen and Saudi Arabia ; and between Iran and Iraq . There are the hostilities within some of the countries based on religious and political differences. The numerous and varied levels of conflict within the Middle East are viewed with favour by the US to maintain the region in a dynamic balance. Indeed it appears that the foreign policy of the US and a number of other states is designed to keep these conflicts alive[13]. Thus, the US at first actively provided Israel and Iran with military and other assistance in as much as these two countries were considered to be stabilizing forces within the region. The US concomitantly provided similar assistance to Saudi Arabia and other Arab regimes.

One of the justifications put forth by the US for its military aid to Middle East was the prevention of former Soviet Union's expansion into the region. The US let it be known that it did not even exclude the possibility of an armed seizure of Middle Eastern oil deposits, if it looked as if the region would fall into the hands of the former USSR.

Following the downfall of the pro-US regime in Iran in 1979, the US took compensatory steps to prepare for an alternative presence in the Middle East region. At the time of the so called Camp David negotiations in 1978 between Egypt, Israel and the US, provisions were made for the US to be able to construct two military bases for Israel in the Negev desert. The presence of the US on the Sinai Peninsula also permitted a continuation of the installation, improvement, and operation of an early warning system in 1980, partly in response to a rapid development force capable of striking the Middle East. Additionally, a number of NATO countries as part of a multilateral United Nations force, quartered military units on the Sinai Peninsula. This enabled these forces to have control over the Suez Canal and the Red Sea region. In 1990, the US attacking Iraq for the latter's attempt at increasing oil prices and occupation of Kuwait, under the aegis of UN in the backdrop of the end of cold war and disintegration of the Soviet Union, further reinforced American presence in Middle East. After dislodging Saddam Hussain from power, aims at deterring any power in the region from ascending to a position of preponderance, that would undermine the interests of the US and its allies. During the Cold War, the spectre of Soviet communism provided America the logic to establish its military presence in the Middle East as a counter to Soviet expansion. But the real intent to bolster up its oil interests lies hidden behind the veil of counterveiling communism. The end of Cold War diminished the ideological pretext to explain American military presence there. The real and vital economic interests have come to the fore, to justify its presence in the guise of a move for nuclear disarmament. To single out Iraq for the purpose is only to show American paradoxical position on world peace and nuclear non-proliferation. Oil in the Middle East has been so vital to American economy that it could not snap its ties with Saudi Arabia, when it found that 15 of the 19 hijackers in the terrorists attack on the US on September 11, 2001 were Saudi citizens helped by Saudi officials [14].

The volatile Middle Eastern conflict situation of today

should be examined from the standpoint of the region's oil deposit and the US and western dependence on its oil. The involvement of US and other western nations in the Middle East conflict has been proportional to their dependence on the Middle Eastern oil.

NUCLEAR ENERGY IS NO ALTERNATIVE AND WORTH ITS EXORBITANT WASTE

What is needed is to reduce emission of $co_{2\ in}$to the atmosphere and to find alternative or renewable sources of energy. The Kyoto protocol, which aimed at cutting co_2 to mitigate climate change, has been used to push nuclear energy for more than two years. The idea is to get legitimacy for nuclear energy, as it does not increase carbon emission. The central problem with atomic power is how to handle millions of tons of waste that it produces and which remains radioacti ve for thousands of years. Thus, expansion of any nuclear power is definitely not worth the high amounts of waste that it would generate. The Kyoto protocol cannot be the pretext for promoting nuclear energy. The nexus of governments and oil cartels is too strong in the US for those making feeble noises about renewable energy. For example, two days before the US Secretary of State Colin Powell was to address the UN summit on sustainable development in August in Johannesburg, negotiators from the US and OPEC blocked proposal by the European Union and Brazil to obtain a set percentage of energy from renewable sources by 2010. This shows the dependence on fossil fuels instead of being lessened is likely to increase and the need for renewable sources of energy gets a short shift.

"One of the ironies at the turn of the century is that in an age when the pace of technological change is almost overwhelming, the world will remain dependent, upto the year 2020 at least, essentially on the same sources of energy – oil, natural gas, coal- that prevailed in the twentieth century "[15].

CENTRAL ASIA: GEOPOLITICAL STRATEGY OF US

This fossil fuel consideration has compelled the US to establish its stranglehold in the Middle East , from where it now eyes Central Asia- the Caspian Sea region which is a cornucopia of oil and natural gas. This region has possibly the third largest oil and natural gas reserves in the world after the Persian Gulf and western Siberia, estimated to be up to 15 percent of the total reserves of the world. The Caspian Sea basin and the three Central Asian Republics- Kazakhstan, Turkmenisten and Uzbekistan – are said to have more than 25 billion barrels of proven oil reserves and at least seven trillion cubic meters of natural gas reserves [16]. Hardly any of this potential has been tapped as yet. It is expected that there are much bigger reserves than have been so far assessed. The Caspian region's introduction to the geopolitics of oil began with the collapse of the Soviet Union in1991. The US vice president Dick Cheney, then the CEO of the oil company Halliburton Corporation told a meeting of oil executions in 1998. "I cannot think of a time when we have had a region emerge as suddenly to become as strategically significant as the Caspian." In the same year, Bill Richardson, the then US Energy Secretary, laid out the US interest in the Caspian region: "This is about America's energy security. It is also about preventing strategic inroads by those who do not share our values. We are trying to move these newly independent countries toward the west. We would like to see them reliant on Western commercial and political interests rather than going another way" [17]. It was very important to the US that both the pipeline map and politics come out right. Several smaller nation-states like Turkmenistan, Uzbekistan, Kazakhstan, Tajikstan and Kirgizstan constitute Central Asia. A handful of former communist party strongmen rule the Caspian region and run them like fiefs. Some of the biggest oil companies of the world court these oligarchs. The region has a former superpower, Russia, to its North. To the east lies China, an emerging superpower. To the east and south lie such politically volatile, strife-torn areas as Chechnya, the Kurd dominated parts of Turkey, Iran and Afghanista . Added to this, the US is directly involved in the region, owing to its business and strategic interests.

OOTW STRATEGY TO TAKE CONTROL OF RESOURCES

As the US Special Forces veteran Stan Goff has pointed out in the Internet magazine "Narconews", the economic might of America rests mostly on its ability to control the prices of oil and gas. In order to keep or gain a hold over fossil fuel resources, Washington has gradually built a strategy based on OOTW (operations other than war) combining secret police raids with military strikes, subversion, disinformation and other kinds of manipulations, now orchestrated by the new Pentagon OSL (Office of Strategic Information), all in the service of what Peter Dale Scott calls, 'parapolitics', in his book *Deep Politics.* Central Asia is now one of the main areas of interest for Washington's strategic planners not only because of its vast energy and mineral deposits, but also on account of its geographic situation between Russia, China, the Indian Subcontinent, and the Persian Gulf [18].

BIN LADEN'S TERRORIST NETWORK: A CREATION AND PROTÉGÉ OF AMERICAN OIL INTERESTS

A review of history of the official and private relations between Saudi Arabia's ruling family, the Bin Laden clan and the American establishment is necessary to show American concerns for oil and gas. The branch of the Bin Laden line that concerns the US, emigrated to what is now, Saudi Arabia in the beginning of the Twentieth Century. The builder of the family's fortune Sheikh Mohammed became very close to King Abdul Aziz, the unifier of the country and was entrusted with the task of building the royal palace. The Al Sauds and the Bin Ladens became further connected through marriage and business associations. The "Bin Laden brothers' for construction and industry", flagship company has extended all over the Muslim world and Europe with a turnover since at least 1996 exceeding $35 billion. The Bin Laden empire, made up of private and diversified secretive companies remains little known and its resources are not clearly separated from the national wealth of the Saudi Kingdom. The assets accessible to the sons and heirs of the late Sheikh Mohamed bin Laden are huge by any standards. It is also worth nothing that, to this date, military facilities in the country including the King Khaled military city and others leased by the US armed forces are maintained and modernized by the Bin Laden companies.

Former President George H Bush visited the Bin Laden corporate headquarters twice in recent years, in his capacity as a paid consultant for the Carlyle Group, a $12 billion company in which the Bin Laden family had an investment until October 2001. Carlyle chaired by Ex-Defense Secretary Frank Carlucci also has on its board James Baker III, Bush's confidant, former Secretary of State, and can presumably rely on the personal support of the US Ambassador to Riyadh, Robert Jordan, Baker's partner in the influential Houston law firm Baker Botts.

These interwoven official and private involvements are to be seen within the context of the oil and gas network which pervades this administration [19]. Many of the top officials came from the energy complex, beginning with the President himself and Vice President Cheney, ex-CEO of Halliburton for which he helped secure large oil infrastructure contracts in Iraq in the last ten years after supervising the destruction of the same country's facilities during Operation Desert Storm as Secretary of Defence. It is not surprising if major economic interests bind this US president and many in his cabinet to the Saudi political and business elite.

In America, some of the Bin Laden brothers have been useful intermediaries between the Saudi Monarchy and influential friends in America, especially the Texas oil and gas oligarchy, including the Bush family. For instance, it is said that

Salem, then the head of the family, played a key role in the secret negotiation between the Reagan team and the Iranian Ayatollahs in 1979, during presidential campaign leading to Republican victory. Salem is believed to have contributed funding to help launch George W Bush's first company, Harken oil, as a gesture of friendship to the present President's father.

BIN LADEN : AN US ACCOMPLICE IN ANTI SOVIET CAMPAIGN

To sum up the review, it may be said that Osama bin Laden was entrusted, when still a young man in the eighties, with the coordination of Arab-American assistance to the anti-Soviet Mujahidden resistance in the Afghanistan. It was a high priority in the agenda of the Reagan administration to weaken and defeat Soviet Union – an "evil empire" in the American eyes. Prince Turki bin Al Faisal to whom he was reporting ensured the coordination with Pakistan's Inter Services Intelligence (ISI). Under the leadership of General Barbar and General Gul, the ISI had taken over from Pakistan's border constabulary, the direction of Islambad's operation against the Kabul communist regime and Soviet occupation troops. Even during the days of General Zia-ul-Haq's military rule, the ISI was closely supervised by the CIA, the DIA (US Defence Intelligence Agency) and other American foreign policy instruments. The very presence of ISI Head General Mahmud Ahmad in Washington DC one week prior to September 11, 2001 and report of his meeting with US top officials including Secretary of State Colin Powell, Deputy Secretary Richard Armitage, under secretary and CIA Director confirms this interwoven network[20]. The *Times of India* report that General Ahmad had ordered wiring of US $ 100,000 to presumed terrorist ring leader Mohammad Atta in New York a few days earlier, has not been denied or disproved hitherto. So the relation between American intelligence, the ISI and Al Qaida and the alleged suicidal attackers, though not officially clarified yet, has a great bearing on American crusade against terrorism. General Masharraf's recruitment while he was an official trainee in the seventies may explain his pro-American attitude and linking Pakistan's defense services with that of the US. This shows Washington at least tacitly supported his rise to power at a critical time and place, where a man of trust was needed. As ex-Pakistani Prime minister Benazir Bhutto put it, "The idea of the Taliban was British , the management was American, the money was Saudi and implementation carried out by Pakistan ". Outlining his carrier, it is said he navigated "like most of the Saudi elites between Wahabi fundamentalist activism and international business, between traditional and modernity he was, and may still be, a very useful intermediary between American strategic policy makers and the rough realities of Middle Eastern conflicts. He and his volunteers "were extensively used wherever Muslim causes called them and Washington's and London's shadowy diplomatic agents wanted them, particularly in the Balkans where they fought the Serbian forces on the side of the Bosnian, Kosovo Albanian and Macedonian Albanian guerillas"[21].

The US government was also aware of Bin Laden's terrorist activities but chose to ignore or even covertly supported them. Even though the Clinton Administration professed to be aware of Qaida's anti American designs, it decided instead to let an admittedly dangerous foe leave aboard a private jet with his family and a part of his team for Pakistan from where they entered Afghanistan. In 1998, similarly a few days after the terrorist attack against the US embassies in Nairobi and Dar-es-Salaam, Secretary of State Madeleine Albright declined Khartum's offer to extradite to the US, two confessed Pakistani members of Bin Laden network. This sequence of events leads one to conclude that the US government did not wish to get rid of Bin Laden or his associates at the time preferring to let him play a part which some of the powers found to be useful.

In the nick of a plot hatched by US in connivance with Pakistan Prime Minister Nawaz Sharife to kill Bin Laden, the sudden coup by General Musharraf led to its cancellation and credence to the view that Pakistan's new ruler acted in chime with the wishes of some American establishment and his ISI colleagues to spare the life of Al Qaida's chief. Lending his full support to Mullah Omar's Taliban faction, Bin Laden could be able to establish a Taliban regime in Afghanistan to the tolerance of the US.

PARAMOUNTCY OF AMERICAN NEED FOR OIL AND NATURAL GAS PLAYS DOWN NABBING TERRORISM

American oil and gas interests penetrated so deeply into US strategic thinking, that it never minded grooming Bin Laden's network despite the probability of the network turning against it, given the US pro-Israel stance in Middle East imbroglio and its much deprecated role in the 1990 Gulf war .The Soviet invasion of Afghanistan in 1979 provided the alibi to the US to strengthen its military presence in the Middle East, blocking the Soviet penetration into the Persian Gulf. Similarly the terrorist attack on the World Trade Centre on September 11 provided US the pretext to enter into Central Asia and Afghanistan. It is said that an important reason behind US action was securing its oil and gas interests. Afghanistan's significance from an energy standpoint stems from its geographical position as a potential transit route for oil and natural gas exports from Central Asia to the Arabian Sea. Since the mid 1990s, it has become the centerpiece of central Asian pipeline politics. The US government's open backing of Unocal company interested in building a pipeline in Afghanistan was an anathema to both Iraq and Russia which were opposed to the Taliban regime. When the Taliban captured Kabul in September 1996, Chris Taggert, Unocal executive told wire agencies that the pipeline project would be easier to implement now that the Taliban had captured Kabul- a statement that Unocal quickly retracted because it implied that Unocal favoured the Taliban. The Taliban was interested in Unocal because it could have brought them US recognition [22]. Two French analysts claim that the Bush administration received the Taliban pipeline connection and that high level talks continued through August 2001 about a month before the September 11 attacks [23].

SEPTEMBER 11 TERRORISTS ATTACK OPENING THE DOOR TO AMERICA STRATEGIC POSITION IN CENTRAL ASIA

With the eclipse of the world war and disintegration of the Soviet Union, the US eyes fell on Central Asia and Afghanistan. With its strategic interests in the Caspian growing, the US became wary of Russia, because the policy makers certainly did not want to see a hegemonic Russia hamstringing its edge into Central Asian natural gas and oil reserves. The Anglo-Saxon alliance in response to 11 September terrorist attack and faced with the new formidable Sanghai Asian pact potentially opposed to its hegemony, acted fast to position itself on the strategic border line between Moscow's and Beijing's spheres of influence, thereby completing the encirclement of Russia and China while increasing the pressure on the Arab world and on India. Setting up extensive military facilities in Asia's heartland supported by a supply line stretched along the old Silk Road all the way to Turkey and NATO bases in the Balkans and in Western Europe was strategically advantageous to the US. This would encircle and replace Russian strategic outposts and also prevent her resurgence as a global power. More importantly, this would secure the US, a sweeping hold over the vast fossil fuel reserves in central Asia edging closer to the Siberian mineral deposits while blocking the likely Chinese commercial and demographic advance towards the Turkestan oil and gas fields.

PIPELINE GEO POLITICS: ANOTHER LUCRE FOR AMERICAN PRESENCE IN AFGHANISTAN

Unlike most major exporters of the world, most Caspian nations are land locked lacking the market, or economy or technology to explore and transport oil and gas over long distance. This is where pipeline politics extends from being economic to geographical. The existing pipeline goes north to Russia, already the repository of the largest gas reserves in the world. A pipeline going west to European markets via the Black sea or the Mediterranean is likely to be too costly and areas such as Chechnya and the Kurdish dominated parts of Turkey do not find favour with the US. A 1755 km. long pipeline from the Azerbaijani capital Baker, to the Turkish port of Ceyhan in the Mediterranean, via Georgia fits well into US foreign policy. Georgia has used US fears of Iran to settle for the western route. But the most economical access to the sea for Caspian oil and gas is through Iran, a political anathema for the US and the west. The second most viable route is through Afghanistan, to Pakistan, and possibly to India. This is the reason explaining the US military attack on Afghanistan to remove the anti US Taliban regime and establish a government that it supports in Kabul. The American stance on resuming bilateral relations between India and Pakistan and not toeing the Indian line against Pakistan, despite the latter's involvement in sponsoring terrorism in India and its alleged nexus with North Korea's nuclear programme, are guided by US geopolitical interest in the Iran-Pakistan-India gas pipe line. Thus, to the US and other multinational companies," the basic question is not about investment in the pipeline, but rather about identifying timely and secures route for getting oil to the market "[24].

NOT CLASH OF CIVILIZATIONS, BUT CLASH OF ECONOMIC INTERESTS

The proxy war launched against the Soviet army in Afghanistan at the behest of the US during the 1980s presented Osama bin Laden a fertile field for the realisation of his un-Islamic vision i.e. Islamic terrorism. It is not an exaggeration to say that he is " an illegitimate product of the US policy during the cold war "[25]. He was fully radicalized during the Jehad against the Soviet army in Afghanistan. Since then he li ved almost in that country training religious fighters drawn from numerous Muslim countries. The Taliban which was installed by the US to decimate Siviet presence there turned against the US. After the defeat of Soviet Union, Bin Laden considers the US the next enemy to the Islamic world. Similarly with the demise of Soviet Union, the United states considers Islamic terrorism represented by Osama bin Laden as the greatest threats to its geopolitical interests in Persian Gulf and the Central Asian region. This is not what Samuel P. Huntington in his article 'The clash of civilization' said that the West is already at war with Islam [27].The threat to American interests could not be laid at the Kremlin's door or at the door of Iraq. The real threat, as perceived by America, is that the region might take control of its own destiny including its own resources. So it has to support oppressive states, like Saudi Arabia and others to make sure that they guarantee that profits from oil flow to the people who deserve it - rich western energy corporations, or the US Treasury Department or Bechtel Construction, and so on. Saudi Arabia has been a client of the United States since its origin. The reason is that it plays the right role to ensure that the wealth of the region goes, to not the people in the slums of Cairo, but people in executive suites in New York[28].

COMBATING TERRORISM AND FOSSILFUEL DEPENDENCE : AMERICA IN LABYRINTHINE MAZE

The United States' sole concern for oil and natural gas in Middle East and Central Asia for and the concomitant pipeline through Afghanistan lubricated the machinery of Islamic terrorism to be used against the former Soviet Union. With the achievement of that what, is perceived as a menace to the US is the very turning back of the wheels of the terrorism towards the US- the mentor, sustainer and creator of Islamic terrorism in the Persian Gulf. The might of the American economy based on fossil fuels of Middle East and Central Asia has put it in the labyrinthine maze of terrorism from which the US at present finds not even a way out. Terming its stance against Islamic terrorism as global terrorism and courting the help of all countries of the world may not go a long way in helping US combat Islamic terrorism, in view of the very fact that, the US' dependence on oil of Persian Gulf and Central Asia is not going to diminish rather increase in future.

GLOBALIZING AMERICAN SCRIPT: THE THREAT TO AMERICAN INTEREST IS A THREAT TO THE WORLD

European politics became international when US joined it and defined the global interest in terms of its own geopolitical interests and that of its allies and in terms of their sovereign right to resources and raw materials found in abundance in the South even at the exercise of that right to use military interventions. The world order whether it was during cold war or during the post cold war period, was defined in American idioms. The prevailing economic and political order has been spelt out by America in its own script and language. The only constancy in American foreign policy is universalisation of its domestic imperative i.e. production of wealth, inordinate consumption and profligate life style. Imitating the US pattern of development and economic structure by most of the world has led to the US unilinear occupation of space and time. That means western pattern of development being ubiquitously followed is universal and there is no alternative because all the nations of the world irrespective of their divergent culture, civilization and societies have with a religious reverence dedicated themselves to the western pattern of development, as eternal for all time to come. So, the American growing economy and pattern of development based on fossil fuels is bound to be dependent on oil and natural gas found in Middle East and Central Asia. America combating terrorism is likely to be constrained by this very fact of its being dependent on the Middle East and Central Asia for oil. Though the Middle Eastern countries and Central Asian states have joined hands with US for economic reasons, in their heart of hearts they are with the Islamic cause advocated by Laden and very much averse to American presence in Middle East [29]. Yossef Bodansky stated, "he is probably the most popular individual in the Muslim world...he is the most lucid and eloquent spokesman of all grievances Muslims have against the west, justified and unjustified [30]. Pakistan sponsored terrorism could not be castigated as a threat to global peace and security in spite of India's frequent appeal to the world. But when the terrorist attack on the World Trade Centre, the US termed these as threats to the entire globe. Threats to American interests were considered as threats to entire humanity. America does not want to remain vulnerable to any domestic upheaval in Middle East resulting in fluctuation in oil price or disruption in production and tanker traffic to the US and its Western allies. The severance of its overwhelming dependence on oil and fossil fuels would mean finding alternative sources of energy or heralding a new thinking in the people towards a different pattern of life, surely not based on profligacy but on modesty and a different vision of life. The question that remains crucial to the American people, are they ready to live the life of a Bangladeshi? Or are they willing to pursue a life pattern that will deprive their future generation of their very right to live on this earth? Mindless industrialization based on fossil fuels and inordinate and exorbitant consumption would not in any way diminish the US dependence on Middle East and Central Asia for oil and natural gas. If the rejection of Kyoto protocol, pressurized by coal, automobile and oil companies of America is any indication, then finding alternative renewable sources of energy and educating the people about the need for envisioning new patterns of development, is not very much on the cards.

CONCLUSION

So far as oil and fossil fuels remain crucial to American pattern of development and luxurious life style of their people, the crusade against terrorism may be a long drawn battle. The global oil consumption is expected to rise from 77 million barrels in 2020- an increase of 43 percent. If these estimates prove accurate, the world will consume approximately 670 billion barrels of oil between now and 2020, or about two thirds of world's known petroleum reserves [31]. In such a situation of burgeoning demand for oil and natural gas, the United States to reduce its vulnerability to such a crisis aims at maintaining its domination over oil resources of the Gulf region and extending its military penetration into the heart of Central Asia for natural gas. So far as fossil fuels remain peremptorily crucial to American economy, taking up the cudgels against terrorism by US will assume the genre of a militant rhetoric in its foreign policy and aim at keeping the cauldron of geopolitics burning in the Gulf and Central Asia so as to maintain a manipulative balance among the warring factions by its heavy military presence in this region. As it is determined to see that terrorism does not vitiate in any way the orchestration of its script of world order, externalization of terrorist threats to its internal economic structure in the name of global threats, remain at present the cornerstome of its strategy. The US claimed in the post cold war world, while giving shape to its fight against terrorism, to have toed the world on its lines "Twice before in this century, the United States and her allies triumphed in the global struggle. Twice before, we earned the right to be arbiter of a post war world. This is our third chance" [32]. The Unites States may have succeeded in installing an anti-Taliban regime in Afghanistan, but its crusade against global terrorism stands flickered in the face of its glowing eyes hovering lucratively on the bonaza of oil and natural gas deposits of these regions.

As seen above, there has been no major change in the objectives of American foreign policy. What has been seen only a change in the pretext. After the collapse of the Soviet Union, the pretext of communism is gone. A new pretext of combating the plague of global terrorism and promotion of nuclear non-proliferation is adduced as a justification for its military build up in the Middle East and Central Asia, which in reality, is only a cover up for its fossil fuel based economy.

REFERENCES

1. *Down To Earth*, vol. II, no. II, October 31, 2002 p.25.
2. L.Turner, Oil Companies in the International System, 3rd edition, (London: George Allen and Unwin, 1983) PP 41-49.
3. Erik Solem and Antony F. G. Scanlan, "Oil and natural gas factors in strategic policy and action : a long term view", in Arthur H. Westing ed., Global Resources and International Conflict (Oxford, New York: Oxford University Press, 1986), P-42.
4. M. V. Champness and G. I. Jenkins, Oil tanker data book (Amsterdam: Elsevier,1985), p.347 : see also D. Steel, "Oil in D. Ezra, ed., Energy debate (London : Ernest Benn, 1983) PP.18-21.
5. *Down To Earth*, 31 October 2002, p.26.
6. Simon Dalby, "Threats from the South? Geopolitics, Equity, and Environmental Security" in Daniel H. Deudney and Richard A. Matthew, ed., Contested Ground (Albany : State University of New York Press, 1999), p.164.
7. Amory Lovins and L. Hunter Lovins, "Brittle Power:Energy Strategy for National Security" (Andover, Mass. : Brick House, 1982).
8. B. R. Inman, J. S. Nye, W. J. Perry, and R. K. Smith, "Lessons from the Gulf war", *The Washington Quarterly*, vol.15, no.I, 1992, PP.67-8.
9. "Down to Earth", 31 October 2002, p.27.
10. David L. Levy and Daniel Egan, "Capital Contents:National and Transnational Channels of Corporate Influence on the Climate Change Negotiations ", *Politics and Society*, Vol.26, no.3, September 1998, PP. 337-61.
11. Newsweek, 14 May 2001.
12. "Down to Earth", October 31, 2002, p.28.
13. Alexander A. Arbatov, "Oil as a factor in strategic policy and action : past and present", in Arthur H. Westing, op. cit., p.29.
14. "Down to Earth ", 31 October 2002, PP.26-27.
15. "The Geopolitics of energy into the 21st Century", Report of the Centre for Strategic and International Studies, February 15,2001.
16. C. Raja Mohan, "Geo-politics and Energy Security ", *Strategic Analysis*, December 1996, p.1271.
17. "Down to Earth ", October 31, 2002, p.31.
18. Come Carpentier De Goudon, "September 11 Events and the resulting Global situations ", *World Affairs*, Vol.6 no.2, April – June 2002, p.106.
19. Ibid, p.110.

20. Ibid, p.112.
21. Ibid, PP.112-13.
22. Ahmed Rashid, Taliban: Islam, Oil and the New Great Game in Central Asia, *Down to Earth*, 31 October 2002, p.32.
23. Jean Charles Brisard and Guillaume Dasique, "Osama bin Laden : The Hidden Truth", quoted in *Down to Earth*, 31 October 2002, p.33
24. Howard Chase, Director of International Affairs for BP AMOCO, Washington, quoted in Anuradha M. Chenoy, "11 September 2001 and After: The Russian and Central Asian Response ", *India Quarterly*, vol.LVIII, no.4, Octo-Dec 2001, p.156.
25. Siddharth Varadarajan , "Osama obsession is Laden with Danger ", *The Times of India*, 22 October 1999.
26. Quoted in Fouad Ajami, "The Sentry's Solitude",, *Foreign Affairs*, November / December 2001, P.7
27. Samuel P. Huntington, "The Clash of civilization?" *Foreign Affairs*, summer 1993, p.32.
28. Noam Chomsky, "Clash of Civilizations?", *Seminar*, January 2002, p.101.
29. L. K. Choudhary, "The United States and Terrorism: Post September 11, 2001 Syndrome", *India Quarterly*, vol.LVIII, no.4, October-December 2001, p.14.
30. Yossef Bodansky, "Bin Laden: The Man who Declared war on America" , quoted in *The Times of India*, 14 September 2001.
31. Michael T. Klare, "The New Geography of Conflict", *Foreign Affairs*, May-June 2001, p.56.
32. Quoted in Satish Kumar, "The Post-cold war International system: An Indian perspective ", *Strategic Analysis*, September 1997, p.826.

9

WESTERN APPROACH TO INTERNATIONAL TERRORISM

Saroj Kumar Rath

First, the ecstasy, and then the agony. It could be that the zeal to gain lone superpower status in the world during the cold war era, that made terrorists and terrorism attractive for the US, to use them as a Trojan horse for intervention in the affairs of other states. But at what point did the dalliance turn dangerous? It is this perilous journey of the US, whose liaison with terrorist outfits, which paved the way to witness a deadly date with destiny. The impact has been widespread and had not remained with in the confinement of New York, Washington and Pennsylvania. The effect of the terrorist attacks exceeded all calculations and imaginations.

Modern terrorism, it is said, originated in the bleak ghettos of Beirut and Belfast. Since then, the phenomenon has come a long way. Suicide to faith chanting, became the major strategic weapon of terrorists. The Tamil Tigers in India and Sri Lanka equipped with cyanide capsules or the Bible-flaunting Timothy Mc Vaigh in Oklahoma City have taken routes less known in the past. Moreover, terror has become the short cut to fame for anyone with a cause and a grievance. The form of terrorism propagated by bin Laden is beyond negotiation, and has denied any kind of solution, even through genuine means.

On September 11, the Muslim world was precariously

poised. The vast majority of decent, law-abiding Muslims throughout the world shared New York's sorrow. But there was a determined minority that walked with an extra bounce. For them, it was Islam's finest hour. There were an equally significant number of fence sitters who looked admiringly at bin Laden's audacity even while dismissing the attack on America as a monumental Jewish conspiracy. For bin Laden, September 11 had a dual significance. It aimed at intimidating the US into an isolationist foreign policy and withdrawing from its commitments in West Asia. Simultaneously, it was targeted at the soul of Islam – to set the pace of a mighty resurgence of militant faith[1].

Once upon a time, the power of the suicide bomber was confined to conflict-ridden parts of the world – Israel, Lebanon, Sri Lanka and perhaps Jammu and Kashmir in India. This precedent no longer remained the same after 9/11, when bin Laden injected a new dimension into the lives of every citizen of world – 'fear'. Suddenly, nothing seemed safe. The dreary security drill people had to endure at airports and other public places no longer seemed an unnecessary irritant. It becomes an indispensable part for safety. For the civilized world, this self-destructive monstrosity bred an unreal climate of fear born out of utter helplessness. As policing became more rigid and intrusive– racial profiling of airline passengers and vetting of tenants, students and employees – civil libertarians raised an outcry. In the normal world, their protests would have been justified[2]. But not after 9/11.

By default, bin Laden aroused the resolve of the US in particular and the western world in general to deal with terrorism in a somewhat new way. The American preparation to deal comprehensively with terrorism covers a larger plan. Such preparation was unparalleled in history. This included diplomatic, military, financial, investigative, homeland and humanitarian steps, in accordance with need and necessity. Due steps were taken to neutralize the economic loss, and measures were taken to regain the momentum of economic growth, at least at the rate that prevailed pre-9/11. The 'Bush Doctrine' has been gradually extended since September 11 to concerned areas and action has been directed at potential area of terrorist activity. The demonstration of US military muscle to counter any upcoming subversive attack was a step in the promised direction by the US. The voice of intellectuals like Noam Chomsky and Michael Perenty seems irrelevant at the security level.

SEPTEMBER 11 AND NEW TERRORISM

More than an end to war;
We want an end to the,
Beginning of all wars.

—*Franklin D. Roosevelt*

History book only shows statistics. Invariably they tell only an incomplete tale. There is no dearth of statistics on terrorism in history books. It seems that terrorism began from the idea "you can't beat brain" once narrated by John F. Kennedy. It is almost impossible on the part of a government or an administration to satisfy every individual's desire in a civilizational journey. At this point man starts searching to find out an outlet to ventilate his suppressed grievances. Terror and hence terrorism has become the short cut to fame for anyone with a cause and a grievance. Terrorism has served its purpose by earning publicity for the perpetrators, creating martyrs for the cause and generating emotive mythologies[3].

In a world polarized along rival power blocs and superpowers, the definition of terrorism posed enormous problems. Terrorist to one man could be freedom fighter to another. Catholicism being in short supply in the world, the end was always seen to be justifying the means. Thus, the IRA that pulled off a spectacular bombing in Brighton in 1984, nearly killing a British Prime Minister, drew its cadres from Londonderry and its sponsors from New York. The LTTE picked up its cannon fodder from Jaffna but its support network extended to Tamil expatriates in Europe and North America. The Palestinian National Charter drafted on July 1-17, 1968 at the Palestine National Council advocated the adequate use of violence and terrorism to meet their demands. The Euskatita ta Askatasuna (ETA) committed to its aim to liberate the Basque region from Spain since 1959. Under the menacing cloud of terrorism, the United Nation sensed its responsibility and drew a cautious definition of terrorism to procure requisite response against those comes under this definition.

"Terrorism is an anxiety-inspiring method of repeated violent action, employed by (semi-) clandestine individual, group or state actors, for idiosyncratic, criminal or political reasons, whereby - in contrast to assassination - the direct targets of violence are not the main targets. The immediate human victims of violence are generally chosen randomly (targets of opportunity) or selectively (representative or symbolic targets) from a target population, and serve as message generators. Threat- and violence-based communication processes between terrorist (organization), (imperilled) victims, and main targets are used to manipulate the main target (audience(s)), turning it into a target of terror, a target of demands, or a target of attention, depending on whether intimidation, coercion or propaganda is primarily sought"[4].

Organization like the Red Army Faction eventually became one of the Europe's most feared terrorist organizations. Its ideology was an obscure mix of Marxism and Maoism, with a commitment to armed struggle as such. The group was organized into hardcore cadres, which carried out terrorist attacks with the aid of a network of supporters who provided logistic and propaganda support. The RAF survived into the mid-nineties despite numerous arrests of top leaders over the years[5].

At the height of its notoriety in the 1970s, the Red Army Faction was seen as Europe's most deadly urban terror group.

Its small and disciplined cells make it a streamlined and effective organization. It attacked not just Germany's rich and powerful, but also US military installations which it saw as emblems of American imperialism. The RAF apparently also harbored ambitious plans of achieving deadlier attacks through use of biological weapons.

In 1984, a safe house belonging to the group was reportedly uncovered in Paris, France. Inside the safe house, an improvised laboratory was found, containing flasks of deadly botulism toxin. Although they apparently never had more than 20 – 40 hardcore members, the RAF is thought to have had several hundred supporters. The group was self-sustaining, but during the Baadar-Meinhof period, they received support from Middle Eastern terrorists. East Germany gave logistical support, sanctuary, and training during the 1980s. In 1997, German authorities observed that the Red Army Faction was no longer a serious terrorist threat. Most of its leaders were dead or in jail, while many of the group's onetime sympathizers had become disillusioned with its brutal methods. In April 1998, the RAF announced that it was disbanding. It sent an eight-page typewritten statement to Reuters news agency, which ended with the guerrillas' emblem of five-pointed star, a stylized machine pistol and the letters RAF. The statement said: "Today we are ending this project. The urban guerrilla group in the form of the RAF is now history.[6] "

The most powerful advocate of guerilla warfare was Ernest "Che" Guevara. He was a Latin American revolutionary and guerilla war theorist. Born in Argentina, and trained as a medical doctor, he became politically active during Peron's dictatorship of that country. In 1953, he went to Guatemala to serve in Jacobo Arbenz Guzman's short-lived reign. After Guzman's overthrow in 1954, Che met Fidel Castro and in 1956 he served in Castro's army providing important strategic leadership until the taking of Havana by Castro's forces on New Year's Day, 1959[7] . After the communist takeover of Cuba, Che served in several capacities, including that of Minister of Industry (1961-1965). In 1965 he left Cuba and went underground to train guerilla forces in Bolivia. In October 1967, Bolivian government forces captured Che and his guerilla forces near Santa Cruz. Che was executed shortly after his capture[8].

The terrorism and terrorist organizations in different parts of the world had been a serious threat and concern for the civil society. The kind of terrorism displayed by the terrorists on September11 requires the accuracy of a shooter striking a rupee coin 10 KM away. Such precision and reliability was not normally associated with terrorist's design earlier. This time that had happened and the consequences are beyond the calculation of the pundits'.

OLD AND NEW TERRORISM- CHARACTERISTICS

Evil has an uncanny habit of blending with fantasy and being garnished with bravado. Adolf Hitler was unquestionably the most evil product of the previous century. His fantastic belief in the Master Race-, which was complemented by the hateful anti-Semitism –was clouded in the boast of a Thousand-Year Reich. "Enjoy The War", his propaganda chief Josef Goebbels asked fellow Germans, and also said "Peace Will Be Terrible[9]."

Osama bin Laden is this century's first inheritor of the mantle of "The New Terrorism." He aroused the subliminal passions of his chosen flock with the dream of an Islamic Utopia – a state of being that would replicate the medievalism of 7th Century Arabia. His instrument of salvation was Jihad, a doctrine of murder as obnoxious as Nazi "Final Solution." He combined dogmatic certitude with total ruthlessness, without even a touch of remorse.

By their sheer scale, the September 11 attacks drew a bright divide between the "New Terrorism" practice by Osama bin Laden and his al-Qaeda and the "Old Terrorism" exemplified by groups like the Palestine Liberation Organization (PLO), the Provincial Irish Republic Army (IRA), Euskadita

Askatasuna (ETA), and the Liberation Tigers of Tamil Eelam (LTTE). Older groups like the PLO or the IRA are generally constrained by nationalist or irredentist goals – a Palestinian state, a United Ireland – that are negotiable. They present their demand clearly, and generally take direct responsibility for their acts in order to make it clear to their adversaries that the bloodletting will stop when those demands are met. What motivates their violence is the desire to obtain a particular political objective and want only to express their wrath and cripple their enemy[10] .

Old terrorism tended to be an outgrowth of national liberation struggles, or of anti-capitalist movements, and frequently had state backing. It was therefore often possible to observe the ideological steps through which the players passed in their conversion from political activism to terrorism. Generally, this transformation would include several of the following elements; opposition to the state or to perceived injustice, expressed through domestic means, a lack of response, or an inappropriate response by authority; extreme but not necessarily violent opposition to that authority; acts of terrorism against a specific target seen as a symbol of that authority[11] .

During the 1990s, old style terrorist groups atrophied due to withdrawal of the cold war's ideological impetus, were compromised when they uncovered records of complicit communist regimes exposed their operations, or were tamed in peace processes. The terrorism of the 1990s and the beginning of the new millennium include some elements of the aforementioned pre-1990s terrorism, but it is also characterized by new ones.

Two types of terrorism now dominate above all others: "new" far right terrorism and religious terrorism. Unlike the traditional far right, the new far right is often not distinguished by membership in visible and well-organized groups with hierarchical structures, the most overt features of which are public manifestations, such as marching in uniform or rioting against immigrants, and an open adherent to Nazi or Fascist ideology. The new ideology stems almost completely from the American far right and is influenced by concepts such as "leaderless resistance" and "Lone-wolf" or "individual" act of terrorism. The ideological mentors are not Hitler and Mussolini, or other far right ideologues of the 1930s and 1940s, but American white supremacist William Pierce, Louis Beam and the Saudi billionaire Osama bin Laden[12].

The new terrorism tends to adopt a networked, less hierarchical fork. Both the anti-capitalist and the national liberation terrorist groups of the 1970s and 1980s, mostly had hierarchical forms and chains of command. Some even had identified operational leaders e.g., Andreas Baader and Ulrike Meinhof of the German extreme left Red Army Fraction; Ahmad Jibril of the Popular Front for the Liberation of Palestine – General Command; Abimael Guzman, of the Perucial Sindero Luminoso.

On the other hand the new terrorists mostly propounded by bin Laden, utilize the leaderless resistance concept, where all individuals operate independently of each other, and never report to a central headquarters or single leader for directional instruction.....participants in a program of leaderless resistance through Phantom Cell[13] or individual action, must know exactly what they are doing and exactly how to do it ....all members of Phantom Cells or individuals, will tend to react to objective events in the same way through usual tactics of resistance. Organs of information distribution, such as newspapers, leaflets, etc which is widely available to all, keep each person informed of events allowing for a planned response that will even out many variations. No one needs to issue an order to anyone[14].

The new terrorism assisted by the growing use of Information and Communication Technology (ICT's). ICT's enable extremists to communicate covertly and to bridge distances, and the new terrorism was the first to understand its potential. The use of ICT's has been one of the major reasons the militia movement expanded so rapidly. The vast size of America represented no communication problem for the new medium, which means that an activist in a remote state in the pacific North West could be as involved in the movement as one on East Coast or Deep South[15].

The new terrorist frequently does not claim responsibility for the action and may even deny it. It is the act that is important and not the claim to it, exemplified by the various bombings and attacks. The new terrorism, especially religiously impelled terrorism, does not confine itself to any boundaries and possessed a terrifying lethality. When terrorism was backed by states, there were limits to the extent to which, the perpetrator would go. These inhibitions no longer apply. Frequently the old terrorism sought out representative targets and made its point by one or two surgical strikes. The new terrorism tends to go for the highest possible body count, such as the Oklahoma City bombing, 1995, US Embassy bombing in Kenya, 1998, and September 11attacks on WTC and Pentagon.

TERRORISM'S HEIGHTENED PROFILE

On the one hand, 9/11 has re-awakened dormant or demoralized terrorist groups and potential recruits to the considerable power of showcasing grievances by lethally attacking unsuspecting civilian targets. Bin Laden himself, of course, is not primarily motivated by grievances pressed by other terrorists or terrorist sponsors. The escalation of the Israeli-Palestinian conflict would seem a natural source of his inspiration, yet the September 11 operation was apparently planned, and other al-Qaeda operations committed, during hopeful phases of the Oslo process[16].

Nevertheless, in the videotapes released shortly after the United States and the United Kingdom began their assault against Afghanistan of 7th October, he and his lieutenants cited the Israeli-Palestinian conflict and US enforcement of sanctions and the no-fly zones against Iraq as reasons for the attacks, and threw in implicit Western backing for Hindus against Muslims in Kashmir for good measure. Presumably the idea was to rally popular Islamic support, incite more localized Arab terrorist operations and weakens the US coalition with moderate Muslim states. To an extent, the gambit worked. Popular protest increased throughout the Islamic World, notably in Pakistan, Palestine and Indonesia[17].

On the other hand, September 11, also has shown most of the world's non-Muslims and Muslims alike, the cruelty and danger that terrorists pose and mobilized wider public opinion against .. Americans, who have been suggestible about whom they deem 'terrorists' as opposed to 'freedom fighters', are now prepared to support substantial curtailments of civil liberties to decrease their vulnerability. Irish-Americans- traditionally a major source of financial, political and occasionally operational support for anti-British groups in Northern Ireland are abandoning their wink-and-nod tolerance of the IRA to disarm, and thus break the impasse in the Northern Irish peace process. In the United Kingdom, an October 2001 Gallup Poll indicated that 80% of the British residents consider the IRA and bin Laden common enemies, and two-third believe the early release of IRA prisoners to seal the Good Friday Agreement, which was signed in April 1998 and has not been fully implemented due to the IRA's refusal to disarm, was a mistake[18].

While this groundswell of disgust for all forms of terrorism is salutary, its significance is tempered by the fact that the small minority of radical Muslims attracted to Al-Qaeda and its ideas still potentially number in the millions. Further, the hallmark of terrorists is that they need only a relatively small core of support for sustenance, and may care little about broader public opinion. Indeed, in most cases, if terrorists enjoyed anything approaching a majority or plurality following, they would have no political need for terrorism. Thus, their very unpopularity can fuel their resolve.

THE POSSIBILITY OF CROSS-FERTILIZATION

Al-Qaeda is far more dangerous to the United States in particular and strategic stability in general, than is the IRA, ETA or even Hamas. Yet it would be a grave mistake to assume that they and al-Qaeda are completely different animals. While these other groups have purposefully been more constrained than al-Qaeda in their violence, and their intent is to persuade their targets rather than to destroy them, the two classes of terrorist do share a methodology: to cow public support for legitimate government objectives by instilling fear in the civilian. The epochal events of September 11 may have hardened the distinctions between new and old terrorists could cross-fertilize.

Al-Qaeda's aims diverge thoroughly and qualitatively from the IRA's and those of most other 'old' terrorist groups. They would not make a ready fit. At the same time, if most terrorist remain fanatically dedicated, they will also forge highly pragmatic and flexible alliances to attain the results they seek. That a potentially frustrated ETA, say, would accept attenuated al-Qaeda assistance – for example, weapons, training or financial assistance rather than actual oversight – should not rule out[19] .

From al-Qaeda's perspective, existing secrete alliances with groups such as Egyptian Islamic Jihad and alumni of Algeria's Armed Islamic Group suggest that the need for new non-Muslim partners is not acute. Nevertheless, backing outfits as divergent as Hamaas and the IRA could be attractive as a means of diverting resources from the heightened international law-enforcement and intelligence effort to thwart al-Qaeda, as well as to help with the work of disrupting and economically impairing western societies. Alternatively, with a mass casualty keynote now emphatically struck, al-Qaeda's operations choose to bide its time until the next major attack with a protracted low-technology terrorist campaign on American soil. This would serve to distract law-enforcement efforts, from planned mass-casualty attacks that serve bin Laden's eschatological vision to corroding US public support for those efforts. For these purposes, groups like Hamas, the IRA, ETA and the Tamil Tigers would make excellent accessories or tutors, and there are quite plausible circumstances in which some of them could be inclined to contract with other groups.

APPLYING DISTINCTIONS

Americans have sometimes accused Europeans of being 'soft on terrorism.' After September 11, it became clear that this accusation was true with respect to the emergence of new terrorism. There are some understandable reasons. European countries have faced mainly ethno-nationalist and left-wing terrorism over the past 30 years. Thus, countries such as the United Kingdom and Spain have had to concentrate anti-terrorist efforts on the more traditional type of terrorist threat, and over the past decade, Europe has perceived the threat from al-Qaeda and related groups as modest, in contrast to the US assessment[20]. As a result, al-Qaeda appears to have found European countries more useful as recruitment and planning points than as direct targets. Existing statutory and operational counter-terrorism resources set-up to deal with old terrorist threats, give European governments a head start in helping to establish an international coalition against terrorism and a transnational law-enforcement and intelligence network to contend with al-Qaeda. Intelligence in response to the September 11 attacks will diminish the operational capabilities of terrorist groups. To liberate those resources for primary application to al-Qaeda, however, political engagement remains a useful tool of counter terrorism for controlling old-style groups. Governments ought to stay engaged with groups that are capable of being restrained.

Contrary to some of the soaring post-traumatic rhetoric, September11 has in fact increased the need to segregate groups that respond to political suasion from those that do not. It will be easier for, Britain- which along with Germany, seems to be a key locale for bin Laden's recruiting and planning – to focus its attention on al-Qaeda, if the IRA is neutralized through a political process. Yet diplomatic resources are also limited and it is not enough to distinguish terrorist groups merely in terms of old and new, political or expressive, apocalyptic or constrained. Old terrorist groups must be further differentiated according to their willingness- as a function of negotiation prospects, financial backing and diplomatic support – to participate in serious political dialogue. Those that are willing will be less likely to impede the global effort against international terrorism (whether by diverting resources through ongoing terrorist operations of establishing some form of synergy with al-Qaeda), provided interested outside powers exploit or create opportunities to bring them to the negotiating table.

A number of questions bear on the likelihood of a terrorist group's linking-up with al-Qaeda. First, are the group's grievances related to Islam? Second, are the prospects of a political solution to its grievances remote? Third, are its indigenous sources of political, financial or other support scarce? Fourth, does the old terrorist group operate in a country or region in which an active al-Qaeda presence has been uncovered? Affirmative answer would indicate a degree of susceptibility on the part of a given terrorist group to al-Qaeda influence and co-optation.

Abu Sayyaf, in the Philippines, would qualify on most of the criteria, and in fact substantial links between the group and al-Qaeda have been established. The radical Muslim make up of Islamic jihad, its military weakness against a US-backed Israel and its political marginalization with in the Palestinian territories may make it ripe for al-Qaeda assistance[21] . Hamas, in contrast, has considerable political support among Palestinians and from outside sponsors, and appears to be more responsive to political developments than the other Palestinian groups, though it does share some ideological roots with al-Qaeda[22] . Hezbollah is supported by Iran, which is hostile to bin Laden, and by Syria, and has recently enjoyed considerable success as a legitimate political party in Lebanon. Hezbollah therefore might not be apt to tilt al-Qaeda's way. Given the fierce mutual hostility between Hindus and Muslims, the Tamil Tigers are broadly unsusceptible to al-Qaeda influence. Chechen rebels are Muslim and have established al-Qaeda links, but many Chechens are uncomfortable with the Islamic law that the rebels have imposed. In the hope that this discomfort could spell political flexibility, the Russian government opened negotiations without preconditions in November 2001[23] .

Among the European terrorist groups, ETA might be moderately susceptible. Although it has nothing to do with Islam, ETA has dismal political prospects and increasingly concern to its indigenous and external support which have been squeezed. At least one al-Qaeda cell is known to have been operating in Spain. Conversely the National Liberation Army (NLA) in Macedonia, while predominantly Muslim in composition does not have a fundamentalist bent, has relatively good political prospects, has partially disarmed and enjoys strong outside support from Diaspora in Europe and the United States. But since the fall of Milosovic, it has become less likely that the Kosovo Liberation Army (KLA), which has close ties with NLA, would attain its goal of independence in the near term. There is also evidence of al-Qaeda's interest in the Balkans as a lucrative drug-trafficking route and fertile ground for spreading the puritanical Wahabi brand of Islam that bin Laden practices. The region is a target of opportunity on account of the deployed American forces there. The KLA therefore merits close attention. The IRA constitutes only a low level threat. The events of September 11 have diminished support among Irish Diaspora in the United States as three Libyans and one Algerian suspected of having ties to al-Qaeda were arrested (but soon released) in Dublin in October 2001. But the chances that the Good Friday Agreement will survive tilts towards the extremes of both pro-British unionism and pro-Irish nationalism have improved since the IRA rendered unusual weapons stored in one or two dumps in October 2001. The group has a large existing arsenal and proven means of generating funds with in Ireland[24].

Burgeoning world opinion against terrorism since September 11 has rendered more credible, threats by governments to old terrorist groups that further terrorist activity. Consequently, these governments, on balance, enjoy greater political leverage over old terrorist groups. Peace processes and other less intensive political instruments, such as the State Department's list of foreign terrorist's organizations, are appropriate vehicles for applying this leverage. Prior to the September 11 attacks, US diplomatic support appeared not only important to the IRA's political strategy for extracting concessions from unionists and the British government, but also seemed to embolden the IRA to commit or threaten violence when politics moved too slowly to suit it.

COALITION CONSIDERATIONS ON COUNTER-NEW TERRORISM

Targeting state sponsors of terrorism, as opposed to the terrorist groups themselves, poses a different set of policy challenges. The military campaign to end state support for al-Qaeda began in October 2001 against the Taliban – the fundamentalist Muslim group that controlled most of Afghanistan, harbored bin Laden and other al-Qaeda commanders, and permitted al-Qaeda training camps to operate in Afghanistan. In prosecuting the wider 'war' on terrorism, Deputy Secretary of Defense Paul Wolfowitz has suggested that the United States should hit Iraq as well as Afghanistan[25].

Yet there are countervailing diplomatic imperatives for waging a campaign against a global terrorist network that claims to draw legitimacy from religious principles. Chief among them is the need to rally a Muslim government leaders against al-Qaeda terrorists. Most American officials – some of them considered 'unilateralist', recognized on September 11, that accomplissement of this end calls for an international coalition that would not be feasible if the United States extended its military campaign into Iraq and other state sponsors of terrorism. They felt it was not advisable, in the absence of incontrovertible evidence of their complicity in the September11 attacks or in the spread of Anthrax. By mid-November, expectations of a lengthy follow on engagement in Afghanistan strengthened the case for holding off in Iraq.

In their own calculations, Muslim states derive moral weight against the United States by virtue of not only US action against Iraq, but also the ongoing Israeli aggression in the Palestinian territories. Diplomatic and moral pressure, for example, President Bush's statement of 20 September 2001 on 9/11 attacks and operational neutrality would be enough to indemnify most countries against US economic or diplomatic retaliation. After registering their obligatory disgust with the World Trade Center and Pentagon strikes, Kuwait has not been penalized for its subsequent reticence, nor Saudi Arabia for its refusal to allow states to sortie from bases there into Afghanistan. So Washington has found it necessary to extend affirmative rewards to fence-sitting Muslim countries in exchange for their active participation in the US-led global campaign.

So far, the most prominent 'deal with evil' has been Washington's enlistment of Pakistan into the coalition, despite the conclusion of a study commissioned by Congress in June 2000 that it was 'not cooperating fully on counter-terrorism.' Pakistan was the only official state sponsor of the Taliban until September 11. Pakistan also backs Islamic terrorist groups in Kashmir.

Distasteful compromises are far from irreversible. The US State Department official lists of terrorist organizations and terrorist sponsors also activate several sanctions. Tools such as political conditionality on economic aid can be re-imposed as well as de-activated. The state sponsor listing system could also be revamped to reflect differing degrees of support for terrorism, for non-cooperation in counter terrorism, which would afford Washington greater precision in punishing undesirable state conduct and rewarding state reform[26].

The events of September 11 argue for foreign policies that employ positive incentives selectively and conditionally subject to credible penalties; with respect to terrorist sponsors. More broadly, certain forms of more open-ended, or 'unconditional,' engagement may prove useful with respect to authoritarian regimes (particularly 'friendly tyrants' like the governments of Egypt and Saudi Arabia) that require political reform if they are to become stable coalition partners or allies and less fertile recruiting grounds for terrorists[27].

The eleventh of September revealed the apocalyptic intent, global scope, organizational sophistication and operational capabilities that make al-Qaeda an unprecedented terrorist threat, and necessitated an equally unprecedented counter-terrorism agenda. Constructive but cautious engagement with lesser evils – be they terrorist groups or their suspected state sponsors – is a price worth paying for the capacity to confront the greater evil without quarter.

AMERICA'S WAR ON TERRORISM

" The unlawful use of – or threatened use of – force or violence against individual or property to coerce or intimidate governments or societies, often to achieve a political, religious, or ideological objectives."

—Definition of Terrorism by the
U.S Department of Defense

The war against Afghanistan was being billed as the first Great War of the 21st century. However, when the US-led "coalition of willing nations" targets the recalcitrant Taliban regime in Afghanistan, the initial tactics for battle was an ancient one of dividing the enemy ranks before the real battle begins. In Dushanbe, the mountain capital of Tajikistan – the strategically located former republic which has for long been the staging ground for Afghan opposition groups, they have a

Russian phrase for this tactic of dividing: 'otkhod podhkod'. Roughly translated, it means knowing how to take the devious route. Afghan war veterans stationed there even have a formula for the strategy that will determine the war. They call it "70 percent money and only 30 percent fighting". The idea is to get many of the tribal warlords loyal to the Taliban to switch sides through bribes and inducements, making the main war easier to fight.

PRECEDENCE OF SEPTEMBER 11 ATTACK ON THE AMERICA

A few weeks after the attack on the World Trade Center and the Pentagon, a top official of the George Bush Administration told closed-door gathering, "Our chickens have come home to roost." The candid submission was more than an attempt to deflect the blame from the present administration. It was a tacit acceptance of the long-term failure of American foreign policy.

It was foreign policy that permitted the fostering of Islamic militant facilities within the US. The aim was to export their ideology in pursuit of strategic objectives. For instance, mosques in New York were allowed in order to help train recruits for the Russo-Afghan war in 1979. It was only a matter of time before these cells turned on the US.

The errors of diplomacy were compounded by a flat-footed secret service, as much out of sync with post-cold war realities as handicapped by red tape and turf wars. As Democratic Senator Bob Kerry of South Carolina asked in the aftermath of the tragedy: "How's it possible that al-Qaeda could operate for so long inside the United States of America without detecting it? How's it possible?" This is the question which has been haunted every American mind for a longer duration of time.

The sheer lethargy of security agencies frustrated the individual investigators who were smart enough to see the clues.

There were enough early warning signals:

* the Manhattan assassination of Rabbi Meir Kahane in the 1990 by a group led by Egypt-born ELSayyid Nossair;[28]
* the decision to allow cleric Shaikh Abdel-Rahman, a leading jehidi figure, to emigrate to the US;
* the first WTC bombing in 1993;
* the attacks in US embassies in Africa and US Naval ship USS Cole.

Each event was seen in isolation. Neither of the security agencies of America bothered with the big picture.

In "The Cell", their recent book, US journalists John Miller, Michael Stone and Chris Mitchell argue investigators had come close to uncovering, at its very infancy, the network that became al-Qaeda. "When the guys from New York office(of the Joint Terrorism Task Force) were trying to hunt down bombing conspiracies halfway around the world, the battle they saw and the one they were asked to fight had become two different things. They tried, but they were unable to make their superiors....adequately appreciate why[29] ."

As far back as 1994, investigators had unraveled an Islamist plot to blow up 12 intercontinental flights almost simultaneously. In addition, the group also planned to hijack and fly a plane into a monument in Washington. The plans came unstuck when the mastermind, Ramzi Youssef – also architect of the 1993 WTC bombing – was arrested in 1995. Shortly after the attack on the Twin Towers, it emerged that the Manila police had alerted the US of such a possibility in New York.

Through the summer of 2001, there were general warnings of an attack on US territory. There were also specific pointers. In mid-July, the Central Intelligence Agency speculated about an al-Qaeda strike at the G-8 summit in Genoa, which Bush was to attend. The White House was told of an Egyptian report that terrorists were conspiring to ram a plane into a US building. On July 10, 2001, Ken Williams, a Federal Bureau of Investigation agent in Phoenix, Arizona, sent his superiors a memo detailing his suspicions about Arab students at a local pilot- training school[30]. He calculated a possible al-Qaeda link. His report got lost in the FBI bureaucracy.

Given this background, it was not surprising the FBI made a mess of its strongest lad, the Zacarias Moussaoui case. There were 19 hijackers on September 11: Moussaoui was allegedly meant to be the 20th. On August 16 this French citizen busy at a flying school in Minneapolis was arrested. Paris passed on a thick folder outlining his radical Islam connections. A week or so before 9/11, an FBI agent working on the investigation on Mousaoui wrote a report how the man could, in theory, fly a plane into the WTC. The feedback about Moussaoui didn't reach FBI headquarters. It was a chronicle foretold. In July 2000, a Congressional Commission had indicted the FBI for failure to communicate with itself. Information collected by field offices often never made it to headquarters. Admittedly, it is easy to be wise after the event. Even if the FBI had acted on leads such as the ones above, it may have not prevented 9/11. The conspiracy was intricate. Nevertheless, America can't forgive itself for its complacency.

POLITICAL FOUNDATION OF THE AMERICAN SYSTEM

Forecasts of post-cold war breakdown and disarray missed an important fact: in the shadow of the cold war, a distinctive and durable political order was being assembled among the major industrial countries. This order might be called the American system – evoking the multifaceted character of this American – centred order organized around layers of security alliances, open markets, multilateral institutions and forums for consultation and governance. It is an order built on common interests and values and anchored in capitalism and democracy.

But it is also an engineered political order built on American power, institutional relationships and political bargains[31].

The American system is a product of two post-war order-building exercises. One – commonly seen as the defining feature of the era, was containment. Truman, Dean Acheson, George Kennan and other American foreign-policy makers were responding to the specter of Soviet power, organizing a global anti-Communist alliance and fashioning an American grand strategy. America's strategy was to 'prevent the Soviet Union from using the power and position it won ... to reshape the postwar international order[32]'.

There was another order created after the Second World War. American officials worked with Britain and other countries to build new relationships among the western industrial democracies. The political order among these countries, aimed at solving the problems of the 1930s, was articulated in such statements as the Atlantic Charter of 1941, the Bretton Woods Agreements of 1944 and the Marshall Plan speech in 1947. Unlike containment, these were a collection of ideas about open markets, social stability, political integration, international institutional cooperation and collective security. Even the Atlantic Pact of 1949 was as much aimed at reconstructing and integrating Europe and binding the democratic world together, as it was an alliance created to balance Soviet power[33].

The American system is based on a vision of open economic relations, intergovernmental cooperation and liberal democratic society. But the most consequential aspect of the order is its security structure. United States extended security guarantees in Europe and Asia, to serve its own motto as well as maintain its dominance in world. This strategy of security binding has provided a structure of commitments, restraints and mechanisms of reassurance.

The American-centred alliances have always been doing more work than is usually appreciated. The traditional understanding of alliances is that they were created to balance against external power and threats. But America's post-war alliances with Europe and Japan were created to achieve a lot more. Stabilizing and managing relations between alliance partners was as much a function of these alliances as countering hostile states. This was true even during the cold war, but it is even more fundamentally the case today. The alliances serve to bind Japan, the United States and Western Europe together and thereby reduce conflict and the potential for strategic rivalry between these traditional great powers. The alliance help these states establish credible commitment to a cooperative structure of relations and provide institutional mechanisms that allow each state to gain access to the policy-making process in the others. Moreover, by binding Germany to Western Europe and Japan to the United States, the alliances help prevent security dilemmas and strategic rivalry that might otherwise break out in Europe and East Asia. These functions of the alliances fit together, constituting a long-term institutional bargain between the United States and its European and Asian partners.

The durability of the American system rests on preponderant American power and a distinctive form of open and institutionalized hegemony. American power has been essential to the building and maintenance of the existing order.

After the Second World War, the United States commanded about 50% of the world's wealth. While the other major powers were destroyed or diminished by war, the United States economy reached new levels of growth and technological advancement. Again today, the United States has only about 4% of the world population but produces approximately 27% of global output. Its nearest rivals – China and Japan – produce about half this amount with four times the population between them. As in the 1940s, today too, America's military and technological supremacy is unchallenged and unprecedented[34].

One explanation for the durability of the American system involves an appeal to a version of the 'democratic peace' thesis: that open democratic polities are less able or willing to use power in an arbitrary and indiscriminate manner against other democracies. The calculations of smaller and warmer states as they confront a democratic hegemon are thereby altered. Fundamentally, power asymmetries are less threatening or destabilizing when they exist between democracies. This might be so for several reasons. Open polities make exercise of power more visible and easy to anticipate. Accountable governments make the exercise of power more predictable and institutionalized. Democracies are more externally accessible than non-democracies. Leaders who rise through the ranks within democratic countries are more inclined to participate in 'give and take' with other democratic leaders than their counterparts in autocratic and authoritarian states. Processes of interaction between democracies make the crude and manipulative exercise of power less likely or consequential. Institutions and norms of consultation and reciprocal influence are manifest in relations across the democratic world.

This system of alliances and multilateral institutions are the core of today's world order. American power has been both under the girds of this system and is transformed by it. By enmeshing itself in a post-war web of alliances and multilateral commitments, the United States is able to project its influence outward and create a relatively secure environment to pursue its interests. However, this order also shapes and restrains American power and makes United States a more genial partner for other states. Likewise, the array of institutions and cooperative security ties that link Europe, the United States, Japan and the rest of the democratic community create a complex and stable order. This order by its sheer size, overwhelms any alternative. Russia, China or any other combination of states or movements is too small to mount a fundamental challenge to the American system. This order provides the ready foundation for a concerted campaign against terrorism.

THE BATTLE PLAN OF UNITED STATES

The Western response to terrorism is being fought at home and abroad through multiple operations including diplomatic, military, financial, investigative, homeland security and humanitarian actions.

Since the beginning of the contemporary wave of terrorism on July 22, 1968, (on that day, the Popular Front for the Liberation of Palestine hijacked a Tel Aviv- bound EL AI flight to Algiers in the first aircraft hijacking by a Palestinian group), the international counter-terrorist community has never seen an organization like al-Qaeda with no historical precedent. Al-Qaeda has proved to be difficult to monitor, target and neutralize by employing the traditional tools of law enforcement[35] .

International efforts made to target al-Qaeda after the simultaneous suicide bombing on two US embassies in Eastern Africa in October 1998 failed. Despite firing 75 cruise missiles into Afghanistan and then arresting its members worldwide, the bombing of USS Cole in October 2000 and the multiple bombing of targets inside continental US in September 2001 could not be prevented.

This demonstrates the difficulty the US-led coalition against terrorism will face in the fight against its the first target al-Qaeda and its leader Osama bin Laden. But the September 11 attacks on various priceless installations of America were an eye opener for the Bush administration. On the evening of September 11, President Bush spoke to the shocked American people from an undisclosed location in a nationally televised address:

"The pictures of airplanes flying into buildings, firing, burning, huge structure collapsing have filled us with disbelief, terrible sadness, and a quiet, unyielding anger. These acts of mass murder were intended to frighten out nation into chaos and retreat. But they have failed; our country is strong. A great people have been moved to defend a great nation. Terrorist attacks can shake the foundations of four biggest buildings, but they cannot touch the foundation of America. These act shattered steel, but they cannot dent the steel of American resolve. America was targeted for attack because we are the biggest beacon for freedom and opportunity in the world. And no one will keep that light from shinning[36] ."

To convert his word in action, President Bush called for formidable battle plans for offensive action. The whole American system was activated to assist the President's plan. The much-calculated steps are:

Step one: America declared war against terrorism. President Bush reiterated, "The deliberate and deadly attacks which were carried out against our country were more than acts of terror. They were acts of war. This will require our country to unite in steadfast determination and resolve. Freedom and democracy are under attack." To achieve victory against the war on terrorism, United States rallies domestic offensive to forge global coalition.

Step two: United States rallies NATO to invoke collective defense obligations. France, Germany and Italy endorsed the military operations and offered to contribute their own forces. Russian government, which has found itself at odds with most major western military operations in the recent past, provided its unequivocal backing. Russia's initiative in aligning itself closely with stated US military and political objectives played an essential role in the coalition-building effort. Vladimir Putin was believed to be disgruntled with the Taliban regime, which he considers instrumental in keeping the conflict in Chechnya raging. China on the other hand maintains a stoic silence due to her own trouble in the Xingjing province. Consequently the silence appeared a support to the American cause. These factors worked in favor of the US plan to counter terrorism.

Step three: The attack inflicted untold damage to the

American economy in general and civil aviation industry in particular. The US stock market had suffered a hefty $9 trillion loss. More than 3 Lakh aviation employee of America were reduced to jobless. To reverse this trend the Federal government immediately offered $15 billion to the civil aviation industry and taken all the desirable steps to keep the moral of financial markets high. On the other hand OPEC was told by America to refrain from any type of fleecing at the crises period[37].

Step four: The US administration's masterstroke was well played, when they successfully enlisted the support of the recalcitrant Pakistan on the war on terrorism. The "deal with evil" policy was worked through the lifting of sanctions on Pakistan, which was imposed after the Chaghai Hill nuclear test in 1998 and rescheduling the debts of Pakistan. The 'carrot and stick' policy found a formidable response in another strategic region when the United States got the logistical support of most of the Central Asian states.

Step five: The most important and crucial step of US in the war on terrorism has been to de-link the financial supply to the terrorist organization. US applied every possible means and technique to target the financial network in Europe and America. The sources and means of financial transactions outsourced by the terrorists are so complex that it is hard to strike the trunk of the tree once and for all. However, the US and its allies had successfully stopped the free flowing of finances of terrorist organizations.

Step six: The talk of the clash of civilization has been gaining ground after the terrorist attack. The US administration has been taking a cautious look to combat the pan-Islamic upsurge by distinguishing Islam from terror. President Bush exclaimed –

"the act to violence on September 11 resulted in the deaths of thousands of innocent people of many races and religions, including Islam. These terrorist acts violate the fundamental tenets of the Islamic faith. America counts millions of Muslims among its citizens and Muslims make a valuable contribution to the United States as doctors, lawyers, law professors, and members of the military, entrepreneurs, shopkeepers, moms and dads. Islam promotes peace, understanding and justice – exactly the opposite the Taliban and the terrorists and their harbor advocate[38]."

Another most important and necessary step taken by the US government was the passage of the PATRIOT Act. There was a beguiling background in the passing of the bill in to an Act. On October 26, 2001, President Bush signed the USA Patriot Act (USAPA) into law. This law has given sweeping new powers to both domestic law enforcement and international intelligence agencies and have eliminated the checks and balances that previously gave courts the opportunity to ensure that these powers were not abused. Most of these checks and balances were put into place after previous misuse of surveillance powers by these agencies, including the revelation in 1974 that the FBI and foreign intelligence agencies had spied on over 10,000 US citizens, including Martin Luther King.

OBJECTIVE OF OPERATION ENDURING FREEDOM

America wounded by the invisible group of Muslim fanatics considered it necessary to show its might and declared war against the perpetrators of the attack on the American mainland under the code name of "Operation Enduring Justice". However, the pontiffs of Islam who are feeling a sense of delight after the attacks on America mobilized the Arabian states to protest the mission code, if not the mission itself. Sensing the vulnerability of unwanted tussles, America readily obliged and renamed it as "Operation Enduring Freedom".

The US has faced an attack from a hostile opponent only for the second time on September 11, 2001, in its history. The British inflicted the first attack against the super power in 1812. However, the absurdity of the latest attack is that it had not come from another superpower or any nation, but from a terrorist organization. The heavy casualty inflicted by the attack attracted strong and firm counter-action from the US government. The objectives of the US action are very clear. Firstly, the Bush administration pledged to bring Osama bin Laden, the architect behind the attacks and his terror network to justice or bring them to justice. Secondly, the US likes to make this war a campaign against a common evil. And thirdly, the conflict is considered as a fight to save the civilized world and values common to the West, to Asia and to Islam. The US administrators have been very keen to see that this war does not turn into a clash between the West and Islam.

As the world waited to see how the United States was planning to retaliate for terrorist attacks in Washington and New York, there was growing anxiety about the tone of American war rhetoric in the Muslim fraternity. President Bush's reference to a "crusade" against terrorism, which passed almost unnoticed by Americans, rang alarm bells in Europe and Arab world[39] .

It raised fears that the terrorist attacks could spark a 'clash of civilizations' between Christians and Muslims, sowing fresh winds of hatred and mistrust. "We have to avoid a clash of civilizations at all costs," French foreign minister Hubert Vedrine retorted. Bush warned Americans that "this crusade, this war on terrorism, is going to take awhile." He and other US officials have said that renegade Islamic fundamentalist Osama bin Laden is the most likely suspect in the attacks. His use of the word "crusade, was most unfortunate" said Soheib Bensheikh, Grand Mufti of the mosque in Marseille, France.

"It recalled the barbarous and unjust military operations against the Muslim world," by Christian knights, who launched repeated attempts to capture Jerusalem over the course of several hundred years. Bush sought to calm American Muslims' fears of a backlash against them by appearing at an Islamic center in Washington. There he assured Americans that "the face of terror is not the true faith of Islam. That's not what Islam is all about. "But his earlier comments, declaring a war between good and evil, shocked Europeans."If this 'war' takes a form that affronts moderate Arab opinion, if it has the air of a clash of civilizations, there is a strong risk that it will contribute to Osama bin Laden's goal: a conflict between the Arab-Muslim world and the West," warned the Paris daily Le Monde in an editorial[40] .

While almost every world leader agrees with Washington that the terrorists who destroyed the World Trade Center were evil, not all of those leaders - especially in the Middle East - identify the United States with good. British Prime Minister Tony Blair has gone out of his way to make it clear that the battle against terrorists is a battle not between Christians and Muslims, but between civilized values and fanaticism. In that battle, he said "the vast majority of decent law-abiding Muslims" opposed fanaticism.

The next objective of US to make it a campaign that is military, diplomatic and humanitarian. The US objectives during the first phase were not for nation building but the end of the Taliban regime, and ensure the war alliance intact.

When Osama bin Laden, the fugitive terrorist claimed the responsibility for the multiple attacks on the American mainland, the war in Afghanistan seemed more of guerilla warfare due to absence of a permanent base of the terrorist group. The hideout of the fugitive is still to be traced, but the Qater based television channel Al Zazeera clandestinely recorded the interviews of the Saudi billionaire in the following word....

"....We calculated in advance the number of casualties from the enemy, who would be killed, based on the position of the tower. We calculated that the floors that would be hit would be three or four floors. I was the most optimistic of them all... due to my experience in this field, I was thinking that the five million liter gasoline in the plane would melt the iron structure of the building and collapse the area where the plane hit and all the floors above it only. This is all that we had hoped for.[41] "

After a serious analysis of the pros and cons of the unintended conflict, the superpower started its military campaign under the code name of "Operation Enduring Freedom". The campaign enjoys the support of countries from the United Kingdom to Australia to Japan. Operation Enduring Freedom unfolds on the night of October 7, 2001, when Kabul plunges into darkness. Some 50 Tomahawk missiles were dropped on Kabul, Kandhar, Jalalabad, and Kunduz by 40 aircraft of the US and UK on the first night of the attack. As the attack screams into preceding nights, the Taliban cut off the electricity of Kabul to counter the US attack. But the superb military technique of US Defense decisively penetrates its target with deliberate precision. After a couple of days, the daylight raids also started. The house of Taliban supremo Mullah Omar was hit with other military bases and oil installations in Kabul, Kandhar and Herat[42].

The Taliban have been forced to surrender major cities. The military has destroyed 11 terrorist training camps and 39 Taliban command control sites. Moreover, al-Qaeda terrorist have been captured, killed or are on the run.

The US motivated its action on other direction also and led a global dragnet to help bring terrorists to justice and help prevent future terrorist acts. The Department of State created the Foreign Terrorist Task Force to prevent terrorist from entering the US, taking steps to arresting and indicting known terrorists. The Bush administration in consultation with the other major power agreed to increase the global sharing of law enforcement information, and implement tough new anti-terrorism laws. The United States does not face any resistanc to the entire offensive campaign, because the list of countries affected by the September 11 attacks comprises most of the major countries of the world. The list of the countries whose citizens were killed by the lethal attacks is....

Antigua&Barbuda	Argentina	Australia
Austria	Bangladesh	Barbados
Belarus	Belgium	Belize
Bolivia	Brazil	Canada
Chile	China	Colombia
Czech-Republic	Dominican-Republic	
Ecuador	Egypt	El Salvador
Ethiopia	France	The Gambia
Germany	Ghana	Greece
Grenada	Guatemala	Guyana
Haiti	Honduras	Hong Kong
India	Indonesia	Ireland
Israel	Italy	Jamaica
Japan	Jordan	Kazakhstan
Kenya	Lebanon	Liberia
Lithuania	Malaysia	Mexico
The Netherlands	New Zealand	Nicaragua
Nigeria	Pakistan	Panama
Paraguay	Peru	Philippines
Poland	Portugal	Romania
Russia	South Africa	South Korea
Spain	Sri Lanka	
St. Kitts & Nevis	St. Lucia	St. Vincent
Grenadines	Sweden	Taiwan
Thailand	Togo	
Trinidad& Tobago	Turkey Ukraine	
United Kingdom	United States	Uruguay
Uzbekistan	Venezuela	Yemen
Yugoslavia	Zimbabwe	

(*Source:* Department of State, US Government)

The Bush administration has claimed success, but results are ambivalent. As the fugitive terrorist is still unapproachable by the US military men, the success of US policy could not be undermined. All the success gained by the US administration by overthrowing the Taliban regime, attributed to superior military technology, modern means of communication, undeniable diplomacy by the administration and genuine and perfect cooperation from the American people especially from the legislator.

CONCLUSION

Let every nation know, whether it wishes us well or ill,
that we shall pay any price, bear any burden,
meet any hardship, support any friend, oppose any foes,
in order to assure the survival and success of liberty.
This much we pledge – and more.

— John F. Kennedy, 1962.

The televised September 11 attacks made a difference to the rest of the world and the American mainland itself. Maybe it would have been different if 4,000 people had perished in an explosion in a crowded Delhi bazaar. But this was New York, the citadel of world capitalism and showcase of the world's greatest power. The outrage here changed the rules of the game.

"Every nation in every region now has a decision to make, either you are with us or with the terrorists", US President George W. Bush told the congress on 23 September 2001[43] . It was forthrightness that struck a chord in all the countries that had suffered the depredation of terrorists masquerading as freedom fighters. However, unwittingly, bin Laden made victimhood the basis of the global coalition against him. "We have to drain the swamp they live in", said the US Defense Secretary Donald Rumsfeld when preparing for the onslaught on terrorism. This new found zero tolerance made all terrorism unacceptable, whether Palestinian or Pakistani. New York

Mayer Rudi Giuliani gauged the pulse and turned down a donation by a Saudi Prince because it was prefaced by gratuitous advice on the need for a "balanced" US policy on Palestine. Anti-terrorism had to be unconditional.

One of the colossal and indelible events in human history was 9/11 attacks. This attack displayed rare sense of imagination and changed the fundamentals of civilian freedom and compelled the governments across the world to give more space to safety and security in their policy making exercise. It was the US foreign policy that permitted the fostering of Islamic militancy within the US. The aim was to export their ideology in pursuit of strategic objectives. For instance, mosques in New York were allowed in order to help train recruits for Russo-Afghan war in 1979. It was only a matter of time before these terror cells turned on the US. The errors of diplomacy were compounded by a flat-footed secret service, as much out of sync with post-cold war realities as handicapped by red tape and turf wars.

The idyll of the fragile world shattered on 11 September 2001 by a committed group of Islamic clergies, masquerading as savior of Islam. The monstrous acts that visited World Trade Center in New York and Pentagon in Washington made a telling transition, so far as US is concerned, from a safe heaven to an ordinary terror ridden part of the world. Backed by a mysterious Shaikh Osama bin Laden, 19 terrorists stormed the citadel of capitalism and the hub of military establishment and wrote an unforgettable chapter in human history. Their sheer action changed the fundamental of American foreign policy and its helmsmen's viewpoint to terrorism. The invincibility of the American mainland in the modern age proved to be a myth. The vulnerability of America unbridled multidimensional change in policy and outlooks of nation states across the globe.

Even if eliminating all terrorist incidents proves impossible, reducing their frequency and lethal potential will make a large difference in their impact on our societies.

Technological progress is putting into the hands of deviant groups and individuals destructive capabilities that were once limited primarily to governments and armies. The world needs a multi-faceted strategy that de-legitimizes attacks on civilians as method of conflict; discourages states from providing resources or safe harbor to those who use such methods; hardens our targets at home; denies terrorists easy access to weapons of mass destruction; and reduces incentives to use terrorism.

Military measures may not deal with the largest part of the problem, but they are essential sometimes. Depriving al-Qaeda of its Afghan safe haven was not sufficient, but it was necessary. The number of states sponsoring terrorism has decreased over the past decade. Diplomacy backed by military threat can reduce the number further. Some failed states are so chaotically organized that they cannot be deterred from providing a haven for terrorists. In such instances, military assistance may be relevant. In others, intervention may be necessary.

Intelligence sharing and police co-operation is often the most effective front line of defense. Because of the sensitivity of sources and the dangers of disclosure, much of this work is carried out through bilateral arrangements. Multilateral cooperation is possible in tracing financial flows, which can help to deprive terrorists of resources as well as provide useful information. Information sharing can also be enhanced by devoting more resources to under-funded organizations like Interpol.

Working to raise the thresholds that terrorists must overcome requires a systemic approach, since plugging one hole can simply divert terrorists to others. Democratic societies are as vulnerable as the weakest international link. It makes no sense to beef up airport security in London if a terrorist can enter the system easily in, Rome or Lagos.

REFERENCES

1. Rath, Saroj Kumar (2003), *Joint Response of US and UK to Terrorism Since 11 September 2001*, M. Phil Dessertation, New Delhi : Jawaharlal Nehru University, p. i.

2. Ibid, p.ii.

3. Rath, Saroj Kumar (2006), "Trans-Atlantic Realization of New Terrorism", *The Atlantic Journal of World Affairs*, Vol. 2 No.1, Jan-Mar 2006, p.8.

4. Schmid, A.P. (1988), UN's "academic consensus definition, accessed on 8th February 07, http://www.unodc.org/unodc/terrorism_definitions.html .

5. *Red Army Faction* (2007), Accessed on 4th Feb 07 at *www.eyespymag.com/terrorgroupsR.htm.*

6. *Press Release* (1998), Federal Criminal Office, Wiesbaden, Germany, 13th April 1998.

7. Che Guevara, Earnest (1966), *Guerilla Warfare: A Method*, Havana: Normount Armament Co. Publication, p.69-70.

8. Che's Medical File (1997), *St. Catharines Standard*, La Paz, 10th July1997.

9. Goebbles, Joseph (1944), The Call of Duty, "Der Befehl der Pflicht," *Das Reich*, 6 August 1944, pp. 1-2.

10. Stevenson, Jonathan (2001), "Pragmatic Counter Terrorism", *Survival* vol.43, no.4, winter 2001-2, London, p.35.

11. While, Michael (2001), "The New Terrorism", Annual *Report*, Stephen Roth Institute, Tel Aviv University.

12. Macdonald, Andrew (1978), *The Turner Diaries,* Washington DC: Hillsboro WV Publication, p.82.

13. Gunaratna, Rohan (2001), "Terrorist Trends Suggest Shift of Focus to National Activities ", *Janes Intelligence Review*, June 2001, p.7.

14. Department of State (2000) 'Pattern of Global Terrorism 1999', *Office of the Coordinator for Counterterrorism*, Appendix C, April 2000.

15. Milton, John (1995), "On Tactics and Strategy for USENET", accessed on 8th February 2007 *http://72.14.235.104/search?q=cache:gmJqpvQCIDMJ:www.nizkor.org/ftp.cgi/orgs/american/adl/recruitment/internet-1995+On+Tactics+and+Strategy+for+USENET%E2%80%9D,1995,&hl=en&ct=clnk&cd=1&gl=in.*

16. Editorial (2001), Oslo Peace Process, *Financial Times*, New York, 2nd October 2001.

17. Horovatz, David (2001), Protest Against US, *Jerusalem Post*, Jerusalem, 10th October 2001.

18. *Daily-Telegraph*, 28th September 2001and *Boston Globe*, 11th October 2001

19. Flakes, E.D and Elliott, Sydney (1994), "*Northern Ireland: A Political Dictionary 1968-93*", Belfast: Blackstaff Publication, p.210.

20. Hoffman, Bruce (1999), "Is Europe Soft on Terrorism?," *Foreign Policy*, New York, No.115, Summer 1999, P. 76.

21. Matus, Victorino (2001), "al-Qaeda's Filipino Branch Office", *Weekly Standard*, London, 26 November 2001).

22. Hroub, Khaled (2000), "*Political Thought and Practice*", Institute for Palestine Studies Publication, Washington DC 2000, P208.

23. Gunaratna, Rohan (2001), "Terror From the Sky", *Jane's Intelligence Review*, London,October 2001,P.8.

24. Pillar, Paul R.(2001), *Terrorism and US Foreign Policy*, Washington DC : The Brooking Institution Publication, p.178-186.

25. Department of State (2001), *Daily Press Briefing*, 15th of Novemer 2001, Washington DC.

26. Pillar, Paul R (2001), *Terrorism and US Foreign Policy*, Washington DC : The Brooking Institution Publication, p.171.

27. Hass, Richard and Meghan, Sullivan (2000), *Honey and Vinegar: Incentives, Sanction and Foreign Policy*, Washington DC: Brooking Institution Publication, p. 43.

28. Robory, Friedman (1990), *The False Prophet*, Chicago: Chicago Review Press, p.14.

29. John, Miller, Michael, Stone and Chris, Mitchell (2002), *The Cell*, New York : Hyperion Publications, p.56.

30. Gerald, Baker (2002), "Flying Institute in Florida", *The Time*, New York, 10 January 2002 p.57.

31. John, Gaddis (1992), *Strategies of Containment: A Critical Apparaisal of Post-War American National Security Policy*, London: Oxford University Press, p.6.

32. Mary N, Hampton (1995), "NATO At The Creation", *Securities Studies*, Florida, Vol.4 No.3, Spring 1995, p.610-611.

33. Cohen, Stephen (1995), *NATO : The Long Entanglement*, New York : Cato Pub. Ink., p. 24.

34. William, Wohlforth (1999), "The Stability of a Unipolar World", *International Security*, New York, Vol.24 No.1, Summer 1999, pp.5.

35. Rohan, Gunaratna (2001), "Terror Unlimited", *Frontline,* New Delhi, 12 October 2001, p.28-29.
36. Bush, George (2001), George Bush's Presidential Address to the Nation on 11th of September 2001.
37. *The Economic Times*, 3rd December 2001.
38. Bush, George (2001), President Bush's address to the Nation From The White House, 7th of October 2001.
39. Ford, Peter (2001), "*Europe Cringes at President Bush's Crusade Against Terrorists*", Christian Science Monitor, Berlin, 19 September, 2001.
40. Editorial (2001), *Le Monde*, 19th September 2001
41. Al Zazeera Broadcast (2001), 23rd of November 2001, Qater.
42. Chengappa, Raj (2001), "Destination Kabul", *India Today*, New Delhi 22nd October 2001.
43. Bush, George (2001), *President Bush's address to the Congress*, 23rd September2001.

10

American Counter-terrorism Measures: An Appraisal

Ashok Sharma

Terrorism has become concern for the United States after the September 11, 2001 attacks on the World Trade towers and Pentagon, the symbols of American economic and military might. Terrorism remains a global threat from which no nation is immune and the US has become aware of the seriousness of this concern. The terrorism that the US is fighting finds its genesis in the wrong interpretation of the Islamic concept of Jihad. Despite ongoing improvements in US homeland security, military campaigns against insurgents and terrorists in Iraq and Afghanistan, and deepening counter-terrorism cooperation among the nations of the world, international terrorism continues to pose a grave threat to the US and its allies. The slaughter of hundreds of innocents in the Beslan school, in the commuter trains of Madrid, on a Philippines ferry, in a Sinai resort, attack on London Metro, continuing terrorists attack in Jammu &Kashmir, explosion in Delhi on the eve of Deepawali, and recently attack on India's IT industry by killing a scientist at IISC Bangalore, and increasing terrorist attacks in South-East Asian countries brings out the truth that the struggle against terrorism is far from over.

Just after the 9/11 attacks, President Bush declared war on terror and said in an address to Congress on September 20,

2001, "Our war on terror begins with al-Qaida, but it does not end there. It will not end until every terrorist group of global reach has been found, stopped, and defeated."[1]

EVENTS LEADING UP TO 9/11 TERRORIST ATTACK

The present Islamic terrorism aims to further the political and religious ambitions of a segment of the Muslim Community in the name of Jihad[2]. Islamic fundamentalism arose in various Islamic states in different forms. For example, Wahabbism was embraced in Saudi Arabia, as the Ottoman Empire declined in the later 18th, early 19th Century. Islamic fundamentalism is a response to many factors, central among which are the domination by the West, relative poverty and underdevelopment of the Muslim world, and lack of political outlets to express discontents.

International developments in the last two-three decades have spawned Islamic fundamentalism in which terrorists have targeted the United States and its allies. US support to Israel in the Arab-Israel conflict is one of the factors that led to the September 11 attack and worldwide attacks on American establishments by the terrorists. All over the world, Islamic countries have criticized and opposed US support to Israel in the Israel-Palestine conflict. The Palestinian cause is linked with religious sentiments and many take it as a holy war. The recent statement issued by Iranian president Ahmadinejad of wiping out of Israel echoes this anti-Iseaeli sentiment of Muslim nations. This also shows their hatred towards American support to Israel.[3]

The perception among Muslims is that Israel can get away with killing and murder and US would turn a blind eye to them. Over the years, Arab channels like Al Zazeera have broadcast countless pictures of Israeli soldiers shooting Palestinian youths, Israeli tanks plowing into Palestinian homes, Israeli helicopters rocketing Palestinian streets. They know that the US sends more than $3 billion a year in military and economic aid to Israel.

The people see their brothers dying in Palestine, and it makes them hate the US. The US diplomacy has been unable to project itself to the Arabs as an impartial or equitable judge in the peace process between Israel and the Palestinians.[4]

Fundamentalist forces see US policy in the Middle-East in the context of Western hegemony and they don't want Western culture to enter into their religious and social belief often linked with religious angle- clash between Christianity and Islam.

American policy in the Middle East, where military might has held the balance of power for 50 years, thousands of US soldiers stationed in the Gulf, and billions of US dollars each year in military aid to Israel, Egypt, and other allies, have antagonized the Muslim world and their concerted attempt to create a Pan Islamic dominance worldwide. This frustration culminated into the terrorists attack of 9/11.

US COUNTER-TERRORISM POLICY

In response to the September 11th terrorist attacks, President Bush laid out the scope of the war on terrorism. Four enduring policy principles is guide to US counter-terrorism strategy.

First, the US Government will make no concessions to terrorists and strike no deals. The US Government will make no concessions to individuals or groups holding official or private US citizens hostage. The US will use every appropriate resource to gain the safe return of US citizens who are held hostage. At the same time, it is the US Government policy to deny hostage takers the benefits of ransom, prisoner releases, policy changes, or other acts of concession.[5]

Second, bring terrorists to justice for their crimes. The US will track down terrorists who attack US citizens and property, no matter how long it takes.

Third, isolate and apply pressure on states that sponsor

terrorism to force them to change their behavior. There are six countries that are designated state sponsors of terrorism: Cuba, Iran, Libya, North Korea, Sudan, and Syria.[6]

Fourth, bolster the counterterrorist capabilities of those countries that work with the US and require assistance. Under the Antiterrorism Assistance (ATA) Program, the US provides training, equipment, and related assistance to law enforcement and security services of select friendly foreign governments. Courses cover such areas as airport security, bomb detection and disposal, hostage rescue, and crisis management. A recent component of the training, entitled the Interdicting Terrorist Organizations Program, provides four courses teaching techniques to identify and apprehend terrorist cells before they have an opportunity to strike. During the past 20 years, the ATA Program has trained over 48,000 officials from 141 countries in various aspects of counter-terrorism.[7]

A broad range of counter-terrorism training resources from other US Government agencies, including military training by the Department of Defense, are in use to bolster international capabilities. The United States is working in cooperation with the world community and seeking assistance from other partner nations as well in the war on terrorism.

EXECUTIVE ORDERS

In response to the September 11 terrorist attacks, President Bush issued an extremely broad Executive Order that prohibits transactions with individuals and organizations deemed by the Executive Branch to be associated with terrorism and allows the government to freeze all assets controlled by or in the possession of these entities and those who support them. The Executive Branch has taken the position that it has the authority to freeze assets while it investigates whether an organization is associated with terrorism.

Agency shortly after the September 11, 2001, terrorist attacks to eavesdrop without a court warrant on Americans suspected of communicating with Al Qaeda members overseas. Bush has since acknowledged the eavesdropping program and defended it.[9]

Immediate action after US administration declaring "War on Terror" was US-led military attack on Afghanistan to hunt down the Al-Qaida terrorists and Osama bin Laden, whom US perceived responsible for terrorist attack on America. In 2003 America declared War on Iraq in 2003. Iraq was attacked on the ground that it possessed Weapons of Mass Destruction and restoration of democracy.

PATTERNS OF GLOBAL TERRORISM

After US declared war on terror Department of State (DoS) has been tracking down the global pattern of terrorism. DoS is responsible for making report on global pattern of terrorism. The annual "Patterns of Global Terrorism" report is submitted in compliance with Title 22 of the United States Code, Section 2656f(a), which requires the Department of State to provide Congress a full and complete annual report on terrorism for those countries and groups meeting the criteria of Section (a)(1) and (2) of the Act.

Report on terrorism activities of 2003 states that there were 208 acts of international terrorism in 2003, a slight increase from the most recently published figure of 198 attacks in 2002, and a 42 percent drop from the level in 2001 of 355 attacks. A total of 625 persons were killed in the attacks of 2003, fewer than the 725 killed during 2002. A total of 3646 persons were wounded in the attacks that occurred in 2003, a sharp increase from 2013 persons wounded the year before. This increase reflects the numerous indiscriminate attacks during 2003 on "soft targets," such as places of worship, hotels, and commercial districts, intended to produce mass casualties. Thirty-five US citizens died in international terrorist attacks in 2003.[10]

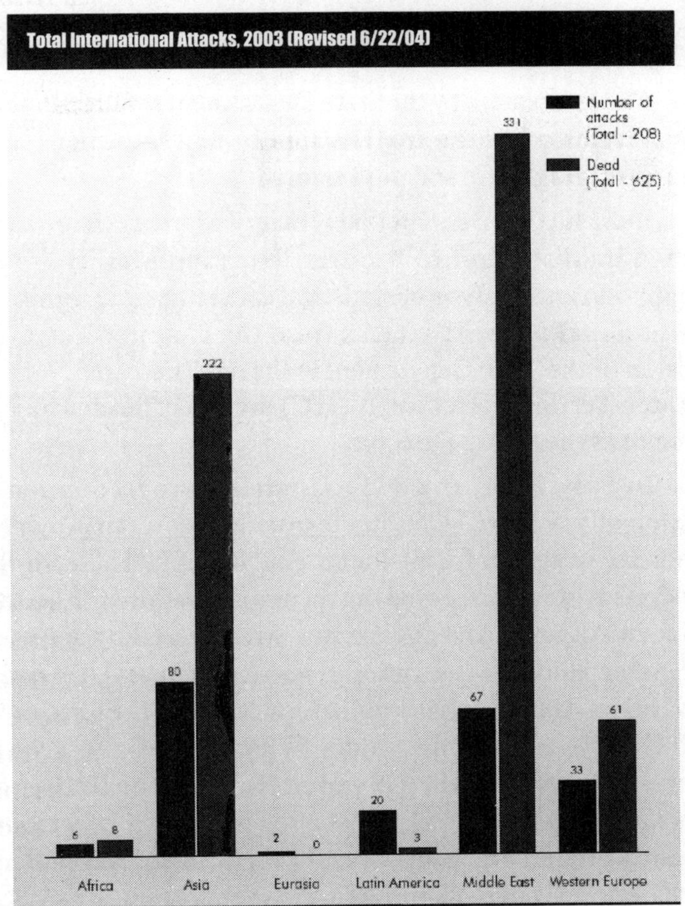

http://www.state.gov/s/ct/rls/pgtrpt/2003/33771.htm

According to National Counter Terrorism Center Report of year 2004 number of total terrorist attack world wide were 651 which took the lives of 1907 people.[11]

PROBLEMS AND DRAWBACKS

Patterns of global terrorism indicate that there has been an increase in the terrorist attacks worldwide. This makes it imperative to find out the drawbacks and inconsistency with the United States counter-terrorism strategy.

(i) Double Standards in Assessment of patterns of terrorism by Department of State

The assessment by the State Department is full of political consideration while the analysis done by newly formed NCTC is realistic, pragmatic and professional.

India has been a major beneficiary of the decision of the Bush Administration to transfer the responsibility for the compilation and analysis of statistical data relating to significant international terrorist attacks from the Counter-Terrorism Division of the State Department to the newly created National Counter-Terrorism Centre (NCTC) presently headed by John Brennan as the acting Director.

In July 2004, the 9/11 Commission recommended creation of a National Counter terrorism Center to provide an authoritative agency for all-source analysis of global terrorism. The President implemented the recommendation by Executive Order in August. And the agency was created by statute in December 2004, in the Intelligence Reform and Terrorism Prevention Act, which is Public Law 108-458". Functions of NCTC included among others 1) serving as the primary organization within the US government for analyzing and integrating all intelligence possessed by the US government pertaining to terrorism and counter-terrorism, (2) conducting strategic operational planning for counter-terrorism activities, (3) assigning operational responsibilities to lead agencies for counter-terrorism activities, and (4) serving as a shared knowledge bank on known and suspected terrorists and international terror groups."[12]

For nearly two decades, the annual analysis of the State Department's Counter-Terrorism Division was influenced more by political rather than by professional considerations. In their anxiety to play down the role of Pakistan's military-intelligence establishment in the sponsorship of terrorism, Jihadi as well as non-Jihadi, against India, the officials of the State Department were very selective in the compilation and analysis of data relating to Pakistan-sponsored terrorism in India. A large number of terrorist attacks carried out by Pakistani Jihadi organisations from their sanctuaries in Pakistani territory were consciously excluded under some pretext or the other.

The professionals of the NCTC, who are apparently under no such political compulsion, have changed this practice and, for the first time in 2004, they took into account many significant terrorist attacks in Indian territory carried out by Pakistani Jihadi organisations, without worrying about its impact on the credibility of the State Department's projection of Pakistani President Gen.Pervez Musharraf as the US' stalwart ally in the so-called war on Jihadi terrorism.

The result is there to see in the statistical analysis of the NCTC. The total number of significant international terrorist attacks in Jammu & Kashmir (J&K) increased from 52 as compiled by the State Department in 2003 to 284 as compiled by the NCTC in 2004. The number of fatalities increased from 111 to 434. These figures indicating a more than five-fold increase in the number of terrorist attacks and a four-fold increase in the number of fatalities do not mean there was a steep deterioration of the ground situation in J&K. They only mean that there is better compilation and analysis of the available data by the professional counter-terrorism analysts of the NCTC uninfluenced by political considerations than by the politicised diplomats of the State Department in the past.[13]

The statistical analysis released on April 27,2005, has been described as an interim one, still with many inaccuracies and anomalies, and the Congress and the public opinion have been promised a more comprehensive and accurate analysis in June 2007. The current analysis was prepared by the NCTC under the supervision of Porter Goss, the Director of the Central Intelligence Agency (CIA) since John Negroponte, the newly-appointed Director of National Intelligence, who would, inter alia, supervise the functioning of the NCTC, had not yet been confirmed by the Senate.

The number of serious international terrorist incidents nearly tripled 2004, according to US government figures, a sharp upswing in deadly attacks that the State Department decided not to make public in its annual report on terrorism due to Congress. Overall, the number of what the US government considers "significant" attacks grew to about 655 last year, up from the record of around 175 in 2003, according to congressional aides who were briefed on statistics covering incidents including the bloody school seizure in Russia and violence related to the disputed Indian territory of Kashmir. Terrorist incidents in Iraq also dramatically increased, from 22 attacks to 198, or nine times the year 2004 total — a sensitive subset of the tally, given the Bush administration's assertion that the situation there had stabilized significantly after the US handover of political authority to an interim Iraqi government last summer. [14]

Perhaps the move was designed to shield the government from questions about the success of its effort to combat terrorism by eliminating what amounted to the only year-to-year benchmark of progress.

April 27, 2005 analysis came out with two version of the state of global terrorism last year— a statistical version as prepared by the professional experts of the NCTC and a somewhat political narrative of the way different countries dealt with the problem as prepared by the State Department. The difference in the approaches of the two was surprising. The NCTC's statistical version did not hesitate to highlight the high level of significant terrorist attacks in J&K by Pakistani Jihadi organisations, the State Department's report praised Pervez Musharraf for dealing with terrorists.

On October 6, 2005, President Bush Addressed the National Endowment For Democracy on "The Nature of the

Enemy We Face and the Strategy for Victory" outlining the ideology. But again even in his speech the focus was on Al-Qaida and Iraq, Middle East and not Pakistan.[15]

The State Department's version said: "Pakistan continues to be one of the United States' most important partners in the war on terrorism. Few countries suffered as much from terrorism in 2004 as Pakistan, and few did as much to combat it. After the two near-miss assassination attempts against President Musharraf in December 2003, groups linked to al-Qa'ida tried to assassinate a corps commander in Karachi in June, and the Finance Minister (now Prime Minister) in July. Nearly 200 people were killed in major Sunni-Shia sectarian attacks. Al-Qa'ida declared the Government of Pakistan to be one of its main enemies, and called for its overthrow. The Government of Pakistan continues to pursue al-Qa'ida and its allies aggressively through counter-terrorist police measures throughout the country and large-scale military operations in the Federally Administered Tribal Areas (FATA) along the rugged Afghanistan-Pakistan border. Pakistani Army and Frontier Corps units destroyed key al-Qa'ida safe havens in South Waziristan Agency (part of the FATA), killing over 100 foreign terrorists and dispersing several hundred more. These operations significantly degraded al-Qa'ida's command and control capabilities in the region, but at a cost of approximately 200 Pakistani servicemen killed in action. In addition to counter-terrorism operations in the tribal areas, Pakistani security services are cooperating closely with the United States and other nations in a successful campaign to eliminate terrorism both within Pakistan and abroad. Over 600 suspected operatives of al-Qa'ida and other groups have been killed or captured by Pakistani authorities since September 2001. The Government also cracked down on several groups that had been active in the Kashmir insurgency."[16]

Not a word about the continuing terrorist infrastructure in Pakistani territory and the sanctuaries which the remnants of Al Qaeda and the Taliban, particularly the latter, continue to enjoy in Pakistani territory. The report justly claims credit for the success of the US in destroying the international Jihadist terrorist infrastructure in Afghan territory, but fails to draw attention to the continuing infrastructure in Pakistani territory.

The State Department says as follows on Bangladesh: "Bangladesh supports the global war on terror, but its ability to combat terrorism is undermined by weak institutions, porous borders, limited law enforcement capabilities, and debilitating in-fighting between the two major political parties. Bangladesh's long tradition of inclusive, moderate Islam is increasingly under threat from extremist alternatives, already offering an attractive breeding ground for political and sectarian violence. Endemic corruption, poverty, and a stalemated political process could further contribute to the type of instability and widespread frustration that has elsewhere provided recruits, support, and safe haven to international terrorist groups. The Government is committed to enforcing UN Security Council resolutions and actions related to terrorism, including the identification and freezing of assets of individuals and organizations designated as terrorists or terrorist supporters, such as the Saudi-based charity al-Haramain Foundation.[17]

It also ordered the closure of the local Rabita Trust office and the departure from Bangladesh of its expatriate staff. The Bangladesh military maintains a large presence in the Chittagong Hill Tracts, and has been successful in locating hidden weapons. In April it seized a large cache of weapons in Chittagong harbor. Bangladesh is taking steps to improve its effectiveness in preventing maritime smuggling and its capabilities in terrorist interdiction operations."

However, it fails to take note of the sanctuaries enjoyed by the United Liberation Front of Assam (ULFA) and other Indian terrorist organisations in Bangladesh territory and of the activities of the Harkat-ul-Jihad-al-Islami (HUJI), a member of bin Laden's International Islamic Front (IIF), from

Bangladesh territory. As in the case of Pakistan, in the case of Bangladesh too, one is struck by a marked reluctance in the State Department to openly articulate concerns over the emergence of the country as a new web of Jihadi terrorism, with serious implications for South and South-East Asia.in fact recently since the first suicide attack on 29 November 2005 in Ghazipur and Chittagong, that killed nine and injured over 50 people, Bangladesh has witnessed a series of militant attacks on symbols of public life like courthouses, government buildings and press clubs. Bangladesh may not be on the brink of disaster, but that possibility cannot be ruled out. The political bickering between Sheikh Hasina-led Awami League and the ruling BNP led by Khaleda Zia has resulted in the weakening of democracy and debasement of the very essence of politics in Bangladesh.

(ii) Over-emphasis on Osama bin Laden

Over-projecting the role of bin Laden in the international Jihadi terrorist movement has given him a larger than life-size image and an air of invincibility. Amongst large sections of the Islamic world, he commands more respect as a good Jihadi commander than as a good religious leader. As a religious leader, Mulla Mohammad Omar, the Amir of the Taliban, commands more respect and following than bin Laden. bin Laden tells Muslims in his messages how to be good Jihadi fighters and not how to be good Muslims. [18]

(iii) Ignoring the Hub of Terrorism: Pakistan

If there is one country in the world which has been systematically violating with impunity all regulations relating to nuclear and missile proliferation and from which there is a real danger of leakage of weapons of mass destruction (WMD) and related technologies to Al Qaeda and other Pan-Islamic terrorist organisations belonging to Osama bin Laden's International Islamic Front (IIF) for Jihad against the Crusaders and the Jewish People, that country is Pakistan. The US double standards in this matter are evident from the alacrity and vigour with which it acted against Iraq despite the lack of any credible evidence against it and the care with which it protects the regime in Pakistan, despite all the evidence available against it.[19]

In fact Pakistan involvement in terrorist activities dates back to late 1980s.Pakistan has aided, abetted, trained and equipped the terrorist groups involved in atrocities in Kashmir and paid lip service to the dead in the 9/11 terrorist attacks against America[20] .Even after the promising Bush to support war against terror it has not lived up to expectation. Pakistan's proliferation activities in Iran, Libya and North Korea were exposed, in 2003 and even then Pakistan Prez did not take any responsibility and put the blame totally on a group of about a dozen scientists headed by A.Q.Khan, the so-called father of Pakistan's atomic bomb.

Too much stress on Al Qaida and giving Osama bin Laden larger than life image was given by America in post 9/11 scenario. But the fact is that since 1995, there emerged a new brand of Jihadi ideology called International Islamism, which advocates a "jihad world-wide" against perceived enemies of Islam in general and against the US and Israel in particular, the significance of the formation of the International Islamic Front (IIF) in Afghanistan in February,1998, under the leadership of Al Qaeda in the conduct of this global jihad, the attempts of the Jihadi elements to take the jihad to US territory and the projection of this global jihad by its proponents as a new third world war which, according to them, would end in the triumph of Islam.

Pernicious role of many Pakistani Jihadi organisations of Wahabi-Deobandi persuasion in the IIF, the secretive role of the Tablighi Jamaat of Pakistan in the spread of this ideology

Was ignored but the fact is that most of these organisations had come into existence long before Al Qaeda. Al Qaeda and Osama bin Laden were inspired by their ideology and not the other way round. Bin Laden's arguments on the right and the religious obligation of the Muslims to acquire and use, if necessary, weapons of mass destruction (WMD) against the USA and Israel were borrowed from the ideology of the Islamic bomb propagated by the Deobandi-Wahabi clerics of Pakistan such as the late Mufti Nizamuddin Shamzai of the Binori madrasa and Fazlur Rahman Khalil of the Harkat-ul-Mujahideen (HUM) etc.[21]

The post-1998 Jihadi terrorist incidents were carried out by the Pakistani and other components of the IIF and not by Al Qaeda and that the Americans were distorting the analysis by trying to see the hand of bin Laden and Al Qaeda in every incident. Over-focussing on Al Qaeda because of its traumatic experience of 9/11 and by not paying adequate attention to the various individual components of the IIF operating from the Pakistani territory, the US diverted attention away from the Jihadi iceberg, while keeping the spotlight only on its Al Qaeda tip.[22]

(iv) Pakistani Game: Keeping the Problem Alive

The global war on terrorism can not be successful unless international community ultimately prevail over international Jihadi terrorism of the Al Qaeda brand and they will have capture or kill the top guns of the movement Osama bin Laden, his no.2 Ayman al-Zawahiri and Abu Musab al-Zarqawi, who co-ordinates the activities of the Al Qaeda and pro-Al Qaeda foreign terrorists in Iraq. Their capture or death would not mean the end of international Jihadi terrorism, but it would convey a strong message to their terrorist hordes, supporters and admirers that the international community means business and that it would ultimately prevail. But its not possible unless complicity and covert support of Pakistan's military and intelligence communities they enjoy is stopped. They do not want the Al Qaeda and other Jihadi terrorist organisations supporting it to ultimately prevail over the US. At the same time, they do not want the US to prevail over them either. The present no-win-for-either-side situation suits them.

President Pervez Musharraf and his advisers in the Pakistan Army and the Inter-Services Intelligence (ISI) look upon Osama-bin-Laden and Al-Zawahiri as the most important strategic assets Pakistan has after its military nuclear capability. In their perception, the newly-acquired importance of Pakistan in the eyes of the international community—particularly in the eyes of the US—is due to their perceived need for Pakistani co-operation in the hunt for them. If the hunt ends successfully for the US with their death or capture, that could mark the beginning of the end of Pakistan's newly-acquired importance. So, they fear. That is the way the Pakistani military mind always works.

WAR ON TERROR- DRAWBACKS

The war on Terrorism, on the one hand, has created a worldwide awareness about the threat of terrorism, cracked down on big terrorist organization links and networking but has not been able to stop terrorist attacks minor or major.

The war on terror has made military and police networks highly intertwined and in the long run seems to form kind of a de facto global police force to tackle terrorism supported by all the states which are facing this problem. "War on Terror" is likely to lead to the gradual decline of large scale terrorist organizations like Al Qaida but has not been able to eliminate terrorist activities in the context of guerrilla warfare in isolated locales or by potentially catastrophic terrorist acts of mass destruction by individuals and small groups. In fact the war on terrorism which is being fought with military technologies of has invited destructive terrorism as resistance, whether organized or random.

It seems that war on terror has somewhere stuck with War on Iraq and has deviated from tracking down the main terrorist organizations which is not only active in Iraq but also creating terror all over the world with their suicide bombing and other terror tactics. The savage attack in London, for which al Qaeda has reportedly taken credit, is just one more indication that the War on Terrorism is not working.[23]

Recently, the Bush administration cancelled the publication of the annual "Patterns of Global Terrorism" report. According to Larry Johnson, a former CIA analyst and State Department terrorism expert who still has many sources within the intelligence community, Secretary of State Condoleezza Rice's office is suppressing data showing that the number of major terrorist attacks worldwide exploded from 175 in 2003 to 625 in 2004, the highest number since the Cold War began to wane in 1985. US officials said that when analysts at the National Counter-terrorism Center declined the office of the secretary's invitation to use a methodology that would reduce the number of terrorist attacks, her office terminated publication of the State Department's annual "Patterns of Global Terrorism" report, which would have embarrassingly revealed that major terrorist attacks worldwide increased. The War Party has been arguing for almost four years that the Bush administration's War on Terrorism has reduced the number of terrorist attacks throughout the globe, but all data seem to demonstrate an increase.[24]

The most loyal Terror Warriors weren't even shaken by the leaked Rumsfeld memo of October 2003, which candidly and simply conceded the most basic limitations inherent in the US government's bureaucratic central-planning approach to wiping out global terrorism: "Today, we lack metrics to know if we are winning or losing the global war on terror. Are we capturing, killing or deterring and dissuading more terrorists every day than the madrassas and the radical clerics are recruiting, training and deploying against us? Does the US need to fashion a broad, integrated plan to stop the next generation of terrorists? The US is putting relatively little effort into a long-range plan, but we are putting a great deal of effort into trying to stop terrorists. The cost-benefit ratio is against us! Our cost is billions against the terrorists' costs of millions".[25]

The Bush administration has bungled the war on

terrorism, doing little to provide security at home while breeding legions of new enemies abroad, the government's former anti-terrorism chief, Richard Clarke.[26]

At the end of November,2005 Pentagon released a report by the Defense Science Board that was highly critical of the administration's efforts in countering terrorism with respect to the wars in Afghanistan and Iraq. Around the same time Richard Clark, the former White House Counter-terrorism tsar under both President Clinton and President Bush, said, "*So much of the US government's attention is on Iraq, that they are really not thinking conceptually about the war on terrorism. President Bush has conflated Iraq and the war on terrorism into one thing, and therefore when they are working on Iraq they think are working on the war on terrorism – which of course they are not because it is a very different thing.*"[27]

In January 2005, the CIA's think tank, National Intelligence Council issued a report describing Iraq as the magnet, training and recruiting ground for international terrorism. The false rationale for the invasion had become a self-fulfilling prophecy.[28]

This is what a Chatham House (Royal Institute of International Affairs. London) Briefing Paper, July 5 said about Iraq and the War on Terror: "*There is no doubt that the situation over Iraq has imposed particular difficulties for the UK, and for the wider coalition against terrorism. It gave a boost to Al-Qaeda network's propaganda, recruitment and fundraising, caused a major split in the coalition, provided an ideal targeting and training area for Al-Qaeda-linked terrorists, and deflected resources and assistance that could have been deployed to assist the Karzai government and to bring bin Laden to justice. Riding pillion with a powerful ally has proved costly in terms of British and US military lives, Iraqi lives military expenditure and the damage caused to the counter-terrorism campaign.*"[29]

Marc Scheur, a former head of the CIA's bin Laden unit, who resigned from the agency last November said, there is a dangerous lack of understanding in the United States about what motivates bin Laden and those who support him. "bin Laden is attacking us because a specific set of US policies that have been in gear for 30 years and haven't been reviewed, haven't been defeated, haven't been questioned," says Scheur. He cited the apparently unquestioning US support for Israel, American presence on Arabian peninsula and support for regimes perceived as oppressing Muslims and for Muslim 'tyrannies'.[30]

There has been a contradiction in countering of terrorism and declaring a war on terrorism. War on Terror seems to have been perceived as the hidden agenda of pursuing American hegemony by the supporters, sympathizers and perpetrators of terrorism. It became major obstacle in stopping terrorism.

PRISONER ABUSE

Article 84 of the Fourth Geneva Convention prohibits housing prisoners of war and "persons deprived of liberty for any other reason" with general criminal populations. The rules also require that enemy prisoners be kept in facilities "affording every guarantee of hygiene and healthfulness." [31]

This very article of the Geneva Convention has been flawed by the forces fighting the war against terrorism. Abu Gharaib Prison incident of torturing Iraqi prisoners (widely circulated photos showing US soldiers abusing prisoners), Guantanamo Bay incident of violating the Quran, recent incidents of torturing of Iraqi prisoners clearly spoils the very spirit of the Geneva Convention. Such incidents have reduced the number of liberal sympathizers for the war against terrorism and above all fuelled the extremist and fundamentalist sentiments of the Muslims worldwide.

Allegations of misuse of Quran at Guantánamo Bay has led to anti-US passions in many Muslim nations and prompted violent protests throughout the world. The US military released details on 3rd June 2005 about five confirmed cases of US personnel mishandling the Quran at the prison in Guantanamo

Bay, Cuba, acknowledging that soldiers and interrogators kicked the Muslim holy book, got copies wet, stood on a Quran during an interrogation and inadvertently sprayed urine on another copy. Brig. Gen. Jay W. Hood, commander of Joint Task Force Guantanamo, who completed the three-week inquiry into alleged mishandling of the Quran, also confirmed five cases of intentional or unintentional mishandling of the holy book, which appear to be unrelated, from among 19 alleged incidents since the detention facility opened in January 2002. His investigation also found 15 incidents of detainees desecrating Quran. Amnesty International is the latest organization to allege detainee abuse at the United States military prison at Guantanamo Bay. Misuse of Quran at Guantanamo Bay again brought the irresponsible conduct of the US military personal in forefront and questioned the very purpose of American war on terrorism.[32]

Although there was a debate in US over this issue and demand was even to shut the Guantanamo Bay detention facility which US had been using after 9/11, that fact is that it fanned the flames of hatred and outrage among Muslim community against America. These incidents of torturing of Iraqi prisoners by US military force at Abu Ghraib prison and Guantanamo Bay incident and recent abuse of detainees questioned the very purpose of war against terrorism. These incidents antagonized the Muslim community against the United States and its allies who are fighting the global war against terror. These incidents have created hurdle in their war against terrorism and produced more terrorists leading to increase in terrorist attack worldwide.

CONCLUSION

Six years have been completed since the United States declared global war on terror. But no major breakthrough has been achieved except tracking down world's biggest terrorist network, Al-Qaida and detaining and killing some terrorists. The counter terrorism measures have not been able to stop terrorists attack worldwide. In last two years in fact there has been an increasing trend in this direction.

International community and especially US will have yto revaluate its strategy to tackle terrorism.

First of all the hub of terrorists activities Pakistan and its leader Mmusharf's role need to be assessed. Musharraf has been blatantly fooling the international community on the matter of cracking down on terrorists. It has to be seen whether he really implements the crack-down against extremists and jihadi terrorists announced by him after the London explosions of July 7,2005. This is the third crack-down announced by him since 9/11.The first two crack-downs announced by him in 2002 were a sham. The terrorist organisations banned by him in 2002 continued to function under different names.

To achieve the progress in tracking down terrorism and progress made by terrorists to acquire the WMD the nations fighting against terrorism must interrogate A.Q. Khan by a group of international experts not connected with Pakistan outside Pakistani territory. This is necessary to prevent or pre-empt the use of nuclear or radiological weapons by the terrorists, it is of the utmost importance for the UN Security Council to force Pakistan to hand over A.Q. Khan to an outside agency for a thorough interrogation.[33]

International community will have to take action against the terrorist infrastructure based in Pakistani territory which has been the continuous source of Jihadi terrorists in India and all over the world.

The Leaders and the linchpin of Al Qaeda and pro-Al Qaeda foreign terrorist network in Iraq like Osama bin Laden, Ayman al-Zawahiri and Abu Musab al-Zarqawi must be captured or killed to convey a strong signal to their terrorist gangmembers, supporters and sympathizers that ultimately the terrorist would be hunt down and peace will prevail.

The Al Qaeda and the International Islamic Front (IIF)

need to be distinguished. Both are not same. The IIF followed the united front tactics of communist insurgencies to suit the operational needs of jihadi terrorist organisations. The IIF, an international Jihadi network, ideology has three elements- loyalty first to religion; religious solidarity; and recognition of only the frontiers of Islam and not national frontiers. The IIF feels that its perception of the Islamic Ummah as an organic whole gives the Muslims the right to go and wage Jihad anywhere to protect their religion and their co-religionists.

It is known that terrorists are well connected not only with similar groups in different countries, but also with groups involved in narcotic trade and drug trafficking and with manufacturers and distributors of deadly weapons. The merchants of death, drug traffickers, terrorist elements, and some of the international criminal syndicates are having some kind of nexus amongst themselves. The international coalition fighting the war against terrorism will have to break that nexus and the targets are not only the terrorist groups but also other groups of this kind who are indirectly supporting them[34] .

Focus has to be given on Bangladesh which in last few years has emerged as a new hub of international jihadi terrorism. The recent explosions—450 of them— on August 17,2005, right across Bangladesh proved it. Also presence of pro-Al Qaeda and pro-Taliban terrorist can be seen in local civil society, local security agencies and armed forces.

South-East Asia region is another area where terrorists are proliferating their terrorist activities. Spread of the prairie fire of jihadi terrorism into Southern Thailand is a case in that point. The embers, which started this fire, originated from Bangladesh and Pakistan and not from Indonesia or southern Philippines.

International community has been focusing too much on Iraq, Afghanistan and Arabian countries, Syria, Iran for its recent fundamentalism and for acquiring nuclear weapons. But as far as controlling terrorist activities are concerned first of all terrorists from outside countries will have to be stopped coming to Iraq. The terrorists are located in Pakistan and the routes of infiltration pass through Iran and Syria.

Also resolving the Israel-Palestinian conflict is crucial to winning the war against terrorism, and US should revaluate Mid East policy but not by distancing itself from Israel.

The Madrid explosions of March 2004, Beslan , London Metro blasts of July, 2005, riots in France, continuing terrorists attack in Jammu &Kashmir despite Indo-Pak peace process , explosion in Delhi on the eve of Deepawali, and recent terrorist attack on India's IT industry by killing a scientist at IISC Banglore, and increasing terrorist attacks in South-East Asian countries indicate serious threats in future from Islamic Jihadi terrorism. Riots in Sydney were not a terrorist activity but has seeds and potential to be one.

The various incidents of terrorism all over the world seem to reflecting a concerted attempt to create a Pan Islamic dominance worldwide. Their objective such as the creation of Islamic Caliphates in South-East, South and Central Asia shows that terrorism has a PAN Islamic angle which can not be countered easily and classical political approach is not sufficient to tackle terrorism in this case.[35]

Fighting terrorism with intelligence and military power is necessary, but the US and its allies must not forget that antagonizing the Muslim community would not serve the purpose. The incidents like torturing of prisoners by Indy England, Guantanamo Bay and insulting the Quran would not serve the very purpose of fighting terrorism. By humiliating the Muslim community, the US and it allies would invited more hatred against themselves. They will have to remember that they are not fighting a traditional war but a war where the enemy is not visible, an enemy who is driven by the very strong force of religious fundamentalism.

In the long run, the spread of democracy, economic and social reform, sustained and encouraged by the United States and others should promote political, economic and social conditions inhospitable to terrorist exploitation. For now, however, the tasks confronting the United States and its allies in this war against terrorism remain formidable.

REFERENCES

1. Patterns of Global Terrorism, *http://www.state.gov/s/ct/rls/pgtrpt/*
2. *http://en.wikipedia.org/wiki/Islamic_Terrorism*
3. Terrorism : Q & A, US Support to Israel, Council on Foreign Relations. http://cfrterrorism.org/cfr/
4. Terrorism: Q&A, US Support to Israel, Council on Foreign Relations, *http://cfrterrorism.org/cfr/*. Also see Rubin, Barry & Rubin, Judith Colp, *Anti-American Terrorism and the Middle East* (Oxford University Press: 2002)
5. Boucher, Richard, International Terrorism: American Hostages, Press Statement, Washington, DC, February 20, 2002. *http://www.state.gov/r/pa/prs/ps/2002/8190.htm*
6. The US Government rescinded Iraq's designation as a state sponsor in October 2004 *http://www.state.gov/s/ct/*
7. Ibid.
8. Handbook on Counter-terrorism Measures: What US Nonprofits and Grantmakers Need to know *http://72.14.203.104/search?q=cache:GAEfk1q6yqoJ:www.cof.org/files/Documents/Publications/2004/Counter-terrorismHandbook.pdf+counter-terrorism+measures+by+US&hl=en&client=firefox-a#6*
9. Cheney: NSA eavesdropping critical to US security, Wednesday, January 4, 2006, *http://www.cnn.com/2006/POLITICS/01/04/cheney.nsa/*
10. Released by the Bureau of Resource Management and the Office of the Coordinator for Counter-terrorism June 22, 2004 , *http://www.state.gov/s/ct/rls/pgtrpt/2003/33771.htm.*
11. National Counter-terrorism Center (NCTC), United States, *http://www.mipt.org/Source.asp?id=80* also http://www.tkb.org/documents/Downloads/NCTC_Report.pdf
12. National Counter-terrorism Center: Implementation, Challenges and Issues for Congress, *http://www.fas.org/sgp/crs/intel/RL32816.pdf*

13. *NCTC's Worldwide Incidents Tracking System (WITS), http://www.tkb.org/Home.jsp.*

14. Glasser , Susan B., US Figures Show Sharp Global Rise In Terrorism, *Washington Post,* Wednesday, April 27, 2005. *http://www.washingtonpost.com/wp-dyn/content/article/2005/04/26/AR2005042601623.html*

15. *http://www.whitehouse.gov/infocus/nationalsecurity/index.html*

16. http://www.state.gov/

17. Ibid.

18. Raman, B., Meeting of a Study Group on Terrorism of the Council on Security Co-operation Asia Pacific (CSCAP) held at Bangkok on April 26 and 27, 2005

19. Raman ,B., International Terrorism Monitor: Paper No. 2 A.Q.Khan & Al Qaeda: Road to Nuclear Jihad, *http://www.saag.org/%5Cpapers17%5Cpaper1638.html*

20. Mahapatra ,Chintamani, *Pakistan?s Response to America?s War against Terrorism, http://www.ipcs.org/Terrorism_kashmirLevel2.jsp?action=showView&kValue=898&subCatID=1022&status=article&mod=g*

21. Raman, B., Jihadi Terrorism: A US Perspective - Part II*, http://www.observerindia.com/analysis/A426.htm*

22. Raman, B., *Jihadi Terrorism: A US Perspective - Part II, http://www.observerindia.com/analysis/A426.htm*

23. Al-Qaeda' group linked to London blasts*, http://www.usatoday.com/news/world/2005-07-07-london-claim_x.htm*

24. Ivan Eland, Evidence that the US May Be Losing the Global War on Terror ,April 25, 2005 http://independent.org/newsroom/article.asp?id=1501

25. Rumsfeld's War-on-Terror Memo, *http://www.usatoday.com/news/washington/executive/rumsfeld-memo.htm*

26. War Against Terror is a Failure, Ex-White House official says , San Fransisco Chronicle, Wednesday, September 8, 2004.

27. "War on Terror Vanishes from Agenda", *BBC News,* 24 November, 2004.

28. Bluementhal, Sydney, "Tunnel Vision", *Salon,* July 28, 2005.

29. Gregory, Frank & Wilkinson, Paul, "Riding Pillion for Tackling Terrorism is a High-risk Policy", in *Security, Terrorism and the UK,* Briefing Paper, July 2005, Chatham House, London, UK.

30. "War on Terror Vanishes from Agenda", *BBC News,* 24 November, 2004.

31. *http://chinadaily.com.cn/english/doc/2004-06/02/content335793.htm*

32. Burns, Robert, "Quran Kicked, Stepped on in Prison at Guantánamo", *Associated Press*, June 4, 2005 *http://www.kuwaitifreedom.org/media/br_news_front3.php* Also White, Josh and Eggen, Dan, "Pentagon Details Abuse of Koran Detainees' Holy Books Were Kicked, Got Wet" *Washington Post*, June 4, 2005

33. *http://www.saag.org/%5Cpapers17%5Cpaper1638.html*

34. Interview with Prof. Chintamani Mahapatra, *News Insight*, Thursday, January 05, 2006, *http://www.indiareacts.com/archivefeatures/nat2.asp?recno=20&ctg=World*

35. Raman, B., *Terrorism: Past, Present & Future*, Paper presented at a conference on terrorism organised by the Institute For Peace and Conflict Studies, New Delhi, on December 16 and 17, 2002.

11

Combating International Terrorism: Afro-arab And Asian Experience

Jagdish P. Sharma

In a firm move aimed at reassuring the Muslim community, Prime Minister Dr. Manmohan Singh made it clear that the muslim community should not be targeted in the fight against terrorism. He described terrorists as, "Traitors and Frauds" and emphasized that terrorism should be stamped out at any cost. Talking to Muslim religious leaders and intellectuals, he sought their cooperation in the task. At the same time, he said that any action against terrorism should be based on concrete evidence. In his Independence day address Dr. Manmohan Singh asked Pakistan to take concrete steps to end cross-border terrorism to enable the peace initiatives to succeed.

"We have taken several initiatives - to be successful, these initiatives need an atmosphere of peace. It is obvious that unless Pakistan takes concrete steps to implement the solemn assurances it has given to prevent cross-border terrorism against India from any territory within its control, public opinion in India, which has supported the peace process, will be undermined, "said Dr. Singh.

Addressing the nation from the ramparts of the Red Fort

after unfurling the tricolour on the occasion of 59th Independence Day on 15 August 2006, the Prime Minister said all countries in our region must recognize that terrorism anywhere is a threat to peace and prosperity everywhere. "It must be confronted with our united efforts."

Observing that there was a larger constituency for peace and shared prosperity "among our people and we must work together to build on that," he said the dream of a South Asian community could hardly be realized if terrorist violence and Politics of hate and confrontation continue to cast a dark shadow.

"We are prepared to work together with all our neighbours to usher in an era of peace and prosperity for our peoples", he said.

In a similar vein, Former Pakistan Prime Minister Benazir Bhutto has asked General Parvez Musharaff to "do more" against terrorism and extremism. In an interview to a British TV channel, she said General Musharaff needed to do more to limit the influence of religious parties and militant groups to tackle extremism. "We need to create a climate within Pakistan where the moderate forces can triumph. At the moment I see that religious parties are gaining strength and the militants, despite several crackdowns are intact", she said. In a travel advisory, the Australian department of foreign affairs and trade urged Australians to reconsider plans to visit Pakistan "due to the very high threat of terrorist attack".

For years the Pakistani intelligence agency the ISI and other outfits have been harbouring fundamentalist militias to further their agenda in Kashmir. For years, they have been fighting a proxy war against India in the Kashmir valley using terrorists. The terrorist groups like Al Qaeda and the other militant varieties like Lashkar-e-Toiba, whose founder had been put under a formal house arrest in Pakistan have made it their lives' mission to kill at random and cause destruction of property in the name of an unholy "Jihad". While the open support and the moral and material assistance extended to sustain and develop these groups in the early stages of their formation have receded into the background on account of growing international condemnation of their activities, the evil has not been eradicated. Many terror outfits are still active, some of them even being able to indoctrinate and misguide youth to undertake terrorist missions. Rashid Rauf, a Briton identified by Pakistan as a key suspect in the London airliner terror plot has links with outlawed Pakistan militant group Jaish-e-Mohammed and is related by marriage to its leader Maulana Masood Azhar who was freed by India in Kandahar in 1999, an intelligence official of Pakistan said£.

Today the world faces three major challenges: the challenges of poverty and under development, the challenge of environmental sustainability and the challenge of security posed by international terrorism. With about 200 innocent railway commuters killed in Mumbai on 11th July 2006 and over ten times that number of air passengers reportedly targeted to be blown up in mid-air, (the plot was foiled by British intelligence). Panic buttons have been pressed for civilians in all walks of life. Given the fact that 17 terrorist organizations have been using suicide bombers in 14 countries including India, accounting for over 50 percent killings, no security system in the world is equipped to tackle suicide terrorism that targets civilians. From the comprehensive database provided by Professor Robert Pape, it can be seen that suicide terrorism is not primarily a product of Islamist extremism, as is often believed in view of 9/11 and 7/7 attacks in the US and UK respectively[1] (refer : The Strategic Logic of Suicide Terrorism). The 'Secular' Tamil Tigers (LTTE), with their localized operations, figure as prominently in his database as the fundamentalist Al-Qaeda. The most prominent among victims of suicide attacks and assassinations were President Anwar Sadat of Egypt in 1981, Rajiv Gandhi, Former Prime Minister of India in 1991 and Ranasinghe Premdasa, President of Srilanka in 1993, and Abu Jihad, the second most important Palestinian leader after President Yasser Arafat by the state of Israel in 1989. Fifteen years later in 2006, the LTTE officially admitted to the killing of the former Indian Premier and apologized for its unpardonable act, thus exposing its mindlessness.

Atleast four major terror plots have been thwarted since the July 7, 2005 attacks in London, It was revealed recently as investigations into the conspiracy to blow up US bound flights showed that terrorists were planning a wave of "apocalyptic" strikes on land and air. Security sources in London estimate that as many as 1,200 people are actively involved with terrorism and that the country is still under "very severe" threat from other potential plots.

As terror plots unfold, bomb scares abound throughout the world. In post-blasts Mumbai, Many people have opted to travel by the state run BEST buses. A large number of Westbound leisure travelers have postponed their trips after the Heathrow airport scare. British Airways and Air India recorded a sharp dip in passengers as families cancelled trips to avoid harassment at European and US airports. Since the September 11, 2001 terrorist strikes on World Trade Centre in New York and the subsequent tragic events in India – attacks on Indian Parliament, attacks on Jammu and Kashmir Assembly, the 2005 Pre-Diwali bombings in Delhi and the recent bombings in Mumbai which killed more than 200 people and injured more than 500, as well as the grenade attacks in Srinagar, the threat to peace and stability of Asia and particularly India has assumed a dangerous proportion. Terrorism has emerged as a global menace and is an assault on human decency. After September 11, 2001, it assumed a global perspective. It is important to note that even before September 11, India had reminded the world about this problem. Nobody was bothered to listen to the Indian point of view then. But, now things have changed, the whole world has realized the potential threat of terrorism. All the major powers including the Afro-Arab and Asian world are facing the threat of terrorism. And the fear of nuclear weapons falling into the hands of the terrorist organizations has put all the major powers of the world on tenterhooks in the war against terrorism.

The world is steadily realizing the fact that terrorism needs to be dealt globally rather than locally, and it is no longer a threat to one or two countries, but to the whole human civilization. It is creating new political equations in the global politics.

Terrorism is actual or threatened use of violence for political and economic goals, directed not only against the victims themselves but also against larger, related groups. International terrorism has acquired the character of undeclared war between the sovereign representative of the victim states and the organized militancy of international fanatics. There are plenty of terrorist groups around the world. The list includes *Abu Sayyaf Group*(Philippines & Malaysia, 1991), *Ansar al-Islam* (Iraq, 2001), *Armed Islamic Group*(Algeria, 1992), *Asbat al-Ansar* (Lebanon, 1990), *Aum Supreme Truth* (Japan & Russia, 1987), *Basque Fatherland and Liberty*(ETA, Spain, France, 1959), *Al Gamaa al-Islamiyya* (Egypt, 1973), *Harakut-al-Mujahiddin* (Pakistan, 1985), *Jaish-e-Mohammed*(Pakistan, 200), *Jemaah Islamiya* (Southeast Asia, 1990), *Al-Jihad* (Egypt, Yemen, Afghanistan, Pakistan etc., 1970), *Kahane Chai*(Israel, 1994), State sponsor's of terrorist acts like the state of Israel (1948 onwards), *Lashkar-e-Tayyiba*(Pakistan, 1989), *Lashkar I Jhangvi* (Pakistan, Afghanistan, 1996), *Liberation Tigers of Tamil Eelam*______ (Srilanka, 1976), *Al-Qaeda* (Afghanistan, 1980), *The Salafist Group for Call and Combat* (Algeria, 1992) and *Sendero Luminoso* (Peru, 1960).

The term terrorism implies action by non-governmental militant groups or by secret units operating outside the usual parameters of warfare aiming at destruction. Terrorists have no fixed territorial limits, no legitimate sovereignty, no visible army, and no known sources of financial income. They operate from their hideouts anywhere in the world. Terrorists indoctrinated with blind belief in fanaticism and radical thinking, use the force of religion to bring into their fold young adolescents and youths and give their minds a thorough brain-washing. The origins of terrorism in West Asia and Arab Africa can be traced to the establishment of the state of Israel on the Arab-Palestinian land and blind and biased economic and military support of the United States to Israel against the Arab-Palestinians. From 1948 to the present crises in Lebanon (The consistent Israeli invasion of Arab-Palestinian lands) the pattern of U.S. support to Israel, right or wrong, has been persisting. This has contributed to increasing militancy in the region.

THE PROBLEM OF INSURGENCY IN AFRO-ARAB WORLD

Algeria

The problem of insurgency in Algeria, Egypt, and Nigeria have been dealt with in greater detail in this following paper.

It is very unfortunate that religion and politics are mixed together to produce a violent cocktail, which should have no place in setting the social, political and economic problems of civil society. There was something sinister in the way Pakistan supported terrorists who attacked the Indian Parliament, the heart of Indian Democracy on December 13, 2001. All the justifications for violence claimed by Jihadi militants and Pakistan cannot blur the fact that the net results of such activity are sorrow and despair to the innocent population, particularly women and children.

Islam as a great religion, sought of the Muslims to create an egalitarian social system where poor and vulnerable would be treated with respect and dignity. This Jihad was indeed a spiritual, political, social and economic struggle. During colonial period, Jihad was essentially a struggle for freedom, justice and equality. The religious solidarity was there in organizing and mobilizing the people. It was a fight, like in the case of Arab Palestinians (against Israeli occupation) of entire people to decide there own destiny. But today, it has narrowed down to violence, extremism and fanaticism. Notwithstanding his denials Osama Bin Laden is still considered as one of the leading and prime suspects of international terrorism.

During the Cold War period, the use of terror in the name of Islam was promoted on pragmatic grounds, to enlist the help of political Islam by the west, particularly the US, which helped hammer the final nails in the coffin of Communism by defeating the Russian Red Army in Afghanistan, led to catastrophe – first for the Afro-Arab Asian world and later for America itself, as was so shockingly brought home by the September 11, 2001 attacks on New York and Washington. After the collapse of Communism, religious extremism or terrorism in the name of Islam is viewed as a major threat to world peace and new global economic order. The Islamic militants gained prominence in the late 1970s and early 1980s as a reaction to what was perceived as the failure of Afro-Asian socialism, Marxism, liberalism and capitalism.

On the occasion of Algeria's Independence day in 1999 President Abdalaziz Bouteflika granted pardon to thousands of prisoners convicted of providing support to Islamic radicals, fighting the government. The release of prisoners was the result of deal between President Bouteflika's newly elected democratic government and the head of Armee Islamique Du Salut(AIS), Madani Mezraq. The commitment of President Bouteflika to democratic and people oriented socio-economic and political policies and pragmatic approach have been succeeded in bringing the terrorist revolt in the country under control. The terrorist insurgency in Algeria which had been simmering for long erupted with a heightened violence when in December 1991 elections, *Islamic Salvation Front*(FIS) won the first round. The second round of elections was halted mid way and the FIS was dissolved by a court order in March 1992. The head of state, Mohamed Boudiaf was assassinated on 29 July 1992 and a campaign of terror was launched by Islamic radicals, which had continued till the recent years. It is estimated that more than 150,000 lives have been lost since the war between the government and the Islamic radicals began in 1992.

Egypt

The triple blasts (April 2005) that ripped through an Egyptian resort brought anguish and calls for an end to violence from Arabs across the Afro-Arab region, many of whom questioned why Muslims have now become a prime target for terrorists. The 26 April 2005 bombings shattered a long national holiday weekend in Egypt, killing at least 24 people – at least 21 of them Egyptians – and wounding more than 60 people.

"They want to change our Government and break our people", said Mustafa Mahmood, 24 who works at a travel agency across the street from the American University of Cairo. Mohieddine Joueidi, a 51 year old lawyer in Sidon, Lebanon, said the attacks seemed "designed to weaken Egypt's role in the region and spread panic and terror throughout the region'."[2] Since the last three decades. Egyptian rulers have grappled with the resurgence of Islam that has significantly challenged the State. The Egyptian experience has witnessed radicalization and institutionalization of Islam socially and politically. In 1979, Muhammad Abdul Salam Faraq, leader of the Egyptian Jihad organization pronounced the government to be apostate and an entity to be fought through a holy war by believers; a return to Jihad was the only way to redemption. Islamic resurgence in Egypt and the Afro-Arab world began with the formation of the society of Muslim Brothers or Islamic brotherhood, Jamiyyat al-Ikhwan al-Muslimin by Hasan al-Banna (1906-1949) in 1928.

Hasan al-Banna's central concern was to analyse the reasons for the decline of Islam in Egypt and elsewhere and to work out a comprehensive and effective remedy. The eviction of the Arab-Palestinians and the establishment of Israel on Palestinian soil had deeply troubled al-Banna and has remained a concern of the Muslim Brotherhood thereafter. With its large size of population, Egypt seems to be vulnerable to this emerging radical Islamic movement. The mass appeal of Islamic radicalism has its roots in wordly frustrations and denials, and those frustrations and denials have been given a religious idiom. In Egypt, Algeria, Saudi Arabia, Kuwait, Jordan and elsewhere, Islamism is basically an indigenous response to prevalent socio-economic and political problems. Islamism here is a product of the failed modernization policies of the past 50 years, which resulted in unfulfilled expectations and consequent militancy. The Hosni Mubarak Government is trying to tackle this problem through socio-political and economic reforms.

Nigeria

The recent developments include a major terrorist strike in Nigeria. Thousands of Nigerian muslims protesting against the publication of caricatures of Prophet Mohammad attacked Christians and burned churches in northeastern Nigeria, killing atleast 45 people in February 2006. It was the first major protest to erupt over the issue in Africa's most populous nation. Three children and a Catholic priest were reportedly among those killed. Nigeria, Africa's most populous country of more than 130 million people, is roughly divided between a predominantly Muslim north and a mainly Christian South. Thousands of people have died in this West African country since 2000 in religious violence fuelled by the adoption of the strict Islamic or Sharia legal code by a dozen states in the north which is seen by most Christians as a move to impose religious hegemony on non-Muslims. The religious cartoons, which first appeared in a Danish newspaper in September 2005, set off violent protests around the Afro-Arab-Asian world sweeping through Libya, Nigeria, Pakistan and other Countries.

CONCLUSION

The challenge of insecurity and terrorism must be addressed first by socio-economic measures securing and commiting greater resources to the poorest countries and regions of the globe. The growing disparity between the rich and the poor on our planet and the gross misallocation of limited resources to vested interests and imposed wars can not be allowed to continue. If they do, we can expect even greater threats and challenges ahead. We need a global glasnost – openness, transparency, and people to people dialogue – on the part of nations, governments and citizens today to build consensus in meeting these threats. In the words of former Soviet President Mr. Mikhail Gorbachev, "We need a policy of preventive engagement: international and individual solidarity, and action to meet the socio-economic roots of the threat, that is, poverty, disease, income disparity and conflict in sustainable and reasonable way.

Terrorist groups challenging established authority surely need to be put down. Equally important is the political aspect and in this context the efforts to establish a separate independent State of Palestine could be a major factor in ending militancy in the Afro-Arab and Asian region.

Although all major powers of the world accept terrorism as a major problem and have taken many steps to save the world from this deadly problem, a lot needs to be done. The whole world should cooperate in nabbing the terrorists who take safe haven in the friendly countries. In the sub-continental context the threat posed by the Taliban terrorists has spread beyond Pakistan's borders. The Pakistani rulers seem to realize that it should not develop into dangerous proportions in their own country. All the countries in the Afro-Arab and Asian region including India, Iran, Karzai's Afghanistan, Pakistan, Turkey, Central Asia, Russia, Algeria, Egypt and Nigeria have a common stake in keeping the terrorists at bay. Religious bigotry and terrorism is not going to serve any religion.

REFERENCES

1. Robert A Pape, "The Strategic Logic of Suicide Terrorism", American Political Science Review Vol. 97, No. 3 August 2003
2. Jamal Halaby, *The Pioneer*, April 26, 2005

12
TERRORISM IN TODAY'S GLOBAL SCENARIO

Sudhira Chandra Jena

The twentieth Century has been very turbulent in the history of the world. It has seen the rise of socialism and collapse of socialist economies. It has also witnessed the rise of fascist regimes and world wars. It has seen the rise of religious fascism or fundamentalism, also known as religion based nationalism. Also it is being witness to globalization, liberalization and privatization as the highest phase of capitalism in the world economy causing havoc on the lives of poor, and above all 'terrorism'-the great threat to humanity. The key question is-whether there is any deeper linkage between these phenomena or their taking place in the same span of time is a mere coincidence? The answer is given in the following. Some countries under the illusion of socialist dream could side track the rules of market economy. Here the emphasis was laid on social welfare but these state proved to be unable, in the global economy where "Free Market" prevailed. Last two decades of 20th century saw the unique phenomenon of collapse of these economies and rise of middle sections of society in the garb of traditionalism, under the banner of religious nationalism, basically to oppose the transitions towards equality, to preserve the process of change, to strengthen the status quo. In some other countries, especially the oil rich, imperialism ensured the sustenance of pre modern authoritarian regimes to fill the coffers of G-7 countries. The simmering discontent, the blockade of democratic channels led to rebellions, which due to the lack of democratic channels are being expressed through 'terrorism' which in a way is the concentrated expression of injustices perpetuated on a large section of people. In this context, terrorism was defined specifically with regimes in mind, more specifically with the totalitarian soviet or communist or East Bloc regime in mind contrasted to the democratic regime of the US and the west. Here terrorism was defined as a negative form of governance or system of rule.

This is not an attempt to conceptualize 'terrorism', but without a proper definition we cannot discuss the trend. But the term 'terrorism' is really difficult to define. It can be described, rather than be defined. To have a clear-cut idea on terrorism, we have to consider terrorist events/acts/activities of terrorists. Acts of terrorism are acts or threats of violence against the ordinary, unarmed civilians carried out in the pursuit of a political objective. However, drawing on the Geneva Convention of 1949, terrorism could be defined as the systematic use of violence and intimidation against civilian populations and the natural and social environments that sustain them. Terrorism may be carried out by individuals, groups (non state actors) or state under conditions of conflict including war. It has often been remarked that terrorism is the weapon of the powerless. But history shows that the most heinous acts of terror have been conducted by warring states, which could be called state terrorism.

Is there a difference in the nature of violence committed by patriots, political extremists, religious fundamentalists and those whom we describe today as terrorists? There were hundreds of others all over the world, fighting for what they see as legitimate causes. History gives them credit for forcing their adversaries to the negotiating table. The common people saw them as brave heroes fighting ruthless despotic regimes. It would be interesting to find out when and why the semantics of violence suddenly changed. When terrorism lost its romance and legitimacy and became just another ugly and violent crime. While other forms of violence, including that inspired by the state, possibly the most dangerous and growing trend in today's world, goes entirely unpublished. What is worse is that it is gaining legitimacy by the day under the garb of the national interest. The US is more belligerently patriotic than ever. So is Israel. So are nations like Pakistan, always up and ready to go to war.

This discussion is confined to terrorist acts at the international level, which is also of general applicability to domestic terrorist acts. In this background, the 9/11 attack on the US is certainly terrorism. It is terrorism at its ugliest. But was Hiroshima any less ugly? Was the bombing of Afghanistan any less terrible? On the other hand, if we illegitimise terrorism, we will have to rewrite all our history. Would Netaji be held under TADA? Would Khudiram be jailed for life? For what we so glibly describe as terrorism today is very often the last attempt of the weak and the poor to be heard. To be heard by a state that is willfully blind, deaf and dumb. So much is boasted about democracy and yet so little is done to ensure that the poor get jobs, homes, medical attention and enough to stay alive. On top of that, we sue religion, caste, ideology to terrorize them. Can they be blamed who out of frustration and anger choose to hit back in the only way they know? One can choose one's own semantics to describe terrorism, but no one can stop it.

In this context, critics of the attack on WTC, say, "these towers were chosen by the terrorists probably because they are symbols of American economic domination and imperialistic designs". The terrorists wanted to convey this message to the world in general and the Americans in particular.

However, terrorism may be linked to violence but violence of poverty, racism, sexism and injustice is not right, rather stricter definition of violence has to be used-the exercise of force such as to physically harm, injure, pain or kill humans. In this context, terrorist acts, which result in mass murder, can additionally be defined as crimes against humanity. Hence any war against terrorism is a terrorist war. Terrorism is understood as having one or a number of the following characteristics:

i. It is organized intimidation;

ii. Violence against civilians or non-combatants;

iii. Indiscriminate use of violence;

iv. Illegitimate use of violence.

Each of these understandings carries grave problems. Intimidation is too loose and broad a concept. There are many kinds or forms of organized intimidation including systems or structures of psychological intimidation at various degrees and levels. Further terrorist acts can also be inflicted on combatants as well. Indefensible violence or extreme disproportion in violence is used against opposing combatants, such as the use of nuclear or chemical or biological warfare, this too can count as terrorism. One does not need to use WMD. Simply using tanks or bombs to destroy a militant hideout-can also count as an indefensible terrorist act. Further more certain civilians (head of the state) given their own very major responsibilities for conducting warfare can be seen by the opposing side with justice as legitimate targets for terrorist efforts at assassination. Terrorist attacks sometimes involve very specific indeed highly discriminate use of violence. Finally, assigning the label of terrorism to only those acts deemed illegitimate begs all questions about the legitimacy of the 'officially' legitimate wielders of violence-the state. Such an approach is far too narrow, for it definitionally outlaws even the possibility of state terrorism.

An appropriate and serviceable definition of terrorism or terrorist act then must posses the following properties:

i. it should be evaluated neutrally,

ii. it should not be too broad or too narrow;

iii. it should be objective. So the judgement of whether an act or event is terrorist or not should be made independently of and without reference to the motives or self perceptions of the perpetrators of that act.

However, from our experiences on events of 20th century and September 11th event of US in 2001, we can draw a working definition of terrorism. It is the calculated or premeditated use or threat of use of violence against an individual, group or large collectivity in such a manner that the target is rendered physically defenseless against that attack or against the affects of that violence. This form of political terrorism is different from criminal terrorism in the sense that the act is harnessed to some political intent or purpose and carries a political meaning. This event of terrorism becomes defenseless due to :

i. surprise war zone;

ii. the nature of the target chosen;

iii. the nature of weapon used;

iv. enormous disproportion in the violence.

In view of 9/11 events we can say that modern technology by its very nature can not be confined to a particular area or a country. US technology was used against it. So the target, method of attack, weapon used and loss-everything became unique and more violent than expected.

So here, we can say that while domestic political terrorism is the righteous revolutionary struggle to overthrow oppressor regimes, international political terrorism may be a struggle or war of liberation from dominance, exploitation, deprivation, psychological trauma and superior attitude. But Musharaff's declaration of cross border terrorism as a freedom struggle is not-appropriate as it does not coincide with above factors. The issue of cross border terrorism will be very clear, when in the following we make a discussion on causes of terrorism to understand it properly.

But the importance of terrorism and terrorist acts vary

from person to person and country to country, because it is relative to the parties (perpetrators and victims). And we can say that it has no border/boundary, no law, no religion. In the last 14 years of terrorist activities in J & K, where terrorist are Muslims, out of 12,400 killings 11,000 belong to Muslim community. But, terrorism has its own ideology and own culture also.

I

Regarding causes of terrorism we can say that it has some general causes besides particular ones due to peculiar settings of different states/ countries. Regarding terrorism there is no comprehensive theory. However, a psychological research in Germany at three levels – individual, group and organisation- indicate that terrorism is seen both in developing and developed countries. The study shows that aggressive political behaviour is found with individuals due to failure to get satisfaction. Out of total respondents 25% of them said that either of parents were dead when they were 14 or below and many of them were in juvenile court due to some crimes. So lack of confidence, frustration, reflection of weakness, obstruction to individual for self development / fulfillment and enjoyment of liberty are cause of the growth of terrorism. So here, we can say that Macro level happenings (International Terrorism or State Terrorism) have Micro level beginnings. So terrorism becomes a culture invaded by the concept that every kind seeks liberty. It is an animal cult which does not yield to rational thinking and it is within the individual.

The next important factor after psychology is the society / social background / setting of individuals / state which make / makes them a terrorist and terrorism will continue depending upon the societal setting of the state, where social values have declined. Socialization process is responsible for this type of behaviour, where socializing the human culture and civilization become failure and society becomes the breeding ground of terrorism.

Terrorism is the weapon of the weak. It is a means to raise wars by racist, ethnic groups, religious groups and minorities to establish their identity and terrorism is an end in itself to damage the enemy's identity. Here comes the question of group; perception of the group determines terrorist activities and group is helpful in risk-taking also. Here we can make a link between religion and ethnic groups. Religion can be both a faith and an identity. As a faith religion becomes spiritual and ritual and performs many functions to strengthen the society, culture and tradition. But religion as an identity acquires political overtones. The terrorists use religion as an identity as ethnicity becomes a powerful function of identity. So ethnic terrorism is as dangerous as religious terrorism and vice-versa. They interpret religion in a distorting way for their own cause and indoctrinate young minds which leads to fundamentalism, fanaticism and finally violence / terrorism. So here religious ideology with strong motivation and training are the cause of international terrorism. Training makes them highly motivated and creates deep sense of commitment for the cause with money and weapon they try to realize and idealism becomes responsible for the survival of terrorism. Hence, modern technology in the hands of such highly ideologically motivated as well as trained individuals can prove as disastrous as in the hands of a country. Big powers of the world should also bear in mind that many nations, of their policies, are remaining silent – for the interests of their ruling classes coincide with those of big power classes – but some angry victim citizens of these countries can retaliate with deadly efficiency and may bring disaster to the humanity. We have seen the rise of Hitler in the history. We have felt the wrath of Laden. The history of Afghanistan shows that they never surrender even to their own co-religionists from outside. The Mughal rulers of India could never hold the Afghans under their own tutelage. In future more US intervention in the affairs of Afghanistan may bring retaliation by some groups / individuals / non-state actors to fight out the presence of US.

In this case the role of weapons are very vital. 91% of weapons are produced by Big (5) power. They are in charge of peace at the global level but they produce weapons of mass destruction. They provide these weapons to their allies. So in future these weapons in the hands of those countries may be used to break world peace. Under the process of globalisation and liberalization the state power is diluted. Splinter groups are dominating the political activities of the state. In any slight deviation, these groups can retaliate, which will lead to terrorism at international level. In the process the democratic countries are worst sufferers as authoritarian system is immune to terrorisms.

Economic considerations are also one of the greatest causes of terrorism at the global level. When deprivation, poverty, backwardness, sufferings, impact of globalisation, negative influence of petro-dollars are responsible for rise of terrorism in developing countries in the case of developed countries like US the economic consideration have equal role to make it a terrorist state. Bush administration is now exploring the possibility of entering in a big way the new oil bazaar of central Asia. US has fought 75 times since 1945, causing 12 million deaths. But when they appear committed to the spread of democracy and freedom but the underlying factor is the economic interests of the US. On the one hand they claim to bring the hope of democracy, development, free markets and free trades to every corner of the world, on the other hand US does not need sanction of the international community and takes pre-emptive action where its interests are threatened. They say "reasons for our actions will be clear and the cause just". But the justness of the cause is determined by the US itself. The US is both the plaintiff and the judge. Regarding Afghanistan and Taliban-Al-Quaida regime US says that the cause of growth of terrorism in that country is weak state. They type of state can pose as great a danger to national interests of US as a strong state. Poverty does not make poor people into terrorists. Yet

poverty, weak institutions and corruption can make weak states vulnerable to terrorist networks and drug cartels within their borders.

Sometimes, extra-territorial power is responsible for the rise of terrorism. The presence of US army in Afghanistan, in Pakistan and at Pakistan and at present in Malaysia violating the earlier agreement, in Kuwait, Turkey, Iraq may cause terrorist activities in future as the nationalist spirit and patriotism will be in danger as per their apprehension.

New world order declared by US is the cause of rise of terrorism at the global level. NOW according to a high level strategy paper prepared for top officials of the Bush (senior) administration envisaged on world in which the US would be able to dominate its European and Japanese allies, isolate its adversaries and sustain its client regimes. The US would be the undisputed world power capable of securing absolute control over strategic resources and a privileged place in the world market. In a systematic fashion in the months prior to 9/11 and the launching of part-II of NOW, the Bush (Jr.) administration abrogated the Kyoto agreement, the anti-missile agreement, the International Court and numerous other accords. The purpose of these unilateral actions was to create optional conditions to favour US MNCs to engage in wars of conquest and to expand military operations. Now a question before all of US. What is New World Order? Who is US to declare so? So those who are neglected in the process, terrorism appeals to them as a reaction against US monopoly over international law and politics. US always defines acts of war / terror exclusively as those directed against itself and its allies while ignoring its own crimes.

In the context of South Asia, terrorism has indigenous stating. There is no such concept as global society. The nature of terrorism in this zone is domestic. Internal factors are responsible for this but external factors entered for their benefits- China in North-East India, earlier Pakistan in Punjab, US in

Pakistan. Further we can say that failure of genuine middle class, failure in governance and failure of civil society are cause of terrorism in South Asia. In the short run globalisation has negative impact in the society and economy of South Asia, which is responsible for furthering terrorism.

II

For any problem the finding of the genuine cause means solution of the problems. In the light of above discussions now we can decide plicy perspectives to challenge the terrorism in the 21st Century to make it a peaceful one free from any violence / terrorist activities in comparison to 20th Century, through we have seen the WTO attack on 11th September, 2001 as the Century, though we have seen the WTO attack on 11th September, 2001 as the most challenged, technical, tactical, heinous, terrible and horrible. And no words can be adequate to condemn as it was directed against innocent civilians who were in no way involved in politics or matters of state policy. In retaliation, US decided to launch a war on Afghanistan in the name of 'War On Terrorism' or 'Operation Infinite Justice'. In Afghanistan only success is change of government but the Taliban, Al-Queda and Osama remain with a future planning. So a big question is before us. Has the mighty US military machine proved inadequate to the challenge of 11th Sept. 2001 despite the massive increase in the defence budget? In post September 11th period we have seen JK Assembly attack in India, attack on Indian Parliament (Dec., 13, 2001) and increasing attack of terrorists in J & K, the Moscow Cinema siege by Chechens, Bali incident in Indonesia. This shows that violence will produce more and much more vicious violence – because if US can send its military into any nation which it perceives as a threat, then Russia use similar justification to send troops into Georgia in pursuit of Chechen rebels. China can invade Taiwan to assert its sovereignty, Pakistan or India can cross the LOC and annex all of Kashmir in the name of 'national security'. The reaction of the US to the deadly attacks on WTC was not of wise matured people but of those who know only of revenge and retaliation. The western and eastern media target Islam as a religion of fanatics and violence. It is co-incidental that the terrorists in many cases are Muslims. But we should keep in mind that terrorists are not product of religion rather they are product of certain state policies. Atack on WTC was not as per the fatwa of the foremost Islamic theologian of Saudi Arabia Bin Bazz. In fact Osama has been thrown out from Saudi Arabia. He is a rebel. All Afghans do not even agree with him. Northern Alliance is a sworn enemy of the Taliban. Violence and fanaticism of Taliban are not products of religion but such religion is product of desperate need of such fringe groups. Most of the Muslim Ulama have condemned these ter ror attacks. Shaykh Hamza Yusuf in US said, "Islam was hijacked on that September, 11, 2001, on that plane, as innocent victims". There was no Islamic approval behind the incident. However, we can say here that US has no pragmatic policy to fight terrorism. Since the attack on Pearl Harbour, US has become a security-led state. Daniel Ellisberg says "Bush is moving in the direction of a police-state." So understanding of past in terms of US security and foreign policies and their co-relation to the principles that US stands for, needs a rethinking. The absence of a strong reaction from Islamic fundamentalists is a great gain in the war on terrorism. While the populations in Islamic countries have not come out in support of Taliban, there is no disputing that anti-America sentiment in all Islamic countries has grown as acknowledged over by leaders of Islamic countries which are co-operating with the US in its anti-terrorist war. This is mostly because the US has treated this anti-terrorism campaign as a military operation and has made no attempt to win the understanding and support of people of the Islamic faith. US policy towards Middle East, West Asia and South Asia has further alienated the US from the people of Islamic countries, if not the ruling classes. When US talks of Iraq's WMD, the world has not forgotten that the use of poisonous gas by the Iraq President against Iran had the tacit support of US. UK supplied the equipment for Baghdad's weapon programmes by circumventing its own laws. Like Laden, Samdm Hussain too was built up by Washington. No attempt is being made to win over the support of the people in Islamic nations. Further, US policy on unilateralism in respect of world trade regulations, the Kyoto protocol, environmental issue and sustainable development has further widened the divide between the US and its traditional democratic allies. One can not preach democracy within nation while ignoring all other democracies on international issues and yet expect to be credible as leader of the democratic world's campaign against terrorism. At the turn of the century (21st) American Muslim Political Organisations intended to foster Islamic values in America and had the freedom to do so. In his 'State of the Union Address', President Bush (Jr.), recently, announced US to foster values in Islamic countries. Although the values meant are those of liberty and justice, education, development, women's rights and others. US unilateral action can only hinder the war on terrorism. An effort must be made to engage the progressive / liberal Islamic clergy to capture the heart of the people. Side by side, Islamic populations must be encouraged to integrate into global value system in the place of fundamentalism and fanaticism. US thus rather than planning a war against terrorism should dispassionately think of policy measures which can ultimately end this brutal kind of terrorism. Arrogance will not be able to defeat Islamic terrorism. Similarly, the WTC attack is a wake up call for the ruling classes in the Muslim countries. They are sitting on volcano. American alliance or American weapons can not save them. The fate of Shah of Iran should be a lesson for them. This can be repeated also. No amount of terrorism and violence will ever help and solve the problems of Islamic terrorism. It will not only attract world-wide condemnation but it will also compound the very problem they seek to solve the problems of Islamic terrorism. It will not only attract worldwide condemnation but it will also compound the very problem they seek to solve. If they really believe in Islam they should do everything possible to project proper image of Islam as a religion of peace and compassions, not of Jehad and violence. In a 40 pages report by Sybrand Van Hulst, the Chief of AIVD, (Dutch Internal Intelligence Service) said, second generation muslims who 'wrestle with their identity' are ripe for recruitment for jehad by radical Islamic groups. Muslim immigrant families comprise around 5% of the 16 million Dutch population. 10 Al-Queda members have been arrested in Netherland since Sept., 11, 2001 and accused of actively recruiting Dutch Youth. Non-violence is the only way to win sympathy of people. They should also think sincerely as to why Muslim world has not produced persons like Gandhi, Mandela? So in the 21st Century, there is relevance of Gandhism. Here problems should be solved in a more civilized and intelligent ways. Wisdom can become much more powerful weapon than even hydrogen bomb. Terrorism recognizes no community. So Muslims must be separated from Islamic terrorist.

Regarding solution of the crisis of terrorism we can say that mechanism of control differs at National and International level. Some alternatives come to our kind.

i. Can we solve it through war?

ii. Can we solve it through diplomacy / boycotting rogue states?

iii. Can we solve it through International Institutions such as SAARC / UN ?

The answer of all these probable is a big 'No'. The problem of terrorism remains elsewhere. It will come to an end when the problem of suffering, health, poverty, economy are solved. We have to strengthen the social value system. So for this purpose, policy should be framed within the state without any outside help. In this process, big powers should not meddle with the states. In every state a department should be established to curb terrorism. The department will work hard in negotiating and solving the basic problems. Tight security and policy / Military operation, alone will rarely end terrorism, whether in US or in India. The possible targets are too many and the methods as varied and unaccountable. The key is avoiding situations where a section of the people gets so alienated that it starts believing that terror and violence are the only means to get justice – or atleast attention. Political solution are a must. KPS Gill of India went Sri Lanka on a special mission and then the world saw the negotiation with LTTE at Oslo with resolution of the continuance of Jaffna in Sri Lanka. So this amicable settlement became possible through negotiation by a specialist in the field of crime / violence etc.

At the global level UN regulations are not properly implemented, due to limited / restricted jurisdiction of UN. After a lot of difficulties, International Criminal Court at the Hague has been established on July 1, 2002. So we have to fight terrorism within the law. India became successful in passing her proposal UN level. But still we have to make a concerted effort to establish certain convention at Internation level to curb terrorism. Big power should come forward to do something / policy decision in this regard. US is violating always the norms of International Law and ignoring UN. Further, at the global level security council should authorize allies against terrorism, Pakistan sealed the border then how could the Taliban, Al-Quida and Laden enter Pakistan?

Oil industries of terrorist countries should be internationalized and controlled by security council and the profits to be spent for the economic development of Oil exporting countries. International purchaser will be there and controlling the purchase of Oil will check the rise and growth of terrorism.

General Amnesty should not be given to terrorists. In European countries through this process they killed terrorists. They should be treated as war crimes to be punished by

International Court. And terrorism should be fought through a humanistic approach as it is a human problem.

States at the global level should be united to take steps against terrorist activities and for the purpose they should rise above their national / parochial interest. Pakistan knows her position in the Asia policy of US, so US fails to take action against her. Further Big powers are not acquainted with the intensity of the problem of cross border terrorism. So they never sympathies with India. So terrorism should be considered as a crime against humanity, not against humanity, not against you and me. So we have to develop secular culture at the global level. Jeff Pettersan says," People of the world are not safe from US and the people in US are not safe from the US." So at the global level there should be a movement to protect human and democratic rights of all those concerned. Regarding terrorist prone countries, the solution of their immediate problem is the stepping stone to curb terrorism.

One thing which urgently needs to be done, in the face of lying politician and mediapersons who, with a few honourable exceptions, gutlessly and mindlessly repeat their lies, is to see clearly and speak and write the truth about what is happening, naming state terrorism for what it is. No doubt these states have the power to harass, arrest, incarcerate and kill us, but let us not allow them to colonies our minds and language or silence our voices. Information and communication should be widespread. Internet should disseminate information more widely in different languages. As a citizen of this world, we have every right to know who is vulnerable and whose humanity is violated / abused.

We have seen terrorism from Hiroshima to New York, WTC to Moscow Cinema Siege, Cross border terrorism to Bali incident. Whatever we have done earlier is adhocism. Now we urgently need for evoluting a hostage policy at the global level, so that Kandahar episode will not allow release of hard core terrorists from India or death of Pearl the journalist or the release of 700 audience of Moscow Theatre Centre.

The need for intelligence about terrorist organizations and their plans is of the essence to prevent such incidents. This calls for promoting greater public awareness about terrorist activities to obtain wider cooperation to detect them before they strike. It also requires greater regional and international co-operation to co-ordinate action against terrorist organization and their links within organized crime and other nefarious activities in society.

The temptation to blame terrorist group / organizations and other for our failure of intelligence, political management, governance and so on is no doubt useful to deflect public attention, but is leading us nowhere in our war against terrorism. That war can only be won if the search light is turned inwards to report on our own inadequacies not remain perpetually focused outwards.

Indian president on NHRC Day observed that children of India need value based education in school and at home to become good citizens and lead an empowered human life to be tolerant of other's views, ways of life, and religious practices. This can curb terrorism and violence at domestic level.

In Asia, the relationship between India, China and Russia is moving in the right track, which in future years will bring out an Axis among these there powers. This Axis will play a very vital role to put a check the US hegemony and also to Islamic terrorism as all these countries are victims of terrorism – Chechen vs : Russia, West China vs: China, Pak. vs : India. So a joint working group will come out challenge unitedly the rise of terrorism in those countries. Their role in future also will influence the working of SAARC, UN and International Criminal Court and US in particular.

Further, we can argue that states have failed to challenge terrorism. So in this perspective a realistic policy demands that we consolidate the gains that have already been made and evolve a well considered multifaceted strategy, make an intelligent study of the pros and cons of the various options and act with a degree of self confidence and faith in national values such as democracy. So in the conclusion we can say that any international problem should be given to state for solution. So reason over appetite, virtue over vice, peace over violence should be the goal of national policy to establish peace and fighting out terrorism. So the only alternative is democratization from the smallest runs to the world level.

REFERENCES

1. Asghar Ali Engineer, "Attack on World Trade Centre and its Implications", *Vikalp*, Vol.IX, No.4, 2001-Vikas PP.47-51.
2. P.R. Chari, "Lessons from the Moscow Seige" *The Hindu* 15 November 2002.
3. J. Venkatesan, "Proxy wars worse" *The Hindu,* 11 December 2002.
4. Balraj Puri, "Not By War Alone", *Economic And Political Weekly,* Vol.XXXVI, No.52, 2002, PP.4781-2.
5. MacArthur, Douglas, "Reminiscences" (Mc Graw Hill Book Company, New York, 1964).
6. Ashgar Ali.Engineer,"September 11: May Messages" in *Economic and Political Weekly*, Vol.XXXVI No.42, 2002, PP.3682-3.
7. Karen Leonard, "American Muslims, before and after September, 11, 2001", *Economic and Political Weekly,* Vol.XXXVII No.24, 2002, PP. 2293-2302.
8. Karem Leonard, "South Asian Leadership of American Muslims" in Yvonne Yazbeck Haddad (Ed.) "*Sigourners to Citizen : Muslim in Western Disporas"* (Oxford, New York, 2002).
9. Peter Ford. "Listening for Islam's Silent Majority", *Christian Finance Monitor,* 5 November, 2001.
10. "Muslims Urged to work on Improving Image", *Los Angles Times*, 7 October 2001.
11. *The Economist*, 13 October 2001.
12. Nayyer Ali M.D, "Winners and Losers", *Pakistan Link,* (2 November 2001.
13. Raana Akbar "Proved of America And President Bush Jr." in *Pakistan Link*, 9 October 2002.
14. Hack Gutman, "Noisome Angle to Bush Doctrine", *The Statesman*, 9 October 2002.

15. Manoj Joshi, "Three wars and A Thousand Funerals", *The Times of India,* 8 September 2002.

16. B. Jhujhunwala, "Bush Double Speak", *The Statesman,* 15 December 2002.

17. Achina Vanatk, "Terrorism : Definition And Ethics" , *Economic and Political Weekly,* Vol.XXXVII, No.40, 2002, PP 4164-68.

18. Mark Selder, "Terrorism: Before And After 9/11" *Economic and Political Weekly,* Vol.XXVII, No.31, 2002, PP.3795-6.

19. Rohini Hensman, "Only Alternative to Global Terror" *Economic and Political Weekly,* Vol. XXXVI, No.44, 2001, PP.4184-9.

20. J. Petras, "9/11 one year of Empire Building", *Economic and Political Weekly,* Vol.XXVIII, No.34, 2002, PP.3504-14.

13

Interpreting National Interest: Bush's War on Terrorism

Pradeep Harichandan

We are living in an age of terror. Terrorism has become a global concern. It seems, with globalization, terrorism is also getting globalized. Terrorist acts, which were earlier sporadic in nature and limited to a few pockets of the world, have become frequent and all pervasive today. There is hardly any part of the world that is left without a real or potential threat of terrorist attacks. Globalization, modern means of communication, information technology and advance explosive technologies have made terrorism truly international.

PERSPECTIVE

There are many reasons for terrorism fast assuming international character. Socio-economic deprivation, political instability, religious intolerance and fanaticism, ethnic strife and cultural alienation make necessary condition for spread of terrorism. Among other reasons, terrorism of today can be conceived as the consequence of the present geo-political situation that has emerged out of de-polarization of international politics in the post-cold war era. After disintegration of Soviet Union, there does not exist any powerful deterrent against American dominance. Amid the debate whether we are heading towards a multi-polar or US-centric unipolar world, one thing is certain that American hegemony has increased substantially. The US has become more arrogant and hegemonic, which has assumed the self-proclaimed status of the 'global police'. Many state and non-state actors, including the terrorists, have not accepted this increasing American hegemony. Samuel P. Huntington's 'clash of civilizations doctrine' can be referred to interpret recent spread of terrorism as the reaction against the predominance of Western civilization and Christianity led by the US over others (mostly Islamic territories).Anti-Western terrorist groups, among others, seek to safeguard their traditional religious and cultural identities from western cultural imperialism. If one subscribes to this view then most forms of terrorism today seem to be organized and violent reactions against of Westernization and globalization. But many would not agree with Huntington's 'clash of civilizations' doctrine.

There is also the thinking, that today's terrorism is the result of rising Third World voice against the supremacy of the developed West. According to this view, religious radicalism has emerged as a 'sole replacement' in the absence of a vocal Third World leadership against Western domination. It has become evident from the decline of forums like the Non Aligned Movement (NAM), in spite of their continuing relevance. Another view point is that, although there is a Pan-Islamic factor in international terrorism, the fact remains that terrorism in this part of the world is spreading because of problem ridden domestic socio-economic and political conditions caused by external factors. Majority of the Afro-Asian Islamic countries have not been able to reap the benefits of technological and economic progress. Many of these countries have also been suffering from prolonged political instability, civil war, repression, economic mismanagement and social animosity. The religious fundamentalists exploit the situation and indoctrinate people into their fold by advocating that the US, the West and non-Muslims are their enemies.

It would be a gross misconception to confine religious terrorism to Islamic fundamentalism alone. Timothy McVeigh who was involved in the bombing of the federal building in Oklahoma City was influenced by the Christian patriotic movement. Aum Shinrikyo, a Buddhist cult member carried out the Sarin nerve gas attack in Tokyo subway. Yigal Amir, a Jewish fundamentalist, assassinated Israeli Prime Miniser Yitzhak Rabin. It is observed that feeling of insecurity and alienation from the global mainstream have made it difficult for some groups to reconcile with a fast advancing world system, which 'they did not create and cannot control'[1]. Since they have no other medium or forum to project their own worldview, they turn towards religious fanaticism.

Although there are various reasons for the spread of international terrorism, a thematic presentation of how pursuance of American national interest has been a major contributor to the spread of such terrorism is being attempted in this article. It is an objective analysis of how the concept of national interest has been misused and abused by the US, time and again because of its hegemonic pursuit of world dominance. It is a sincere attempt to relate the effects of the American pursuit of national interest with spread of international terrorism as it has determined the course of action and debate on international terrorism in the recent years.

IN PURSUIT OF NATIONAL INTEREST

The concept 'national interest' has been misused and abused not only by the US, but most of the major players in international politics. It has been misused as a façade to justify the unjustifiable and legitimize the illegitimate actions. It seems to be the most abused term in power play among the major players of international politics. Statesmen have always used it in ways suitable to them and to justify their actions. Hitler justified Nazism in 'Germany's national interest', Stalin justified expansionist policies in 'Soviet Union's national interest' and both the erstwhile Soviet Union and the US justified their respective intervention in Afghanistan in their 'national interest'. Two emerging powers of 1930s- the US and the USSR fought the Second World War together in their 'national interest' and after the world war they were engaged in the Cold War against each other in their 'national interest'. Germany was divided into East and West, not in German national interest, but for the interests of the major powers. Thus the term national interest has been grossly misused and thoroughly abused by the major players in international politics throughout history. It seems, for this reason, Raymond Aron went to the extent of suggesting altogether abandoning the concept of national interest, in the greater interest of peace and justice.

In their attempt to define national interest many, scholars have made it more ambiguous and controversial by using phrases such as 'what a nation feels to be necessary for its security and well being' and 'that which states seek to project or achieve in relation to each other' or 'desires on the part of sovereign states.' But even a staunch realist like Morgenthau, who strongly advocates that foreign policy of a state must be based on its national interest, observes in his book, *Dilemmas of Politics,* that 'national interest is similar to the principles of general welfare and due process.' According to him, survival - safeguarding physical, political and cultural identity against encroachments by other nation states, constitutes 'national interest' of a state. Thus 'survival' is inherent in the concept of national interest and not 'attack' or 'expansion' or 'love for dominance'. Beyond survival, the concept of national interest stands for meanings that are logically compatible with its residual meaning i.e. survival. However, it remains an open question, whether the major powers subscribe to the 'survival' definition of the concept. Survival means protection from encroachments and aggression, certainly not attacks on others, expansion and domination.

The US policy on terrorism has changed in perception and pursuit of (what it considers to be) its national interest. The American foreign policy and diplomacy, which are based on the realist concept of national interest, but has neither cared for the "general welfare", nor have any respect for the "due process". It has not only abused the concept of national interest, but has violated international conventions and practices by bypassing the United Nations on collective security matters, on various occasions. As fight against international terrorism has become top priority in US foreign policy agenda, it needs to be objectively analyzed how national interest has been determining the US stance on issues like terrorism, human rights and democracy, which has varied from time to time. If the pursuit of national interest has necessitated double standards, there must be a revelation of such hypocrisy.

PURSUIT OF NATIONAL INTEREST AND SPREAD OF TERRORISM

The objectives of terrorism might have often rationalized on ethnic, religious, regional, political and ideological grounds. But, the prime targets of terrorist acts are the innocent civilians and legitimate state authorities. Striking terror in the minds of the people has been the principle intuition of terrorist organizations. Major Western powers, including the US, have aided and abetted terrorism to erode state authorities and weaken legitimate governments in many parts of the developing world. Some believe that assassinations of Prime Ministers Indira Gandhi and Rajiv Gandhi were planned and funded by some Western powers as both of them stood against Western hegemony. There are several instances, which point towards the fact that not the national interest in its true sense, but sheer craving for hegemony by the US has contributed to growth of international terrorism. Examples are plenty.

To start with, towards the end of December 1979, the Soviet Union directly intervened in Afghanistan on the plea of achieving its so-called national interest. After the Soviet forces marched into Afghanistan, the US supported the *Mujahideens* with advanced weapons and resources to fight against the Soviet forces and the Soviet- backed government in Kabul. Then the US saw the *Mujahideens* as freedom fighters rather than terrorists. The US had supplied sophisticated weapons including stinger missiles, financed and trained the *Mujahiddens* for guerilla warfare. The huge infrastructure that was built up then, with the active US help, later came to be used by Osama Bin Laden and his *Al Quaida* organization against which the US and its allies have waged a war since September 2001. Pakistan, which is a frontline partner in this so called war, is the country which has a major role in making *Al Quida* and other dreaded terrorist outfits strong and truly international.

Secondly, the Indian government's attempt to curb terrorism in Punjab in the 1980's was then projected in the US Congress as 'gross human rights violation.' The Amnesty International then came out with regular annual condemnation of India's record on human rights. Sikh *Gurudwaras* in the USA, Canada, Britain and West Germany were involved in fanning terrorism in Punjab. A number of terrorist camps were traced in Canada and massive fund raising for terrorist activities were reported from Western countries like England. This was the time when India was fighting its lone battle against terrorism and the Western countries, led by the US supported the terrorist outfits in the name of 'the right to self-determination'. The Western love for the democratic value of 'self-determination' was preferable to insurgency and terrorism because they were not direct targets of terrorist groups or insurgents.

Thirdly, the American and Western policy towards insurgency and terrorism in Kashmir provides another instance of sheer opportunism and double standards. Even after the cold war ended, the Soviet troops withdrew from Afghanistan and the US faced no real threat to its awesome military power and political dominance since disintegration of the Soviet Union,

Pakistan continued to remain Washington's close ally in South Asia. As terrorism gained momentum in the Kashmir valley in the early 1990s with full support from across the border, the senior Bush administration expressed concern over human rights violation by the Indian security forces and ignored the cross-border support to terrorism. The White House down played the issue of terrorism by linking it with human rights. While expressing concern over human rights violation in the valley, the US Administration deliberately chose to ignore the plight and rights of innocent people including Kashmiri *Pundits.* Islamabad was encouraged by this US stance and attempted to internationalize the Kashmir issue with propaganda that Indian security forces were the worst violators of human rights. With the coming of the Clinton administration in 1993, there was a shift in American policy on Kashmir. For the first time, a US official source acknowledged that there was outside support to Kashmiri terrorists. John Malot, the then acting Director of the South Asian Bureau in the State Department, in his testimony before the Asia-Pacific Sub-committee of the House of Representatives on April 20, 1993 acknowledged that there was outside support for 'militants' in Kashmir. The American double standard was exposed in this whole episode when the then Pakistani Prime Minister Balakh Sher-Mazari, being let down by this testimony remarked, "When Arabs were trained in Pakistan and were going to Afghanistan they were heroes. Now when they are going to Kashmir they are being called terrorists"[2]. Mazari's despair revealed how US soft-pedaled terrorism for its own interest. But Malot's testimony could not change the US policy on terrorism in Kashmir and it continued to maintain that it was indigenous and again criticized India for human rights violation[3]. After Robin Raphel assumed the office of Assistant Secretary of State and the Director of the Bureau of South Asia, the US policy tilted even more towards Pakistan. She contended, "Whatever outside support, there is a strong indigenous element to the insurgency. I can also argue that it is self-sustaining"[4] Thus in overall analysis, the US has been soft-pedalling Pakistan's role in cross-border terrorism.

In the present scenario, when the US is left with no other option but to declare a war against terrorism in which the actual target is Osma Bin Laden and Al Qaida, it cannot afford to antagonize Islamabad. The US continues to need Pakistan as a front-runner Islamic country that unequivocally supports and facilitates the US hegemonic interests. In exchange of its support, Pakistan has gained immensely in terms of massive military and economic aid. The episodes of nuclear weapon technology being smuggled or sold from Pakistan to North Korea and Iran are being down played by the US, precisely because Pakistan is the culprit.

THE CHANGED PURSUIT

It was a series of direct attacks on American interests in the late 1990s that compelled the US to initiate its actions against terrorism. Attacks on American embassies in Tanzania and Kenya by Al Qaida, the bombing of federal buildings in Oklahoma city and finally the September 11, 2001 terrorist attacks on World Trade Centre and the Pentagon made the US realize that terrorism knew no boundary. 9/11 attack made the US realize the dangers of terrorism, which transcendent the boundaries of nations, religions, cultures, and faiths. Before 9/11, countries like India were unsuccessfully trying to convince the US and the West to de-link terrorism from its ideological, religious and strategic considerations and to wage an all out war against it. The realization that terrorism is indivisible and must be fought globally dawned late in the minds of the US and Western statesmen.

The American love for democracy and democratic values is again marred by double standards. It is well known that a military coup established the present military regime in Pakistan by ousting a legitimate, democratically elected government led by Nawaz Sharif. It is also known that Pakistan continues to be a safe heaven not only for terrorist outfits such as *Laskar-e-Toiba, Harkat-ul-Anssur, Harkat-ul-Majahideen, Al Bader* and *Al Qaida,* but international terrorists like Dawood Ibrahim and his men- who are responsible for deaths of thousands of innocent people, for extortion, murder in several parts of the world. The Pakistani regime has been so soft towards them that, for these terrorists and their outfits, the border between Pakistan and Afghanistan simply does not exist.

Nations like India have been fighting their own battle against terrorism even much before the US and its Western allies woke up to this reality to form a international coalition against terrorism. The US dictates the mission and regulates the course of the said mission without any reference to the United Nations, the legitimate body of the international community. The unilateral promulgation of doctrines such as 'pre-emptive military strike' on Iraq is an exemplary American arrogance that completely bypassed the United Nations.

Democracy in Pakistan continues to be illusory, but the US continues to strongly support General Musharaf's military regime. The defenders of democracy have become blind to the fact that the military regime in Pakistan eludes the hopes of millions of Pakistani people. It seems that the US thinking on democracy, human rights and terrorism have completed a full circle. In a changed context, they do not hesitate to sacrifice their love for democracy for fighting against terrorism, even by embracing dictatorial military regimes.

In spite of great variations and differences of opinion in interpreting and defining terrorism, its common connotation seems to be the deliberate killing of innocent people, often irrelevant to their objectives by an organized uncommon act of violence that sends shock waves in society and leaves the body wounded and mind shattered. Zero tolerance for terrorism of any kind, from any quarter, against any society, person or group of persons must be the motto to win the war against terrorism.

NOTES

1. Bruce Lawrence, *Shattering the Myth: Islam Beyond Violence*, (Princeton: Princeton University Press, 1998) PP.34-51.
2. *Times of India*, New Delhi, May 19, 1993.
3. *Reports of the Asia Pacific Sub-Committee of the House of Representatives* Committee on Foreign Affairs; reported by Aziz Hanifa in *Hindustan Times*, June 7, 1993. But in contrast to this report, The Report of the Research Committee of the House of Representatives produced solid evidence of Pakistan's involvement in terrorist activities in the valley. It stated how 20,000 Kashmiri youths had been trained, armed and pushed by Pakistan to the Kashmir valley. The US State Department's Annual Report on 'The Pattern of Global Terrorism' also stated that there were credible reports in the year 1992 about official Pakistani support for Kashmiri militants. But in spite of all these revealing confirmations, the Clinton administration did not declare Pakistan as a state sponsoring terrorism.
4. *Robin Raphel's Foreign Centre Briefings*, Washington D.C., USIS, October 28, 1993.

REFERENCE

1. A.S. Narang & Pramila Srivastava, *Terrorism: The Global Perspective*, Kaniska : New Delhi, 2001.
2. B.P. Singh Sehgal (ed), *Global Terrorism: Socio-Politico and Legal Dimensions*, Deep & Deep: New Delhi, 1995.
3. Dipankar Sengupta and Sudhir Kumar Singh, *Terrorism in South Asia*, Authors Press: Delhi, 2004.
4. Lakshmi Krishnamurti et.al (eds.) *Responding to Terrorism: Dilemmas of Democratic and Developing Societies*, Book Venture: Madras, 2003.
5. Samuel P. Huntington, *The class of Civilizations and the Remaking of World Order*, Penguin: New Delhi, 1997.
6. V.D. Chopra (ed.) *Rise of Terrorism and Secessionism in Eurasia*, Gyan : New Delhi, 2001.
7. Yoram Schweitzer and Shaul Shay, *The Globalization of Terror: Response of the International Community*, Viva : New Delhi, 2004.

14

FEAR OF THE GOD-FEARING: MYTH AND REALITY OF ISLAMIC TERRORISM

Saumyajit Ray

Even if Salman Rushdie repents and becomes the most pious man of all time, it is incumbent on every Muslim to employ everything he has got, his life and wealth, to send him to Hell.

Said Ayatollah Ruhollah Khomeini, founder of the Islamic Republic of Iran, after Indian-born British author Salman Rushdie apologized for hurting Muslim religious sentiments in his novel *The Satanic Verses* in early 1989. The Ayatollah had earlier pronounced a *fatwa* (a religious edict) calling upon Muslims to kill Rushdie for his alleged blasphemy against Prophet Muhammad. That *fatwa* is yet to be revoked. Of late, protests have broken out in the Kashmir valley against the knighthood granted to Rushdie (the author is of Kashmiri origin), reminiscent of the violent protests that had marked the release of Rushdie's book. The Indian government was among the first in the world to ban it.

What is important here is not what Rushdie wrote or the public anger against him. Most Muslims who participated in violent demonstrations against Rushdie's book had not read it. The book was written in English, and most of the Muslim youth who destroyed public property in the name of their religion could not read, let alone read English. The issue here is the *fatwa* given by the late Ayatollah; he considered—and the *fatwa* pronounced—that it was a religious duty of every Muslim to kill Rushdie for his sin. The Ayatollah's assumptions are clear in issuing such a *fatwa*. First, any living person who has blasphemed against Islam is deserving of death. Second, it was incumbent upon every Muslim to avenge the insult done to Islam and its Prophet. Third, and this is most dangerous, any Muslim individual—regardless of nationality—is free to take up arms for the purpose of killing someone who has allegedly blasphemed Islam. In other words, Muslims can act alone against anyone deemed to have sinned against their faith. And fourth, and this is dangerous too, whatever be the legal consequences of such actions in the countries in which they are committed, in the eyes of Allah they are completely lawful. Even though the Ayatollah was Shia, Sunni Muslim leaders had no objection to the *fatwa* issued by him; the sin committed by Rushdie was too grave to start squabbling on sectarian grounds.

What is evident is the federal and individualistic nature of Muslim religious action. The fact that the Ayatollah's *fatwa* said that it was the duty of every devout Muslim to murder Rushdie precludes the need for similar *fatwa*s in the future; if anything done by any individual, group, or government is deemed to be anti-Islam, then Muslims with similar beliefs can be expected to act alone—that too violently—in defense of their faith. Such actions can—and surely will—lead to death and destruction on a large scale and create fear in the minds of those purported to have acted against Islam and of those who have not. People of all nationalities will be convinced that there was a need to fear Muslims, especially the devout within the *umma*. By definition, all Muslims are required to be devout, to submit themselves to Allah and declare that there was no God but Allah and Muhammad was his only prophet. Then, the objective behind issuing such a *fatwa* will be fulfilled: first, the non-Muslim world will refrain from persecuting Muslims and criticizing their faith; second, all attempts at religious debate and discussion within the Muslim community will be stifled. Islam will then be tethered to the whims of local imams (it had become a truly federal religion after the demise of the caliphate in early 20th century), and local religio-political leaderships will get complete control and direction of Muslim religious action, including acts of violence. Whether done alone or in concert with co-believers, such violent action directed at enemies of the faith—both Muslim and non-Muslim—has acquired a name that has come to dominate discourse on world politics in the later part of the 20th and the early 21st centuries: Islamic terrorism. Some use terms like pan-Islamism, others call it fundamentalist Islam. But all agree on one point: that of Muslims perpetrating violence against innocent civilians, wreaking havoc on life and property for the ostensible purpose of setting right some religious wrong or of getting back at anyone—individual, group, or government—perceived to have acted unjustly against Muslims and their faith. Whenever there is a terrorist act involving Muslims, either the *mazhab* (faith) or the *umma* (community) is perceived to have been insulted or are in danger of being physically eliminated.

Even though the Ayatollah's *fatwa* called upon individual Muslims to kill Rushdie, terrorist violence involving Muslims have seldom been the result of individual efforts. Some organization or the other—whether pan-Islamic (like Al Qaeda), local (like Hizb-ul-Mujahedin), or transnational (like Lashkar-e-Toiba)—have meticulously planned, authorized, sponsored, and executed terrorist operations. As such, Islamic terrorism—that is, terrorist acts committed in the name of Islam and purported to be blessed by Allah—has emerged as the most powerful and dangerous form of organizational terrorism. Secular terrorists like Maoists (in Nepal and parts of India) and national liberation fighters (like the LTTE of Sri Lanka) are also prepared to readily die for the cause they believe in, but what distinguishes Islamic terrorists are the multiple enemies they have taken up arms against: the Other may be a government perceived to be occupying Muslim lands (like India and Israel), infidel civilizations and their armies (like Americans), or individuals blaspheming Islam (like Rushdie and the Danish cartoonist alleged to have caricatured the Prophet).

But why do Muslims, of all people, take up arms in the name of religion? Certainly, they are not the first religious community to do so. The Middle Ages have seen Christian padres—blessed by the Pope—undertaking violent expeditions to reclaim Jerusalem and the Holy Land for Christendom. The Crusades were religious wars conducted in the name of Christianity to deliver the Holy places from what was then perceived to be Muslim tyranny. But that was a long time ago. More importantly, the Crusades cannot, by any stretch of imagination, be categorized as terrorist activity. Suicide bombings and killing of innocents in sudden violent attacks is of latest origin. Experts say that a "lunatic" fringe—that they call "fundamentalists"—within the Muslim community is responsible for such attacks.

ISLAMIC FUNDAMENTALISTS

Karen Armstrong, an acknowledged expert on Islamic history, tries to trace the reasons behind the rise of fundamentalism, not only in Islam, but in all religions:

> At first religious people try to reform their traditions and effect a marriage between them and modern culture, as we have seen the Muslim reformers do. But when these moderate measures are found to be of no avail, some people resort to more extremist methods, and a fundamentalist movement is born. (Armstrong 2001: 140)

Then she makes the more important point, in fact an eye-opener for those who associate only Islam with fundamentalism:

> Of the three monotheistic religions, Islam was in fact the

> last to develop a fundamentalist strain, when modern culture began to take root in the Muslim world in the late 1960s and 1970s. By this date, fundamentalism was well established among Christians and Jews, who had had a longer exposure to the modern experience. (Armstrong 2001: 141)

Again, as another author wrote:

> Colonialism and the advance of Western modernity have nurtured the modern version of Islamic fundamentalism: if Islam is perfect and its kingdom is in retreat, it must be that its practitioners have strayed from the fundamentals of the faith. This notion gained increasing currency after 1979, when a popular uprising overthrew the corrupt, Westernizing, U.S.-backed Shah of Iran and paved the way for the Ayatullah Khomeini to launch an Islamic revolution in Iran and beyond. Khomeini called Muslims to violence to conquer "the land of the infidel." (Beyer 2001)

Islamic fundamentalists believe that the tenets of Islam must inform all dimensions of individual and communal existence, that the life of every Muslim individual and that of the *umma* must be guided by the principles laid down in the Holy Quran (the Book of Revelation sent down by Allah to mankind through his Messenger, the Prophet Muhammad) and the Hadith (traditions relating to the words and deeds of the Prophet). It is said that Islam demands complete supplication of the individual to the will of God beginning with the Muslim confession of faith: "*La ilaha illallah wa anna Muhammad-ur-Rasul Allah*" (There is no God other than Allah and Muhammad is the Messenger of Allah). Muslims everywhere, regardless of their nationality, and physical and economic condition are required to open their prayers with this confession of faith. But is it wrong to demand complete devotion and loyalty to one's religion? Can there be a Christian who does not believe in the divinity of Jesus Christ, the Immaculate Conception, and the

Resurrection and still call himself Christian? Then why should Muslims be expected not to be loyal to their faith? The problem arises if the display of such loyalty is accompanied by acts of aggression. Or, for that matter, aggression against non-Muslims becomes a measure of loyalty to Islam. In other words, the test of fundamentalism lies in the extent to which political and military action are deemed absolutely necessary to the practice of faith. There is no doubt that the Holy Quran talks of military action against infidels and non-believers, but only against those among them who have publicly ridiculed the Islamic faith, preached the worship of false gods in the form of idols, and attacked Muslims.

> "And fight in the Way of Allah those who fight you, but transgress not the limits. Truly, Allah likes not the transgressors...And kill them wherever you find them, and turn them out from they have turned you out. And *Al-Fitnah* (polytheism) is worse than killing...But if they attack you, then kill them...And fight them until there is no more *Fitnah* (disbelief and worship of others along with Allah) and (all and every kind of) worship is for Allah (Alone). But if they cease, let there be no transgression except against *Az-Zalimun* (polytheists, and wrong-doers)". *Surah* 2, *Al-Baqarah* Part 2: 190-93

There is no doubt that such scriptural stipulations present a grim picture of Islam as a faith. It also runs the danger of conveying that Islam believes in a jealous God. But to say that Islam enjoins all Muslims to kill non-Muslims all the time is a travesty of truth. "Transgress not the limits", says the Holy Quran. And, what the Holy Quran sanctions are religious wars, to be conducted to establish the glory of Allah in every human heart. Surely, there is nothing to prove in these oft-quoted verses that Islam sanctions terrorism. In fact, terrorism is a product of complex modern societies, not of the simple society in which Islam was born.

HOLY WAR

There is no doubt today that Islam and *jihad* has become synonymous. As author Sam Harris writes:

> "The feature of Islam that is most troubling to non-Muslims, and which apologists for Islam do much to obfuscate, is the principle of jihad. ...Jihad—war against infidels and apostates—is a central feature of the faith. Armed conflict in "defense of Islam" is a religious obligation for every Muslim man (Harris 2006: 111).

According to the Holy Quran and the Hadith, religious wars—or *jihad*—are obligatory for every Muslim. As seen above, the Holy Quran requires all Muslims to fight whosoever fights them: "And fight in the Way of Allah those who fight you" (Surah 2, Al-Baqarah Part 2: 190). Then there is a clear stipulation: " *Jihad* (holy fighting in Allah's Cause) is ordained for you (Muslims) though you dislike it" (Surah 2, Al-Baqarah Part 2: 216). Leading commentators on the Holy Quran have pointed to the obligatory nature of *jihad* (holy war) for every devout Muslim:

> *Al-Jihad* (holy fighting) in Allah's cause with full force of numbers and weaponry is given the utmost importance in Islam and is one of its pillars. By *Jihad* Islam is established, Allah's Word is made superior, and His religion (Islam) is propagated. By abandoning *Jihad* Islam is destroyed and the Muslims fall into an inferior position, their honor is lost, their lands are stolen, their rule and authority vanish. *Jihad* is an obligatory duty in Islam on every Muslim, and he who tries to escape from this duty, or does not in his innermost heart wish to fulfill this duty, dies with one of the qualities of a hypocrite.

Even the Hadith quotes the Prophet of Islam as supporting the idea of *jihad* as laudatory:

> Narrated Abdullah bin Masud: I asked Allah's Messenger, "O Allah's Messenger! What is the best deed?" He replied,

"To offer the *Salat* (prayers) at their early fixed stated times." I asked, "What is next in goodness?" He replied, "To be good and dutiful to your parents." I further asked, "What is next in goodness?" He replied, "To participate in *jihad* in Allah's Cause." *Sahih Al-Bukhari*, Vol. 4, *Hadith* no. 41

The Holy Quran also requires Muslims to spend in Allah's Cause (*Jihad*) [*Surah* 2, *Al-Baqarah* Part1: 3]. Surely, Islam appears to be a militaristic religion from these. Fighting—whether in Allah's cause or otherwise—is based on need. If Muslims are actually attacked by enemies of Islam to the extent that the survival of the Muslim *umma* comes into question, then *jihad* becomes obligatory. "By abandoning *Jihad*, their (Muslims') honor is lost, their lands are stolen, their rule and authority vanish." Even in the hour of need, if Muslims refuse to fight, then the consequence would be a loss of honor, occupation of their lands by infidels, and overthrow of their government (ostensibly by infidels). But what is worth noting is that even though *jihad* is made compulsory for every Muslim, it is not designated as one of the five principles of Islam: confession of faith, five daily compulsory congregational prayers (*Salat*), charity (*Zakat*), pilgrimage to Mecca (*Hajj*), and fasting during the holy month of Ramadan. The relative unimportance of *jihad* for individual Muslims and for the Muslim *umma* is evident. In other words, *jihad* is not one of the principal strands of Islam.

Clearly, *jihad* is for the protection and defense of Islam against its enemies ("If they attack you, then kill them"). *Jihad* as a form of military aggression is expressly forbidden in the Holy Quran ("But transgress not the limits. Truly, Allah likes not the transgressors"). Nothing can be more fallacious than equating *jihad* with terrorism for the simple reason that terrorism is a form of aggression.

THREATS TO ISLAM

From time to time, Muslims have perceived threats to

themselves and their faith. Before India's independence and partition on communal lines, a favorite slogan of the All India Muslim League was "Islam in danger." Presently, there are Muslims who see grave dangers threatening Islam. Osama Bin Laden, supreme leader of the Al Qaeda terrorist network has a similar story to tell the Muslim world. Bin Laden sees danger to Islam from the West, from Western imperialism and Western culture. The threats to Islam, though, are actually threats to Muslims—as perceived by them—and can be broadly categorized into the threat of loss of honor, the threat of occupation of Muslim lands by "infidels", and the threat of overthrow of Islamic states.

Loss of honor

The sources of the loss of Muslim honor are many: the Crusades that gave control of the Holy Land—especially Jerusalem—to the infidels, the defeat and dissolution of the Ottoman Empire in the First World War, the division of Arabia into mandates under European powers, the establishment of the Jewish state of Israel. In all these cases, Muslims had lost out to an inferior people, and therein lies the root of the Muslim humiliation.

As Lisa Beyer put it in a brilliant essay in *Time* magazine, written within a fortnight of the attacks on the Twin Towers:

> The brutality of Christendom's efforts to conquer the Holy Land from the Muslims in the Crusades of the 11th, 12th and 13th centuries is not forgotten in the Middle East (making President Bush's early use of the word crusade to describe America's antiterror effort an unfortunate choice). An even greater sore is the sense that, in the centuries since, so much dignity has been lost, and to an inferior people. In Islamic belief, Muhammad is God's last prophet; he built upon the revelations of Moses and Jesus to propound a superior, perfect faith. But the world that faith created was broken apart: after the defeat of

the Ottoman Empire in World War I, the colonial powers of France and Britain carved the Middle East into arbitrarily drawn mandates and states governed by handpicked local leaders (Beyer 2001)

New York Times correspondent Thomas L. Friedman is to be believed, Muslim humiliation was at the root of Muslim terrorism. In a piece written for the paper in November 2003, Friedman declared: "If I've learned one thing covering world affairs, it's this: The single most underappreciated force in international relations is humiliation". He cites a speech made by former Malaysian Prime Minister Mahathir Mohammad on October 16 that year to support his case:

> "I will not enumerate the instances of our humiliation,...We are all Muslims. We are all oppressed. We are all being humiliated. . . . Today we, the whole Muslim [community], are treated with contempt and dishonor. . . . There is a feeling of hopelessness among the Muslim countries and their people. They feel that they can do nothing right...Our only reaction is to become more and more angry. Angry people cannot think properly....We sacrifice lives unnecessarily, achieving nothing other than to attract more massive retaliation and humiliation." (Friedman, "The Humiliation Factor", *New York Times*, Nov. 9, 2003)

But nowhere has Mahathir advocated the taking up of arms—or terrorism, for that matter—for the purpose of ending Muslim humiliation.

Friedman also says that Iraqis feel humiliated that they did not liberate themselves from the tyrannical rule of Saddam Hussein and the American presence on their soil forever reminds them of that. The only way Americans can improve the situation in Iraq was by the "dehumiliation and re-dignification" of Iraqis.

Lord Meghnad Desai—in his thought-provoking work on Islamic terrorism—points to the decline and ultimate disintegration of the Ottoman Empire as the primary reason behind Muslim misery; the West was not to be blamed in this case, whatever Bin Laden may say. The fault lay within:

> The origin of Muslim misery is arguably due not to foreign machinations but entirely to the weakness of the Ottoman Empire, mainly because of its failure to adapt to modern trends of industrialization with the shift to a scientific and rational mode of thinking. This weakness of the Ottoman Empire could not be solved by a return to the faith, but only by moving forward to receive the benefits of Enlightenment. (Meghnad Desai, *Rethinking Islamism: The Ideology of the New Terror*, I.B. Tauris, New York, NY, 2007, pp 122-23)

He goes on to castigate Bin Laden and his ilk—Global Islamists as he calls them—for dwelling on "an 83-year-old story (the defeat of the Ottoman Empire in the First World War that led to its dissolution and the abolition of the caliphate) recalling every slight and every betrayal." No effort has been made, he laments, to search within for the causes of Muslim decline:

> There is no introspection as to whether the failure to develop could have anything to do with the people themselves and the nations which emerged from the Ottoman Empire or with the unreformed nature of the society, sunk in religiosity. (Desai 2007:124)

Clearly, Lord Desai points to the Muslim failure to reform themselves as a society in the aftermath of the disintegration of the Ottoman Empire. This failure to modernize themselves is at the root of the decline of Muslim societies in Arabia. Though the Malaysian Mahathir seemed to be talking on behalf of all Muslims, Lord Desai believes that the problems of Muslims in Arabia and those of Muslims elsewhere in the world were different; he criticizes Bin Laden for trying to universalize the plight of Arab Muslims:

The majority of Muslims of the world live outside Arabia,

> outside the boundaries of the former Ottoman Empire....The trick that Global Islamism performs is to include all Muslims in the plight of the Arab Muslims. For this reason local conflicts such as Kashmir are made part of the global story. (Desai 2007: 124-25)

But the universalization of the Muslim condition is at heart of the pan-Islamic ideology professed by Bin Laden. According to that ideology, Kashmir, Chechnya, Iraq, and Afghanistan have become a matter of protecting Muslim honor for Muslims everywhere in the world. More importantly, there is need for every Muslim to fight for the protection of that honor. And that would mean conducting war against those deemed to be responsible for humiliating Muslims in various parts of the world. Bin Laden's Al Qaeda network is presently doing just that: recruiting Muslim youth from across the world to build up a powerful army for fighting the "infidels" (the United States, Israel, India, Russia).

Occupation of Muslim territory by non-Muslims

"Get out of our lands, do not force us to send you back as cargo in coffins," said Bin Laden, in a statement posted on the Internet in 2002. The statement was addressed to American troops stationed in Saudi Arabia. In fact, Bin Laden had started his Holy War against the United States for having troops in Saudi Arabia and for supporting the Israeli occupation of Al Quds (Jerusalem). He had issued a *fatwa* titled "Declaration of war against the Americans Occupying the Land of the Two Holy Places" in 1996. Those who were swayed by this so-called religious edict overlooked the fact that Bin Laden—who was neither a priest nor an Islamic jurist—had no authority to issue such a *fatwa*.

The deployment of American troops on *Hijaz* (Holy) land—the region in northwest Saudi Arabia consisting of Jeddah and the Islamic holy sites of Mecca and Medina—was considered by Bin Laden as a sacrilegious act in which the Saudi royal family had cooperated:

> The presence of non-Muslim troops on Hijaz land was the spark that inspired Bin Laden to launch his long war against the Americans. From the abolition of the caliphate to the occupation of the holy land by non-Muslim troops was a steep decline. This was the abyss. For the Islamist ideologue that Osama Bin Laden had now become, this was more than he could tolerate. The Saudi royal family, in his view, had besmirched itself and the holy land. It had to be removed. A series of attempts to attack the American mainland and American interests abroad began. (Desai 2007: 52)

Seriously, Bin Laden had thought about the removal of the family of Saud from power and its replacement by someone who would rule according to the dictates of Allah's Book. The fact that the American troops were in Hijaz land on the invitation of the Saudi royal family was not lost on him.

But the European colonization of Muslim lands had started in the 19th century itself. The European powers colonized one Islamic country after another within a span of eighty years. Beginning with the French occupation of Algeria in 1830, the Europeans went on to capture Tunisia (1881), Egypt (1882), Sudan (1889), Libya and Morocco (1882). The Sykes-Picot agreement of May 16 1916—drawn up by Sir Mark Sykes of the British Foreign Office and Georges Picot of the Quai d'Orsay—divided the territories of the Ottoman Empire between Britain and France. Since Jerusalem housed the holy sites of the three Abrahamic religions, it was put under an international regime. But the agreement was reversed soon after, and Jerusalem fell to British forces. Britain came to acquire the Palestine Mandate.

Bin Laden has also not overlooked the significance of Jerusalem. Considered by Muslims as the third most important sacred place in their tradition, Jerusalem (called *Al-Quds*, or sacred place), is revered by Muslims as the land of many prophets of the Abrahamic religions; it is also the site of the Al-

Aqsa (farthest) mosque. It is also at the heart of the Arab-Israeli dispute. In Islam, Palestine was always holy.

The British Imperial War Cabinet—in a resolution moved by then Foreign Secretary Arthur Balfour—declared on October 31, 1917: "His Majesty's Government views with favour the establishment in Palestine of a national home of the Jewish people, and will use its best endeavours to facilitate the achievement of this object" (Quoted in Desai 2007: 33-34).

The establishment of Israel by the United Nations in 1948 with Anglo-American support constituted not only a loss of Muslim territory to non-Muslims, but a deep humiliation of not only Arab Muslims but all Muslims:

> In 1948 the Arabs of Palestine lost their homeland to the Zionists, who set up the Jewish secular state of Israel there, with the support of the United Nations and the international community. The loss of Palestine became a potent symbol of the humiliation of the Muslim world at the hands of the Western powers, who seemed to feel no qualms about the dispossession and permanent exile of hundreds and thousands of Palestinians. (Armstrong 2001: 127)

As Beyer wrote in the essay mentioned above:

> Certainly the greatest single source of Arab displeasure with the U.S. is its stalwart support of Israel: politically (notably at the U.N.), economically ($840 million in aid annually) and militarily ($3 billion more, plus access to advanced U.S. weapons). To a majority of Arabs, Israel, as a Jewish state, is an unwelcome, alien entity. Even to those who accept its existence, Israel is an oppressor of Arab rights; despite the Oslo peace process, it still occupies most of the Palestinian territories. Particularly egregious to Muslims is Israel's control over Islamic shrines in Jerusalem, the third most sacred city to Islam (Beyer 2001)

Palestine is perhaps the only issue involving occupation of Muslim territory by non-Muslims that became a matter of global Muslim humiliation. Over and above, the holy land of Palestine was lost to Jews, regarded by the Holy Quran as a scheming community ["And verily, you will find them (the Jews) the greediest of mankind for life and even greedier than those who ascribe partners to Allah", *Surah* 2, *Al-Baqarah* 1: 96]. The Jews are said to have earned Allah's anger ("Guide us to the Straight Way. The Way of those on whom you have bestowed Your Grace, not of those who earned Your Anger", *Surah* 1, *Al-Fatihah* 1: 6, 7]. The *Hadith* says that when asked by Adi bin Hatim, Allah's Messenger—Prophet Muhammad, that is—replied that "those who earned Your Anger" meant the Jews. In other words, the enmity between Muslims and Jews is scriptural. Though Jews have been regarded by Quranic tradition as *Ahl-e-Qitab*—People of the Book, or People of an earlier Revelation—this belligerence of the Jews evidenced by the setting up of the State of Israel has earned the anger of Muslims, not to speak of the anger of Allah.

According to the pan-Islamic ideology of Osama Bin Laden, the definition of "Muslim lands" has been expanded to include those territories outside Arabia and the Hijaz land that have a Muslim majority or are wholly Muslim: Afghanistan, Kashmir, Chechnya. Non-Muslims—Jews, Christians, pagans—are to be driven out from these lands and Islamic governments established in these places. That is why Bin laden fought alongside the Afghan *mujahedin* (liberation fighters) against Soviet occupation of the country in the late 1980s.

Interestingly, though Bin Laden regarded the secular socialist Ba'ath Party government of Saddam Hussein as "sinful", he openly called for support to the Iraqi dictator in 2003 because the latter was fighting an invasion of his land—a Muslim territory—by American "infidels". Saddam, true to his political ideology, neither hobnobbed with nor sought the support of Bin Laden ever.

What is of significant importance is that territories that have once been captured by Muslims can never be ceded to others, writes Princeton University professor Bernard Lewis, in his book *The Crisis of Islam*: "(F)or Muslims no piece of land once added to the realm of Islam can ever be finally renounced". (Lewis 2003: 32) Already, Palestine—part of the Holy land—had been taken away by the Jews supported by the "Crusader armies", shameful matter of political defeat of the Muslim *umma*. Of late, Bin Laden made his disapproval public of the separation of East Timor from Muslim Indonesia.

Overthrow of Islamic states

Till date Pakistan remains the only state launched in the name of Islam. Ironically, Pakistan is outside Arab territory. The Objectives Resolution, passed by the Pakistan Constituent Assembly in March 1949, intended Pakistan to be a state wherein the principles of democracy, freedom, equality, tolerance and social justice, as enunciated by Islam, shall be fully observed;

> wherein the Muslims shall be enabled to order their lives in the individual and collective spheres in accordance with the teachings and requirements of Islam as set out in the Holy Qur'an and Sunnah.

The Constitution of 1956—Pakistan's first indigenuous Constitution—declared Pakistan an Islamic republic. The 1973 Consitution—Pakistan's latest effort to write a fundamental law—reiterates much of the sentiments expressed by the 1949 Objectives Resolution.

Though Bin Laden is unwelcome in the Islamic Republic of Pakistan—many, though, belive him to be hiding in the hilly areas bordering Afghanistan and Pakistan—an Islamic republic is what Bin Laden would have liked to head. In fact, he was closely associated with a more radical Islamic government—that of the Taliban in Afghanistan, known as the Islamic Emirate of Afghanistan—from the time of its coming to power in 1996 to its fall in the aftermath of the US invasion in 2001. When in power, the Taliban is believed to have implemented the "strictest interpretation of Sharia law ever seen in the Muslim world" (Rashid 2000: 29). The Taliban also destroyed the Bamiyan Buddhas—statues of the Buddha carved in the Hindu Kush mountains near the town of Bamiyan—claiming that idolatry which was contrary to Islamic beliefs had no place in Afghanistan.

Bin Laden helped the Taliban government with men and money. At the time of the terror attack on the Twin Towers of the World Trade Center at New York City on 11 September 2001, Bin Laden was in Afghanistan. His close association with the fundamentalist Taliban regime and Taliban's reciprocal support for his Al-Qaeda terror network inspired the American attack on Afghanistan and force a "regime change" in that country. Bin Laden's activities are also directed toward the reversal of such regime changes. The Al Qaeda is believed to be actively assisting the Taliban to regroup inside and outside Afghanistan (McCarthy, 2002)

Of late, a Bangladeshi Islamist group, calling itself the Jamaat-ul-Mujahideen, spoke of its plan to carry out car-bomb attacks "to establish Allah's rule in the soil of Allah" in a television interview. Surely, "Allah's rule" means an Islamic theocracy, of the type that the Taliban had inaugurated in Afghanistan in 1996. The "soil of Allah" in all probability means Saudi Arabia. Though Hijaz land is governed strictly according to Islamic law by the Saudi royal family, it has fallen from grace of Bin Laden and other Islamists because of its invitation to station American troops there.

More importantly, the resolve of a Bangladeshi group can no longer be ridiculed. For two reasons: one, such Bangladeshi Islamic militant groups are very active not only in their own country but even outside, eg. in India; two, this points not only to the international networking capabilities of Islamic militants, but also to the potency of Bin Laden's pan-Islamist appeal.

An Islamic State based on the Shariah is also the best guarantee against the spread of American culture which Bin Laden hates as un-Islamic. In another of his so-called religious edicts, he called upon Americans "to be a people of manners, principles, honor, and purity; to reject the immoral acts of fornication, homosexuality, intoxicants, gambling, and usury" (Quoted in Desai 2007: 119). Though fornication, homosexuality, drugs, drinking, gambling, and usury are not the hallmarks of the American civilization, there are fundamentalists of other religions—including Hindu fundamentalists—who regard the United States as the birth place of such social ills. In the rhetoric of Bin Laden, it acquires a new dimension of cultural hatred. And it is this hatred against the West that drives all Muslim terrorist attacks in its direction.

THE NATURE OF ISLAMISM

It is politically correct in secular states like India to declare—in an attempt not to antagonize the Muslim minority—that terrorists have no religion. Even President George W. Bush and Prime Minister Tony Blair had told the world that they were not in war with Islam. However, there are opinion makers in the world, who–encouraged by the "clash of civilizations" thesis of the venerable Samuel P. Huntington—believe that not only is the West in war with Islam, it was Islam which was the real culprit:

> We are at with Islam. It may not serve our immediate foreign policy objectives for our political leaders to openly acknowledge this fact, but it is unambiguously so. It is not merely that we are at war with an otherwise peaceful religion that has been "hijacked" by extremists. We are at war with precisely the vision of life that is prescribed to all Muslims in the Koran, and further elaborated in the hadith, which recounts the sayings and actions of the Prophet (Harris 2006: 109-10).

Harris is emphatic in holding Islam singularly responsible

for Islamic terrorism: "Nothing explains the actions of Muslim extremists, and the widespread tolerance of their behavior in the Muslim world, better than the tenets of Islam (Harris 2006: 137). The author quotes extensively from the Holy Quran passages which he believes prove Islam to be a cult of hatred, even more so a cult of death. And then he declares about the Holy Quran and Islam:

> On almost every page, the Koran instructs observant Muslims to despise non-believers. On almost every page, it prepares the ground for religious conflict. Anyone who can read passages like those quoted above and still not see a link between Muslim faith and Muslim violence should probably consult a neurologist (Harris 2006: 123)

In 2002, President Vladimir Putin of the Russian Federation claimed that Islamic radicals were pursuing a systemic annihilation of non-Muslims in their attempt to create a "worldwide caliphate". Putin also said that the western civilization faced a mortal threat from Muslim terrorists; according to him, the world no longer faced isolated acts of terrorism but a "concerted effort and program" by a global network bent on slaughter (Ambrose Evans-Pritchard and Julius Strauss, 12/11/2002)

History will tell whether Putin was correct or not. At the moment, though, "Islam is the solution" is the slogan of the Islamist movement and many in the Arab world regard it as a better alternative than Arab nationalism of the Iraqi and Syrian varieties which had brought both poverty and corrupt despotic governments. A return to the simple life of the early years of Islam—governed by the tenets of Allah's religion—is the message of Bin Laden's Islamist network.

Lord Desai puts forth a powerful thesis on the issue of Islamic terrorism. He disagrees that the war on terrorism was a war against Islam. In fact, the terrorism faced by the world today was based on an ideology fashioned by Osama Bin Laden that feeds on Islam; Desai calls it Global Islamism:

> What we face in the recent upsurge in terrorism is not a religion but an ideology. That ideology wears religious garb, but we have to see through the garb and discern the political lineaments beneath. The ideology is Global Islamism. It is the ideology of global terrorism. No matter how evil it may be, we have to learn that it has a coherent story to tell which has inspired thousands of Muslims, and make them take absurd risks even to the act of suicide bombing. (Desai 2007: 12)

Desai stresses on the need to treat Global Islamism as a violent, destructive, and murderous political ideology distinct from the religion of Islam and then elaborates on the nature of global Islamism:

> Global Islamism confronts the entire world, both Western and Eastern, North and South. Its terrorist activities have covered the USA, the UK, Spain, India, Indonesia, Kenya, Egypt, Saudi Arabia and Jordan. Its rhetoric is of a worldwide struggle against the Judeo-Christian 'Crusader' regimes, yet its victims have been Muslims, Hindus, Christian and Jews and all other religious communities. Yet its vision is a call to Muslims to defend their community, their *umma.* It recalls previous crises in the history of Islam when there were appeals by learned men to the community as to how to meet the challenge. Its rhetoric is meant to be heard or read by Muslims since there are allusions to the Qur'an and the traditions (*hadith*) of the Prophet, to historic events which every Muslim will know about such as the *hijra* (migration) of the Prophet from Mecca to Medina. (Desai 2007: 97)

CONCLUSION

Islam is the world's biggest monotheistic religion. Not only is it characterized by one God, one Book, and one Prophet, it believes that it is the most refined of all the Abrahamic religions and superior to both Judaism and Christianity.

According to the Islamist ideology, if Muslims were God's chosen people, there was no way that they could suffer political defeats at the hands of Jews and Christians. More so when both Jews and Christians had incurred the wrath of Allah by refusing to accept His revelation as sent to mankind through His messenger, the Prophet Muhammad. Modernity was the product of the Judeo-Christian Western world and as such was anathema to Muslim fundamentalists, whether Shia (like Ayatollah Khomeini) or Sunni (like Osama Bin Laden). In fact, Muslim societies had acquired a modicum of modernity only under secular dictators, like Kamal Ataturk in Turkey and Saddam Hussein in Iraq. In fact, the United States had, at one point of time, backed Saddam Hussein against Islamic Iran. Bin Laden also had no love lost for the Iraqi dictator. The 2003 American invasion on Iraq changed all that.

Islam is the perhaps the only modern religion that is linked with terrorism. Nearly two decades back in India, terrorism started in the name of Sikhism, but it was for the purpose of seceding from India and setting up a separate sovereign Sikh state called Khalistan. But no scholar—Western or Indian—made any attempt to search the Guru Granth Sahib (the Sikh Holy Book) for evidences in support of terrorism. (In fact, speeches were made in the American Congress supporting the Khalistani cause.) Then why search the Holy Quran for such evidence? Not only is the Holy Quran being dissected to prove that it is a faith that naturally breeds terrorism, even websites have been launched to defame the Prophet and, citing instances from his life, show that he was the first Islamic terrorist.

This malicious campaign in the Western media has forced many Muslim scholars on the backfoot, painstakingly citing Quranic stipulations to establish that Islam was a peaceful religion. To many in the Western world, Islam and peace do not go hand in hand; *jihad* is the actual face of Islam. But as Karen Armstrong has written: "Because the Koran was revealed in the context of an all-out war, several passages deal with the conduct of armed struggle" (Armstrong 2001) True, all religions are products of societies they are born in. The Holy Quran was revealed to Prophet Muhammad in a war-torn Arabia. Even the Prophet's own tribe of Qureish had turned against him for preaching a rigid unidolatrous monotheistic religion. The strength of the Prophet's beliefs in his God and his mission made him take up arms against his adversaries. He had fought in Allah's Cause and had become the first *jihadi* (holy warrior). His bitter experience—that involved his flight from Mecca to Medina—during the initial years of declaring Islam convinced him that the only way to spread the Word of God was through the sword. Accordingly, there was no peacetime missionary activity in Islam. But there is no denying that the Prophet had established peace in his realm within a few years of declaring God's Revelation.

There is no doubt that there are passages in the Holy Quran that appear intolerant of other faiths, and seem to non-Muslims as supportive of religious conflict between Muslims and the rest of the world. Unfortunately, Islamists refer to those sections only to inspire Muslim youth to take on the might of powerful Western states like the US and the UK. References to the Holy Quran and the *hadith* are made to illustrate and analyze modern problems and find solutions to them. The reason is simple: Islamists need to legitimize their nefarious activities through some authority. The Holy Quran is that authority. The failure of the so-called secular and pacifist Muslims to condemn Islamic terrorism has further convinced Muslim youth about the wisdom behind Bin Laden's activities.

The problem has been compounded by the absence of a central spiritual authority in Islam like the Pope of the Roman Church. Lord Desai may be right in saying that Global Islamism is a modern political ideology, but Islam had been used as a political ideology earlier as well. Sixth Mughal Emperor Moinuddin Mohammad Aurangzeb used Islam to legitimize his rule; he was actually a usurper who killed his brothers to ascend the Mughal throne. In other words, the use of Islam for political purposes is not a modern phenomenon. Directed against the world's superpower and seeking to annihilate it, the political use of Islam has acquired a global dimension. As Lord Desai has pointed out, globalization itself has helped the rise of Global Islamism. Bin Laden can now hope to recreate a global Muslim *umma.* He can even look forward to lead it. Surely, the ideology of Islamism is going to stay. The conditions in which the Holy Quran was revealed had made it an overtly political religion. May be for this reason Islam is susceptible to be used as a political ideology. Seldom did Christian or Hindu rulers run the affairs of the state with continuous reference to their holy books. This is not the case with Islam. In Islam, Allah is the head of state in any Islamic country. The king or president rules on His behalf. For a devout Muslim, such a state is spiritually desirable. For the Islamist, such a state is politically attainable and worth fighting for. In the view of the Islamist, the only way to acquire state power is through war. That such a war may not be in Allah's Cause is a different matter altogether.

REFERENCES

1. Al-Hilali, Muhammad Taqi-ud-din and Muhammad Muhsin Khan, *Translation of the meanings of The Noble Qur'an in the English Language* (Madinah, K.S.A.: King Fahd Complex for the Printing of the Holy Qur'an, ?)
2. Armstrong, Karen, *Islam: A Short History*, (London: Phoenix Press, 2001)
3. Armstrong, Karen, "The True, Peaceful Face of Islam", *Time*, September 23, 2000
4. Beyer, Lisa, "Roots of Rage", *Time*, September 23, 2001
5. Meghnad Desai, *Rethinking Islamism: The Ideology of the New Terror* (London: I.B. Tauris, 2007)
6. Evans-Pritchard, Ambrose and Julius Strauss, "West in mortal danger from Islam, says Putin", November 12, 2002 http://www.telegraph.co.uk/news/main.jhtml?xml=/news/2002/11/12/wput12.xml, *(accessed on 6/21/07)*
7. Friedman, Thomas L. "The Humiliation Factor", *New York Times*, November 9, 2003

8. Harris, Sam, *The End of Faith: Religion, Terror, and the Future of Reason* (London: Simon & Schuster, 2006)

9. Jihad Watch, *http://www.jihadwatch.org/archives/016510.php*(Accessed on 6/22/07)

10. Lewis, Bernard, *The Crisis of Islam: Holy War and Unholy Terror*(New York, NY: Modern Library, 2003)

11. *McCarthy, Rory "Kabul fears Taliban regrouping", The Guardian, March 12, 2002,* http://www.guardian.co.uk/afghanistan/story/0,1284,665980,00.htm *(accessed on 6/22/07)*

12. Ahmed Rashid, *Taliban: Militant Islam, Oil, and Fundamentalism in Central Asia* (London: IB Tauris, 2000)

15

NUCLEAR TERRORISM: MYTH OR REALITY

Sitakanta Mishra

The apprehension of "increasing probability of terrorists using radiological weapons"[2] mainly emanates from the negative popular perception regarding anything nuclear, the projected reach of the terrorists and the vocabulary of 'nuclear terrorism' itself. As the magnitude of the threat of nuclear terrorism is unknown and there has not been such a precedent, this apprehension bound to emerge. But a realistic introspection on different facets of nuclear terrorism, accessibility of required materials, and affordability of the terrorist entities entail that the feasibility of such an incident at the micro level seems in the offing than a nuclear attack of a macro level.

This paper takes a position contrary to the conventional wisdom on nuclear terrorism – acquiring, fabricating, and detonating of a bomb by terrorists as pronounced by political leaders, academia and the media. It attempts to identify the nuances of the apprehensions of a possible nuclear-terror catastrophe. It goes on to analyze the potential nexus between nuclear proliferation and international terrorism, its different facets, the fallacies in popular perception, possible factors that may lead to such an incident by examining the availability of the required ingredients, the psyche, strength, and weaknesses of terrorist entities to carry out such an act.

NUCLEAR TERRORISM: WHAT, HOW, WHY, AND WHO

The phenomenon of nuclear terrorism is "neither a single entity nor a narrow category".[3] It encompasses a broad spectrum from low-level incidents of threats involving radioactive material through attacks on the reactors to a detonation of a full-fledged terrorist nuclear bomb.[4] It could also range from spreading very small amount of radioactive material by post to the use of a large powerful weapon misappropriated from the state arsenal. While some form of this variety would deliver no harm, other forms may make cities completely garbage heap. In a comprehensive sense of the term, nuclear terrorism connotes:

1. The theft or sabotage of nuclear items for demonstration or blackmail.
2. Environmental contamination with radioactive material.
3. Attack or sabotage of nuclear reactor or other facility.
4. Capture or sabotage of fuel storage or other nuclear facility short of meltdown or a fuel fire.
5. A widely published nuclear threat that prove to be hoax
6. Detonation of Radiological Dispersal Device (RDD)
7. Damage to spent fuel storage pool
8. Detonation of a low-yield Improvised Nuclear Device (IND)
9. Detonation of a intact nuclear weapon from a state arsenal
10. Fabrication of nuclear device by terrorists on availing all required means and materials through the black-market or state sponsorship.

The beginning of any form of nuclear terrorism is the terrorists' access to radioactive materials without which virtually there can be no nuclear terrorism. Terrorists' access to radioactive materials is possible in many ways: the most common path is illicit trafficking, state sponsorship, obtaining unauthorized assistance from the senior officials of the establishment, assistance from custodians of nuclear materials, or by seizure. Chances of access to nuclear devices are more when a nuclear capable country undergoes political unrest.

Thus, terrorists' have broadly four ways to carry out their objectives:

* theft and detonation of an intact nuclear arsenal.
* theft or purchase or trafficking of fissile material leading to the fabrication and detonation of a crude nuclear weapon.
* attack and sabotage of a nuclear facility, power plant, research laboratory or medical facility where radioactive sources are used.
* fabrication of a "dirty bomb" – RDD – or radiation emission device (RED) by unauthorized acquisition of industrial or medical radiation sources.

Among these four forms, the first two are horrific forms of nuclear terrorism or macro-level nuclear terrorism that would inflict incorrigible damage to life, property and the environment. The rest two forms are considered as low level of terrorism that probably would cause less damage, hence can be categorized as micro-level nuclear terrorism. There is an agreement among the experts that nuclear terror with the highest consequences are the least likely to occur owing to the difficulty in their accomplishment but those acts with the least damaging consequences are the most likely to take place as they are relatively easy to carry out.[5]

Literature on nuclear terrorism of pre-Cold War era was primarily concentrated on the reasons and the means by which the terrorists might resort to the nuclear path. A definite shift can be perceived in the post-Cold War era, not only in the means of accessing radiological material but also both in the very nature and motivation of terrorism itself.[6] The paradox of post-Cold War period is the substantial growth of terrorism perpetrated by many groups which cannot be pigeon-holed into any clear-cut category such as, nationalist-separatist, left-wing, right-wing, religious, etc. Though many terrorist groups in the past pronounced to resort to nuclear path, they could not overcome their conservativeness regarding their tactics and level of violence in the pursuit of their goals. But the newer terrorist groups in the post-Cold war period are more violent, more innovative, and more willing to use mass-killing weapons.[7]

The question of why terrorists might resort to nuclear weapons lies in some of the following assertions:

Failure of Deterrence Theory

While a state possessing nuclear weapons can effectively deter its adversary, it can not deter a non-state actor since it does not have a return address. But a terrorist organization possessing nuclear arsenal can bring down a state to its knees. Nuclear weapon seems to be an effective deterrent for the terrorist organizations against coercive state action. With the possession of the ultimate weapon, a terrorist outfit can effectively blackmail a state and bargain for its cause, standing on the platform of ultimate strength.

Manipulating Negative Societal Perception on Nuclear

Nuclear terrorism has the feature of achieving a unique type of public fear and trauma because of the negative societal association with almost anything nuclear. Terrorists can well exploit the public's irrational fear of radiation. Terrorists consider that pursuing some type of nuclear terrorism would be perceived as crossing a major threshold and would cause enormous horror.

Unique Identity

The prestige and unique identity factor involved in the possession of nuclear power would instigate a terrorist organization to acquire it. By acquiring nuclear capability a terrorist outfit could assume a quasi-state nature. That would apart the entity from other entities since mere identity of 'being nuclear' would certainly ensure that it had vast coercive power and can inflict considerable impact on the public and government's imagination, fear and response.

Proportionate Value

The popular fear involved with nuclear weapons and the panic involved with such an act exactly matches the aims and objectives of terrorism. Nuclear weapon today is the highly feared weapon and mere possession by any sub-state actor would better serve its purpose.

Enduring Impact

Of all other weapons, only a nuclear detonation would guarantee immediate massive destruction. Also the resultant impact would continue

The psycho-dynamic aspects of terrorism in the post-1990s and the increasing instances of nuclear smuggling[8] strengthened the apprehension of terrorists resorting to nuclear weapons. Though the probability of nuclear terrorism is much smaller, the danger of high-end terrorism is on the rise, one day it might acquire the nuclear content. Concern for this high-end terrorism can well be perceived in the policy pronouncements at the highest level of many states. Within a few weeks of September 11, 2001, the US President George Bush reportedly "ordered his national security team to give nuclear terrorism priority over every other threat to the United States".[9] The US *National Strategy for Combating Terrorism* (2003) warned that "(t)he probability of terrorist organization using a chemical, biological, radiological, or nuclear weapon ... has increased significantly during the past decade".[10] On the eve of Indian Independence Day celebration, India's Defence Minister, Pranab Mukherjee and National Security Advisor, M.K. Narayanan raised their concerns over the intelligence news of the country's nuclear installations on Lashkar-e-Toiba's (LeT) hit list.[11] In response, the Indian Army along with the National

Security Guards (NSG) took over security of the Indira Gandhi Centre for Atomic Research (IGCAR) at Kalpakkam, imposing an 'informal curfew' in and around the facility within a radius of 8 kms.[12] To that extent, the Indian Army organized teams of specialists ready to respond to attacks involving biological, chemical or nuclear weapons.[13]

Not only this, the post-9/11 world community is deeply concerned about the increasing trafficking of radioactive materials and the terrorists' nuclear weapon ambitions. The Illicit Trafficking Data Base (ITDB) on radiological materials released by International Atomic Energy Agency (IAEA) on September 27, 2005, reveals that out of 662 confirmed incidents, 196 involved nuclear materials, 400 involved other radioactive materials and 24 incidents involved both nuclear and radioactive materials.[14] According to the report, the number of incidents reported by states to the ITDB substantially increased during 2003–04. Taking note of the post-9/11 concerns and the increasing incidents of trafficking, an international convention for the suppression of acts of nuclear terrorism was convened in 2005 to meet the urgent need to enhance international cooperation in devising effective and practical measures for the prevention, prosecution and punishment of the perpetrators.[15]

As like the varied forms of nuclear terrorism, there are also different splintering groups who might resort to the nuclear path. Charles D. Forguson and William C. Potter have broadly categorized them into the following four groups:[16]

1. Apocalyptic Groups
2. Politico-Religious Groups
3. Nationalist/Separatist Groups
4. Single Issue Terrorists

The apocalyptic group believes in purifying the world *via* violent upheaval since the end of the current world order is close, use of nuclear weapon would be the best option to accomplish their objective. The politico-religious groups have come to dominate the post-9/11 dialogue on terrorism. This group ranges from a very broad network like al Qaeda to the more geographically focused Hezbollah, Lashkar-e-Toiba and the Hindu fundamental extremist groups, which are hybrids of both political and religious motivations.[17] The nationalist/ separatist terrorist groups include those organizations whose purpose is to achieve some political objectives on the basis of their ethnic, regional or separate identity. The LTTE in Sri Lanka, the Kurds in Turkey, the Irish Republican Army in Ireland, etc. are some such outfits who might consider at certain point to inflict harm on their oppressors through nuclear means and to force state authorities to concede to their demands. The single-issue terrorist category includes the animal liberation activists, anti-abortion advocates, pro-environmentalist groups, and the anti-nuclear activists who could resort to nuclear terrorism as a way to force the public and government to recognize their concerns.

Terrorist organizations bear no postal address though terrorism thrives in different geographic locations and their linkages are cross-regional. In one way, while their anonymity helps them to operate clandestinely, in another way their mobile character owing to the states' hunt for them, becomes a liability for them to think nuclear as developing nuclear arsenal requires a stable establishment. The minimum criteria to pursue nuclear terror- a terrorist group must have extreme desire to acquire nuclear device, organizational and technical skills, adequate financial resources and multi-country operation capability. While the transnational terrorist groups have greater ability to get access to nuclear weapons and are also financially sound, the splintering terrorist groups confined within certain geographic location might only manage to sabotage a nuclear installation or can resort to the dispersal of radiological device owing to their limited operability.

SCRUTINIZING THE LIKELIHOOD OF A NUCLEAR TERROR ATTACK

This section examines the merit of the apprehension of a nuclear catastrophe by the terrorists by evaluating both implicit and explicit assumptions made thereof to substantiate this paper's stated position stated in the beginning, i.e. nuclear terrorism is overstated and popular wisdom is flawed.

To start the enquiry, it is pertinent to chuck-out the chain of necessary conditions for nuclear terror act to occur. The first form of nuclear terror as identified earlier, i.e. theft and detonation of an intact nuclear weapon, necessitates a terrorist group with an extreme objective to acquire necessary technical and financial resources for carrying out the operation. It must prepare a blue print as how to bypass or defeat any safeguards in and around an intact nuclear weapon. Then the appropriated device must be transported to a high-value target for detonation. So the route to successful carry out of the plan is quite long, thus the chances of this long chain being severed is high and would easily be thwarted at many points if their plan is leaked.

STATE SPONSORSHIP

A (rogue) state might deliberately transfer, share or sell nuclear weapons to a terrorist group, but such combination is a 'worst case scenario'. Prior to 9/11, the US Department of Defense concluded in its January 2001 analysis of proliferation threats that, "the likelihood of a state sponsor providing such a weapon to a terrorist group is believed to be low".[18] Potential cases are Pakistan, North Korea, Iran and such other "rogue states". The apprehension is that leaders supportive of radical Islamist groups may come to power in these countries and transfer an intact nuclear weapon to their patron terrorist organization. Chances of slippage are high during a coup or at the time of extreme political unrest. Although the chances of possible loss of control over nuclear arsenals cannot altogether be refuted, in spite of a coup, all regimes can be expected to regard nuclear weapons as crucial symbols of power and to employ the most reliable military or state security forces to guard them. Though the chances of slippage of nuclear weapons are high during and after the political instability, "the elite security forces are most likely to perform their protective duties".[19] If the coup is successful, the new regime will have the same drive as its predecessors to guard its nuclear arsenals.

DEFYING SECURITY ARRANGEMENT

Nuclear weapons are under tight security during their entire life cycle, including production, transit, storage, and deployment. This system has a number of mutually reinforcing components like personnel reliability programmes to verify the loyalty and emotional stability of custodians, physical protection measures (barriers, alarms, controlled access arrangements, armed guards, and response forces), careful weapon accounting practices and other measures to prevent unauthorized use.

Even if terrorists get access or acquire an intact nuclear bomb, the in-built security system with the bomb would be difficult for them to penetrate. Most countries now use Permissive Action Link (PAL) system designed to ensure maximum security of their warheads. The PAL is an electronic locking system with multiple six or twelve-digit codes integrated into the warheads design. These locks allow only a limited number of tries to enter the correct codes: if the limit is exceeded, circuits in the arming mechanism self-destroy or disable the warhead.[20] Weapons are also safeguarded against unauthorized use through safing, arming, fusing, and firing (SAFF) procedures. For instance, the arming sequence for a warhead generally designed to ensure that the warhead can be used only according to a specific mission profile, not for all missions in general. Finally, weapons are also protected from unauthorized use by a combination of complex procedural arrangements and authenticating codes authorizing each individual to activate the weapon.[21]

The nuclear weapons of the United States, Britain, France, and Russia are safeguarded using all these mechanisms. Chinese nuclear weapons are not believed to be using PALs but they have sought US assistance for PLAs.[22] The warheads of other countries like India, Israel, North Korea and Pakistan appear rely on procedures and codes rather than PLAs.[23] Both India and Pakistan's nuclear arsenals are in disassembled form thus reducing the chances of their inadvertent use.[24] Also, the US is very much concerned about the upgradation of the security system of arsenals by providing the necessary technical support to these countries.

ACQUISITION OF RADIOACTIVE MATERIALS AND KNOW-HOW TO FABRICATE THE BOMB

The second argument on the possibility of nuclear terrorism to occur is the fabrication of a nuclear bomb by accessing the required materials, know-how and technical support. This apprehension has been strengthened with the revelation of the AQ Khan network. Though chance of state sponsorship is less, the elite officials and the security personnel in charge of security of the radiological materials and the bomb may facilitate the slippage to the terrorists. Through trafficking channel, the terrorists can get required radiological materials and hire technical personnel to fabricate their own bomb. Two types of fissile material could be used for making the bomb – highly enriched uranium and plutonium. These materials have been produced in great quantity in the nuclear weapon and civilian nuclear energy programmes around the world. Russia alone possesses more than 34 metric tonnes of weapons-usable materials annually.[25] According to the IAEA, about 25 kilograms of HEU or 8 kgs of plutonium would be needed to manufacture a first-generation weapon.[26]

However, acquiring the required radioactive material, technology and know-how by terrorists is not that easy. Nuclear materials or weapons are considered as a national treasure and are provided with lifetime security in every country. Though the number of cases of illicit trafficking is on the rise in recent days, the quantity of weapons-usable radiological material trafficked is very less. Out of 662 confirmed incidents of illicit trafficking in the past twelve years, there have been 18 confirmed incidents involved HEU and plutonium.[27] The data reported to the ITDB in 1993–2004 shows a long-term downward trend in the occurrence of incidents involving nuclear materials. Though the ITDB recorded a substantial increase in the number of such incidents from the year 2000 to 2004, none involved HEU or Plutonium which are necessary for making the bomb.[28]

During the 1990s, after the collapse of the Soviet Union, chances of slippage of its radiological materials in its poorly guarded, scattered facilities was severe because of political uncertainty. Though there were some reports on alleged selling of radiological materials by the unpaid workers,[29] most of these attempts were foiled. Now the Russian facilities are secured and both Russia and the US are cooperating with each other to safely secure all materials and facilities of the former Soviet Union.[30] Officials of the 12th Main Directorate of the Ministry of Defense responsible for the security and safety of Russia's nuclear weapons have repeatedly stated that Russia's arsenal is secure from terrorists..[31]

Even if the terrorists get access to the radiological materials, a sizeable infrastructure and extremely complex technology would be required to produce sufficient quantities of weapon-useable materials. Even if terrorists manage to get HEU, but they cannot use it directly asHEU is generally available in the form of uranium hexafluoride or oxide. It needs to be processed into a form usable in a nuclear device and for this terrorist group need nuclear reactors. Building a reactor or stealing it is almost impossible as it technically complex and involves huge resources. It is argued that high officials in charge of the devices or materials might transfer them to terrorists for example the AQ Khan network. But it should be kept in mind that AQ Khan provided the blueprints for a plant to produce the HEU, raw material and weapon design, not uranium as such or any ready-made nuclear device to any terrorist organization. Further, he provided all these to the friendly countries of Pakistan, not to any terrorist organization. It is feared that North Korea and Iran might transfer their nuclear technology to the terrorist organizations. There is no known tie between North Korean government and extremist terrorist groups now. There is also report that North Korea is prepared to reassure the US that it has no intention of providing nuclear materials to terrorists.[32] However, it is unlikely that states sympathetic to certain terrorist groups would transfer such materials to terrorists. The transferring state would risk massive retaliation from the international community. So the fear of being traced would serve as an effective means of deterrence.. The Khan expose appears to make such transfers from Pakistan less likely in the future.

One instance of a terrorist group's attempt to build its own nuclear weapon was the Japanese terrorist group Aum Shnrikyo which tapped its vast financial resources to buy Australian properties and conducted an investigation for purchasing uranium-enrichment technologies.[33] But it failed, largely because enrichment is an extremely challenging process, requiring state-level resources. Other such attempts[34] have been:

* November 1995 cesium-137 discovered in a Moscow park
* December 1998 RDD found near Argun, Chechnya
* Multiple attempts by al Qaeda to acquire material for a radiological device
* UK intelligence – al Qaeda prioritized RDD from 1999+
* Jose Padilla, Arrested May 2002 & accused of planning to develop a uranium-based RDD & targeting of apartment blocks using conventional weapons. Khalid Sheikh Mohamed & Abu Zubaydah key sources of information & encouraged Padilla to focus on

conventional weapons. Padilla detained as an enemy combatant in spite of his US citizenship

The worldwide stockpiles of HEU are plentiful with about 1,850 metric tons enough to make tens of thousands of nuclear weapons.[35] A major chunk of this is under military control. Like enriching uranium, making plutonium, without state sponsorship, is beyond the capability of terrorists. The US, Russia, Britain, and France have stopped producing plutonium for weapons purposes and China might have also stopped military plutonium production.[36] No doubt since 1999, global stocks of plutonium have increased, but HEU stocks are declining.[37] Again, the highly radioactive spent fuel is not easy to be acquired by terrorist groups if they don't have the access to 'special handling gear'. Thus it is clear that though fissile materials are theoretically accessible to terrorists, the required resources and expertise to utilize them for fabricating a device are staggering and extremely hard for them to mobilize.

It is apprehended that radiological materials present in the countries like Russia, former Soviet Republics and Pakistan are prone to slip into the terrorist groups. As of March 2003, Russia possessed roughly 600 metric tons of weapon usable plutonium and HEU stored at more than 50 military and civilian sites.[38] It is true that the state of Russian nuclear infrastructure is decaying. Inadequate accounting of nuclear materials, impoverishment of Russian nuclear workers and scientists entails that most of the nuclear materials are unsecured. The widely perceived notion about the state of Pakistani nuclear materials is the possible slippage or taken over by the domestic extremist Islamic groups and in the surrounding region coupled with political instability, fractured civil-military relationship.

However, the world is not a passive onlooker. At least the fear of a possible nuclear terror catastrophe has raised the awareness of the international community to locate and work upon such possible cases. All over the world now, there is a concern for the security of radiological materials and consequent partnerships are being built for reducing the chances of terrorists' access to nuclear arsenals. The Global Initiative to Combat Nuclear Terrorism (GICNT) launched by US President George W Bush and his Russian counterpart Vladimir Putin on July 15, 2006, with an aim "to prevent the acquisition, transport, or use by terrorists of nuclear materials and radioactive substances or improvised explosive devices using such materials, as well as hostile actions against nuclear facilities"[39] illustrates such co-operation. Other two US programmes are already in operation to hinder the process of slippage of radiological materials into the hands of terrorists. The Material Protection, Control and Accounting (MPC&A) programme of the US Department of Energy (DOE) provides equipment and training to upgrade security at existing sites of the Russian Federal Agency of Atomic Energy (RFAAE) housing fissile materials.[40] The US Department of Defence (DOD) programme to construct the Mayak Fissile Material Storage Facility intends to provide a highly secure location for plutonium and HEU taken from dismantled Russian nuclear weapons.[41] The DOE also manages the Russian Surplus Fissile Materials Disposition Programme, commonly known as the Plutonium Disposition Programme to facilitate implementation of the September 2000 Plutonium Disposition Management and Disposition Agreement under which Russia and the US will each dispose of 35 tons of excess weapons-grade plutonium by immobilization or utilization in MOX fuel.[42] Many such programmes are in full operation now to locate and secure orphan radiological materials scattered in the former Soviet states.

In the case of Pakistan, the fissile material stockpile is relatively small thus easy to guard, than the case of Russia. Little information is available about the Pakistani security measures covering fissile materials. However, according to some press reports, the US had been assisting Pakistan with improving the security of its nuclear material.[43] It is also known that during peace time Pakistani nuclear arsenals are kept disassembled form reducing the chances of slippage.

IN the worst case scenario, even if terrorists acquire fissile materials they cannot fabricate a bomb owing to the degree of engineering and the amount of financial resources required. Also the acquisition of militarily significant nuclear capability involves a more than simply the purchase or construction of a single nuclear device or weapon. It requires attention to the issues of safety and handling of the weapons, reliability and predictability of entire systems and their efficient use. To that extent, the international nuclear black market is almost entirely driven by supply, not by demand. And except conceptual outlines, the detailed plans and engineering required to fabricate a bomb is not easily available.

SABOTAGE

One of the conceivable chances of nuclear terrorism is the sabotage of a nuclear facility, power plant, laboratory or medical facility by any terrorist group that would lead to nuclear explosion and release of radiation. Various techniques might be employed by the terrorists in this regard ranging from the lunching of a rocket, mortar, throwing of a grenade to crashing of an airplane. The event of 9/11 has strengthened this apprehension. Such an action would inflict large scale psychological stress and social disruption, radioactive contamination, and financial damage, but not large number of deaths.

Not only commercial power plants, but also research reactors, are potential terrorist targets. About 280 of these reactors are operating in 36 countries.[44] Internationally, there is no binding mandate that states should meet minimum security standards for research reactors or commercial power plants. Though the International Atomic Energy Agency (IAEA) has issued voluntary guidelines which have been widely adopted, these are very broad and lack specificity.

Spent fuel storage facilities are potential terrorist targets. Most countries store spent fuel adjacent to the nuclear reactor site where it is produced. Worldwide, more than 200,000 metric tons of such spent fuel has been accumulated.[45] A successful terrorist attack on spent fuel storage could create a radioactive disaster..

Waterborne attack is another form of nuclear terrorism. Every nuclear plant requires some means of supplying external cooling water. Generally power plants are accessible by sea, lake, or river. A terrorist group can reach vital water intakes and attempt to block the water flow. An interruption to this flow for long period could force the plant to shut down.

Research facilities, medical establishments, food processing units, etc., using radiological materials are also prone to terrorist targets. Though the amount of radiological material used is less, the level of security is uneven in these facilities. Nearly 100 civilian facilities around the globe operate with small amounts of weapon-grade HEU (uranium enriched up to 90 per cent or greater). Commercial radioactive sources are used in virtually every nation, in various applications, such as cancer treatment, industrial radiography, oil well logging, and scientific research. In numerous medical centers radiological materials, like Cobalt 60, are used for treatment of cancer, which are virtually out of any national security structure. These facilities are soft targets for terrorists for spreading radiation. Same is the case for food processing units where radiological materials are used for preserving and processing food items. Though the damage or radiation contamination level would be less compared to the attack of a nuclear reactor or detonating a bomb, its psychological effect would be far greater.

RADIOLOGICAL DISPERSAL DEVICE (DIRTY BOMB) OR RADIATION EMISSION DEVICE

Another possible tactic of terrorist groups is to explode a conventional explosive coupled with radioactive material known as "dirty bomb". Whatever the amount of radioactive material that is accessible to terrorists would be sufficient to fabricate a Radiological Dispersal Device (RDD), which is much easier than an Improvised Nuclear Device (IND). Conceptually, RDD is a very simple device. It's a mixture of conventional explosive with radiological material, for example, TNT (trinitrotoluene) packaged with radioactive material. When the explosion takes place, the radioactive material spreads in a sort of dust cloud, carried by the wind that reaches a wider area. Unlike a nuclear weapon explosion, use of RDD would not involve a nuclear chain reaction or a massive release of energy, but it would kill people in the near term for the ionizing radiation. This would boost radiation level above normal levels, increasing the risk of cancer and radiation sickness to some degree. Cobalt 60, cesium-137, iridium-192, and strontium-90 isotopes are RDD usable weak nuclear materials generally trafficked internationally.[46]

In an IND, highly enriched uranium is used that inflict severe damage and radiation. But developing an IND represents the most challenging type of nuclear terrorism. An attack involving an IND requires extensive financial and technological resources, in addition to a secure facility in which to develop and construct the weapon. The construction of an IND demands a well-organized international network for collecting fissile material and tapping skill and know-how to develop the device, which is much more completed than the fabrication of an RDD.

The builders of a dirty bomb wouldn't find much trouble getting their hands on high explosives – dynamite is readily available, and TNT is not too hard to come by. The main limitation of the bomb would be the availability of radioactive material. It's not nearly as accessible as explosive material, but there are a number of sources for radioactive material around the world. For instance,

* Hospitals use small quantities of radioactive material, such as cesium-137, in nuclear medicine. Cancer treatment institutes use Cobalt-60 for radiotherapy of

cancer.

* Universities use similar materials to conduct scientific research.
* Food irradiation plants use radiation from cobalt-60 to kill harmful bacteria in food.
* Natural radioactive uranium isotopes are mined for use in nuclear energy. Terrorists could conceivably acquire uranium from various mines.
* There are a number of abandoned "nuclear batteries" scattered around the former Soviet Union. These portable thermoelectric generators contain a sizable amount of strontium-90, a highly potent radioactive isotope.
* People could also collect spent radioactive fuel from Russian reactors, which have been abandoned in old nuclear submarines, among other places.
* They could also put something together using various low-level radioactive materials available to anybody.[47]

PSYCHO-DYNAMIC FACTOR OF NUCLEAR TERRORISM

The subject of terrorism does not end with the technical and resource dynamics of any terrorist outfit. Nuclear terrorism is very much related to terrorists' psychology and motivation. All terrorists have a theoretical ability to cause mass casualties, but resort to the nuclear path involves the psychodynamics of the group, not just any individual's choice.[48] The popular belief of the image of terrorists is that they are psychopathic or psychotic, sick, crazy, etc. but this is a misleading assumption. Resorting to terrorism is not an aberration. Most terrorists are psychologically sound and rational and they do not reveal major psychopathology. So, their strategy and decisions to resort to the nuclear path would be well calculated. "A possible motivation for nuclear terrorism would be the group's belief that it has nothing to lose."[49] Since every terrorist group's core priority is its survival, there is a second thought before resorting to the nuclear path because the post-attack actions of the concerned state and international community might simply wipe out the outfit.. A group might resort to nuclear terrorism when its survival is at stake, dissolving or fading and through the nuclear attack, it hopes to regain its status. It might also go in for nuclear attack to prevail over another group. For the sake of the status of being nuclear-weapon capable organization, it might acquire nuclear capability to distinguish itself from other groups.

Another psychological aspect of nuclear terrorism is that "terrorists are technologically conservative" and probably that's why there is no instance where terrorists have resorted to nuclear weapons.[50] They prefer to use tried and tested methods to achieve their aims they don't follow trial and error method since the chances of success in their every operation is fifty-fifty. The act involves high risk, but low probability of success. Owing to huge technical and financial hurdles involved in nuclear terrorism, terrorists would prefer biological and chemical weapons, which are relatively easy to acquire than nuclear devices. Also the lead time between "desiring and acquiring" a usable capability is shorter for other WMD materials than for their nuclear equivalent. To that extent, some writers have the opinion that terrorists do not want a lot of people to watch their actions go futile. But the trend in terrorism in the post-1990s shows that mass casualty has been a normal phenomena. It seems that the phase of idealism has already ended.

CONCLUSION

Above all, nuclear terrorism in the post-1990s, specifically in the post-9/11 era is a conceivable phenomenon. It is not because of the easy availability of fissile material or micro-proliferation but the changing nature of political, psychological and organizational characteristics of terrorism itself. So the very nature of the terrorist behaviour is at the core of the problem.

As there are no precedents for nuclear terrorism, except few aborted attempts, one cannot draw a definite conclusion on this subject. As of now, the only terrorist entity that has the capability to resort to the nuclear path is the al-Qaeda. Documents found in Afghanistan reveal that while al-Qaeda's efforts to make nuclear weapons were far less sophisticated than known state programmes, it is determined to get them and willing to use them.[51] One report says that the idea of attacking nuclear power stations by al-Qaeda perceived to be raised in the early stages of the development of the 9/11 attacks, but was vetoed, apparently by bin Laden himself.[52] But assuming al-Qaeda not going down to the nuclear path is also erroneous. Except in few cases, the behaviour of terrorist groups cannot be predicted all together. They may not use the nuclear weapon but the possession of one such a device is sufficient to create havoc.

From the above discussion it is clear that it would be difficult for terrorists to fabricate or steal a nuclear weapon, but a nuclear sabotage or use of RDD is conceivable. As the objective of any terrorist act is creating fear,, use of radiological weapons (RDD or dirty bomb) seems to be the best option for terrorists as just the news of possession of these would serve their purpose. Growing international awareness on the issue is a positive factor and a national-regional-global strategy would contain the menace.

REFERENCES

1. 53 The author is Research Associate, Centre for Air Power Studies (New Delhi). He is also a Doctoral Candidate in Jawaharlal Nehru University and Editorial Associate of *Indian Foreign Affairs Journal*(New Delhi).
2. The US National Security Strategy for Combating Terrorism (Feb. 2003) warned that "the probability of a terrorist organization using a Chemical, biological, radiological or nuclear weapon or high yield explosives has increased significantly during the past decade" and consequently within a few weeks of 9/11 President Bush ordered his national security team to give nuclear terrorism priority over every

other threat to the US. For details see *National Strategy for Combating Terrorism*, February 2003, available at: http://www.whitehouse.gov/news/releases/2003/02/counter_terrorism/counter_terrorism_strategy.pdf

3. Robin M. Frost, *Nuclear Terrorism After 9/11*, Adelphi Paper 378, (New York: Routledge, 2005), p. 11

4. Gavin Cameron, *Nuclear Terrorism: A Threat Assessment for the 21st Century*, (London: Macmillan Press Ltd., 1999), p. 1

5. See Mathew Bunn and George Bunn, "Strengthening Nuclear Security Against Post-September 11 Threats of Theft and Sabotage", *JNMM* (Spring 2002), pp. 48–60 and "Nuclear and Radiological Threats", Chapter 2 of Committee on Science and Technology for Countering Terrorism, National Research Council, *Making the Nation Safer: The Role of Science and Technology in Countering Terrorism*(Washington, D.C.: National Academy Press, 2002)

6. Gavin Cameron, n.3, p. 13

7. "Terrorism: Motivations And Causes", available at: http://www.terrorism.com/modules.php?op=modload&name=News&file=article&sid=5693&mode=thread

8. There were unprecedented instances of nuclear leakage from the former Soviet Union in 1994 that exacerbated the apprehension of slippage to the hands of terrorist entities. For more details see, "Nuclear Smuggling: How Serious a Threat?", *Strategic Forum banner*, Number 59, January 1996, available at: http://www.ndu.edu/inss/strforum/SF_59/forum59.html

9. Quoted in Charles D. Ferguson, William C. Potter, *The Four Faces of Nuclear Terrorism*, (New York: Routledge, 2005), p. 4

10. See the US *National Strategy for Combating Terrorism*, February 2003, p. 9, available at: http://www.whitehouse.gov/news/releases/2003/02/counter_terrorism/counter_terrorism_strategy.pdf

11. "India's nuke installations on LeT hit list: Mukherjee", available at: hhttp://news.monstersandcritics.com/india/article_1185448.php/Indias_nuke_installations_on_LeT_hit_list_Mukherjee, July 31, 2006.

12. "8-km strong security clamp on Kalpakkam", *The Indian Express*(New Delhi), August, 15, 2006, p.5

13. "Indian Army Prepares for WMD Attacks", available at: http://www.nti.org/d_newswire/issues/2006_8_4.html#12ADF92D, August 4, 2006

14. *IAEA Illicit Trafficking Database*, p.2, available at: http://www.iaea.org/NewsCenter/Features/RadSources/PDF/itdb_31122004.pdf

15. *International Convention for the Suppression of Acts of Nuclear Terrorism*, 2005, United Nations, available at: untreaty.un.org/English/ Terrorism/summary.pdf
16. Ferguson, n.8, pp. 18-20
17. Ferguson, n.8, pp. 18–19
18. US Department of Defense, *Proliferation: Threat and Response* (Washington: Government Printing Office, 2001), p. 62
19. Ferguson, n.8, p. 60
20. Peter Stein and Peter Feaver, *Assuring Control of Nuclear Weapons*, CSIA Occasional Paper # 2, Centre for Science and International Affairs (Harvard University, 1987).
21. Gurmeet Kanwal, "Comand and Control of Nuclear Weapons in India", *Strategic Analysis*, 23, January 2000.
22. Ferguson, n.8
23. *Ibid.*
24. Rajesh Rajagopalan, *Second Strike: Arguments of Nuclear War in South Asia*, (New Delhi: Viking/Penguin, 2005), p. 169.
26. Kalpana Chittaranjan, "The IAEA as a Safeguards Regime", available at: http://www.nuclearfiles.org/menu/key-issues/nuclear-energy/ history/article-chittaranjan-kalpana.htm
27. "Nuclear Trafficking Latest Statistics Released", Staff Report, 27 September 2005, available at: http://www.iaea.org/NewsCenter/ News/2005/traffickingstats.html
28. Illicit Nuclear Trafficking: Facts & Figures, available at: http:// www.iaea.org/NewsCenter/Features/RadSources/Fact_Figures 2004.html
29. For details on Russian activities see "The Human Factor and Security Culture: Challenges to Safeguarding Fissile Materials in Russia", Preliminary Report, November 2002, Center for International Trade and Security, The University of Georgia, USA, available at: http:// www.uga.edu/cits/documents/pdf/Humanfactor.pdf.
30. Kenneth N. Luongo, "The Uncertain Future of U.S.-Russian Cooperative Security", *Arms Control Today*, January/February 2001
31. See for example, statements by Gen. Igor Valynkin, *Interfax*, September 4, 2002
32. Gregory Elich, "The Nuclear Frame-up of North Korea", 4 July 2003, http://www2.gol.com/users/coynerhm/nuclear_frameup_of_north_ korea.htm

33. for details see "The Demand for Black Market Fissile Material" available at: http://www.nti.org/e_research/cnwm/threat/demand.asp

34. "Nuclear Terrorism", available at: www.comm.cornell.edu/als481/Nuclear.ppt

35. Mohamed ElBaradei and Jonas Gahr Støre, ;'How the World Can Combat Nuclear Terrorism", Disarmament Documentation, The Acronym Institute, available at: http://www.acronym.org.uk/docs/index.htm

36. Charles D. Ferguson, *Preventing Catastrophic Nuclear Terrorism*, CSR NO. 11, Council on Foreign Relations, March 2006, pp. 6–7.

37. Charles D. Ferguson and William C. Potter, "Improvised Nuclear Devices and Nuclear Terrorism" available at: http://www.wmdcommission.org/files/No2.pdf.

38. Russia Profile: Nuclear Overview, available at http://www.nti.org/e_research/e3_8b.html

39. "UK joins global initiative to combat nuclear terrorism", available at: http://www.irna.ir/en/news/view/menu-234/0608011297165947.htm

40. for details see "Plan for securing the Nuclear weapons, material, and expertise of the states of the former soviet union plan for securing the Nuclear weapons, material, and expertise of the states of the former Soviet Union", available at: http://www.carnegieendowment.org/pdf/npp/Nuke%20Security%20Report%202-5-3%20(1).pdf

41. "178 STC 05 E-The Security Of Wmd Related Material In Russia", http://www.nato-pa.int/default.asp?SHORTCUT=695

42. S.G. Cochran and et al., "Fissile Material Disposition Program Final Immobilization Form Assessment and Recommendation", October 3, 1997, Lawrence Livermore National Laboratory, available at: http://www.osti.gov/bridge/servlets/purl/605164-bSbqmb/webviewable/605164.pdf.

43. David Albright, "Securing Pakistan's Nuclear Infrastructure", in Carnegi Endowment for International Peace, *A New Equation: US Policy towards India and Pakistan after September 11*, Working Papers, No. 27, May 2002.

44. *Nuclear Power in the World Today*, Nuclear Issues Briefing Paper 7, February 2005, available at: http://www.uic.com.au/nip07.htm

45. George Bonn, Fritz Stenhausler, and Lyudmila Jaitseva, "Strengthening Nuclear Security Against Terrorists and Thieves Through Better Training", *The Non-proliferation Review*, Fall/Winter

2000, available at: http://cns.miis.edu/pubs/npr/vol08/83/83bunn.pdf.

46. Robin Frost, "Nuclear Terrorism Post 9/11: Assessing the Risks", available at: http://www.cda-cdai.ca/symposia/2003/frost.htm

47. *Ibid.*

48. Robin M. Frost, n.2, p. 41 and Gavin Cameron, n.3, p. 135.

49. Cameron, n.3, p. 135.

50. *Ibid*, pp. 135-36.

51. David Albright, *Al Qaida's Nuclear Programme: Through the Window of Seized Documents*, Nautilus Institute Special Forum 47, 6 November 2002, available at: www.nautilus.org/fora/special-Policy-Forum/47_Albright.html#sect2

52. *The 9/11 Commission Report: Final Report of the National Commission on Terrorist Attacks Upon the United States*, Official Government Edition (Washington, DC: US Government Printing Office, 2004), available at: http://www.gpoasccess.gov/911/pdf/full-report.pdf, p. 172

16

Naxalism and Terrorism: Assessing Departures and Similarities

Arvind Kumar

"On 13th November, at around 9 pm, to coincide with the great November Russian Revolution...Nearly a thousand Naxalites armed with weapons like self-loading rifles and machine guns and clad in police uniforms, launched near simultaneous assaults on the police lines, jail and a CRPF camp located in the heart of the South Bihar town of Jehanabad...341 of the jail's 600 odd prisoners, including Ajay Kanu, state secretary of the proscribed CPI (Maoist) and several other cadres of the outfit were set free and around twelve men of the Ranvir Sena, which is locked in a bloody feud with the ultra-left organisation for the last several years, have been kidnapped..."[1]

This audacious act of one of the extreme left outfits,[2] moves us to ask certain difficult questions regarding how our institutional mechanisms have fared against this most long-running of blood-baths our country has been witnessing since its independence. Post-9/11, the question of terrorism, i.e. use of un-provoked violence against non-combatants, has assumed bigger significance. States are being called upon to deign all kinds of violence against the democratic-sovereign states as 'terrorism' and are asked to take more pro-active action to weed it out. Now, with the growing concerns over the Maoist imbroglio in Nepal, and fears of linkages of the Nepalese Maoists with their Indian counterparts being ever present, we should look into this violent political struggle, which has lasted for almost 60 years in India and look for ways to come to grips with it.

Coming from a primitive urge to resort to violence in order to defend oneself against perceived threats, the circle of violence has vitiated the space for negotiations among aggrieved parties all over the world. Demarcation of political space continues to be a slave to coercion- the advocated use of violence- for settling contentions in the exercise of political power. It seems as if the post-9/11 world is plunged anew into a flurry of violence, with contending parties standing at the fault-lines of diverse political aspirations and societal positions, going at each other's throats to settle their scores. This world order has been reinforced by the renewed belligerence of the global powers against the so-called rogue states, or the states in the axis of evil[3].

Karl von Clausewitz, the great war-theoretician, was one of the first to formulate the use of 'terror'- as distinct from 'war', and as a form of premeditated violence, which aims to strike the opponent's psyche, cowing her into submission. Terrorism, as a form of political violence, may or may not be justified, but the recent spate of Naxalite violence in Bihar, and its projection as a simple act of terrorism forces us to ask certain theoretical questions regarding the categorisation of political violence. The obvious and heuristic relativity of context[4] notwithstanding, 'terrorism' is still very much an amorphous category, even in its recent enunciations as violence against structures of the state.

Against this background, the troubled but stable third world democracies such as India face the brunt of terrorism in various forms, from the ethnic violence for secession in the North-East, to the spates of Naxalite violence close at hand in the heartlands of Bihar and Andhra Pradesh. Some of the insurgencies are largely of a post-colonial nature, over disputes inherent in the accession of disparate political entities into a nascent democracy like India[5]. But, the most striking cause here in India is its abject poverty and inequality in material conditions. The existence of this cauldron of redundant but obstinate feudal structure, along with an incipient neo-liberal capitalist economy in its teething-trouble phase, has created a unique situation in India. When seen through the prism of hunger and incommensurable aspirations, all kinds of 'perceived threats' glean public coinage and legitimacy.

Labelling of any political violence as 'terrorist', or 'religious', or in any other category, is largely conditioned by the relative hegemony-potential of the involved parties in terms of their respective positions in the political hierarchy. Even, a democratic welfare state as a construct, though ideally reified and secular, is actually a hierarchical construct with pronounced differences in power relations among its subjects. Therefore, wherever state is an actor poised as a coercive enforcer of law and order, it would be at odds with the dissenters. Because of this, the state is not always perceived as an unbiased arbiter on political violence. There will always be an element of contextual prejudice as follows in this couplet by Telugu revolutionary poet Sri Sri,

Yesterday the white man called you Bhagat Singh'
Today the brown man calls you Naxalite,
Tomorrow the whole world will call you 'Morning Star'.

The use of the proximate understandings about the nature of political violence or 'terrorism' in the context of Naxalism, can actually obfuscate and decentralise the attempts to deal with it effectively. From a post-modern view of ontology,[6] it is argued in this paper that the variant ontological positions on the exercise of violence in Naxalist[7] and terrorist movements have points of convergence as well as points of divergence. It is imperative that we understand these ontological positions in their entirety, given the complexity of the issues at hand. The categorization of Naxalism as straightforward terrorism is sought to be questioned on these grounds.

THE SPECTRE OF NAXALISM: A BRIEF SKETCH

While contemporary Naxalism takes its popular title from the failed peasant revolt that commenced at Naxalbari in the Darjeeling district of West Bengal in 1967, Left Wing extremism has had a more persistent and sound base in the Telengana region of Andhra Pradesh than in any other part of the country. It is here that it has been crushed again and again, to rise with unyielding tenacity, and "(e)ach time official circles begin to write an obituary of the Naxalite groups, the latter have struck even more ferociously."[8] It was here that the great and futile Telengana uprising first challenged the might of the newly independent Indian state, leading an estimated 4,000 men and women to death. It is here again, that the campaigns of murder have escalated once again to secure new heights over the past months.

With the exception of the State capital, the twin-cities of Hyderabad-Secunderabad, the entire Telengana region stands out for its poverty and underdevelopment. Adilabad, Karimnagar, Warangal and Khammam, ranged in the north of the State, along its borders with Maharashtra, Madhya Pradesh and Orissa, are the Naxalite heartland, its command zone, where their writ remains unquestioned. Their influence, however, extends across the entire Telengana region, into the drought prone expanse of the Rayalseema area to the South, and across to Srikakulam at the Northeastern tip of the State along the Bay of Bengal. More significantly, this area of influence and operation extends well beyond the State's borders across the entire Dandakaranya forest and tribal region in the North, and into the territories of the three bordering States. Beyond these, a merger of the CPI (ML) - Party Unity group with the PWG has extended this dominion into the chaos of Central and South Bihar.

The PWG's merger with the Bihar and Jharkhand based

Maoist Communist Centre (MCC) on September 21, 2004, leading to the formation of Communist Party of India (Maoist) (CPI-Maoist), has given it new teeth recently. The late 1990s leading up to now has been "the most cohesive phase of the 'armed struggle' in spite of the persistence of disparate groups such as the CPI(M-L) Janashakti, the CPI(M-L) New Democracy and the CPI(M-L) Provisional Committee.[9]

There are cur rently some 18 extreme Left or Naxalite groups operating in Andhra Pradesh, but the hegemon here is, without doubt, the PWG. Over the past decade, all Naxalite groups together have reportedly been responsible for over 3,800 murders, including 364 security personnel. In turn, the Security Forces have killed over 1,557 Naxalites. Property, worth over Rs. 1.12 billion, has also been destroyed by the extremists, and the costs to the State in terms of the counter-terrorism effort and developmental opportunities lost is incalculable.[10]

The recent adventures of Naxalites in Jehanabad, is only one of the instances of the steadily increasing influence of Naxalities, as they continue to spread their operations in new states, i.e. Karnataka, Maharashtra, Chattisgarh. There is seen markedly better coordination between these outfits these days. All this bodes badly for the stakeholders at both the ends.

TERRORISM: THE VARIOUS DISCOURSES

Terrorism is the organised use of violence for political ends and is directed primarily at non-combatants. We generally think of terrorist violence as being organised by non-state actors of various kinds- nationalists, anarchists, fundamentalists, leftists, secessionists, and so on. Terrorist violence is also an instrument of governments often to combat non-state terrorists.[11] Generally terrorism involves ....the use of premeditated and planned acts of violence to achieve certain goals for the good of a collective -the aristocracy and princely court, the nation, the ethnic group, the working class. Terrorism uses force or threatens to use force primarily against non-military targets, in order to frighten the other into capitulating: the word 'terrorism' comes from the Latin, *terrere,* to frighten.

Liberals argue that terrorism has to be understood as a response to economic, social and political misery. Conservatives, by contrast, attribute it to the 'natural' stresses and strains of nation building. Realists see terrorism as arising out of the competition between states and/or the contending parties. Not surprisingly, liberals, conservatives and realists also differ on how states and societies should respond to terrorism. Liberals believe that timely and imaginative social, economic, political, and administrative engineering can fix the grievances of rebellious populations, isolate the terrorists who are fighting on their behalf and allow the authorities to capture or eliminate them. Violence, for conservatives is a regrettable fact of social life, particularly pluralistic post-colonial countries, and governments must use this instrument not necessarily as a last resort and with great restraint, as liberals would prefer, but instead as quickly and as firmly as possible. The prescriptions of realists are much closer to those of conservatives. Since terrorism is just another instrument in the hands of rival parties and since there is no other recourse but to defend oneself by force, governments are justified in using violence to put down insurrections.[12]

While liberals, conservatives, and realists can be criticized on various grounds, each also contains an explanation for why terrorism occurs. Liberals certainly seem to be right in suggesting that a sense of economic, social, and political grievance creates the basic conditions in which terrorism takes root and grows. People who perceive that they have suffered because of the government's acts of commission or omission and who nurse a sense of being wronged over a long period of time will eventually turn to violence. Conservatives are right in pointing to the resentment of an ethno-religious group as being the most important condition of terrorism, as it would come into conflict with the government's desire to foster national identity at all costs. Finally, realists are justified in claiming that external influences[13] on terrorism are a matter of historical record.

Apart from these, geographic considerations, as well as ideological considerations can induce qualify terrorism.

NAXALISM AND TERRORISM: THE ONTOLOGICAL DEBATES IN POLITICAL VIOLENCE

The broad approach, while dealing with Naxalism, by and large, draws inspiration from a somewhat uncritical acceptance of the general theory that all political violence is rooted in economic and social deprivation - relative or absolute as the case may be. The more extreme formulation of this thesis contends that, in conditions of extreme poverty, inequality or inequity, all political violence, irrespective of its immediate or proximate motivation and impact, is remedial or catalytic of positive reform. Ted Gurr, in his authoritative exploration of the question *Why Men Rebel*, gives masterful expression to this coldly 'objective' calculation:

> *It is likely that high magnitudes of violence destroy more than they create, at least in the short run. When the time dimension is taken into account, however, intense political violence, though it destroys much in the short run, may have the long-run payoffs either of stimulating rulers to increase outputs or of restructuring society in such a way that total satisfactions are substantially increased.*[14]

Every act of mass violence is inevitably followed by changes - both positive and negative - which may be consequent upon such violence, or may be the result of entirely independent variables. Given this ambiguous pool of data, and depending on the time frame selected (needless to say, arbitrarily), any conclusions desired can safely be arrived at. Apart from the historical record of most new revolutions laying the foundations of a new tyranny, who is to determine whether the appropriate time frame of evaluation, for instance, of the Russian revolution was Gurr's timeframe[15] , or the seven years that brought Stalin to power, or the seventy-odd that culminated in the collapse of the Soviet Union? And who is to define what *could have been*, had the revolution not occurred, and had a more even, non-violent evolutionary process of social, economic and technological change been pursued? The fact is, the sum of evidence in favour of the salutary social and economic effects of revolutionary violence is at least equivocal, if not entirely suspect - especially where such evidence is arraigned against the record, even of the imperfect but consistent democracies of the Third World.

The application of utilitarian criteria to the evaluation of long-term historical trends suffers from another defect: there is no 'objective' or correct way to determine whose 'utility' or satisfaction is to be evaluated. Which generation is to be the beneficiary? Is the present to be automatically and inevitably sacrificed to the future? And where does the process stop? The problem was, in another context, succinctly expressed by Keynes: in the long run, we are all dead.[16]

Those who take the Naxalites' political and ideological pretensions seriously insist "the movement gets sustenance because the government does not treat it as a politico-ideological and socio-economic problem,"[17] and that the movement is "symptomatic of a society which is anxious to usher in social change."[18]

'Revolutionary' violence that persists for decades, as has Left extremism in India, must be evaluated by criteria other than the general 'causal' approach that seeks to justify it in terms of historical wrongs and contemporary inequalities, or the presumption of its intrinsic beneficence. As one commentator observes, "Since this movement has had a controversial and turbulent existence on India's political stage for close to six decades, its leaders must attempt a socio-political audit of their efforts - from the point of view of their own objectives and its impact on the people they are fighting for."[19]

Another perspective on the 'basic realities' that are often ignored, notes that the causal link between absolute, or even relative, deprivation and 'revolutionary violence' is, at best, tenuous. Extreme Left movements have found justification for random and indiscriminate violence in the most affluent and among the most equitable societies of Western Europe, as also in modern Japan. Within India, it has been observed that the districts in central Bihar that were most affected by Naxalite violence - Patna, Nalanda, Gaya, Jehanabad, Aurangabad, Nawadah and Bhojpur - were characterised by "farm prosperity and literacy... higher than in the rest of the State... thus in some ways the violence in central Bihar is not the offshoot of stagnation and poverty, but is instead a reflection of development and growth, however stunted."[20](Mohanty, N. 22)

The *choice of violence*, moreover, is in most cases made, not by the deprived, impoverished or victim communities, but by better-educated and relatively affluent 'ideologues' and mobilisers, who purport to speak on their behalf. This is natural, of course. But, given the extreme complexity of the patterns of violence, of both voluntary and coercive mobilisation, and the overlap of a range of purely criminal and 'revolutionary' activities undertaken by various extreme Left groupings, it is important to understand that the claims of such 'representation' have, in all these movements, never been tested or seriously questioned.

Another aspect of the unexamined 'basic realities' of Naxalite violence is the widening hiatus between the proclaimed intention and the actuality. Those who, overtly or otherwise, sympathise with the broad objectives of these movements, or with some of the organisations and individuals connected with them, are eager to point out that, "the PWG[20] is now engaged in constructive programmes, such as building irrigation facilities, ensuring primary education and primary healthcare, besides demanding full benefits of government programmes for tribals."[21] Others, however, insist that this is mere political posturing and tokenism, and that the extreme Left formations are a lawless, depredatory force, and that "about 90% of the persons killed by Naxalites are from poor and labour classes and coming from SC, ST and BC castes. The sense of insecurity is therefore more in the poorer sections of the population."[22] There are also basic structural constraints that limit the capacity of benign intervention on the part of the extremist: Naxalism is not an alternative system of governance or development, as it degenerates into dogmatic and hierarchic local rule. The caprice of the local leader is, within this system, the final law and arbiter for those who are at its mercy, and an institutional structure and mechanism of ensuring accountability are non-existent. The MCC in Bihar, for example, has maimed people for defying its orders on poll-boycott and co-operation with the State administration with impunity. They have struck terror with similar tactics in Andhra Pradesh and other States too. Not surprisingly, the existence of the Marxist groups has exacerbated social conflict in a queer combination of caste and class war.[23]

Revolutionaries tend to be impatient with democracy and its institutions, believing that they can, at a stroke, dismantle all the evils of the system - and that this alone is an adequate corrective. This is a perspective that has much in common with the *tanto peggio, tanto meglio* principle of Italian Fascism that amounted to little more than a visceral rejection of everything that the *status quo* represented.[24]

An aspect of this self-perpetuating cycle of violence that is seldom noticed, and that has become a critical element in the persistence of most insurgencies and terrorist movements in India, is the creation, complexity and continuous expansion of the underground terrorist economy, and the magnitude and power of the collusive arrangements that come into being between the extremists, on the one hand, and the political, administrative and business elite, on the other. To take the case of Andhra Pradesh, the relationships of the PWG with the various dominant political parties in the State has been far from unambiguous, and each of these has, from time to time, found it expedient to seek the support of this extremist organisation to secure an electoral advantage, as have many individual politicians.[25] These arrangements are often transient, and political alliances have frequently degenerated into fierce campaigns of repression and retaliation within a brief interval. More insidious and persistent, however, is the web of financial and commercial interests that emerges over time. As the Advocates' Committee on Naxalite Terrorism in Andhra Pradesh noted,

> *The extremist groups are collecting crores of rupees from all types of traders, contractors or any other persons engaged in any economic activity. They are also imposing levy on the farmers. Collection of money is so easy that many unemployed local rowdies are finding it an easy way of making money.*[26]

A final 'justification' of extreme Left violence also demands attention here. "The violence that we indulge in," declares Muppala Lakshmana Rao 'Ganapathy', the present head of the CPI-ML-People's War, "is only as a counter to the mindless violence perpetrated day in and day out by the state's mercenary forces."[27] The claim merits serious evaluation. It is certainly the case that the agencies of the state do adopt extra-legal methods in the conflict in various theatres of extremism in the country, and the Naxalite affected areas are no exception. While the magnitude and frequency of such actions can hardly be authoritatively documented or confirmed, it is the case that Ganapathy's statement was made in the context of allegations of one such incident, in which three prominent leaders of the PWG were allegedly executed in a 'fake encounter', and of the rash of retaliatory killings by the Naxalites that followed. The question, very clearly, cannot be settled by counting casualties on either side of the conflict, or by seeking to identify the point at which the conflict was initiated, or indeed, as supporters of the government often do, by justifying extra-legal methods in terms of the collapse of all the institutions of civil governance - including the criminal justice system - in a situation of widespread terrorism. The fact, however, that the Naxalites consciously choose the path of violence against the state may, in some measure, impose a moral responsibility on them. But this line of argument is contentious, since evidence of the 'violence' of the state against its people can easily be selectively culled from the historical record to justify such a choice.

It is, consequently, the *nature* of Naxalite violence against which the movement's claims must be tested; and in this, it would be found wanting. As with all the other militant 'saviours' of various class and sectarian groupings in India, the largest proportion of the victims of Naxalite violence are drawn from the very classes and communities they claim to be protecting or fighting for.[28] Such killings are justified on the grounds that the problem arises only "when there is an informer. The party has to decide between the life of a revolutionary and the life of the informer."[29] It is important, nevertheless, to remind ourselves that, "(w)here revolutionaries find it necessary to kill more people on their own side than the enemy, it must be presumed either that their cause is widely opposed or that, at least, it leaves the population indifferent."[30] While the violence of the state may, at least on occasion, be conceded to be 'mindless', Naxalite violence cannot escape the charge of an equal, if not disproportionate mindlessness.

The sweep of the preceding analysis is far from comprehensive, and there would be many other aspects and 'basic realities' that demand detailed examination if we are to arrive at an adequate understanding of the complexity of socio-economic, ideological, political, tactical and strategic issues raised by the Naxalite movement. Such a study, however, falls beyond the scope of the present paper. What is sought here, is a demonstration that a reductionist approach that conceives of poverty alleviation and developmental programmes, investments and reforms as the panacea for extreme Left violence, is roughly as myopic as the competing viewpoint that the whole problem can be subsumed under a simple 'law and order' approach that depends overwhelmingly on the use of para-military and police forces to crush extremism. Equally myopic, moreover, is the position that seeks a simple-minded juxtaposition of these two in a 'carrot-and-stick' policy that offers some developmental sops, even as it goes after the Naxalites with a continuously augmenting force of arms.

CONCLUSION

Terrorism is characterised by a form of violence, which is completely illegitimate and dehumanised, and the state is justified in clamping down on it without any space for ideological negotiation. In its multifarious forms violence is an ethical offence and is decried universally. We tried to see political violence as seen in case of Naxalism in the rubric of terrorism. In the process, we were able to prove many disquieting facts about the legitimacy claimed by the Naxalites for use of violence. At the same time, we could also see that instrumental definitions of terrorism can never subsume Naxalism in all its aspects.

The fact that Naxalism has a strong appeal for countless people disadvantaged to the point of alienation from the mainstream is irrefutable. The ideological and theoretical underpinnings of this political struggle, though at times millenarian, are real humanistic ideals. This, and the fact that violence comes to the fore when all other options for negotiation has been exhausted, entails a re-evaluation of our policies towards stemming this self-perpetuating spreading swathe of blood-bath in our country.

The vacuum left behind by the state is not a perceived reality in Naxalite-infested areas- it is a bitter cold reality. The failure and the contradictions of the universalistic development programme coupled with fact that the democratic political structure continues to reflect the skewed power relations in India, mean that there will always be space for the revolutionary elements. Legends, myths and martyrs for the cause of the people, would always be created at the cost of lives. Terrorists may come and fade away after they exhaust their legitimacy, but, since, Naxalite movements base their violence in the politics of these basic needs- not for a few, conventional terrorism cannot hope to subsume Naxalism wholly. On the other hand, romantic metaphors cannot justify violence and the consequent 'terror'.

A *Jehanabad,* based as it is on such an anomic premise as violence, can give only an adrenalin rush of a very transient nature. No lasting societal revolution can be built through such acts.

REFERENCES

1. Monday, November 14, 2005 09:33:07 am PTI, as reported in *The Times of India.*
2. CPI (Maoist)
3. We allude to the belligerence of the US and its allies in the Gulf and Afghan wars, as also against countries like Iran, South Korea etc. (these are also the states accused of forming an axis of evil against the US), justifying the use of terror to maintain their hegemony.
4. The import that any act of violence carries, impinges on the relativity of context- be it temporal (today's terrorist may be tomorrow's patriot/ martyr), geo-politics (Kashmiri terrorists are freedom fighters in Pakistan), etc.
5. Like that of the North East and Jammu and Kashmir.
6. For a debate on ontological stances in political theory, see, Moore, Will H. 2001. "Evaluating Theory in Political Science." Florida State University.
7. We shall use the phrase 'revolutionary violence' interchangeably with 'political violence'
8. "Naxal Violence", *The Hindustan Times,* Feb.12, 2003.
9. Ramakrishnan, Venketash, October 21, 2005, *Frontline,* p-11.
10. Figures as quoted in Ajai Sahni's paper "*Naxalism: the retreat of Civil Governance*" in www.satp.org
11. See, Bajpai, Kanti P. (2002), "*Roots of Terrorism*", Penguin Books: New Delhi, for an in-depth and general definition of terrorism.
12. Ibid, pp— pp-6-16
13. A case to illuminate this, in our context of Naxalism, would be the endorsement shown to the Naxalites by the People's Republic of China.

In fact the editorial in *People's Daily*, July 5, 1967 (the day Naxalbari erupted), described that the "revolutionary group of the Indian Communist Party has done the absolutely correct thing". This is as quoted from Ramakrishnan, Venketash, October 21, 2005, *Frontline*, p-11.

14. Gurr, Ted Robert, (1970), *Why Men Rebel*,Princeton:PUP, footnote no.4, pp 4-5.
15. Ibid.
16. Keynes, John Maynard, (1923), *A Tract on Monetary Reforms*, ch-3.
17. Das, Ashok, "Naxalism: Y2K Problem sans Solution?", New Delhi, *Hindustan Times*, Feb 10, 2000.
18. ibid
19. Mehra, Ajay K., "Failing Revolution", *The Pioneer*, March 10, 2000.
20. It has since merged with MCC in Bihar to reborn as CPI (Maoist).
21. Mohanty, Manoranjan, "The Civil War is Growing", *Hindsutan Times*, New Delhi, Feb.13, 2003.
22. *Report of the Advocate's Committee on Naxalite Terrorism in Andhra Pradesh*, 1997, April 4. This is quoted in Ajai Sahni's paper "*Naxalism: the retreat of Civil Governance*" in *www.satp.org*
23. Mehra, Ajay, *op cit.*
24. Sahni, Ajay, *op cit.*
25. *Report of the Advocate's Committee on Naxalite Terrorism in Andhra Pradesh, op cit.*
26. ibid.
27. "The Rediff Review: Their Murders Will be Avenged", *www.rediff.com*
28. Cf. *Report of the Advocate's Committee on Naxalite Terrorism in Andhra Pradesh, op cit.*
29. Rao, Dr. Vara Vara, "The Rediff Interview", www.rediff.com
30. Crozier, Brian, (1974), *A Theory of Conflict*, London: Hamish Hamilton, p-129.

17

Cyber Terrorism: Fact or Fiction

Dr. Padmalaya Mahapatra

Terrorism is the calculated and unlawful use or threat of use of force or violence against persons or property to induce fear, intimidate or coerce a government, civilian population or any segment thereof in furtherance of goals which are generally religious, political or ideological. Tomorrow's terrorist may be able to do more damage with a keyboard than with a bomb. The combination of two of the great fears of the twenty-first century is combined in the term 'cyber terrorism'. The fear of random and violent victimization is well associated with distrust and outright fear of computer technology. Both capitalize on the fear of the unknown. It is easy to distrust that, which one is not able to control.

Terrorism, with its roots in the periphery of mainstream society is feared. It is perceived as being random, incomprehensible and uncontrollable. Groups with obscure names and origins exercise catastrophic attacks on the innocent.

The word "Cyber terrorism" refers to two elements; cyberspace and terrorism. Cyber terrorism is the premeditated, politically motivated attack against information, computer systems, computer programmes and data, which result in violence against non-combatant targets by sub-national groups or clandestine agents.

NEW PERSPECTIVES OF CYBER TERRORISM

Cyber terrorism requires some new perspectives. The following concepts must be considered in order to fully understand threats of cyber terrorism.

1. The motivations behind a cyber terrorist may be the same as any other type of terrorist attack. Cyber terrorism is another tool, as are explosives and automatic weapons.
2. The individuals or organizations executing these acts may not necessarily be those committed to the outcome of the act. Cyber terrorism can require technical expertise that exists outside the realm of a terrorist organization.

   Frequently, a system cracker may be hired to execute an act of Cyber Terrorism. This might be a professional looking for money or it might be a teenager looking for a challenge. The recruitment process may or may not include "the cause".
3. Like many terrorist attacks, there may not be a warning. However, with cyber terrorism, one may not even know that the act has taken place until sometime after the attack.

   Attacks on computer systems can go unnoticed even after penetration. A cyber terrorist may be in the system several times before the act takes place for reconnaissance or experimentation. Also, the act may be tied to a delay much like a bomb timer, set to execute when a certain time span or a certain event takes place.
4. The cost of such an act is minimal and the tools and information are ubiquitous.
5. Intelligence gathering on cyber terrorism is difficult. Tradecraft and intel gathering is complicated by virtual of meetings, drop sites and encryption.
6. Finally, the prevention of attacks requires more coordination than almost any other form of terrorism.

   The explosion of inter-networks, the connection of trusted

to non-trusted systems and myriad other factors, along with reliance and dependence on computerized systems, makes cyber terrorism one of the most difficult threats to prevent.

When we speak of where a cyber terrorist act may occur, we are not specifically referring to a physical location.

Geography is limitless and irrelevant when dealing with cyber terrorist threats. We must think in terms of cyber terrorism acts as happening in cyberspace, regardless of locale or origination or target. The systems that are most likely to be attacked are at the point where we are most vulnerable: the point at which the physical and virtual worlds converge. Let us first define theses two domains.

The physical world is matter and energy – light, dark, hot and cold, all physical matter – that place in which we live and function.

The virtual world is symbolic – true, false, binary, metaphoric representation of information – that place in which computer programs function and data moves.

The physical and virtual worlds are inherently separate worlds. However, it is at the intersection, the convergence, of these two worlds, that stands as the most likely location of a Cyber Terrorist Act.

EXAMPLES OF ACTS OF CYBER TERRORISM

Let's take a look at a few examples of potential cyber terrorist acts. These examples are not potential acts we may see in the future. These are all situations that could happen today, with today's technology.

* A cyber terrorist could remotely access the processing control systems of a cereal manufacturer, change the levels of iron supplement, and sicken and kill the children of a nation enjoying their food.
* The cyber terrorist could then perform similar remote alterations at a processor of infant formula. The key: the

cyber terrorist does not have to be at the factory to execute these acts.

* A cyber terrorist could place a number of computerized bombs around a city, all simultaneously transmitting unique numeric patterns, each bomb receiving each other's pattern. If one bomb stops transmitting, all the bombs detonate simultaneously.
* A cyber terrorist could disrupt the banks, the international financial transactions, the stock exchanges.
* A cyber terrorist could attack the next generation of air traffic control systems, and collide two large civilian aircraft.
* A cyber terrorist could remotely alter the formulas of medication at pharmaceutical manufacturers. The potential loss of life is unfathomable.
* The cyber terrorist may then decide to remotely change the pressure in the natural gas lines, causing a valve failure and a block of sleepy suburb detonates and burns.

FACTORS FOR THE RISE OF CYBER TERRORISM

Terrorism and Internet are related in two ways. First, the Internet has become a forum for terrorist groups and individual terrorists both to spread their messages of hate and violence and to communicate with one another and with sympathizers. Secondly, individuals and groups have tried to attack computer networks including those on the internet which is known as Cyber Terrorism or Cyber warfare.

At least 12 of the 30 groups on the US State Department's list of designated foreign terrorist organizations maintain websites on the Internet. While US officials believe that some terrorists use encrypted E-mail to plan acts of terrorism, most groups appear to use the Internet to spread their propaganda. Most Internet sites of terrorist groups seek to advance the organization's political and ideological agenda. Immediately after the Peruvian terrorist group Tupac Amaru stormed the Japanese Ambassadors's residence in Lima and held diplomatic, political and military officials hostage in December, 1996, Tupac Amaru sympathizers in the US and Canada established several solidarity Internet sites, one of which included detailed drawings of the terrorists' plan of assault on the Japanese Ambassador's residence. Latin American guerrilla movements are among the most electronically sophisticated extremist groups according to a study in the Wall Street Journal.Mexico's Zapatista guerrillas have been rallying support online since their 1994 uprising. The Revolutionary Armed Forces of Colombia (FARC) fields press inquiries through electronic mail. The Website of Peru's primary terrorist organization, "Shining path" contains scrolls of Marxist-Leninist propaganda.

Islamic militant organizations also use the Internet to disseminate their anti-western, anti-Israel propaganda. Hezbollah, the pro-Iranian Shiite terrorist organization based in South Lebanon sells books and publications through its website. Other sites actually provide information on how to build bombs as well as instructions for making dangerous chemical and explosive weapons. Many of these sites post the "Terrorist's Handbook" and "The Anarchist Cook Book", which offer detailed instructions for making dangerous chemical and explosive weapons. Al Qaeda has developed a communications network that is based on the Internet, electronic bulletin boards, and e-mail in an attempt to avoid capture by counter terrorism agencies.

Another terrorist group is Aum Shinrikyo. Aum Shinrikyo mainly operates from Japan and Russia. The group seeks to bring about the Apocalypse, and is responsible for the 1995 sarin gas attack on a Tokyo subway. The attack resulted in 12 dead and 5,000 injured civilians. The extent of Aum Shinrikyo's cyber terrorism capabilities was discovered in 2000, when a Japanese police department realized that one of their computerized vehicle tracking programs was created by Aum Shinrikyo. Until this discovery, Aum Shinrikyo had been compiling classified data concerning the whereabouts of both marked and unmarked Japanese police vehicles through the program that they had created for the police.

The fear surrounding cyber terrorism is that terrorists and other criminals could attack and penetrate our nation's critical infrastructure, computer systems and endanger human lives by disrupting military networks, emergency medical services, land and air transportation systems, telecommunications and utilities.

Cyber crime has already assumed a political agenda. In August 1997, a group calling itself the Internet Black Tigers (affiliated with the Liberation Tigers of Tamil Eelam) claimed responsibility for E-mail harassment of several Sri Lankan missions around the world. The group claimed in Internet postings to be specialists in "suicide e-mail bombings" with the goal of countering the Sri Lankan Government.

Elsewhere, Internet saboteurs defaced the Home Page and stole E-mail from India's Bhabha Atomic Research Centre in May and June 1998.

A major ongoing debate related to terrorism and the Internet is the question of encryption. Encryption is software technology that locks computerized information to keep it private. Only those with an "electronic Key" can decipher the information. On the one hand encryption protects individual and corporate privacy and is a fundamental building block of electronic commerce. On the other hand, police and intelligence agencies oppose denying the government access to electronic information because terrorists and other criminals can use encryption technology to conduct illegal activities while avoiding government monitoring. World Trade Centre bombing mastermind Ramzi Ahmed Yousef utilized encryption technology in his foiled plot to blow up airliners in the Far East.

CONCLUSION

Cyber terrorism is a fairly recent threat; therefore, there

is still speculation as to who is ultimately responsible for combating cyber terrorism. However, the government's inability to deal with cyber terrorism is part of the problem.

For every fifty complaints given to law enforcement by private corporations, only one was prosecuted. This is due to the government's lack of resources, both of human specialists and financial funding. This fact is especially frustrating to provide corporations who lose an estimated 10 billion dollars a year to electronic crime. In an attempt to generate a preparedness for cyber terrorism, the U.S. government has developed the National Strategy to Secure Cyberspace. The three objectives of the plan are to "prevent cyber attacks against America's critical infrastructures, reduce national vulnerability to cyber attacks and minimize damage and recovery time from cyber attacks that do occur.

The strategy also sets out five priorities that are critical to defending against cyber terrorism. First, the plan calls for the development of a national cyberspace security response system. Second, the strategy calls for a national cyberspace security threat and vulnerability reduction program. Third, the plan calls for the development of a national cyberspace security awareness and training program. Fourth, the strategy seeks to secure all systems and networks used by the government. Finally, the plan calls for national and international cyberspace security cooperation.

For the strategy to be effective, it requires active participation by all cyberspace users, including the average home user, small businesses, large corporations and enterprises, all critical infrastructures, and all government agencies. Because of the nature of the threat, and the nature of the strategy to defeat the threat, it appears that to have an effective defense against cyber terrorism, a combined effort between international, federal, state, and local law enforcement agencies will be necessary.

REFERENCES

1. Donn Parker, *Crime by Computer*, New York, Charles Scribner's Sons, 1976.
2. United States Department, "Patterns of Global Terrorism", Washington D.C., 1996.
3. Neil Barrett, "Digital Crime", Kogan Page Limited, London, 1997.
4. Walter Reich, ed., *Origins of Terrorism: Psychologies, Ideologies, Theologies, States of Mind*, Washington D.C., Woodrow Wilson Center Press, 1998.
5. Walter Laquer, *A History of Terrorism*, London, Transaction Publishers, 2002.

18

Transnational Terrorism: Challenges For The Media

Chitra Kanungo

Soon after the horrors of September 11, 2001, the international community led by the United States had solemnly vowed to completely root out terrorism from the face of the earth. Five years hence, the menace of terrorism persists, with greater intensity and alarming regularity. The attacks, more daring by the day, are designed to be transnational, in so far as actions by terrorists, in one country imposes uncompensated costs on people or property of another.

Terrorist attacks appear to be random; as a result targeted states expend a large amount of resources and concern to project a wide range of vulnerabilities. Rather than aim at high security targets, terrorists now choose to carry out horrifying attacks on thousands of innocent people, like the "7/11 death on wheels", as the commuter bombings on Mumbai's railway network was described. It was a sickening repeat of Madrid and London attacks.The intention was to disrupt normalcy and completely demoralize the country and its people. "Al-Qaeda", called "terrors leading transnational corporation", rising to fame after 9/11, continues to be the brutal face of modern terrorism; the complexities of this Network, more often than not, going beyond journalistic capture.

"Publicity is the Oxygen of Terrorism", Margaret

Thatcher had rightly said. One of the main purpose of terrorists is the use of extra-normal violence or brutality to capture news headlines for attaining their political objectives. As the public gradually becomes numb to their acts of violence, the terrorists respond with more gruesome acts to recapture media attention. The challenge for the media is therefore to comprehend the dynamics of the terrorist enterprise and to develop options that would serve the interests of government, the media itself and the society at large.

"The media are known to be powerful forces in confrontations between terrorists and governments. Media influence on public opinion may have an impact not only on policies of governments but also on terrorist groups. From the terrorist perspective, media coverage is an important measure of the sources of a terrorist act. Governments can use the media in an effort to arouse world opinion against a country or group using terrorist tactics. Public diplomacy and the media can also be used to mobilize public opinion in other countries, to pressurize governments to take, or reject action against terrorism".

Terrorists, Governments and Journalists view the role and responsibilities of the media, when covering terrorist events from different and often opposing perspectives. The prescription for the desired role of the media, therefore varies amongst there three major players.

TERRORISTS' PERSPECTIVE OF THE MEDIA

Terrorists thrive on publicity. An act of violence of such magnitude sways the focus of the world on them. This is what they need to serve their purpose of using terror as a tool in destroying an existing order and bringing it under its control. Religion is simply a means to bring blind passion and legitimacy to the terrorist imperial vision. Therefore publicity and that too free publicity is invaluable for terrorist groups. From the terrorist's perspective, an interview with a terrorist leader is a treasured prize. Visuals of Osama Bin Laden, rising like a phoenix, spewing venom against American imperialists, telecast by the 'Al Jazeera', was the ultimate triumph for terrorists. After the 9/11 manhunt against him and his terrorist outfit Al Qaeda, he was given up as dead by many,. Such telecasts enhance the morale of terrorists.

"They seek a favourable understanding and appreciation of their cause, if not their act. Terrorists believe the public "needs help" in understanding that their cause is just and terrorist violence is the only course of action available to them against the superior evil forces of state and establishment. Good relationship with the press is important here and they are often cultivated and nurtured over a period of years"[2].

* Terrorist outfits seek to court and woo sympathetic personnel in media. In some cases, they also try to have control over smaller news organisations through funding.
* Observers would conform that every terrorist organisation years for legitimacy. They wish the press to give legitimacy "to what is often portrayed as ideological or personal feuds or divisions between armed groups and political wings. For the military tactician, war is the continuation of politics by other means; for the sophisticated terrorist, politics is the continuation of terror by other means, IRA and Hamas are examples of groups having "political" and military components"[3] Such divisions are also designed for financial contribution from the people to this fund and to entice people to join their ranks.
* Terrorist organisations desire press converge for public sanction and legitimacy to the views of specially created non-government organisations and study centers that serve as covers for terrorist activities fund raising, recruitment, training and travel to target cities are vital activities impossible to carry out without covers. These NGOs or Institutions are created to shield such activities. The Palestine Islamic Jihad and the Islamic Association

of Palestine in Texas are a few example. The terrorist organisations want the media to highlight the legal activities, albiet not the others.

* In case of terrorist acts that lead to hostage situations, terrorists are heavily dependent on the media to provide them details of identity and value of hostages as well as details of rescue operations and retaliations by the government. In such high profile attacks, media coverage of the event and public exposure becomes the life-breath of terrorism.

* Terrorist outfits seek media coverage that "causes damage to their enemy". They want the media to spread fear and panic, to facilitate destruction of a country's economy by scaring away investment and tourism. The strategy is attacks on a country's economy through attack on transport system and tourists as in Bali , Madrid, London, Mumbai and the battle scarred Srinagar, where tourism is the mainstay of the state economy. The attention of the media, both electronic and print stays put on events for a long time-the detailed narration of the incidents, the rescue operations, the tragedy and the sorrow of the victims, the background and mode of operation of the suspected terrorist organisations, interviews with public, politics leaders, with defence analysts and academia and panel discussion on available options takes centre stage, much to the delight of the terrorists and the discomfiture of Governments.

GOVERNMENT'S EXPECTATIONS FROM THE MEDIA

Along with Government, Opposition and Judiciary the Press stands as the fourth pillar of democracy. It has a vital role in keeping the system alive and kicking. Governments, therefore, seek cooperation, restraint and loyalty from the media while dealing on the subject of terrorism.

* Governments always like to have the media on its side

while covering terrorist events. They want media coverage of their manifest not that of the terrorist. From the government's perspective, it is important that the media disseminate government provided information during a crisis.

* Governments also expects that the media never allow itself to be used as a platform for the terrorists to vindicate their views and actions.

* Some media channels tend to glamorize the terrorists. The government expects the press to display maturity while commenting on such incidents and present the terrorists as criminals, which they are, regardless of their cause. There is nothing glamorous about blowing up airlines, trains or buildings and kidnapping prominent persons.

* The governments would like to exclude the media from the scene of action in hostage situations

  (Ms. Barakha Dutt of NDTV was disallowed, as we learnt, by the former external affairs minister, Sri Jaswant Singh, to travel on the plane to Khandahar for the rescue of the hostages)

* It is role of the press to "diffuse the tension of a situation and not contribute to it." An important policy olycitive is to keep the public reasonably calm.

* It is irresponsible media coverage, when they telecast emotional scenes of relatives of victims, angry and weeping demanding action. It certainly builds pressure on the authorities and the latter would prefer if the media exercises restraint in its reporting. The Kandahar hostages case is an example again, where public pressure to make concessions, weighed heavy on th government.

* Just as the terrorists would like to have access to information in hostage situations, the government would on its part wish to bar all information to terrorists. The

government strongly desires that the media does not reveal any anti-terrorist actions or provide any other data to the terrorists.

* After incidents, governments would expect the media not to reveal the techniques and secrets of successful government operation. They would also not like the technological achievements of terrorists to be publicized, or else other anti-socials and outlaws may emulate them anti socials.
* The media should have the ability to discern and then keep away from disinformation and false propaganda, intentionally floated by terrorist groups to mislead governments.
* The governments would want the media to boost the image of government agencies.
* When journalists have reasons to believe that some terrorist attack is in the offing, or have traced suspected terrorist, the government asserts that it is the prime duty of the media to immediately inform them.
* The government expects the media to cooperate by spreading disinformation, when the situation urgently demands, in the interest of the security and integrity of the nation.

The role that media adopts while covering terrorists incidents or issues.

* The media to carry out its function must be essentially free and independent. A free press is the very essence of democracy. The survival and nature of democracy prevalent in a state is determined largely by the freedom the press enjoys in that state. A healthy media can be sustained wherever there is a free flow of information. Media persons want the freedom to cover an issue or an incident without any restraints from media owners, editors, advertisers or from government.

* Every newspapers and every television channel would want to be the first with the news. It is a matter of pride for the media to present a scoop to the public. There is pressure to convey real time news instantly in the world of competitive hi-tech communications.
* The journalists aspire to be truthful and responsible while reporting news. The reporting should be objective, without taking sides. Inaccuracy and distortion is not the hallmark of a true journalist. The horrors of distortion is severe, particularly while covering incidents of hijackings and hostages.
* Media persons seek to be professional and expect to be treated as such, by their employers as well as the government.
* The media invariably attempts to present a story from an angle that is novel and pragmatic, making the news piece exemplary.
* A journalist loyal to his profession will always be fearless. This essential trait often puts his life in danger. Braving pressure from all quarters; he expects protection for his safety from the government, particularly when the incident involves the life and security o the nation. There have been numerous instances of journalists having been kidnapped and later murdered by terrorists. They have exhibited exceptional courage in covering incidents, in fact personally opting for such assignments. Dodging bullets has become a way of life for some. Seeking protection and security therefore is legitimate.
* If requested by the government, the media generally has no objection in playing a constructive role in solving specific terrorist situations, provided the request does not require too much compromise of values.

The media in the subcontinent, particularly in both India and Pakisthan has never attempted to make a serious analysis of the failure of their respective Intelligence Agencies. "The role of intelligentsia and media including politicians is also found wanting in a few other areas. They have failed to provide clarity on crucial issues and have diverted attention by raising irrelevant ones". The Journalists should educate themselves on disturbing subjects like terrorism before attempting to report, let alone comment on it. Terrorists avoid confronting a regular army and attack only unarmed civilian targets, unlike the guerillas. The media should not confuse between the two. As a matter of fact, terrorism is equated with Islamic terrorists today. It is a tragedy that social and educational activities, essential for the upliftment of the community are neglected by Muslim activists. The vacuum, has been filled by the Islamic clergy and Madrasahas that have become the breeding ground for Jehadi thinking. MS Rajaran writes that it "is vital that Indian scholars and the media familiarize themselves with sources like the 'Quranic concept of war' by Brigadier SK Malik, which is a required reading for all Pakistani officials, both military and civilian. The Urdu version of the book called "Jihad" as the manifesto followed by all Islamic terrorists." Many a times, a copy of this book has been found on slain terrorists.

Having long gone soft on Islam and Terrorism, the media in India views the recent terrorist attacks as a threat to its own credibility, for not having foreseen them. A sense of paranoia prevails in society today. Islamic terrorism is not a result of victimisation and misunderstanding, but is a cold calculated game plan, a Jehad, to demoralize and demolish the enemy. The media establishments must have their own intelligence think tanks and a smart journalist should be able to smell attacks. " For the first time in April this year, Al Qaeda overlord Osama Bin Laden mentioned India when he ranted about a Zionist-Christian – Hindu conspiracy against Islam". The warning came close the heels of US President Bush's visit to India and reflected a familiar global hate campaign, which going by past instances, inevitably cultivates in spectacular attacks: both the Madrid and

London blasts were preceded by Al Qaeda hate campaigns". Yet the Mumbai attack caught every one by surprise, though it was already established that Lashkar-E-Toeba and the JeM had close links with Al Qaeda.

The involvement of locals in all such attacks, resembling the modes operandi of the LTTE[1] , makes it doubly difficult for the intelligence and the media. However, the media's regular expose of Pakistan's infidelity, makes it easier for the government to handle policy matters in International forums.

EMERGING TRENDS

A series of recent terrorist acts indicates the emergence of trends that impact on the relationship between the Media, the Terrorist and the Government.

1. **Trend towards anonymity in terrorism. There are instances of anonymous terrorism where no one claims responsibility and no demands are made**
2. **Trend towards more violent terrorists attacks.**
3. **Trend towards attack on media personnel and institutions. Attacks on journalists who are outspoken on areas of concern to the terrorists seem to be on the rise. Attacks accused in Algeria, Mexico, Russia Chechnya and London. There have also been cases as well, in Washington at the National Press Building and the United Nations in New York.**

Some general guidelines may be considered for adoption by the media.

* **Limiting infor mation on hostages, which could harm them: e.g., number, nationality, official postings, how wealthy they may be, or important relatives they have;**
* **Limiting information on military, or police, movements during rescue operations;**
* **Limiting or agreeing not to air live unedited interviews with terrorists; wherever regained;**

* Checking sources of information carefully when the pressure is high to report information that may not be accurate—as well as limiting unfounded speculation;
* Toning down information that may cause widespread panic or amplify events which aid the terrorist by stirring emotions sufficiently to exert irrational pressure on decision makers;
* Encouraging citizen journalists.

By its very nature, democracy offers operational advantages for terrorists. The media, the government and the public have common interests to guard against any one of the public institutions being manipulated by the terrorists, particularly the institutions of the press. Communication between the government and the media is of vital importance in any strategy designed to prevent terrorism and in preserving the stability of nations and freedom of its people. If terrorism flourishes, freedom shrinks and a free media the vital pillar of democracy becomes the first casualty.

REFERENCES

1. Raphael F. Perl, "Terrorist, the Media and the Govt: perspectives, trends and options for policy makers" .... CR.S. Issue Brief Pg. 2, 1997.
2. Ibid, p. 2.
3. Ibid, p. 3.
4. N.S. Rajaram, "Fighting Terrorism", 2003.
5. Unnithan, Shukla, Mohurkar-"India Uner Attack" 'India today', July 24, 2006.
6. Raphel F. Perl, terrorism, the media........... P.6.
7. Ibid.

19

Suicide Terrorism in Sri Lanka

Smita

Over the past two decades suicide terrorism has become an ever-spreading phenomenon. Fifteen different terrorist organizations in twelve different counties resort to the use of suicide tactics against their enemies.[2] Although the tactic may present itself as unique and innovative, it is a combination of familiar method, targets and motives. During 1980s, suicide terrorism was witnessed in Lebanon, Kuwait and Sri Lanka and during 1990s, it had spread to Israel, India, Panama, Algeria, Pakistan, Argentina, Croatia, Turkey, Tanzania, Kenya and many other countries. These developments vindicate that suicide bombings have become a favourite and an effective mode of terrorist strategy to successfully penetrate the target and create lasting injuries and socio-political chaos.[3] Sri Lanka's is a typical case in point where the separatist group – Liberation Tiger Tamil Elam (LTTE) – has the dubious character of attempting maximum number of suicide attacks in the world within the country and in its neighbourhood.

Locating the discourse in a broad framework there are broadly ten identified religious and secular terrorist groups in the world that are capable of resorting suicide terrorism as a tactic against their governments or foreign governments. They are: the Islam Resistance Movement (Hamas) and the Palestinian Islamic Jihad of the Israeli occupied territories; Hezbollah of Lebanon; the Egyptian Islamic Jihad (EIJ) and

Gamaya Islamiya (Islamic Group - IG) of Egypt; the Armed Islamic Group (GIA) of Algeria; Barbar Khalsa International (BKI) of India; the LTTE of Sri Lanka; the Kurdistan Worker's Party (PKK) of Turkey; and the Osama bin Laden network (Al Qaeda) of Afghanistan.[4] The groups engaged in suicide operations in Lebanon alongside Hezbollah were the Natzersit Socialist Party of Syria; the Syrian Nationalist Party; the Lebanese Communist Party; and the Baath Party of Lebanon.[5]

The threat of suicide terrorism is likely to spread with time. It has emerged as 'deadly weapons' in the arsenal of terrorism.[6] Terrorist groups are increasingly relying on suicide attacks to achieve their major political objectives.[7] They are providing intensive training to their bombers with the intention of increasing their endurance. For instance, the suicide bomber who destroyed the US embassy in Nairobi in 1998 had been resident in Kenya for four years. He had married in Kenya and lived in the capital before carrying out the suicide operation.[8] Similarly, the suicide bomber who assassinated President Premadasa of Sri Lanka had lived in the capital Colombo, for three years before carrying out the attack.[9]

DEFINING SUICIDE TERRORISM

Suicide terrorism is one of the most extreme and indiscriminate methods used by terrorist groups. Acts of terrorism that require the death of the perpetrator for successful implementation is typically known as 'suicide terrorism'.[10] The suicide terror attack is defined as *a politically motivated violent attack perpetrated by self-aware individual (or individuals) who actively and purposely causes his own death through blowing himself up along with his chosen target. The perpetrator's ensured death is pre-condition for the success of his mission.*[11] It is the readiness to sacrifice one's life in the process of destroying or attempting to destroy a target to advance a political goal. The aim of the psychologically and physically war-trained terrorist is to die while destroying the enemy target. Thus, a suicide attack is an 'operational method'[12] in which if the very act of attack is dependent upon the death of the perpetrator. The terrorist is fully aware that if he does not kill himself, the planned attack will not be implemented. The attack is carried by terrorists in the form of a portable explosive charge or in a vehicle he is driving.

Assessment of suicide terrorism across a range of groups has revealed that terrorist groups use suicide bombers when they are both strong and weak. In terms of military and economic power, Hezbollah and the LTTE lead the list of suicide operations. In terms of numbers, the LTTE has conducted the largest volume of suicide operations, followed by Hezbollah, Hamas and the PKK.[13] In terms of range, only some of the groups have operated beyond their territories.

There are two types of suicide operations: battlefield and off the battlefield.[14] In battlefield operations, suicide bombers are integrated into the attacking groups. Most off-the-battlefield operations have involved single suicide bombers. In the case of the LTTE and Hamas, there have been multiple suicide bombers. The targets have been static and mobile, against infrastructure and humans. Suicide bombers have destroyed military, political, economic and cultural infrastructure. They have committed terrorist attacks by killing civilians in buses, crowded places and in buildings. Suicide bombers have also assassinated political and military VIPs.

According to Robert Pape, 'the total number of terrorist incidents of all kinds had been falling - from a peak of 666 in 1987 to a low of 274 in 1998. But, in contrast, suicide attacks are proliferating'.[15] There were 98 suicide attacks in the past four years, as compared to 212 attacks during 1983–2000.[16] Why suicide bombers are being favoured than other terrorist attacks? First, in their ability to implement the attack at precisely the time and place where it will cause the maximum number of casualties and greatest damage, the suicide bomber is virtually guaranteed success. Even the least deadly of such attacks succeed in striking a devastating blow to the public morale. Second, it is all more threatening because of the difficulty of combating it, the large number of casualties it creates and the ideological and religious zeal it inspires. Third, planning and executing the escape route after a terror attack has occurred, is usually most complicated and problematic aspect of any terrorist attack. Suicide attack requires no escape plan. Fourth, besides material convenience the suicide bombs can be simple to manufacture. Simplicity is an attribute in many suicide bombings, since terrorist agents' acts as the detonator, thus obviating the need for a sophisticated timing device.[17] The fifth advantage is that the perpetrators have a good chance of avoiding detection. Risk for the organisation and the individual can be kept low. However, there has to be strong emotional appeal for the purpose. Due to these, the degree of success is very high in suicide attacks.

TARGETS

Target is the crucial element in any kind of the terrorism. Assuming that terrorists are rational individuals they are often less discriminative in the selection of the targets. Sandler and Lapan analyse the choice of targets in non-bargaining situations.[18] If the potential target increases its defensive measures, terrorism will be shifted to a different target. Thus, terrorists' choices are sensitive primarily to what governments do to protect themselves. When new techniques and policies are applied to prevent terrorist event, terrorists transfer their efforts to new but related targets.[19] Thus, when primary sets of targets harden, terrorists move to softer and easier targets that are less risky.

The LTTE's principal targets have always been political and military leaders; killing of innocent people is perceived as collateral damage. The mandate for the Black Tiger is always a single person, a leader, political or military, who was adversely associated with the LTTE. The list of LTTE suicide attacks reveals that it never used its Black Tigers against innocent bystanders.[20] As the quality of targets chosen by the LTTE is high, it has a sophisticated training program that lasts for about a year. As well as training the bomber, the LTTE research unit tests the effects of explosives on dogs and goats to ensure that the attack is successful. In other words, elimination of the target has a special focus and significance for the LTTE. Contrarily, the victims of *jihadi* suicide attacks have not been specific leaders, but civilians who, to an extent, were in no way linked with the organization or actively involved against the perpetrators.

MOTIVATION

By its very nature, suicide terrorism is motivated by desperation. Some of suicide groups are motivated by religion and religious or ethnic nationalism. While suicide attacks led by the LTTE are nationalistic and secular in character, the motives behind attacks led by various other *jihadi* organizations seem to be religious and at times even sectarian. Al Qaeda's religious philosophy transcends territorial borders. Hamas, the PIJ and Hezbollah are primarily religious groups, but they are also driven by ethno-nationalism. BKI is the only non-Islamic religious group. While the LTTE and the PKK are driven by ethno-nationalism, the PKK is also infused with Marxist-Leninist ideology. As such, the motivation of Hamas, the PIJ and Hezbollah suicide bombers is primarily Islam. The motivation of the LTTE and the PKK suicide bombers is mainly Tamil and Kurdish nationalism respectively. Thus, the preponderance to associate suicide terrorism as something that is somehow unique to Islam and Middle East is wrong, the perpetrators and organizers of suicide bombings transcends all religion and cultural traditions. Suicide terrorism has continued to be employed by religious and secular groups alike.[21] The background of suicide terrorist reveals that they are neither fanatics nor mentally deranged or uneducated; instead they seem to have come from higher economic and educational background.[22] Their motives may be tactical goals by disrupting peace processes to acquire political recognition or status.

PSYCHOLOGICAL FACTORS

Suicide is generally associated with hopelessness and depression.[23] The desire to end the intense and unbearable psychological pain motivates the actor to commit the act.[24] The individual terrorist's willingness to face not just risk but certain death has a psycho-cultural explanation. The function of martyrdom for resistance movement demonstrates legitimacy and authenticity of the cause. The truth of the cause is established by the individual's willingness to sacrifice everything on its behalf. The martyr self- consciously creates a model for future emulation and inspiration. He has a motive to impress the audience and to be remembered. For those whose life otherwise has little significance, transcendent fame can be a powerful motive to establish themselves as legend for all the time. Martyrdom is identified with the heroism and glory of the act of self sacrifice. It is a way of legitimizing a cause and inspiring imitation.

In LTTE's case, the motivation for suicide attacks seems to be a kind of *en masse* cult hysteria that LTTE consciously cultivates by rituals like martyr's week.[25] They prompt a cult of martyrdom, building of special cemeteries, naming of weapons after Black Tigers and, in short, promise of honour after death.[26] These promises are attractive to those who have nothing to gain in their life. It becomes as significant as most of the LTTE cadre who now come from lower middle class and easily accept such propaganda. The family and the loved ones typically support this behaviour and if the event occurs, the family is honoured.[27]

MODUS OPERANDI

Planning and organization of a suicide operation is extremely secretive. The success of the mission depends on a number of elements: level of secrecy; thorough reconnaissance; and thorough rehearsals. Secrecy enables the preservation of the element of surprise, reconnaissance enables the group to plan, often by building a scale model of the target and rehearsals allow the bomber to gain stealth and speed. There are other elements, such as getting the bomber to the target zone and then to the target itself. A comprehensive knowledge of the target is essential for the success of a suicide operation. For this purpose, terrorist groups depend on building solid agent-handling networks, so the bomber can reach and destroy a valuable target – human or infrastructure. In such cases, even the presence of a bodyguards or guards assigned to protect sensitive installations cannot serve as a counter measure. The reason is well acquaintance with the target.

There are six types of suicide improvised explosive devices (IEDs). These are[28] : the human-borne suicide IED, also known as the suicide bodysuit; the vehicle-borne suicide IED; the motorcycle-borne suicide IED; naval craft-borne suicide IED; scuba diver-borne suicide IED; and aerial (microlight, glider, mini-helicopter) borne suicide IED. All these categories have been used in South Asia and the Middle East. Furthermore, in suicide attacks, there is no need to provide an escape route for the attacker/attacking force. Therefore, a suicide terrorist could enter a high security zone and accomplish his/her mission without worrying about escape.

Comparison Profile of LTTE with Other Groups

Activities	*LTTE*	*HAMAS*	*ETA*	*PIJ*	*IRA*	*PKK*	*Shining Path*
Bombing	20.7	6.1	37.3	9.3	25.0	27.6	5.0
Car Bomb	10.3	4.3	35.3	18.5	37.5	0	45.0
Knife Attack	3.4	7.8	0	1.9	0	0	0
Shooting	10.3	37.4	23.5	27.8	31.5	13.8	35.0
Suicide bombing	41.4	34.8	0	35.2	0	13.8	25.0
Kidnapping	6.9	5.2	0	1.9	0	20.7	10.0

Source: R. Ramasubramanian, "Suicide Terrorism in Sri Lanka", *Institute of Peace and Conflict Studies (IPCS) Research Paper*, August 2004.

ROLE OF WOMEN

Women have played an important role in the terrorist activity of some of the prominent group that uses suicide terrorism. In general, women's participation is limited to the organizations with a nationalist orientation. The fundamentalist Islamic terror groups have never let women to take part in their terrorist activities. Nevertheless, about five of the suicide operations in Lebanon were women.[29] The nationalist groups, such as PKK, the LTTE and the PPS, enable women to participate in their most extreme attacks. The leaders of these groups often exploit female members' profound desire to prove equality with their male peer.

Women account for high percentage of suicide attacks. In the LTTE they participated in about 30 to 40 percent of group's overall suicide activities. In the PKK women carried out 11 out of 15 successful attacks, in all 66 percent of the total were women.[30] In the PPS, women took part in 5 out of the group's 12 suicide activities.[31] A higher percentage of women have featured in off-the-battlefield suicide operations, which requires infiltration, invisibility and deception. For many reasons, women are the preferred choice of secular groups when it comes to infiltration and strike missions. First, women are less suspicious because being 'a gentle sex'[32] . Second, in the conservative societies of the Middle East and South Asia, there is a hesitation to body search a woman. Third, women can wear a suicide device beneath her clothes and appear pregnant.

SUICIDE TERRORISM AND LTTE

The LTTE is widely regarded as the world's deadliest and fiercest terrorist group and the most ferocious guerrilla organization in South Asia. Out of 118 suicide attacks in South Asia in 1990–2000, Sri Lanka alone suffered 88 attacks.[33] It is the only terrorist group to have assassinated three heads of the governments- Indian Prime Minister Rajiv Gandhi in 1991, Sri Lankan President Ranasinghe Premadasa in 1993 and former

Prime Minister Dissanayake in 1994. It has also assassinated several prominent and military figures. Other than the loss of leaders, the country's national, political, economic and cultural infrastructure has been severely damaged by suicide attacks. [34] The LTTE's ill-conceived Gandhi assassination, however, resulted in the LTTE's loss of a substantial logistical infrastructure and also the loss of the popular support for LTTE among mainstream Indian Tamils.

Also known by 'Tamil Tigers' the LTTE is a by-product of Sri Lanka's ethnic conflict between the majority Sinhalese people (74 per cent) and minority ethnic Tamils (12.5 per cent). As a result of the government action that violated the rights of the Tamils in Sri Lanka in the 1948-77 period, a large number of educated and unemployed young people on the island rose up against the government in 1972, under the leadership of Velupillai Prabhakaran. Founders of this military youth movement formed the 'Liberation Tigers of Tamil Eelam' on May 5, 1976. The LTTE is only of the five groups that have achieved dominance over more than 35 Tamil guerrilla groups. Nationalism remained the driving force behind the tiger movements.

The bloody ethnic riot of July 1983 polarised the Sinhalese and Tamil communities and became a watershed in the history of Sri Lanka. The riot resulted in evacuation of Tamils, around 500,000 who left for India and West to seek asylum. They become the backbone of the terrorist campaign and the years that followed, the Tigers established offices and cells allover the world. They built a network unsurpassed by any other terrorist group. By 1987, the LTTE had emerged as the strongest militant group in Sri Lanka.

LTTE SUICIDE ATTACKS

The organizational culture of the LTTE provided the internal conditions ripe for the use of suicide terrorism. Further, when it combined with popular support of the Tamil community, there existed legitimate motivational factors for Black Tiger missions. Emile Durkheim's study of suicide can be used as a valuable tool to understand these underlying motivations.[35] The LTTE suicide follows most closely the form that Durkheim calls "altruistic suicide," where the individual commits the act of suicide because he is deeply connected to a community and willing to die for this community "because it is his duty." The Black Tigers are so committed to the LTTE and the Tamil society which supports them that they are willing to die for the cause of the Tamil homeland.

LTTE's suicide units 'Black Panthers' is comprised of both men and women. In fact, the women LTTE terrorists play a key role in the unit. Members of this unit are designated as 'suicide commandos' and carry around their neck a glass vial containing potassium cyanide.[36] The suicide capsule, which LTTE members view as the ultimate symbol of bravery and commitment to cause, is issued at final initiation ceremony. A LTTE commando who wears the capsule must use it without fail in the event of an unsuccessful mission.

The first LTTE suicide operation was conducted on July 5, 1987, to stall the advance of the Sri Lankan military to Jaffna town.[37] It was not an LTTE cadre wearing a suicide body-suit, but a vehicle laden with explosives that was used. Captain Millar volunteered to drive the vehicle bomb into the makeshift army camp in Nelliaddy.[38] LTTE claimed Captain Millar's success in killing 40 soldiers in Nelliaddy by frustrating the intentions of the Government to recapture the Tamil heartland. After that LTTE did not conduct suicide operations during the IPKF period. But immediately after that it initiated a series of suicide attacks with the assassination of Wijeratne and Rajiv Gandhi in March and May 1991, respectively. Since then it is unequivocally the most effective and brutal terrorist organization ever to utilize suicide terrorism.

On the eve of the 1994 Sri Lankan elections, the LTTE assassinated UNP presidential candidate Gamini Dissanayake who enjoyed close ties with India. Interrogation of LTTE cadres revealed that V. Prabakaran, the LTTE's supreme leader, had decide d to target Dissanayake for fear that a government under Dissanayake would receive Indian assistance. Further, both intelligence and interrogation of LTTE cadres reveal that the LTTE intended to assassinate Chandrika Kumaratunga in order to ensure the victory of leader of the Opposition Ranil Wickremasinghe. Wickremasinghe's United National Party (UNP) had initiated a dialogue with the LTTE with the intention of declaring a ceasefire, which would have enabled the LTTE, as it had done during three previous cease fires, to strengthen its organisation both politically and militarily. The political context of each suicide operation reveals how the LTTE manages to survive and advance its aims using this lethally accurate tactic.

The LTTE deployed with deadly accuracy suicide bombers to destroy the Joint Operations Command, the nerve-centre of the Sri Lankan security forces; the Central Bank; the World Trade Centre; the Temple of the Tooth Relic, the most hallowed Buddhist shrine; and the oil storage installations in Kolonnawa.[39] The LTTE used suicide bombers to kill a number of service personnel, apart from political leaders and outstanding intellectuals such as Neelan Thiruchelvam. Two officers engaged in the "hearts and minds" campaign, Brigade commander of the Jaffna peninsula Brigadier Larry Wijeratne and Jaffna town commandant Brigadier Ananda Hamangoda, were killed in two independent suicide attacks.[40] In order to paralyse the security apparatus, the LTTE singled out and targeted individuals who were at the forefront of counter-insurgency operations.

WOMEN SUICIDE BOMBERS

In LTTE presence of women cadres in Black Tigers is distinct phenomenon. The *Vituthalai Pulikal Makalir Munani* (Women's Front of the Liberation Tigers) was formed in 1983, which had begun as a support group and was later absorbed into the fighting formations. The first group of Women Tigers had their training in Tamil Nadu camps by 1985, and had their first taste of combat in July 1986. In October 1987, Prabhakaran set up a training camp exclusively for women in Jaffna for the second and successive batches. By 1989, this unit secured its own leadership structure. In the same year they were recruited for the Sea Tigers, which was then in an embryonic stage. As in the case of selecting males for Black tiger operations, the LTTE central military command selects, rather accepts, volunteer women for suicidal missions.[41] Women undergo the same tough training as men. Tasks are assigned that break taboos such as riding bicycles, driving motor vehicles, swimming and sea faring that have given women a sense of empowerment that could stand them in good stead even outside their military roles.[42] Women in the LTTE are allegedly forced to suppress their femininity and sexuality, which is regarded as a crime and an evil force that could sap their strength.[43] Marriage is not allowed for women cadres up to the age of 25 and for men up to the age of 28.

Suicide Commandos of LTTE

Black Tigers	*Men*	*Women*
Total strength	312	92
Black Sea Tigers	152	22
Successful Mission	58	27
Training Camp	Red Garden, Mullaitivu Forest	Red Garden, Mullaitivu Forest
Mode of Operation	Truck laden with bombs, Bicycles, Abdominal belt bomb, Scuba diving	Abdominal belt bomb, Body suit, Brassiere bomb

Source: R. Ramasubramanian, "Suicide Terrorism in Sri Lanka", *Institute of Peace and Conflict Studies (IPCS) Research Paper*, August 2004.

STRUCTURE AND RECRUITMENT OF MEMBERS

The LTTE leadership has two wings – a military wing and a subordinate political wing, governed by a central governing committee, headed by the LTTE chief, Velupillai Prabhakaran.[44] The Military wing has four major units viz., *the Sea Tigers, the Black Tigers, an elite fighting wing,* known as the Charles Anthony Regiment and a *highly secretive intelligence group.*[45] The political wing is headed by Thamilselvam and Anton Balasingham. The LTTE an exclusively ethnic organization consisting almost entirely of Tamil Hindu youth. The early supporters of Tamil Eelam were in their thirties, but the level has declined sharply in recent days. In 1970's quotas on university admission for Tamils prompted younger Tamils to join the insurgency.[46] By 1980, a majority of LTTE combatants were reportedly between 18-25 years of age and in 1990, approximately 75 percent were from second generation.[47] The majority of rank and files members belong to the lower middle class.[48] It is said that LTTE had implemented compulsory military training for all people over the age of 15 in areas under LTTE control in the Vanni region. The feature that attracts young minds to the LTTE was the glamour and the perceived respect it was paid by society. LTTE has inculcated the nationalist spirit amongst its cadres, who are carefully indoctrinated into the authorized position that they are fighting for a separate Tamil Eelam. The cadres must banish all fear of death from their minds and be prepared to lay down their lives fighting the Government forces, or consume the cyanide pill carried around their necks when capture is imminent.[49] Unlike religious indoctrination, the LTTE has been successful in infusing ethno-nationalism in the minds of its members. This has led to the formation of LTTE's elite commando unit known as the Black Tigers, which is trained for suicidal missions

CONCLUSION

To sum up, suicide terrorism is a complex phenomenon

rooted in its own time and place. Organizations will continue to employ martyrdom operations in the face of stronger and more powerful enemies. The challenge is to remove the conditions of conflict that foster such acts. Peace talks between the Sri Lankan Government and Tamil Tigers have seen the cessation of such attacks. However, events in the Middle East remain deeply worrisome. In the absence of a settlement in either Iraq or Palestine, such violence is likely to continue. Unless there is substantial and sustained global engagement that delivers peace and justice, the bloodletting associated with these conflicts will continue to supply groups such as al Qaeda and allies with volunteers prepared for martyrdom. Unless there is a change in the mindset of the perpetrator, nothing can stop suicide bombings.

REFERENCES

1. The author is a Research Scholar in South Asian Studies Division, School of International Studies, Jawaharlal Nehru University, New Delhi.
2. Yoram Schweitzer, "Suicide Terrorism: Development and main characteristics", in *Countering Suicide Terrorism: An International Conference,* (Herzliya, Israel: The International Policy Institute for Counter Terrorism at the Interdisciplinary Center, 2001), p. 75-76.
3. R. Ramasubramanian, "Suicide Terrorism in Sri Lanka", *Institute of Peace and Conflict Studies (IPCS) Research Paper,* August 2004.
4. Rohan Gunaratna, "Suicide Terrorism: A Global Threat", *Frontline,* October 2000.
5. *Ibid.*
6. Scott Atran, "Genesis of Suicide Terrorism", *Science,* March 7, 2003, p. 21. http://search.epnet.com.direct.asp?an=9355002&db=aph
7. Josie Glausiusz, "The Surprises of Suicide Terrorism", *Discover,* October 2003, p. 17. http://search.epnet.com/direct.asp?an=10841171&db=aph
8. Rohan Gunaratna, n. 3.
9. *Ibid.*
10. Martha Crenshaw, "Sucide Terrorism in Comparative Perspective", in *Countering Suicide Terrorism: An International Conference,* (Herzliya,

Israel:.The International Policy Institute for Counter Terrorism at the Interdisciplinary Center, 2001)

11. Yoram Schweitzer, n.1.
12. *Ibid.*
13. Rohan Gunaratna, n. 3.
14. *Ibid.*
15. Robert Pape, "The Strategic Logic of Suicide Terrorism", *American Political Science Review*, Vol. 97, Vo. 3, August 2003, p.1.
16. Michael Kurton, "Why Human Bombs?", *Journal of Defence Strategy*, Vol. 42, No. 4 , July 2001, p. 56.
17. Martha Crenshaw, n. 9.
18. Todd Sandler and Harvey E. Lapan, "The Calculus of Dissent: An Analysis of Terrorist' Choise of Targets", *Synthesis* 76, 1988, pp. 245-261.
19. Walter Enders, Todd Sandler and Joe Cauley, "UN Conventions, Technology and Retaliation in the Fight Against Terrorism: An Econometric Evaluation", *Terrorism and Political Violence*, 2, 1990, pp. 83-105.
20. Suba Chandran, "Suicide Terrorism in South Asia: From Promised Land to Presumed Land", *Peace & Conflict*, vol. 6, no. 5, 2003, p. 8.
21. Julian Madsen, "Suicide Terrorism: Rationalizing the Irrational", *Strategic Insights*, vol. III, issue 8, August, 2004.
22. Suba Chandran, "An Inquiry into Suicide Terrorism: Sociological Perspectives", in P.R. Chari & Suba Chandran (eds.) *Terrorism Post 9/11: An Indian Perspective* (New Delhi: Manohar, 2003), p. 133.
23. Prabhan, "Historisation of Martial Ideology of Liberation Tigers of Tamil Eelam (LTTE)", *Journal of South Asian Studies*, vol. 20, no. 1, p. 38.
24. R. Ramasubramanian, n. 2.
25. Sabil Francis, "The Uniqueness of LTTE's Suicide Bombers", in P.R. Chari and Suba Chandran (eds.), *Terrorism Post 9/11: An Indian Perspective* (New Delhi: Manohar, 2003), p. 143.
26. *Ibid.*
27. Kodikara, "The Seperatist Eelam Movement in Sri Lanka: An Overview", *India Quarterly*, April 1981, pp. 194-212.
28. Rohan Gunaratna, n. 3.
29. *Ibid.*
30. Yoram Schweitzer, n.1.

31. *Ibid.*
32. Julian Madsen, n. 18.
33. Rohan Gunaratna, " Suicide attacks", in Michael Green (Edt) 'Global Rebels: Terrorist Organizations as Trans-National Actors', *Harvard International Review,* (Fall 2001), p 64
34. Rohan Gunaratna, "A strategic failure", *Frontline,* Vol 17 - Issue 10, 13 May 2000, p.43
35. Durkheim, Emile. Suicide: A Study in Sociology, trans. John A. Spaulding and George Simson. New York: Free Press, 1951. 219.
36. Yoram Schweitzer, n.1.
37. Rohan Gunartana, "The LTTE and Suicide Terrorism", *Frontline,* vol. 17, issue. 3, Feb 08, 2000.
38. *Ibid.*
39. *Ibid.*
40. *Ibid.*
41. Liberation Tigers of Tamil Eelam, Institute of Conflict Management, http://www.satp.org/satporg/countries/shrilanka/terroristoutfits/Ltte.htm
42. Miranda Alison, "Female combatants of the LTTE and IRA: A comparative study" Northeastern Monthly - July 1, 2004. http://www.tamilcanadian.com/pageview.php? ID=2430&SID=456
43. Tim Mc Girk, 'Running away from the Tigers', *Time,* 17 November 1997.
44. R. Ramasubramanian, n.2.
45. Peter Chalk, "LTTE's international organization and operations – a preliminary analysis" *The Island,* 2 May 2000. http://www.is.lk/is/clips/sp0443/clip5.html
46. Rohan Gunaratna, 'The LTTE and Suicide Terrorism', *Frontline*, Vol 17, Issue 03-05 February 2000, p.42
47. *Ibid.*
48. Oberst,'Sri Lanka story', *The Island,* 23 June 2002.
49. R. Ramasubramanian, n.2.

20

Trans-national Terrorism: A Concept Paper

Ashwini Kumar Tiwari

INTRODUCTION

The 9/11 attacks on the United States has added a new dimension to the dynamics of Modern Terrorism. It has transformed contemporary transnational terrorism into truly "catastrophic terrorism" with possible access by terrorists to weapons of mass destruction, chemical and biological weapons and high-tech equipment of communication. Today's terrorist acts on a variety of motives than ever before and possesses an advanced ability to make precise strikes on most vulnerable targets, be it the killing of embassy lifeline, and vital installations or even challenging the might and sovereignty of the great super-power by smashing its economic symbol – the World Trade Centre.

B. Peter Rosendorf and Todd Sandler in "The Political Economy of Transnational Terrorism" have analysed the impact of 9/11. They have observed that the events of Sept. 11, 2001, heightened the public awareness of the threat posed by modern day terrorism. For global security, 9/11 was a defining moment for a number of reasons. First, the sheer magnitude of the attack and the resultant death of almost 3000 persons was unprecedented in terms of terrorist attacks. Second, the associated financial losses and repercussions of over $80 to $90 billion were far greater than those associated with most catastrophic natural disasters to date. Financial consequences were particularly heavy on the airline industry, tourism and insurance. Third, 9/11 aptly underscored the vulnerability of modern society to terrorist attacks that could use an everyday object to cause havoc and terror. Fourth, 9/11 created an ongoing financial commitment to homeland security that devours scarce resources. Fifth, 9/11 sets the bar for future attacks, as terrorists try to outdo the magnitude of past attacks to capture and maintain media attention. In their quest to eventually top 9/11, terrorists will resort to large conventional attacks or even weapons of mass destruction, most likely chemical and radiological in nature.

TERRORISM IN HISTORY : EVOLVING A COMMON IDENTITY

No phase of history can be said to have been free from the scourge of terror. But, it is only recently that terror has been elevated to the level of an "ism". On a global scale, there may be nothing common between one terrorist group and the other in terms of motivation, objective and tactics.

The Naxalites in Andhra Pradesh may not have anything in common with Al-Fatah of the Middle East or Al Qaida. But at a deeper level, there are convergences, which are striking. The most prominent point of convergence is a belief in violence as an instrument of achieving objectives. This has led to widely dispersed terrorist groups, seeking support from each other in terms of supply of arms, training and resources. There have been recent instances of the People's War Group (PWG) and Maoists in Andhra Pradesh, receiving arms from the LTTE and there have been reports of similar links between the terrorist groups of the North East in India and the LTTE. The terrorist outfits operating in Jammu and Kashmir in India have links with terrorists in Afghanistan, Sudan as well as China.

Most terrorist groups take advantage of the worldwide availability of deadly arms and weapons – a pernicious legacy of the cold war. Terrorist groups employ guerrilla tactics, which with local variations are generally identical. These organizations derive sustenance from the support of the sections of the population who may have nursed certain grievances against the established order of the Government.

In spite of the generally local nature of the terrorist movements, there is a strange commonality in their approach, which creates an amorphous identity for world terrorism.

TRANS – NATIONAL TERRORISM

Terrorism comes in two varieties: domestic and transnational terrorism. Domestic terrorism is homegrown and home directed, with consequences for just that country, its institutions, citizens, property and policies. For domestic terrorism, the perpetrators, the victims and audience are all from the host country. There are no spill-over effects across the border in terms of costs and benefits.

Through its perpetrators, victims or audience, trans-national terrorism has implications for two or more countries. If an incident starts in one country, but terminates in another (e.g. 9/11), the incident is a transnational terrorist event, as it is the case for hijacking of a plane in country 'A' that is diverted to country 'B'. In the World Trade Centre tragedy, citizens from 80 countries lost their lives at the hands of the terrorist who crossed into the US from abroad.

An act of terrorism when carried out by autonomous non-state actors, whether or not they enjoy some degree of support from sympathetic states can be called transnational terrorism.

DEFINING THE CONCEPT OF TERRORISM

By its nature, the term 'terrorism' is bound in political controversy. It is a concept with a very negative connotation. As terrorism implies killing and maiming of innocent people, no country wants to be accused of supporting terrorism or harboring terrorist groups. At the same time, no country wants what it considers to be a legitimate use of force to be considered "terrorism". An old saying goes "One person's terrorist is another person's freedom fighter".

Today there is no universally accepted definition of terrorism. Countries define the term according to their own beliefs and to support their own national interests. International bodies, when they craft a definition, do so in the interest of their own states. Academics striving to define terrorism are also subject to their own point of view.

Title 22 of the US code defines terrorism as "pre-mediated, politically motivated violence against non-combatant targets by sub-national groups with the goal to influence an audience."

The US department of defence uses a definition that highlights another element of western concept of terrorism. Terrorism is "the calculated use of violence or the threat of violence to inculcate fear; intended to coerce or to intimidate governments or societies in the pursuit of goals that are generally political, religious or ideological". In other words, terrorism is viewed as "violence designed to advance some cause by getting a government to change its policies or political behaviour".

An Iranian religious leader Ayatulla Tashkhiri offers a contrasting definition of terrorism. In 1987, at a conference called for by the Organisation of Islamic Conference he defined terrorism as "an act carried out to achieve any inhuman and corrupt objective and involving threat to security of any kind and in violation of the rights acknowledged by religion and mankind". On September 14, 2001 the U.N. passed resolution (No. 1624/2005) calling on the Member States to prohibit "Terrorism" without defining the term. This has added greater chaos to already existing confusion as far the definition of the term "terrorism" is concerned.

On the face of it, the current impasse in defining terrorism appears to have arisen partly out of some (Muslim) countries' sympathies with armed campaigns like that being waged by PLO against Israel. Such campaigns, say some, represent legitimate resistance and should not be claimed as terrorism. However, the US and the UK have been appealing to the UN to draft a definition that must include "deliberate and unlawful targeting, and killing as terrorism without giving it any legitimacy or justification in the name of any cause or grievance".

Dr. Boaz Ganor, Director, International Council against Terrorism (ICT) has proposed a definition of terrorism which could constitute an accepted or agreed upon foundation for academic research, as well as facilitating operations on an international scale against perpetrators of terrorist activities.

He defines Terrorism as "The intentional use of threat to use violence against civilians or against civilian targets in order to attain political aims". This definition is based on three important elements.

(i) The essence of the activity is the use of or threat to use violence: According to this definition, an activity that does not involve violence or a threat of violence will not be defined as terrorism (including non-violent protests – strikes, peaceful demonstrations, tax revolts etc.)

(ii) The aim of the activity is always political: Normally the goal is to attain political objectives, changing the regime, changing the people in power, changing social and economic policies etc. A violent activity against civilians that has no political aim is, at most an act of criminal delinquency, a felony or simply an act of insanity unrelated to terrorism. Some scholars tend to add ideological or religious aims to the list of political aims. The concept of "Political Aim" is sufficiently broad to include these goals as well. The motivation, whether ideological, religious or something else being the political objective is irrelevant for the purpose of defining terrorism.

(iii) The targets of terrorists are civilian: Terrorism has to be distinguished from other types of political violence (Guerilla Warfare, Civil insurrection) etc. Terrorism exploits the relative vulnerability of the civilian "underbelly" – the tremendous anxiety and the intense media reaction evoked by attacks against civilian targets. The proposed definition emphasizes that terrorism is not the result of an accidental injury inflicted on a civilian or a group of civilians who stumbled into an area of violent activity, but stresses that this is an act purposely directed against civilians. Hence, terrorism should not be ascribed to collateral damage to civilians used as human shields or to cover military activity or military installations, if such damage is incurred in an attack originally aimed against a military target. In this case, the responsibility for civilian casualties is incumbent upon whoever uses them as human shield.

INDIA'S DRAFT CONVENTION ON INTERNATIONAL TERRORISM (2000)

Long before the September 11th attack, India has been vigorously campaigning at the United Nations for an early adoption of its comprehensive draft convention on suppression of international terrorism. The underlying spirit of the Indian draft is that "terrorism is the emerging global threat which calls for concerted international action". Two rounds of discussions of the draft have been held by the concerned UN committees. The highlights of the draft convention are

(i) It has called for the prosecution or extradition of terrorist elements and their co-conspirators.

(ii) Sponsors and co-sponsors of such acts must be termed as terrorists.

(iii) All contracting nations to the convention must cooperate with each other and coordinate their activities in fighting terrorism.

(iv) The draft identifies terrorism in specific term viz. unlawful seizure of aircraft, unlawful acts against the safety of civilian aviation, crimes against internationally protected persons, taking of hostage, threat to maritime navigation and terrorist bombings.

(v) It calls upon the member states to enact appropriate domestic legislation to check and discourage criminal acts of terrorism viz. undertaking, organizing, sponsoring, facilitating and financing of terrorist activities against another state.

(vi) A member state shall refrain from activities against another state tantamount to its interest.

(vii) No such acts of terrorism shall be justified by considerations of political, philosophical, ideological, racial, ethnic, religious or of reasons similar in nature.

INCESSANT CYCLE OF FORCE SUSTAINS TRANS-NATIONAL TERRORISM

The foremost fundamental aspect of war is that of force. If the element of force did not exist, there would be no motivation for battle. With this in mind, it is relatively easy to apply this concept to the notion of terrorism, as the ultimate goal of any terrorist is to obtain the desired commodity through drastic and often deadly means of force.

By understanding this obvious correlation, one can effectively argue that without the support of force on their side, terrorists would not have the ability to pursue their violent protests, which for most part have historically been political. Part of the problem is that terrorists' active demands to be noticed, a fact that ultimately constitutes the need of force. However, if the terrorist is not acknowledged, this may lead the need to greater force for getting their demands answered. And this incessant cycle of force continues.

The terrorist succeeds every time he makes a strike questions the ability of the state to maintain inter nal order.

Creating a perception of the weakness of the State or its diminishing ability to protect the lives and properties of its citizens as well as the states' vital interests, brings success to terrorist activites on the one hand and makes terrorism attractive and romantic on the other.

FACTORS THAT HAVE FACILITATED THE GROWTH OF TRANS – NATIONAL TERRORISM

The CIA of the US has identified the following 5 factors that have facilitated the growth of trans –national terrorism.

(i) The technological advances that have provided the terrorist with new mobility, new weaponry and (through the introduction of TV – Capable Satellite connection) the near certain prospect of their more dramatic and worldwide publicity.

(ii) The growth of global and regional ties, fed by modernizing change, dependencies and obligations that have both provided terrorists with a host of new and potentially highly disruptive targets for attack (e.g. power grid, Nuclear installation, Jumbo Aircrafts etc.) and fostered a reactive upsurge in nationalism and ethnicity.

(iii) An increasingly permissive political environment born of the challenges raised to the post war order by the developing nations of the world – and also the subsequent breaking up of the communist world.

(iv) The persistent of uneven behavior of those states, less than score in number, that have furnished practising or potential terrorists with funds, arms, training, documentation and other operational support.

(v) Changes in the overall economic environment that have fanned local dissidence and fed the countries of émigré workers that can provide terrorists with cover, recruits and various forms of operational support.

TERRORISM IN THE PERSPECTIVE OF 9/11 TERRORIST STRIKES

Evaluating post 9/11 terrorism can only be defined by its methods and not by its goal, which have always been far too diverse and chaotic. Terrorist groups in the contemporary era have identified themselves with anarchism, revolutionary communism, fascism, secessionism, religious fundamentalism and romantic idealism. Democracies can suffer from one or many type of these manifestations of terrorism.

Terrorism therefore, has emerged as a "radical method". The theory behind this method is achievement of the goals of an organized group of saboteurs through systematic violence for a cascading effect. Persistence of violent attacks, on some date promises either to overthrow the government or to weaken it. Thus terrorism is politics of blackmail, coercion and a design to impose the will of a minority on that of the majority. Consequently, transnational terrorism has emerged as a great threat to all democracies.

DEMOCRACY'S RESPONSE TO TRANS-NATIONAL TERRORISM

All democracies face terrorists threats, but the one's least plural are less affected. Terrorism erodes the environment of pluralism, tolerance and liberty, which comprise the basic ethos of democracy. Terrorists expect and calculatedly provoke, a repressive reaction on the part of the democratic state, which effect free debate and political liberty. Thereby, terrorism attempts to rob democracy of its core values by increasing self-doubts and fermenting disaffection among people and the state.

Terrorism least affects authoritarian states. Neither Hitler's Germany nor Mussolini's Italy suffered from terrorism, nor closer in time the dictatorship of Myanmar or North Korea counted terrorism as a threat.

9/11 exposed the vulnerability of democracies to trans-national terrorism. The attack on the Indian parliament, blasts in the streets of Berlin, attacks on the Western diplomats and embassies, London bomb blasts or the attacks on the innocent people of Moscow by the Chechen rebels reveal the apparent softness of democratic institutions and society, which easily become tempting targets for terrorist attacks.

Trans-national terrorism has emerged as one of the worst fears of western democracies largely because these democracies have had a long run of peaceful existence having succeeded in insulting themselves from the turmoil elsewhere in the world. They have developed strong economies and technologically advanced infrastructure, which are vulnerable to terrorist acts and violence.

Democracatic states' response to such violence is quite often incoherent and halting. Despite extensive counter-terrorist attacks by powerful Western democracies and countries in Asia, Africa and Latin America, control of terrorist activities has remained elusive. The degree of terrorist attacks has been on the increase, as democracies are concerned. In 1986, only 64% of terrorist attacks were directed against democracies. In 2004 this figure stood at about 80%.

By strange coincidence, the phenomenal growth of democracy coincided with the growth of terrorism. Arguably, since democracy offers tempting targets, the urge to reach those targets through terrorist acts has been increasing. The methods of democracy are often slow. Socio-economic grievances of specific groups of people may not always be accommodated within the democratic process, though the people's mandate may invest the government with legitimacy, it may not necessarily enhance its acceptability by all sections of people. Civil Society in democratic countries is not sufficiently developed to address the major grievances nursed by its people. Many countries which have established political democracies, have not succeeded in establishing economic democracy. Terrorism feeds on disaffection prevalent in the state. There is a strong need for democracies to strengthen civil societies, ensuring economic democracy and providing opportunities to citizens for grievance redressal.

SECULAR LIBERALISM AND FUNDAMENTALIST TERRORISM

Some commentators have argued that terrorism and its alliance with despotism are the response of believers in fundamentalism against the growing power of the secular democratic state. There is a fear that westernized secular democracies are built upon a fundamental aversion to religion and faith, which compete with religions for the adherence of the people. Terrorism, thus, is the response of a besieged belief which dreads obliteration. As such, there could be nothing wrong with fundamentalism per se. But there is everything wrong with fundamentalism, which attempts to sustain itself through terrorism because of its assumed failure to compete with the secular, liberal state. There is anger against the West for what it has done to sweep all competing beliefs away. Exponents of fundamentalism like Hassan Abdullah al-Turabi of Sudan and Sheikh Muhammed Husien Fadlallah of Lebanon, have used the self-esteem of religion as the reason for a terrorist response. Osama-bin-Laden, the Chechen war lord Basayev and Khattab have projected Faith as an emblem of defiance against the secular order.

The fundamentalist Islamic terrorists in Central Asia, Chechnya, Dagestan, Alegeria and Egypt aim at nothing short of complete overturn of the Western model of secular state and to replace it with a romanticised version of their own beliefs. This explains the campaign to kill writers and intellectuals, unveiled women, foreigners who are painted as the cat-paw of western liberalism. This also explains the attempts to describe the West through imageries drawn from sacred texts as the Great Satan, the Devil's Empire, etc.

The modern-day Islamic terrorist is nostalgic about the Islam of the 8th and the 9th centuries, when pan-Islamism built both power and influence.

The word 'Talibanisation' has introduced a new expression in the vocabulary of fundamentalist terrorism. The Taliban dominance of Afghanistan has introduced a wholly new variant and unpredictable terrorist element into international relations. The dismantling of Taliban Regime has not eased the pressure of violence at home. While Trans-national terrorism has gained more committed terrorists to its rank.

There would be no Taliban, if there were no cold war. The American who intervened in Vietnam in retaliation to the erstwhile Soviet Union, created and promoted Taliban. This today, has emerged as a platform for every brand of radical fundamentalism originating from diverse countries to raise holy wars against enemies of the Faith. The world had a first-hand glimpse of the Taliban variety of terrorism when Chechnya based militants took over parts of Russian Dagestan. Their ranks included Arabs, Afghans and Pakistanis who had experience of fighting against the Soviets in Afghanistan. The 800 Uzbeks and Tajiks who took over parts of southern Kyrgystan in August 1999 had received Taliban training. The failed state of Afghanistan has given training to militants of Pakistan, Iran, Central Asia and China's Muslim Xinjiang province sanctuary and financial support through smuggling.

A combustible combination is fast emerging, including the failed state of Afghanistan and the unstable geo-strategic politics in the states bordering Afghanistan. Drug trade and other forms of smuggling, free availability of deadly weapons, burgeoning influence of fundamentalist Madarssas plus poverty and unemployment among youth, create conditions of lasting terrorist violence within and outside Afghanistan and in far flung areas.

The fledgling republics of Central Asia, Kazakstan, Kyrgystan, Tajikistan, Turkmenistan and Uzbekistan have been halting in their attempt to establish full-fledged democracies in their states, due to apparent fear of Taliban like attacks on them.

They fear flow of drugs and weapons and a possible flood of refugees if the northern alliance is defeated.

This mindset has given to the rulers of these republics the raisond'etre for their authoritarianism. Rigged elections and restrictions on political parties have undermined democratic alternatives, leaving underground Islamist movements as the only political opposition. Widespread poverty and unemployment provide a fertile recruiting base for young militants.

In February 2003, a terrorist bomb aimed at the Uzbek President, Islam-e-Karimov, killed 16 people and wounded 128. The main suspect in these bombings, Tahir Yuldashev, the leader of the Islamic movement of Uzbekistan found shelter in Afghanistan. Islamic militants are being trained in Afghanistan to attack regimes in Central Asia.

The Taliban terrorism holds a threat also to Iran. The Taliban regime freely harbours Iranian dissidents, such as Ahl-e-Sunnah Wal Jamaat and the Iraq-based Mujaheedin-e-Khalq. Even China fears the Taliban brand of fundamentalist terrorism. Heroin money is enabling Taliban to support terrorist outfits in Xinjiang and certain other provinces of China.

EMERGING DIMENSIONS OF TRANSNATIONAL TERRORISM

(i) Terrorism has become completely global

The 9/11 attacks on the US are a symbol of a total 'globalization of terrorism.' "An attack on Manhattan, inspired from a cave in Afghanistan and planned in Hamburg and Kuala Lumpur, that has turned the fabric of Western life, triggered combats in Central Asia, caused unrest from Nigeria to Indonesia and fed tension between Pakistan and India, all this and much more is etched on the ruddy role of 9/11" –(Habitat Focus – July 02).

(ii) A striking point of convergence between diverse Terrorist groups

There may not be anything common between one terrorist group and the other in terms of motivation, objective and tactics but there are emerging convergences, which are striking. The most prominent point of convergence is a belief in violence as an instrument. This has led to widely disperse terrorist groups seeking support from each other in terms of supply of arms, training and resources. There have been recent instances of the PWG. groups in Andhra Pradesh receiving arms from the LTTE. There have been reports of similar links between the Militants of North East with the LTTE. Terrorist outfits in Kashmir have links with terrorists in Afghanistan, Sudan and Pakistan. Inspite of the generally local nature of terrorist movements, there is a strange commonality in their approach, which creates an amorphous identity for world terrorism.

(iii) International terrorism derives substance from their local support base

The terrorist organizations derive sustenance from the support of the sections of the populations who may have nursed certain grievances against the established order or the government. Of the 9000 persons arrested in the US in the after math of 9/11 attacks, majority of them were American citizens. The ISI has been able to establish links with the 'locals' in India who in turn carry out terrorist activities. This has been the case in large parts of the world experiencing terrorism.

(iv) Terrorism Sponsored by Nation-States and Governments

A new genre of terrorism is the variety supported by nation – states and Governments. It is possible that certain forms of terrorist outfits acquire such strength and means, as to perpetuate violence in far flung areas. Ideology or faith, real or assumed historical grievances provide the motivation for terrorist actions which have demonstrated an amazing power to sustain themselves for long years. The support of the erstwhile Taliban regime for terrorism world over, Pakistan sponsored terrorism in Kashmir are variants of this type of world terrorism. The network built by Al – Qaida was possible due to such support.

(v) Projection of Terrorism as an Alternative Ideology:

Ideologies are a broad framework of ideas to reshape societies. Most of the ideologies of the 20th century have been discredited by historical events and have proved to be insufficient to be an ideal blue-print for social, economic and political reconstruction. Communism and the ideologies of the left, liberal democracies have all exposed their limitations in the testing demands of the modern era.

Religious fundamentalism and terrorists sponsored by it are attempting to project themselves as an alternative model of reconstruction. They believe that before you begin to reconstruct, you must destroy that which exists. There is a tinge of 'romanticism' in these beliefs. But when the modern day ideologies and social processes fail to meet the demands of people of all religions, faiths and colours, the fundamentalist ideologies will continue to be attractive to many sections of global society, so will be the terrorism associated with these ideologies. Islamic fundamentalism has attracted world wide attention due to its sheer spread and persistence.

(vi) Narcotics , Money laundering and Terrorism:-

Terrorism is funded by the proceeds of Narcotic Trade, money thus earned is used to buy and distribute weapons to terrorists all over the world. Money laundering and unfair and unlawful transfer of currency help the international terrorists to strengthen their base. The failed state of Afghanistan, the unstable fundamentalist Pakistan narcotic trade and other forms of smuggling including arms, free availability of deadly weapons, growing influence of Madarasas plus poverty and unemployment among the youth, create conditions of lasting terrorist violence within and outside Afghanistan, Pakistan and far flung areas.

(vii) International Terrorism and Media

Media coverage is proving to be a welcome carpet for international terrorism. By granting them celebrity status, experts say, intense and infiltrating news – reports only benefit the terrorist, for it is that exact public access he is after to present his political platform. Terrorists plan their acts to get as much media exposure as possible. Media coverage magnifies the terrorist act by spreading fear among a mass audience and giving attention to the terrorist cause. The attacks on Israeli athletes at the 1972 Munch Olympics assured a world wide television audience, as crashing planes did into the World Trade Center.

There is a distinct bias in reporting as for as Western media is concerned. An attack by terrorists on the World Trade Centre or the streets of London are described in the Western Media as "Terrorist attack" where as "Violence" in Kashmir is categorized as "militant attacks". More often, Western media coverage of terrorist violence in other parts of the world shifts attention from terrorism to the "grievance of the terrorists".

This only encourages terrorism all over the world. It is essential that the media plays its role objectively and impartially.

(viii) Terrorism – an end in itself

There is a new kind of terrorists who view destruction as and end in itself. Whereas old terrorists sought to change the world – however misguided – the new sort is often practised by those who believe that the world is hopelessly beyond redemption and hence needs to be destroyed.

(ix) Technology Savy Terrorists

Todays' terrorist groups are more like techno-savy businessman than bandits of yester years. Armed with lap-tops, satellite phones and internet access, they have embraced technology to further their objective.

The entry of high technology into international terrorism enables killers to remain far away from their victims as they are

equipped with remote control devices or missiles racing towards aircrafts. From online maps that show detailed location to specific information sarine gas, all the information they want is just a click away. Also with satellite telephony, communicating and accessing the internet is no problem – even from hilly and inaccessible areas with no telecom infrastructure.

Why the increasing dependence on IT by the terrorist? First, and perhaps the most important factor is that it ensures anonymity. The satellite phones bypass the state owned – networks, e-mail encryption keeps away the peeping Toms, different layers of passwords keep the internet virtually impenetrable and so on. They can access any information anywhere any time and compare the cost and time involved in flying a personal messenger.

Most importantly, many young educated jobless and disillusioned people have made entry into terrorist groups. They bring with them fresh mindset and have a high level technology acceptance.

CONCLUSION

Terrorism is a great challenge to national and international security as well as law and order. Development and security are truly mutually inter-related. We need to, therefore evolve a combined strategy to deal simultaneously with the twin challenges of development and security within the framework of a democratic polity committed to respect for all fundamental freedoms and rule of law. The growth process must, therefore, be made more even.

The 9/11 attack has placed the war on terror firmly on the agenda. International terrorism is currently one of the international community's most urgent challenges. Everyone agrees that we must do what we can do to combat and prevent terrorism. A broad range of measures are being brought to bear against terrorism including political, diplomatic, economic, financial and military measures. However, fight against

terrorism must not be used as an excuse to ignore human rights. The UN must play a leading role in the global terror efforts. In addition, regional groups and organizations such as the European Union (EU), Association of South East Asian Nations (ASEAN), South Asian Association for Regional Co-operation (SAARC) must also play a central role in fighting terrorism.